This study examines one significant theological theme in Luke–Acts, that of 'the plan of God'. It traces the way this theme is developed throughout Luke–Acts, both through direct statements made by the writer and through various associated means such as divine appearances, signs and wonders, the fulfilment of prophecy, and indications of fate or of divine necessity. Dr Squires locates Luke's use of this theme in the context of the history-writing of the hellenistic period, noting numerous passages in those works which illumine Luke's theological purposes. His book shows how the notion of the plan of God is used by Luke as he writes to confirm his readers' faith, encouraging them to bear witness to this faith, and equipping them for the task of defending it.

SOCIETY FOR NEW TESTAMENT STUDIES

*MONOGRAPH SERIES*

General Editor: Margaret E. Thrall

**76**

THE PLAN OF GOD IN LUKE–ACTS

# The plan of God
# in Luke–Acts

**JOHN T. SQUIRES**

*Lecturer in New Testament Studies,*
*United Theological College, Sydney*

CAMBRIDGE
UNIVERSITY PRESS

BS
2589
.S75
1993

Published by the Press Syndicate of the University of Cambridge
The Pitt Building, Trumpington Street, Cambridge CB2 1RP
40 West 20th Street, New York, NY 10011–4211, USA
10 Stamford Road, Oakleigh, Victoria 3166, Australia

© Cambridge University Press 1993

First published 1993

Printed in Great Britain at the University Press, Cambridge

*A catalogue record for this book is available from the British Library*

*Library of Congress cataloguing in publication data*

Squires, John T.
The plan of God in Luke–Acts / John T. Squires.
    p.    cm. – (Monograph series / Society for New Testament
Studies: 76)
Includes bibliographical references and index.
ISBN 0–521–43175–1
1. Providence and government of God–Biblical teaching.  2. Bible. N.T.
Luke–Theology.  3. Bible. N.T. Acts–Theology.  I. Title.  II. Series:
Monograph series (Society for New Testament Studies):76.
BS2589.S75 1993
226.4'06–dc20   92–9603   CIP

ISBN 0 521 43175 1 hardback

CE

# CONTENTS

# ACKNOWLEDGEMENTS

This book is a revised version of my 1988 Yale University PhD dissertation. I wish to acknowledge my gratitude to those people who have encouraged and assisted me in my studies. The late Revd Dr Robert Maddox introduced me to Lukan theology while I was a student, preparing for ordination, at Sydney University. He gave me a fascination of Luke–Acts which has increased over the years. My understanding of the hellenistic milieu of the New Testament has benefited greatly from seminars conducted at Yale University by Professor Wayne Meeks and Professor Abraham Malherbe. The general approach that I have taken in this work is largely due to insights gleaned from their teaching. I can only hope that this work does not fall too far short of their high standards. I am especially grateful to my dissertation adviser, Abraham Malherbe, for numerous bibliographic suggestions and for his perceptive and provocative comments.

I have had opportunity to try out my ideas in graduate seminars at Yale, and more recently in faculty colloquia at United Theological College. Comments offered on my dissertation by Wayne Meeks, Richard Hays and Rowan Greer have all helped me to formulate the argument more concisely. Whilst I have not accepted all of their criticisms, I have valued their incisive observations.

Support for my studies has come in various ways. A Yale University Fellowship and a *With Love to the World* scholarship provided me with some means for undertaking intensive research. Throughout my years of study, and especially whilst I was at Yale, my parents have been supportive of me in very tangible ways, for which I am most thankful. In particular, Debbie gave me support, understanding and encouragement throughout those years of research and writing, for which I will always be indebted to her. More recently the proof-reading efforts of both my parents and Elizabeth Raine have been greatly appreciated.

Finally, to my parents, Joan and John Squires, who have nurtured me right from the start of my academic and ministerial training, to them I dedicate this book with deepest gratitude, appreciation and love.

# ABBREVIATIONS

| | |
|---|---|
| AJ | *Antiquitates Judaicae*, Josephus |
| *ANRW* | *Aufstieg und Niedergang der römischen Welt* |
| *AusBR* | *Australian Biblical Review* |
| BDF | Blass and Debrunner (trans. Funk), *A Greek Grammar of the New Testament* |
| BH | *Bibliotheke Historike*, Diodorus Siculus |
| *Bib* | *Biblica* |
| BJ | *Bellum Judaicum*, Josephus |
| *BJRL* | *Bulletin of the John Rylands Library* |
| BTB | *Biblical Theology Bulletin* |
| CA | *Contra Apionem*, Josephus |
| *CBQ* | *Catholic Biblical Quarterly* |
| ETL | *Ephemerides theologicae lovanienses* |
| *EvQ* | *Evangelical Quarterly* |
| *ExpTim* | *Expository Times* |
| FRLANT | Forschungen zur Religion und Literatur des Alten und Neuen Testaments |
| HDR | Harvard Dissertations in Religion |
| *HTR* | *Harvard Theological Review* |
| HTS | Harvard Theological Studies |
| *JBL* | *Journal of Biblical Literature* |
| *JJS* | *Journal of Jewish Studies* |
| *JQR* | *Jewish Quarterly Review* |
| *JSJ* | *Journal for the Study of Judaism* |
| LCL | Loeb Classical Library |
| LSJ | Liddell, Scott and Jones, *A Greek–English Lexicon* |
| LXX | Septuagint |
| *NovT* | *Novum Testamentum* |
| NovTSup | Novum Testamentum, Supplements |
| *NTS* | *New Testament Studies* |
| PW | *Paulys Realencyclopädie der classischen Altertumswissenschaft*, ed. G. Wissowa |

| | |
|---|---|
| RA | *Romaike Archaiologia*, Dionysius of Halicarnassus |
| *RPLHA* | *Revue philologique, littéraire et historique de l'antiquité* |
| SBLDS | Society of Biblical Literature Dissertation Series |
| *SBLSPS* | Society of Biblical Literature Seminar Papers Series |
| SBLMS | Society of Biblical Literature Monograph Series |
| *SJT* | *Scottish Journal of Theology* |
| *ST* | *Studia Theologica* |
| Str–B | Strack and Billerbeck, *Kommentar zum Neuen Testament* |
| *SVF* | *Stoicorum Veterum Fragmenta*, coll. von Arnim |
| *TDNT* | *Theological Dictionary of the New Testament* |
| *ThZ* | *Theologische Zeitschrift* |
| V | *Vita*, Josephus |
| *VC* | Vigiliae Christianae |
| *ZAW* | *Zeitschrift für die alttestamentliche Wissenschaft* |
| *ZNW* | *Zeitschrift für die neuetestamentliche Wissenschaft* |
| *ZRGG* | *Zeitschrift für Religions- und Geistesgeschichte* |
| *ZThK* | *Zeitschrift für Theologie und Kirche* |

# 1

# THE PLAN OF GOD IN LUKE–ACTS

## 1.1 The plan of God as a central theme in Luke–Acts

The plan of God is a distinctively Lukan theme which undergirds the whole of Luke–Acts,[1] becoming especially prominent in the speeches of Acts. A variety of thematic strands are woven together to emphasize the certainty and consistency of the plan of God as it is worked out in the life of Jesus and the history of the early church. This theme serves as a multifaceted means by which Luke strives to explain, strengthen and expand the faith of the readers of his two-volume work.

Luke first presents this distinctive theme[2] in his Gospel, where he links this plan of God (ἡ βουλὴ τοῦ θεοῦ) with accepting the baptism of John, which the people and the tax collectors did (Luke 7.29), thereby 'justifying God', in contrast to the Pharisees and lawyers, who rejected such a baptism (Luke 7.30). In the first major speech reported in Acts, Peter claims that Jesus' crucifixion occurred as part of God's 'definite plan and foreknowledge' (τῇ ὡρισμένῃ βουλῇ καὶ προγνώσει τοῦ θεοῦ, Acts 2.23), and the early believers acknowledged to God that the plot against Jesus which led to his death was 'whatever thy hand and thy plan (βουλή) had predestined to take place' (Acts 4.28). When the apostles come before the Sanhedrin, the Pharisee Gamaliel asks a rhetorical question whether this plan (ἡ βουλὴ αὕτη) is really of men (Acts 5.38) or of God

---

[1] The unity of authorship and purpose of the two volumes is assumed; see the recent discussion of R. J. Maddox, *The Purpose of Luke–Acts* (FRLANT 126; Göttingen: Vandenhoeck und Ruprecht, 1982) 3–6, 24 n. 14. The author is referred to as 'Luke' without equating him with the companion of Paul of ecclesiastical tradition.

[2] The term βουλή appears five times in Acts and once in Luke with reference to the plan of God. It is used also at Luke 23.51 and Acts 27.12,42 (and Acts 19.1 in some MSS) to refer to human plans. The word appears elsewhere in the New Testament only at 1 Cor 4.5, Eph 1.11 and Heb 6.17.

(5.39), implying the latter. Paul also knew of the overarching plan of God. In his first reported sermon, he says that David carried out the plan of God (τῇ τοῦ θεοῦ βουλῇ) in his life (Acts 13.36). In his farewell speech to the Ephesian elders, Paul declares, 'I did not shrink from declaring to you the whole plan of God' (πᾶσαν τὴν βουλὴν τοῦ θεοῦ, Acts 20.27).

Alongside this primary strand, other indications of the plan of God are to be found throughout Luke–Acts. God is portrayed as being well pleased with Jesus,[3] and references to the obedience to the will of God shown by Jesus[4] and Paul[5] reinforce the ongoing outworking of the plan of God. Luke frequently uses the term 'it is necessary'[6] and occasionally 'is about to'[7] to depict the unfolding of the plan of God throughout his story. The history of Jesus and the early church can be understood as fulfilling the scriptures,[8] and thereby being in complete accord with the plan of God. In addition, a cluster of προ- compounds and related verbs[9] describes the intentions of God and the execution of the plan of God, as do a sequence of epiphanies in which God or divine messengers are manifested.[10]

For purposes of analysis, these various expressions of the primary theme of the plan of God can be grouped in five broad areas. (1) God is the primary actor throughout Luke–Acts, for the actions of God extend throughout the whole span of history, from creation to final judgement. (2) God directs the life of Jesus and the mission of the church, performing signs and wonders and enabling healings and exorcisms to take place. (3) Epiphanies of God occur in the life of Jesus and throughout the Gentile mission, declaring God's will

---

[3] εὐδοκία at Luke 10.21; εὐδοκέω at Luke 3.17; 12.32.

[4] See Jesus' prayer on the Mount of Olives at Luke 22.42, πλὴν μὴ τὸ θέλημά μου ἀλλὰ τὸ σὸν γινέσθω.

[5] God appointed Paul to know his will (γνῶναι τὸ θέλημα), Acts 22.14, and see also Acts 21.14, where Paul submits to the will of God.

[6] δεῖ is used 18 times in Luke and 24 times in Acts, 42 times in all out of a total of 102 times in the entire New Testament. Significant for our purposes are Luke 2.49; 4.43; 9.22; 13.33; 17.25; 21.9; 22.37; 24.7,26,44; Acts 1.6,21; 3.21; 4.12; 5.29; 9.6,16; 14.22; 16.30; 17.3; 19.21; 20.35; 23.11; 24.19; 25.10; 26.9; 27.24.

[7] μέλλω, Luke 9.31,44; 22.23; 24.21; Acts 17.31; 26.22,23.

[8] πληρόω, Luke 4.21; 9.31; 21.24; 22.16; 24.44; Acts 1.16; 2.28; 3.18; 12.25; 13.25,27,52; 14.26; 19.21; and τελέω, Luke 12.50; 18.31; 22.37.

[9] προορίζω (Acts 4.28); προκαταγγέλλω (Acts 3.18; 7.52); πρόγνωσις (Acts 2.23); προχειρίζομαι (Acts 3.20; 22.14; 26.16); προχειροτονέω (Acts 10.41); ὁρίζω (Luke 22.22; Acts 2.23; 10.42; 17.26,31); τάσσω (Acts 13.48; 22.10); and τίθημι (most notably Acts 1.7; 13.47,48; 19.21; 20.28).

[10] See Luke 1.11–22,26–38; 2.9–15; 3.22; 9.30–2; 22.43; 24.4–7,15–31,36–49; Acts 1.3,9–11; 2.3; 5.19–20; 9.3–6; 10.3–7,10–16,30–2; 11.5–10,13–14; 12.7–11,23; 16.9–10; 18.9; 22.6–8,17–21; 23.11; 26.13–18; 27.23–4.

and guiding the events of history. (4) The life of Jesus, especially his passion, and the mission to the Gentiles, fulfil what had been prophesied. (5) Inherent in the life and passion of Jesus and in the missionary deeds of the apostles, there is a necessity which had been foreordained by Jesus. Juxtaposed alongside this theme of necessity is the role of human agents in carrying out the plan of God; some may oppose this plan, but those who are obedient to the will of God play key roles in God's plan.

Such an analysis of the strands we have identified, whilst to a degree artificial, is useful for heuristic purposes. These indicators of the plan of God are woven together throughout the two volumes of Luke's work in a variety of combinations. The interweaving of such strands was, as we shall see, part of a standard complex of ideas in hellenistic culture. By separating and examining each strand in turn, we shall note the role each part plays in the development of the overall argument that everything narrated by Luke comes under God's providence.

## 1.2 Previous scholarship on the plan of God in Luke–Acts

In the scholarly literature on Luke–Acts, numerous references to the plan of God can be found. Many of these are made in passing, and contribute little to an understanding of the role played by the theme in the overall work. Some studies pay more attention to the theme and its constituent strands, outlining major aspects or examining particular features in more detail. Differences of opinion are to be found when scholars address the cultural context within which the theme is best understood, or the theological significance of the theme.

### 1.2.1 Cluster of thematic strands

Some studies have noted the cluster of thematic strands associated with the plan of God. In discussing the purpose of Luke–Acts, H. J. Cadbury[11] refers to 'the evidence of divine guidance and control that pervades it'.[12] As he briefly discusses the evidence, he notes the presence of themes related to this divine guidance[13] and suggests

---

[11] *The Making of Luke–Acts* (New York: Macmillan, 1927) 303–6.

[12] *Making* 303.

[13] Fulfilment, necessity, the guiding hand of God, the προ- verbs, miracles (including the work of the Holy Spirit) and visions.

that such a conjunction of motifs serves an apologetic purpose. He does not investigate why these pieces of evidence cohere around the central theme.

Subsequently, a number of scholars have noted the combination of these themes. The most detailed examination of the evidence is made by S. Schulz,[14] who interprets the presence of a number of themes[15] as indicating the pervasive nature of providence in Luke's writings. Yet his overriding concern at all times is to argue for an exclusively deterministic understanding of providence which he sees Luke as holding. H. Flender[16] treats Luke's concept of 'the divine plan of salvation' more briefly under the heading of the Holy Spirit as the presence of salvation. He lists a number of the strands we have identified[17] as evidence for Luke's presentation of divine providence, although his primary concern is to deny that Luke merely depicts a past-tense 'redemption history'.

J. Navone[18] considers that 'the way of the Lord' is the fundamental theme for Luke's portrayal of history, and he relates this to various of the themes already noted.[19] Although he claims an interrelationship of these themes through 'the way of the Lord', he does not explore the reasons Luke may have had for so doing. D. Adams[20] pays attention to Luke's emphasis on necessity, divine protection in adversity, and the overt guidance of God in his exploration of the literary framework of Luke–Acts. Whilst he provides a most useful and detailed discussion of these features in Luke's presentation of Paul,[21] especially as they relate to his central concern, the theme of suffering, he does not pursue the relation of these themes to others we have noted, nor does he place Luke's use of these themes in any wide context beyond this one document.

[14] 'Gottes Vorsehung bei Lukas', *ZNW* 54 (1963) 104–16, and 'Der Heilsplan Gottes', *Die Stunde der Botschaft* (Hamburg: Furche, 1967) 275–83.
[15] πρo- compounds, nouns indicating the will of God, verbs indicating the carrying out of that will in history, the prominence of δεῖ, and the use of the hellenistic theologoumenon of Acts 26.14. Schulz also notes aspects of Luke–Acts which are to be interpreted providentially, namely the kerygma, epiphanies, visions, scripture proofs and apologies.
[16] *St Luke: Theologian of Redemptive History* (London: SPCK, 1967) 142–6.
[17] The plan of God, πρo- compounds, necessity and predestination.
[18] 'The Way of the Lord', *Scripture* 20 (1968) 24–30, reprinted in *Themes of St Luke* (Rome: Gregorian University, 1976) 188–98.
[19] Necessity, predestination, the plan of God, fulfilment of prophecy, God's universal acts and the Holy Spirit.
[20] 'The Suffering of Paul and the Dynamics of Luke–Acts' (Yale Ph.D. diss., 1979).
[21] 'Suffering' 37–46, 55–69.

In the introduction to his recent commentary, J. Fitzmyer[22] collects the evidence for 'the author's conception of salvation-history' under five headings.[23] However, he does little more than simply provide a handy concordance for these themes in Luke–Acts, for his main interest is to debate the thesis of Conzelmann with regard to salvation history. A similarly comprehensive list is provided by R. F. O'Toole[24] as he explicates his claim that the primary theological theme of Luke–Acts is that 'God who brought salvation to his people in the Old Testament continues to do this, especially through Jesus Christ'.[25] O'Toole incorporates each of the elements we have already noted[26] and relates them to divine salvation, but explicitly excludes any analysis of these themes in the wider context.[27]

Deliberately limited is the discussion by E. Richard[28] in his examination of 'the divine purpose' in Acts 15, for although he notes various aspects of that divine purpose,[29] he considers them only in so far as they appear within Acts 15. None of these studies have addressed the issues of how these various themes relate to one another, or what function is served by the weaving together of such a range of elements within Luke's writings.

### 1.2.2 Individual strands

Other studies have explored one or another of these themes in more detail. W. Grundmann[30] explored the term δεῖ throughout the New Testament, noting that 'the usage of Luke has the widest

---

[22] *The Gospel According to Luke* (Anchor Bible 28, 28A; New York: Doubleday, 1981); see 'Salvation History' 1.179–81.

[23] Necessity, predestination, the plan of God, fulfilment of prophecy, God's universal acts and the Holy Spirit.

[24] *The Unity of Luke's Theology: An Analysis of Luke–Acts* (Good News Studies 9; Wilmington, Delaware: Michael Glazier, 1984).

[25] *Unity* 17.

[26] The first chapter includes sections on the scriptures, God's foreknowledge, 'certain verbs' (do, determine, set, destine, must), the Holy Spirit, angels and visions.

[27] 'Any effort to interpret Luke's double work primarily in terms of Hellenistic literature is mistaken' (*Unity* 12). O'Toole regards the Septuagint as the primary background to Luke–Acts, but his detailed analysis fails to substantiate this claim adequately.

[28] 'The Divine Purpose: The Jews and the Gentile Mission (Acts 15)', *Luke–Acts: New Perspectives from the Society of Biblical Literature Seminar* (ed. C. H. Talbert; New York: Crossroads, 1984) 188–209.

[29] Necessity, supernatural intervention, temporal expressions and interpretation of the Old Testament.

[30] 'δεῖ', *TDNT* 2 (1964) 21–5.

implications'.[31] Grundmann interpreted this Lukan usage in a most restrictive manner, however, viewing the evidence solely through the lens of 'the necessity of the eschatological event'. E. Fascher[32] explored δεῖ in the New Testament in more detail, noting that Luke links it with fulfilling the scriptures and the Holy Spirit, and equating it with the will of God. Yet because his study ranges widely across so much material, he does not probe the Lukan reasons for its prominence, and concludes rather lamely that in Acts δεῖ is used in the same way as in the LXX and in Paul.[33]

The will of God in Luke has been studied only in passing, usually in the context of the synoptic tradition and the words of Jesus,[34] rather than in the context of Luke–Acts as a literary entity in itself. The importance of the phrase designating the plan of God (βουλὴ τοῦ θεοῦ) in the overall structure of Luke–Acts was recognized by P. Schubert[35] but he failed to relate this theme explicitly to the wider linguistic evidence noted by others. A significant comment in his earlier study on proof by prophecy in Luke 24, that 'in most cases Luke's δεῖ had fully technical, theological denotations and connotations', remains undeveloped in his later writings.[36]

G. Stählin[37] takes a thematic approach to Fate (*Schicksal*) in the whole of the New Testament and in Josephus. Discussing the conjunction of certain key terms, he notes that this complex of terms occupies a central position in the theology of Luke; but again,

[31] Grundmann, 'δεῖ' 23.

[32] 'Theologische Beobachtungen zu δεῖ', *Neutestamentliche Studien für Rudolf Bultmann*, (ed. W. Eltester; Berlin: Alfred Töpelmann, 1954) 228–54.

[33] See also Fascher's article, 'Theologische Beobachtungen zu δεῖ im A.T.', *ZNW* 45 (1954) 244–52.

[34] G. Segalla, 'Gesù revelatore della volontà del Padre nella Tradizione Sinnotica', *Rivista biblica italiana* 14 (1966) 467–508; and C. L. Mitton, 'The Will of God in the Synoptic Tradition of the Words of Jesus', *ExpTim* 72 (1960–1) 68–71.

[35] 'The Place of the Areopagus Speech in the Composition of Acts', *Transitions in Biblical Scholarship* (Essays in Divinity 6, ed. J. C. Rylaarsdam; Chicago: University of Chicago Press, 1968) 235–61, and 'The Final Cycle of Speeches in the Book of Acts', *JBL* 87 (1968) 1–16. In this latter article he declares that 'the theology of Luke is a many-sided development of the theme of the ὡρισμένη βουλὴ τοῦ θεοῦ' (p. 2).

[36] 'The Structure and Significance of Luke 24', *Studien* (ed. Eltester) 165–86. In similar fashion, R. C. Tannehill ('Israel in Luke–Acts: A Tragic Story', *JBL* 104 (1985) 69–85) considers that the various episodes of Luke–Acts 'are part of a unitary story because they are related to a unifying purpose, the βουλὴ τοῦ θεοῦ, to which the writing refers with some frequency'; but he limits his development of this statement to the 'tragic story' of Israel.

[37] 'Das Schicksal im Neuen Testament und bei Josephus', *Josephus-Studien: Untersuchungen zu Josephus, dem antiken Judentum und dem Neuen Testament. Otto Michel zum 70. Geburtstag gewidmet* (ed. O. Betz, K. Haacker and M. Hengel; Göttingen: Vandenhoeck und Ruprecht, 1974) 319–43.

because of the scope of his study, he fails to provide a distinctively Lukan profile regarding the theme. None of these studies, then, attempt to relate their conclusions to other dimensions of the plan of God, nor do they offer any comprehensive reason as to why Luke uses these particular aspects of the plan of God in his work.

### 1.2.3 The cultural context

The precise cultural context within which to view the theme has been interpreted in radically different ways. Fascher argues that Luke–Acts reflects a Jewish understanding of the divine control of history, mediated particularly through Old Testament texts, where for Schulz a hellenistic understanding of providence shapes the story of Luke–Acts. Both Schulz and Fascher assume that a heavily deterministic understanding of Fate as an impersonal entity was held consistently throughout the hellenistic world, and contrast this sharply with the Old Testament view in which God is involved with Israel in a personal struggle of wills. Each of these studies thus relies on a false dichotomy between Jewish and hellenistic environments, and overlooks much evidence to suggest that Judaism was substantially hellenized well before the first century.[38]

Fascher's effort to distance Luke's δεῖ entirely from an impersonal entity is insensitive to the processes of adaptation which were at work amongst the Jews from early in the hellenistic period, and thus to the range of opinions concerning Fate which existed anywhere in a hellenistic Jewish environment. Schulz's effort to prove the presence of a hellenistic 'blind Fate' in Luke–Acts is itself blind to the differences, both sharp and subtle, in the understandings of Fate and necessity within the hellenistic world. The result of this polemical treatment of the context within which to understand the plan of God in Luke–Acts is that we must explore in more detail, and with greater openness to the evidence, the understandings of providence which existed in Luke's time.

---

[38] One need only cite the pioneering studies of S. Lieberman, *Greek in Jewish Palestine: Studies in the Life and Manner of Jewish Palestine in the II–IV Centuries CE* (New York: Jewish Theological Seminary of America, 1942) and *Hellenism in Jewish Palestine: Studies in the Literary Transmission, Beliefs and Manners of Palestine in the I Century BCE – I Century CE* (New York: Jewish Theological Seminary of America, 1950), and the comprehensive treatment by M. Hengel, *Judaism and Hellenism: Studies in their Encounter in Palestine during the Early Hellenistic Period* (2 vols.; Philadelphia: Fortress Press, 1974).

E. Plümacher,[39] in his careful treatment of Acts in the context of hellenistic historiography, shows how certain dramatic episodes in Acts function in a manner similar to such episodes in hellenistic literature. In discussing those episodes related to the gentile mission,[40] he makes frequent reference to the direct intervention and ongoing providence of God, but the only texts he uses with which to compare the content (rather than the function) of the material are later Christian apologetic writings, not earlier non-Christian historiographical works.

### 1.2.4 Theological interpretations

A variety of theological interpretations of the plan of God in Luke–Acts have been proposed. In his epochal study on Lukan theology, H. Conzelmann[41] saw the theme of 'the role of God in redemptive history'[42] as a pivotal point in his overall schema of the three epochs of salvation history. Recognizing the importance of the plan of God in Luke's work, Conzelmann related it to Luke's characteristic theological perspective: 'the delay [of the parousia] has to be explained, and this is done by means of the idea of God's plan which underlies the whole structure of Luke's account'.[43] Conzelmann refuted the false eschatological interpretation of δεῖ offered by Grundmann,[44] but continued to uphold the misleading dichotomy between Jewish and hellenistic environments, and injected other inaccuracies into his discussion, notably his treatment of 'election'.[45]

I. H. Marshall[46] continued the dichotomy by concluding 'that Luke's idea of God is drawn from the Old Testament tradition, and that hellenistic influences are peripheral',[47] but certain theological objections that he raised against Conzelmann[48] alert one to the

[39] *Lukas als hellenistischer Schriftsteller: Studien zur Apostelgeschichte* (Göttingen: Vandenhoeck und Ruprecht, 1972).
[40] *Lukas* 86–91, 105.
[41] *The Theology of St Luke* (London: Faber and Faber, 1960).
[42] *Theology* 149–57.
[43] *Theology* 131–2.
[44] *Theology* 153 n. 2.
[45] *Theology* 154–6.
[46] 'God My Saviour', *Luke: Historian and Theologian* (Exeter: Paternoster, 1970) 103–15.
[47] *Historian* 115.
[48] See also the critical (but sympathetic) evaluation of Conzelmann by U. Wilckens, 'Interpreting Luke–Acts in a Period of Existentialist Theology', *Studies in Luke–Acts* (ed. L. E. Keck and J. L. Martyn; Philadelphia: Fortress Press, 1966) 60–83; the more direct repudiation of Conzelmann's interpretation by W. G. Kümmel, 'Luc en accusation dans la théologie contemporaine', *ETL* 46 (1970)

dogmatic presuppositions inherent in Conzelmann's work which interfere with his reading of the text. Necessity, both eschatological and historical, is related to the scriptures even before Luke writes (for we see this in Mark), especially to the Spirit in the book of Acts.[49] The concept of election has not been replaced by a hellenistic notion of predetermination, for election words are not as rare in Luke–Acts as Conzelmann claimed.[50] Marshall accordingly refutes this aspect of Conzelmann's construction of a Lukan *Heils-geschichte*.

More recent treatments of the theme are to be found in three further studies. The thesis of D. L. Tiede[51] is that Luke–Acts is an indication of the widespread soul-searching in late first-century Judaism, seeking to assert God's providence even in the wake of the destruction of the Temple. Tiede does not arbitrarily separate Jewish and hellenistic contexts, but locates key passages of Luke–Acts within ongoing Jewish midrashic debates, offering helpful suggestions as to the function of this theme in hermeneutic, theological and pastoral contexts. Whilst he acknowledges the hellenistic influences on Luke, Tiede pays much more attention to analysing Luke's midrashic techniques as a means of dealing with the crucifixion of Jesus, the fall of Jerusalem and the rejection of the Jews in favour of the Gentiles.

C. H. Cosgrove[52] addresses the question of the relation of divine necessity to human free-will in Luke–Acts and outlines the shape of providence as Luke understands it. Although he provides a larger framework for Luke's expression of providence, Cosgrove does not seek to relate his exegesis to philosophical concerns in other literature of the time, nor to the occurrence of the theme in contemporary historiography, nor does he directly address the broader theological implications of this theme.

T. Radcliffe[53] analyses the Emmaus story of Luke 24 with particular reference to the problem of necessity and freedom, and provides a philosophically oriented discussion in which he concludes that Luke used this theme to undergird the identity of his

---

265–81; and the survey of other reactions to Conzelmann's view by F. Bovon, *Luc le théologien: vingt-cinq ans de recherches (1950–75)* (Neuchâtel et Paris: Delachaux et Niestlé, 1978) 21–84.

[49] Marshall, *Historian* 107–11.
[50] Marshall, *Historian* 111–13.
[51] *Prophecy and History in Luke–Acts* (Philadelphia: Fortress Press, 1980).
[52] 'The Divine ΔΕΙ in Luke–Acts', *NovT* 26 (1984) 168–90.
[53] 'The Emmaus Story: Necessity and Freedom', *New Blackfriars* 64 (1983) 483–93.

community by affirming its links with its Jewish roots. This is a useful contribution which again is limited in its scope.[54]

### 1.3 A comparative approach to the theme of providence

Our survey of these interpretations, many of which have contributed useful items of information, demonstrates that we lack a comprehensive statement of the understanding which Luke had of the plan of God, and the role that it played in his two-volume work. In particular, three questions need to be addressed in order to make such a statement:

(i)   What logic holds together the various strands of the plan of God?

(ii)  What understanding of providence and Fate lies behind and informs Luke's use of this theme?

(iii) What is the function of the plan of God, in all its various strands, within Luke–Acts?

We will proceed towards answers to each of these questions by treating five strands of the primary theme which we have distinguished, namely the primary strand of providence, how God is at work in history; divine interventions through portentous events; epiphanies in which God is manifested; prophecies which are given and whose fulfilment is later noted; and the divine necessity of certain key events. In considering this last strand, the question of the freedom of the human will to exercise its own intentions will be explored in its relation to the plan of God.

Two related approaches will be taken to each of these strands. After a brief survey of each of the strands in Luke–Acts, noting where specific terms or themes are to be found, a comparative analysis will be made of each strand in turn, in order to shed light on the ways in which Luke's readers might have understood the theme and the interrelations of the various strands. This comparative analysis will explore works of the same general period in order to discover the function of these themes and their interrelationship one with another. Then, in a more theological and exegetical vein, we shall explore the use of each strand by Luke in his writings. Throughout this exploration, specific passages will be dealt with in

---

[54]  E. Richard gives further bibliographical references to studies in which the theme appears in passing, in 'Luke – Writer, Theologian, Historian: Research and Orientation of the 1970s', *BTB* 13 (1983) 3–15.

more detail, to demonstrate how each strand, although isolated for ease of consideration, is in fact an integral part of the overall cluster of strands making up the theme of 'the plan of God'. In the light of our comparative analysis, we shall draw conclusions as to what function is performed by this theme in Luke–Acts, and what roles the various strands play in that overall function.

Some justification for the comparative aspect of our approach is required. An increasing trend in recent scholarship has been to relate Luke–Acts to the hellenistic world, reflecting a wider acknowledgement of the influence of hellenization on the world of the early Christians.[55] For our purposes, it is important to take note of the ways in which the concept of divine providence (in its various terms) was dealt with in that context,[56] in order to understand how an ancient reader of Luke–Acts might have understood the theme of the plan of God. For this reason, then, the writings of Flavius Josephus[57] are important evidence, for Josephus exhibits a distinctive perspective: providence and the will of God is a central theme in his *Antiquitates Judaicae* (AJ).[58]

Josephus makes use of certain historiographical conventions which are found in hellenistic histories, indicating his awareness of this genre and his deliberate attempt to present Jewish history in a manner congenial to educated readers of Greek and Roman histories.[59] Two major hellenistic histories written within the century

[55] On this issue more generally, see W. C. van Unnik, 'First Century A.D. Literary Culture and Early Christian Literature', *Nederlands Theologisch Tijdschrift* 25 (1971) 28–48; for Luke in particular, see H. J. Cadbury, *The Book of Acts in History* (New York: Harper, 1955), esp. 32–85.

[56] C. H. Talbert ('Promise and Fulfilment in Lucan Theology', *Luke–Acts* (ed. Talbert) 91–103) rightly points out the necessity of examining Luke–Acts within the wider cultural context of his time, and asking 'how a Mediterranean person would likely have heard the Lucan presentation', referring explicitly to 'divine necessity' (*ibid.*, 96–7).

[57] The importance of Josephus for the study of Acts in the context of contemporary historiography is noted by H. J. Cadbury, F. J. Foakes Jackson and K. Lake, 'The Greek and Jewish Traditions of Writing History', *The Beginnings of Christianity: Part I, The Acts of the Apostles* (F. J. Foakes Jackson and K. Lake, eds.; 5 vols.; London: Macmillan, 1920–33, reprinted Grand Rapids, Mich.: Baker, 1979) 2.15, 25–9. On the relation between Josephus and Luke, see H. Schreckenberg in 'Flavius Josephus und die lukanischen Schriften', *Wort in der Zeit, Neutestamentliche Studien, Festgabe für Karl Heinrich Rengstorf zum 75. Geburtstag* (ed. W. Haubeck and M. Bachmann; Leiden, Brill, 1980) 179–209, and the bibliography he assembles. On the common apologetic purposes of Luke and Josephus, see J. C. O'Neill, *The Theology of Acts in its Historical Setting* (London: SPCK, 1970 (2nd edn) 146–7.

[58] Abbreviations used for the other works of Josephus are as follows: BJ (*Bellum Judaicum*), CA (*Contra Apionem*) and V (*Vita*).

[59] In AJ 20.263, Josephus comments on his knowledge of Greek literature, and in CA 1.37, he refers to earlier authors who wrote historical works on the Jews in the

prior to Josephus' own work reveal the prominence of providence as a theme in this genre. In his universal history, the *Bibliotheke Historike* (BH), Diodorus Siculus calls historians 'ministers of divine providence' (BH 1.1.3), making substantial use of the idea throughout his work. A similar concern with the activity of the gods in guiding human history is to be found in the *Romaike Archaiologia* (RA) of Dionysius of Halicarnassus. By exploring this thematic area in these works, we shall gain a sense of what was the popular belief about providence, and where Luke's presentation might be placed in the contemporary discussion. In this way, this study will make a further contribution, it is hoped, to the ways in which Luke's work shows similarities with hellenistic methods of historiography current in his day.[60]

Furthermore, the other strands associated with the primary theme of the plan of God in Luke–Acts, which we have noted above, are to be found in the hellenistic histories already noted, often in connection with the idea of providence or divine guidance of history. Portents were considered to have been signs given by the gods and

---

Greek language. Concerning the conventions of hellenistic histories, Cadbury, Foakes Jackson and Lake consider that 'Josephus ... is largely under the spell of these principles' ('Traditions', *Beginnings* 2.15); similarly, T. Rajak, *Josephus: The Historian and His Society* (Philadelphia: Fortress Press, 1983) 102; H. W. Attridge, 'Josephus and His Works', *Jewish Writings of the Second Temple Period* (Compendia rerum iudaicarum ad Novum Testamentum 2.2; Assen: Van Gorcum, 1984) 206, 217. Attridge surveys earlier attempts to relate Josephus to hellenistic historiography and pronounces them all 'disappointing' (*The Interpretation of Biblical History in the 'Antiquitates Judaicae' of Flavius Josephus* (HDR 7; Missoula: Scholars Press, 1976) 24–5); but now, see the excellent analysis by R. G. Bomstead, 'Governing Ideas of the Jewish War of Josephus' (Yale Ph.D. diss., 1979) 62–73. On the sources used by Josephus, see E. Schürer, 'Josephus', *The History of the Jewish People in the Age of Jesus Christ (175 B.C.–A.D. 135)* (trans., rev. and ed. G. Vermes and F. Millar; Edinburgh: T. & T. Clark, 1973) 49–52; R. J. H. Shutt, *Studies in Josephus* (London: SPCK, 1961) 75–7, 79–109; T. Rajak, 'Josephus and the "Archaeology" of the Jews', *JJS* 33 (1982) 471–4.

[60] The most thorough discussion to date is that of E. Plümacher, *Lukas* (*passim*). See also M. Dibelius, 'The First Christian Historian', *Studies in the Acts of the Apostles* (ed. H. Greeven; London: SCM, 1956) 123–37; C. K. Barrett, *Luke the Historian in Recent Study* (London: Epworth, 1961) 9–12; W. C. van Unnik, 'Luke's Second Book and the Rules of Hellenistic Historiography', *Les Actes des Apôtres: traditions, rédaction, théologie* (ed. J. Kremer, Bibliotheca Ephemeridum Theologicarum Lovaniensium; Gembloux: Duculot, 1979) 37–60; G. W. Trompf, *The Idea of Historical Recurrence in Western Thought: From Antiquity to the Reformation* (Berkeley: University of California Press, 1979) 121–2, 321–4; and the discussions of genre in W. S. Kurz, 'The Function of Christological Proof from Prophecy for Luke and Justin' (Yale Ph.D. diss., 1976) 7–9, and D. E. Aune, *The New Testament in its Literary Environment* (Library of Early Christianity 8; Philadelphia: Westminster, 1987) 77–80, 116–31, 138–41.

were therefore subjected to intense scrutiny in the hellenistic world.[61] Both dreams or visions, and prophecies made concerning the future, were also carefully interpreted because they were seen as ways by which the gods guided events.[62]

The relation of providence to Fate or necessity was also an occasional topic of discussion in the popular historical writings.[63] Accordingly, the relationship of these themes in the wider cultural context, as reflected in the literature of Diodorus, Dionysius and Josephus, will illuminate the interweaving of the various strands in Luke–Acts[64]. Josephus, in particular, at certain points indicates his awareness of the more intellectual discussion of issues concerning providence and Fate, portents and prophecy. His presentation of the three major Jewish sects of his day in the manner of Greek philosophical schools, with particular reference to their views on Fate, shows his knowledge of the various philosophical perspectives.[65] His discussion of Daniel's prophecies is a glimpse into the way the issues were debated in the philosophical schools of the day,[66] as is a speech he places in the mouth of Moses.[67]

Both Diodorus[68] and Dionysius[69] give similar indications of their knowledge of the philosophical debates. In the philosophical literature itself extensive consideration is given to these questions in

[61] See, amongst many examples, Dionysius, RA 1.23.1–3; 2.56.6; 3.16.2; Diodorus, BH 2.25.5; 17.66.7,114.5; Josephus, AJ 2.332; 4.128; 10.177; 11.279–81; see further in chap. 4.

[62] Dreams: Dionysius, RA 5.56.1; Diodorus, BH 4.43.1–2,48.6–7; 17.103.7; Josephus, AJ 4.110; 5.277; 17.354; see further in chap. 5. Prophecies: Dionysius, RA 2.32.1; 3.70.5; 10.9.4; Diodorus, BH 31.10.1–2; Josephus, AJ 10.277–81; 15.373; see further in chap. 6.

[63] Thus, Dionysius, RA 3.5.1–2; 5.54.1; Diodorus, BH 2.30.1; Josephus, BJ 4.622; CA 2.245; AJ 16.397–8; see further in chap. 7.

[64] Some indication of this is given, very briefly, by Aune, *New Testament* 131–6; many elements of the themes noted here are mentioned as common to Luke and 'pagan historiography' by W. den Boer, 'Some Remarks on the Beginnings of Christian Historiography', *Studia Patristica* 4 (1961) 348–62.

[65] See AJ 13.171–3; 18.11–25; BJ 2.119–66.

[66] AJ 10.277–81. See W. C. van Unnik, 'An Attack on the Epicureans by Flavius Josephus', *Romanitas et Christianitas: Studia Iano Henrico Waszink* (ed. W. den Boer, P. G. van der Nat, C. M. J. Sicking and J. C. M. van Winden; Amsterdam and London: North Holland, 1973) 351; L. H. Feldman, 'Hellenizations in Josephus' Portrayal of Man's Decline', *Religions in Antiquity: Studies in Memory of Erwin Ramsdell Goodenough* (ed. J. Neusner; Leiden: Brill, 1968) 342–3; see further in chap. 3.2.2.

[67] AJ 4.47. Van Unnik ('Attack' 349) notes that reading the prayer as a philosophical polemic by Josephus, rather than as a confession by Moses, 'shows how dear the ideas [of providence] were to Josephus and how the Epicurean doctrine is here implicitly condemned'.

[68] BH 15.48.4.

[69] RA 2.68.1–2; 8.56.1.

treatises on providence[70] and Fate[71] and in discussions on the
relation between divination of omens and divine providence.[72]
When the material with which we are concerned reflects this philosophical discussion, we will investigate this literature also.

Luke himself gives very few clues as to his knowledge of such
discussions, for it is only in the second century that Christians
directly address matters of necessity and free will.[73] The methods of
the apologists, however, bear some resemblance to the way in which
Josephus deals with the matter, and may also have a role to play in
helping us to understand what Luke does, or does not, do in this
regard. Accordingly, we shall explore the arguments of the Christian apologists who first dealt directly with philosophical criticisms
of Christianity in the area of providence and free will.[74] More
generally, the ways that the apologists counter the various kinds of
criticism levelled against Christianity by pagans (once Christianity
had become well known and widespread enough to warrant such
attention) are instructive when we consider Luke's apologetic tendencies and methods.[75]

It is hoped, therefore, that this wider contextual investigation will
enable us to see the meanings inherent in Luke's use of the plan of
God, to understand the ways in which the various strands of that
theme were interwoven by Luke, and to propose reasons as to why
Luke presents his story in this way.

[70] Seneca, De prov., Philo, De prov., and Plotinus, Περὶ εἱμαρμένης I and II.

[71] Cicero, De fato and the relevant sections of De nat. deor. and De div., Ps-
Plutarch, Περὶ εἱμαρμένης, and Plotinus, Περὶ εἱμαρμένης.

[72] See Cicero, De div..

[73] First found in Justin Martyr, First Apology 28; 43–4; Second Apology 7;
Dialogue with Trypho 141; and then in Tatian, Oratio 7; 9; 11; Athenagoras, Legatio
25.

[74] The similarities between the writings of Luke and the apologist Justin are
explored by F. Overbeck, 'Über das Verhältnis Justins des Märtyrers zur Apostelgeschichte', ZWT 15 (1872) 305–49. O'Neill develops this connection in various
ways, especially with regard to the use of similar apologetic arguments by Luke and
Justin (Theology 14–15, 166–71, 176–8); but for problems with the dating adopted by
O'Neill, see J. Jervell, Luke and the People of God: A New Look at Luke–Acts
(Minneapolis, Minn.: Augsburg, 1972) 175 and the literature noted by Kurz, 'Proof
from Prophecy' 1 n. 2. Kurz provides a useful study of the apologetic functions of
proof from prophecy in Luke and Justin (see esp. 174–84, 250–1). On the apologetic
purposes of Luke–Acts in the context of the late first-century church, see E. Trocmé,
'The Beginnings of Christian Historiography and the History of Early Christianity',
AusBR 31 (1983) 7–11. On political apologetic, see chap. 3 n. 83.

[75] Reference is made to second- and third-century literature with due caution,
acknowledging the perils of an anachronistic interpretation of Luke–Acts. Nevertheless, the pagan writers cited are representative of a general hellenistic viewpoint on
religion, and for this reason are useful for gaining a perspective on Luke–Acts.

# 2

## THE PROGRAMMATIC ROLE OF PROVIDENCE IN HELLENISTIC HISTORIOGRAPHY

### 2.1 The histories of Diodorus Siculus and Dionysius of Halicarnassus

'It is fitting that all men should ever accord great gratitude to those writers who have composed universal histories',[1] writes Diodorus Siculus in the latter years of the first century BCE, as he commences his own mammoth attempt at a universal history, the *Bibliotheke Historike*.

> Such historians have therein shown themselves to be, as it were, ministers of divine providence (ὑπουργοὶ τῆς θείας προνοίας), for just as providence, having brought the orderly arrangement of the visible stars and the natures of men together into one common relationship, continually directs their courses through all eternity, apportioning to each that which falls to it by the direction of fate (ἐκ τῆς πεπρωμένης μερίζουσα), so likewise the historians ... have made of their treatises a single reckoning of past events and a common clearing-house of knowledge concerning them.
> (BH 1.1.3)[2]

---

[1] For Diodorus' dependence on earlier historians, see J. Palm, *Über Sprache und Stil des Diodorus von Sizilien* (Lund: Gleerup, 1955) 15–63; J. R. Hamilton, 'Cleitarchus and Aristobulus', *Historia* 10 (1961) 448–58; R. Drews, 'Diodorus and his Sources', *American Journal of Philology* 83 (1962) 383–92; R. K. Sinclair, 'Diodorus Siculus and the Writing of history', *Proceedings of the African Classical Association* 6 (1963) 36–45; F. W. Walbank, 'The Historians of Greek Sicily', *Kokalos* 14–15 (1968–9) 491–3; and F. Bizière, 'Comment travaillait Diodore de Sicile', *Revue des Etudes Grecques* 87 (1974) 369–74.

[2] On the development of universal history in Greek historians, see F. Jacoby, 'Über die Entwicklung der Griechischen Historiographie und den Plan einer neuen Sammlung der Griechischen Historikerfragmente', *Klio* 9 (1909) 80–123, esp. 99–106; J. B. Bury, *The Ancient Greek Historian* (London: Macmillan, 1909) 162–3, 178, 199, 235–40; A. Momigliano, 'The Origins of Universal History', *The Poet and the Historian: Essays in Literary and Historical Biblical Criticism* (ed. R. E. Friedman; Harvard

Diodorus thus envisions the ideal historical work as one in which
the historian's ordering of disparate events into one account is
comparable to the way that providence orders the elements of the
cosmos into one scheme. In practice, however,

> when we turned our attention to the historians before our
> time, although we approved their purpose without reserva-
> tion, yet we were far from feeling that their treatises had
> been composed so as to contribute to human welfare as
> much as might have been the case. For although the profit
> which history affords its readers lies in its embracing a vast
> number and variety of circumstances, yet most writers have
> recorded no more than isolated wars waged by a single
> nation or a single state, and but few have undertaken ... to
> record the events connected with all peoples. (BH 1.3.1–2)[3]

Diodorus' own work is an attempt to rectify this situation by writing
a history in which divine providence plays a dominant role.[4]

With the same intentions, Dionysius of Halicarnassus undertook
his pioneer work on the early centuries of Roman history, the

Semitic Studies 26; Chico, Calif.: Scholars Press, 1983) 133–54; C. W. Fornara, *The
Nature of History in Ancient Greece* (Berkeley: University of California Press, 1983)
42–67; and Aune, *New Testament* 86–9.

[3] The need for history to be useful (ὠφέλιμος or χρήσιμος) is asserted by Thucydides, 1.22.4; Polybius, *Hist.* 1.35.9; 15.36.3; 33.1.10–13; Dionysius, RA 1.2.1; and
Lucian *Hist.* 9; 42; 53. On edification as the purpose of history, see Fornara, *Nature*
104–20; G. Avenarius, *Lukians Schrift zur Geschichtsschreibung* (Meisenheim/Glan:
Anton Hain, 1956) 22–6.

[4] Providence is widely recognized as an organizing principle of Greek history from
the time of Herodotus; see Arrian, *Anab.* 5.1.2; Fornara, *Nature* 78; van Seters, *In
Search of History* 34, 361; W. den Boer, 'Graeco-Roman Historiography in its
Relation to Biblical and Modern Thinking', *History and Theory* 7 (1968) 70; 'Some
Remarks' 358–9; and Bury, *Historians* 46–7, 68, although Bury admits Herodotus
may simply be showing 'a formal homage to orthodox dogma' (*Historians* 49). Cf.
A. Momigliano ('Greek Historiography', *History and Theory* 17 (1978) 7), who con-
siders that 'metaphysical explanations' were usually avoided in hellenistic histories.
For further bibliography, see Rajak, *Josephus* 101 n. 40.

A century prior to Diodorus, Polybius had claimed this as his distinctive contribution to the historiographical enterprise (*Hist.* 1.4.1–2). But the role of Fortune in
Polybius' work has occasioned modern scholarly debate, particularly over the matter
of Polybius' knowledge and use of Stoic concepts of Fate and Providence. See
S. Zeitlin, 'A Survey of Jewish Historiography from the Biblical Books to the Sepher
ha-Kabbalah', *JQR* 59 (1969) 181–2; Momigliano, 'Historiography' 7; Bury, *Historians* 203; and Fornara, *Nature* 81. F. W. Walbank explains the contradiction
inherent in Polybius' assessment of Fortune as being due to the common usage of the
word which had rendered it 'unsuitable for conveying precise ideas' (*Polybius: The
Rise of the Roman Empire* (Harmondsworth: Penguin, 1979) 30).

*Romaike Archaiologia*. He, too, writes to refute earlier historians[5]
who 'are careless and indolent in compiling their narrative' (RA
1.1.4), and to correct those who ignorantly claim that Roman
superiority came about only 'through some chance (αὐτοματίσμον)
and the injustice of Fortune (τύχην)' or who maliciously 'are wont
to rail openly at Fortune for freely bestowing on the basest of
barbarians the blessings of the Greeks' (RA 1.4.2).[6]

Dionysius thus sets forth the theoretical foundation for his work
as he explains that he writes

> to the end that I may instil in the minds of those who shall
> then be informed of the truth the fitting conception of this
> city [i.e. Rome] ... and also that they may neither feel
> indignation at their present subjection, which is grounded
> on reason (for by an universal law of Nature, which time
> cannot destroy, it is ordained that superiors shall ever
> govern their inferiors), nor rail at Fortune for having wan-
> tonly bestowed upon an undeserving city a supremacy so
> great and already of so long continuance.        (RA 1.5.2)[7]

In short, he writes that his readers may 'lay aside all resentment'
(RA 1.5.3); but the positive dimension of his programme is to
present the workings of Fortune in such a way as to win the
admiration of the Greeks for the Romans,[8] whom Dionysius depicts
as their distant cousins hailing from the same good Greek origins.[9]

---

[5] For criticisms of previous historians as a *topos* in Greek history, see Avenarius, *Lukians Schrift* 50. Polybius explicitly criticizes various of his predecessors throughout his work; see, for example, his remarks concerning Philinus and Fabius at *Hist.* 1.14, Phylarchus at 2.56, Chaereas and Sosylus at 3.20 and Timaeus throughout Book 12.

[6] Whilst Dionysius shares with Diodorus a polemical view of earlier historians, the programme he here unfolds differs from that claimed by Diodorus, who attempted to provide a universal history in some organized fashion. Dionysius' purpose is more limited, namely to provide an accurate account of Roman origins. The means to these divergent ends, however, include the common factor of divine guidance and control of history.

[7] On Dionysius' 'reverence for Τύχη', see Drews, 'Sources', 386 n. 15. On these claims for the apologetic role of τύχη, see the analysis in chap. 3.1.3.

[8] Dionysius refutes the claim that the ἀρχαιολογία of Rome is a period 'so barren of distinction' (RA 1.4.1) and emphasizes that 'Rome from the very beginning (ἐξ ἀρχῆς) ... produced infinite examples of virtue in men' (1.5.3).

[9] 'I engage to prove that they were Greeks and came together from nations not the smallest nor the least considerable' (RA 1.5.1). In 1.10.1 he describes the Romans as αὐτόχθονας, the very word which reflects Attic pride in their aboriginal status in Athens (see Euripides, *Ion* 29, 589–90; Aristophanes, *Vespae* 1076; and Isocrates 4.24; 8.49; 12.124–5)

## 2.2 The history of Josephus

In his *Antiquitates Judaicae*, Josephus reflects many of the same conventions found in hellenistic historiography,[10] making use especially of the motif of providence.[11] Although the prominence of the idea of God's guidance of history may be attributed to the Jewish upbringing of Josephus,[12] the particular form in which he presents the motif of providence is to be ascribed to his acquaintance with, and use of, methods of hellenistic historiography. Jewish writers prior to Josephus had indicated their awareness of this theme in Greek literature,[13] but only in Philo's writings was it

[10] See chap. 1 n. 59. Specific evidence for this has been seen in the features held in common by Dionysius and Josephus, such as their shared plan (both RA and AJ are in 20 volumes), purpose (an apology for Rome to the Greeks, an apology for the Jews to the Romans), method (not merely to present the truth but also to entertain and gratify the reader, RA 1.6.5 and AJ 1.17; 14.2) and style (many small features, notably the formula of RA 1.48.1, etc., which is similar to that of AJ 1.108 etc.). See Thackeray, *Josephus* (LCL; vol. 4; Cambridge, Mass.: Harvard University Press, 1930) ix–x; Shutt, *Studies* 97–101; and further bibliography in S. J. D. Cohen, *Josephus in Galilee and Rome; His Vita and Development as a Historian* (Columbia Studies in the Classical Tradition 8; Leiden: Brill, 1979) 26 n. 5. In fact, Josephus exhibits many features which are found not only in Dionysius, but throughout hellenistic historiography (see Cohen, *Josephus* 24–33; Rajak, 'Josephus' 465–77).

[11] On providence in Josephus, see C. G. Bretschneider, *Capita theologiae Judaeorum dogmaticae e Flavii Josephi scriptis collectae* (Lipsiae: Bahrdtium, 1812) 25–30; A. Schlatter, *Wie Sprach Josephus von Gott?* (Beiträge zur Förderung christlicher Theologie 14; Gütersloh: C. Bertelsmann, 1910) 49–55; D. A. Carson, *Divine Sovereignty and Human Responsibility: Biblical Perspectives in Tension* (New Foundations Theological Library; Atlanta: John Knox, 1981) 110–19; Attridge, *Interpretation (passim)* and 'Josephus' 218–19.

[12] See J. A. Montgomery, 'The Religion of Flavius Josephus', *JQR* 11 (1920–1) 286. However, the precise terminology of πρόνοια appears in the Septuagint only at 2 Macc 4.6, referring to the watchfulness of the king Seleucus IV, whilst προνοέω similarly refers to human oversight at Num 23.9; Job 24.15; Prov 3.4; 2 Macc 14.9. J. Freudenthal overstates the case when he claims that 'the idea of divine Providence ... is presented in every page of Scripture' ('Are there Traces of Greek Philosophy in the Septuagint?', *JQR* 2 (1890) 217), although as J. van Seters (*In Search of History* 52) notes, referring to both Greek and Hebrew traditions, 'divine providence ... [is one of the] basic concerns of both historiographic traditions ... and constitutes a major motivation for their existence'.

[13] The word πρόνοια is used of God at 3 Macc 4.21; 5.30; 4 Macc 9.24; 13.18; 17.22; Wis 14.3; 17.2; προνοέω is used of God at Wis 6.7. Most significant is Wis 14.3, where the noun appears in a philosophical commonplace contrasting a sailor vainly trusting in the wooden idol at the prow of his ship, with 'your providence (πρόνοια), Father, that steers its course (διακυβερνᾷ)'. For the use of διακυβερνάω by the Stoics, see Cleanthes' *Hymn to Zeus, apud* Marcus Aurelius 7.64; Plutarch, *Der virt. morali* 450C; and further references in Pease, *De Natvra Divinatione* 332. See the discussion of D. Winston, *The Wisdom of Solomon* (Anchor Bible 43; New York: Doubleday, 1974) 214, 265.

employed in a fully developed manner.[14]

The programmatic significance of this theme in the *Antiquitates Judaicae* is established in the prologue to the work:

> the main lesson to be learnt from this history, by any who care to peruse it, is that men who conform to the will of God (θεοῦ γνώμῃ), and who do not venture to transgress laws that have been excellently laid down, prosper in all things beyond belief, and for their reward are offered by God felicity; whereas, in proportion as they depart from the strict observance of these laws, things practicable become impracticable, and whatever imaginary good thing they strive to do ends in irretrievable disasters. (AJ 1.14)

The full force of this purpose is expressed in the first reported speech of God, addressed to Adam:

> I had decreed for you to live a life of bliss ... all things that contribute to enjoyment and pleasure were, through my providence (πρόνοιαν), to spring up for you spontaneously (αὐτομάτων) ... but now you have flouted my purpose (γνώμην) by disobeying my commands. (AJ 1.46)[15]

In Fragment 1 of the Sibylline Oracles we find concentrated expressions of divine providence without the technical terminology found in Wisdom of Solomon and 3 and 4 Maccabees. God is descibed as the ἐπίσκοπος (frag. 1.3; see also *Sib. Or.* 3.29, and cf. πανεπίσκοπος, *Sib. Or.* 2.177) who alone rules (frag. 1.7; see also *Sib. Or.* 3.11) and leads (1.15; 1.35; see also frag. 3.13 and *Sib. Or.* 8.430). In Fragment 3, God watches over all (see also frag. 1.8, and *Sib. Or.* 3.12, 4.12). In the prayer in chap. 12 of *Joseph and Asenath*, there are similar indications of divine providence, without the technical terminology.

[14] On providence in Philo, see H. A. Wolfson, *Philo: Foundations of Religious Philosophy in Judaism, Christianity and Islam* (2 vols.; Cambridge, Mass.: Harvard University Press, 1947) 2.290–4; S. Sowers, 'On the Reinterprettion of Biblical History in Hellenistic Judaism', *Oikonomia, Heilsgeschichte als Thema der Theologier, Oscar Cullmann zum 65. Geburtstag gewidmet* (ed. F. Christ; Hamburg-Bergstedt; Reich, 1967) 18–25; S. Sandmel, 'Some Comments on Providence in Philo', *The Divine Helmsman: Studies on God's Control of Human Events, presented to Lou H. Silbermann* (ed. J. L. Crenshaw and S. Sandmel; New York: KTAV, 1980) 79–85; and D. A. Carson, 'Divine Sovereignty and Human Responsibility in Philo: Analysis and Method', *NTS* 23 (1981) 148–64.

Philo affirms his belief in providence against those who would deny its existence (*De opif. mundi* 2.9; *De ebr.* 1990, and upholds providence in explicitly philosophical terms (*De sobr.* 63 and throughout *De prov.*), but also depicts the workings of providence in history: providence guides Abraham (*De virtut.* 215), Joseph (*De Ios*, 99, 236) and Moses (*Vita Mosis* I.6,13,67,162; *De mut. nom.* 25).

[15] For the depiction of the original bliss of humanity in classical Greek authors, see Feldman, 'Hellenizations' 341, 347–8. On its special affinities with the Stoic notion of ἀπάθεια, see 'Hellenizations' 344.

Providence is thenceforth a key factor in the history of the Jewish nation, as Josephus reports it.

## 2.3  Luke's history of Jesus and the early church

In chapter one, we noted that one of the features of Luke–Acts which points to the similarities it shares with hellenistic historiography is the role accorded to providence in this work. Although it is never stated as explicitly as we find in Josephus, Diodorus or Dionysius, the theme is significant for Luke. However, before we consider some of the indications of its central role, we shall note the ways in which Luke presents his work as a history.

### 2.3.1  Luke's historiographic purpose

Luke begins his account of Jesus and the early church with a preface (Luke 1.1–4) which discloses his intentions in writing. When read in the context of hellenistic historiography, this preface indicates Luke's historiographic purpose.[16] Thus, Luke the historian acknowledges his use of sources,[17] which he claims have been faithfully handed down to him,[18] and emphasizes that the authors who

---

[16] See E. Norden, *Agnostos Theos* (Leipzig and Berlin: B. G. Teubner, 1913) 313–27; Foakes Jackson and Lake, *Beginnings* 2.489–510; W. den Boer, 'Some Remarks on the Beginnings of Christian Historiography', *Studia Patristica* 4 (1961) 348–62; Kurz, 'Proof from Prophecy' 11–12; D. J. Sneen, 'An Exegesis of Luke 1.1–4 with Special Regard to Luke's Purpose as a Historian', *ExpTim* 83 (1971) 40–3; W. C. van Unnik, 'Remarks on the Purpose of Luke's Historical Writing (Luke I 1–4)', *Sparsa Collecta: The Collected Essays of W. C. van Unnik* (3 vols.; Leiden: Brill, 1973) 1.6–15; I. J. du Plessis, 'Once More: The Purpose of Luke's Prologue (Lk 1.1–4)', *NovT* 16 (1974) 259–71; T. Callan, 'The Preface of Luke–Acts and Historiography', *NTS* 31 (1985) 576–81. Luke's Preface has been compared with those of hellenistic biographies, by V. K. Robbins ('Prefaces in Greco–Roman Biography and Luke–Acts', *SBLSPS* 14 (1978) 2.193–207) and with the 'scientific tradition' of the period, by L. Alexander ('Luke's Preface in the Context of Greek Preface-writing', *NovT* 28 (1986) 48–74).

[17] Luke refers to the many (πολλοί, 1.1) who have written on his subject before him, calling them 'eyewitnesses and ministers' (αὐτόπται καί ὑπηρέται, 1.2). Acknowledgement of earlier histories is likewise made by Diodorus (BH 1.1.1–3) and Dionysius (RA 1.1.1–2); Josephus frequently acknowledges that he uses earlier (Hebrew) records (AJ 1.5,13,17,26; see 20.263 and the literature cited at chap. 1 n.59). Diodorus calls historians 'ministers of divine providence' (ὑπουργοὶ τῆς θείας προνοίας, BH 1.1.3) and emphasizes that he has been an eyewitness (αὐτοπται, BH 1.3.1) of many of the places about which he writes; see also Herodotus 2.99,147; 4.81; Polybius, *Hist.* 12.25; Josephus, V 357–60; Foakes Jackson and Lake, *Beginnings* 2.498–500; du Plessis, 'Once More' 265.

[18] παρέδοσαν (1.2) is a technical term used of the passing down of traditional material; see F. Büchsel, 'παραδίδωμι', *TDNT* 2.171–3; Str–B 1.691–5; Foakes Jackson and Lake, *Beginnings* 2.497; I. H. Marshall, *The Gospel of Luke* (Exeter:

preceded him were eyewitnesses 'from the beginning'.[19] Much of the material he includes in his narrative account[20] is already known to his first reader, Theophilus,[21] and whilst Luke himself has carried out the historian's task of carefully scrutinizing his sources,[22] it is clear that he has arranged them according to his own purposes,[23] in order that Theophilus 'may know the certainty' of these things.[24]

Apart from the preface, there are other signs that history is the genre which best describes Luke–Acts. Aune[25] has argued that

Paternoster, 1978) 42; Fitzmyer, *Luke* 1.296–6. Trompf (*Idea* 321) notes that 'the appeal to reliable authorities is reminiscent of classical historiography'.

[19] ἀπ' ἀρχῆς (Luke 1.2); cf. the apologetic use of this phrase by Dionysius (RA 1.5.3, and see ἐξ' ἀρχῆς, RA 1.3.4), and his emphasis on the antiquity (ἀρχαιολογίαν, RA 1.4.1) of his subject; see above, n. 8. Josephus makes the same emphasis at AJ 1.5. On the similar function of ἄνωθεν, see Foakes Jackson and Lake, *Beginnings* 2.502–3; du Plessis, 'Once More' 267–8.

[20] διήγησιν (1.1) is a common description of histories; cf. Josephus, AJ 1.67; 10.157; V 336; and see du Plessis, 'Once More' 263; Fitzmyer, *Luke* 1.173–4, 292. On the rhetorical understanding of the διήγησις in antiquity, see E. Güttgemanns, 'In welchem Sinne ist Lukas "Historiker"?', *Linguistica Biblica* 54 (1983) 14–20.

[21] Since Theophilus has already been instructed (κατηχήθης, 1.4) about this material, Luke writes in agreement with his precursors; see Foakes Jackson and Lake, *Beginnings* 2.4.94; Marshall, *Historian* 40–1; S. Brown, 'The Role of the Prologues in Determining the Purpose of Luke–Acts', *Perspectives* (ed. Talbert) 104; van Unnik, 'Remarks' 13 n. 4; du Plessis, 'Once More' 162–2. (*Contra*, Conzelmann (Theology 14): Luke does not seek 'to instruct as, for example, Thucydides'.) Contrast this with Josephus' purpose to correct those who 'preach ignorance of important affairs' (AJ 1.3; and see CA 1.26).

[22] He claims that he has παρηκολουθηκότι ἄνωθεν πᾶσιν ἀκριβῶς (Luke 1.3); cf. the critical assessment of earlier histories offered by Diodorus (BH 1.1.4,3.1) and Dionysius (RA 1.1.3–4,4.2–3,5.4); and see above, n. 5. Josephus showed the same attitude towards others who had reported the war between Rome and the Jews (AJ 1.40; but his treatment of his scriptural source is sympathetic rather than critical (AJ 1.17, and see the discussion of this formula at chap. 5 n. 50). Callan ('Preface' 580) sees 'mild criticism' in Luke's reference to earlier accounts.

[23] καθεξῆς (1.3) reflects the 'Historisierung' of Luke's work (Schulz, 'Vorsehung' 112–13); cf. the clear explanations of purpose given by Diodorus (BH 1.1.3,3.5–8), Dionysius (RA 1.4.1,5.1–3) and Josephus (AJ 1.14–15). For examples of explicit statements in the preface of a history, concerning the plan of the whole work, see D. Earl, 'Prologue-form in Ancient Historiography', *ANRW* I.2.842–56.

[24] ἵνα ἐπιγνῷς ... τὴν ἀσφάλειαν (1.4); the emphatic position of ἀσφάλειαν is noted by Foakes Jackson and Lake, *Beginnings* 2.509–10; Maddox, *Purpose* 22; Fitzmyer, *Luke* 1.289. This purpose is equated with the common view in antiquity that history must instil the truth, by du Plessis ('Once More' 265, 267, 270–1); this is perceived as Luke's purpose by van Unnik ('Remarks' 8–9, 13, 14). See Lucian, *Hist.* 53; Polybius, *Hist.* 1.14.6; 2.56.12; Dionysius, RA 1.1.2,5.2; Josephus, AJ 1.4; 14.1–3; BJ 1.30; 7.455; CA 1.24; V 336–9. See also τεκμήριον (Acts 1.3) and the comments by Trompf (*Idea* 321–2) on its use in historiography. Callan ('Preface' 579) sees Luke's aim as related to the function of history as teaching what is useful; see Lucian, *Hist.* 7–14; Diodorus, BH 1.1.2,4,3.1; Josephus, AJ 1.3; CA 1.23; and n. 3 above.

[25] *Literary Environment* 116–19. For other useful discussions of Luke–Acts as hellenistic history, see W. A. Beardslee, *Literary Criticism of the New Testament*

Luke–Acts would certainly have been perceived as an historical work on the basis of four major features: (1) the somewhat refined language and style reflect 'elevated literary standards'; (2) the arrangement of two books follows the convention of historians who divide their works into (approximately) equal parts; the recapitulatory preface in book 2 (Acts) is also typical of histories; (3) precedents for the 'unsatisfactory' ending of Acts can be drawn from hellenistic histories; (4) the recurrence of similar literary patterns was frequent in histories, as were direct repetitions of the same event, told differently; parallelisms between volumes; and the same thirty-year span of each volume.

There are other features of hellenistic histories which are found in Luke–Acts.[26] The dominant role of speeches in Acts (where they form 25% of narrative) and the device of interrupting speeches at key points (Luke 4.28; Acts 7.53; 17.32; 23.7) both reflect common historiographical practice. The reporting of miracles in histories was common; to the ancient mind, 'history' was not a dry, 'rationalistic' enterprise, for the 'supernatural' was an ordinary part of everyday living and belief. Shipwrecks – and miraculous escapes (cf. Acts 27.14–44) – were part of such histories, as were accounts of travel and the various curiosities or wonders that were encountered on the way (cf. Paul on Malta, Acts 28.1–9). The use of doublets or triplets was not unknown; historians would often tell the same incident two or three different ways, adding a comment that the reader should determine which version is preferred – or stating their own preference. Luke reports the conversion of Saul thrice (Acts 9,22,26) and the visions to Peter and Cornelius twice (Acts 10,11), each time with minor, subtle differences.

Many speeches conform to standard hellenistic rhetorical patterns, as, for instance, the forensic speech of Acts 26.2–23. A common feature in histories was the symposium, or discourse framed around a meal setting, such as we find in Luke 7.36–50; 11.37–54; 14.1–24. There are two letters quoted in Acts (15.23–9; 23.26–30) in standard Greek form. Historians often quoted letters with the same function as speeches, to illustrate events. Classical

(Philadelphia: Fortress Press, 1970) 42–52; H. C. Kee, *Miracle in the Early Christian World: A Study in Sociohistorical Method* (New Haven and London: Yale University Press, 1983) 190–200; L. T. Johnson, *The Writings of the New Testament* (Philadelphia: Fortress Press, 1986) 200–4; E. P. Sanders and M. Davies, *Studying the Synoptic Gospels* (London: SCM, 1989) 276–98.
[26] The features listed here are investigated by Aune in *Literary Environment* 120–31.

allusions are also common in histories; certain turns of phrase or sayings evoke classical literature, such as the sayings of Peter before the Sanhedrin (Acts 5.29), Paul before the Areopagus (Acts 17.28) and even God to Saul on the Damascus road (Acts 26.14). Some forms of Jesus' sayings also evoke classical literature (e.g. Luke 22.25). The use of summary episodes in both volumes (Luke 4.37,44; 6.17–19; 9.6; Acts 2.43–7; 4.32–5; 5.11–16; 9.31; 12.24) reflects a common feature of histories, used to link together more detailed sources about different events. Finally, the oft-noted manner in which Luke provides clear historical settings for his narrative (Luke 1.5; 2.1–2; 3.1–2; Acts 11.28; 18.12) also reflects his historiographical tendencies.[27]

### 2.3.2 Luke's interest in providence

We have noted above the role played by providence in hellenistic histories. An explicit focus on divine providence, such as is evident in the prefaces to the works of Diodorus, Dionysius and Josephus, is lacking from Luke's preface, but becomes increasingly prominent throughout his work.[28] This narrative development sheds light back onto some of the significant terms of the preface, subtly indicating an interest in providence from the start.[29] This is seen most strongly in two phrases by which Luke introduces important motifs which summarize the content of his account.[30] By describing his subject matter as 'concerning the things (περὶ τῶν πραγμάτων) which have been accomplished among us' (1.1), Luke evokes the motif of

---

[27] Cf. the similar notes in Josephus, AJ 10.1; 11.1; 14.4.

[28] See Aune, *Literary Environment* 134–6. E. Dinkler ('Earliest Christianity', *The Idea of History in the Ancient Near East* (ed. R. C. Dentan; New Haven: Yale University Press, 1955) 197) incorrectly claims that 'the secularization of history in Christian theology begins with Luke'; see the criticisms of Kümmel, 'Luc en accusation' 278, and my argument below.

[29] R. J. Dillon ('Previewing Luke's Project from His Prologue (Luke 1.1–4)', *CBQ* 43 (1981) 205–27) sees an interest in the divine plan exhibited in Luke's use of the terms διήγησιν (pp. 208–9), καθεξῆς (pp. 219–23) and ἀσφάλειαν (pp. 224–6), as well as πεπληροφορημένων (pp. 211–12; see below, n. 31). Du Plessis considers Luke's purpose to be 'to serve Christianity with a true report of God acting in history', which he sees as implicit in the terms γενόμενοι ('Once More' 265) and ἄνωθεν ('Once More' 268). Sneen ('Exegesis' 42) interprets ἀσφάλειαν in connection with 'God's purpose and will for all mankind'.

[30] Alexander ('Preface' 72) considers the content of the work to be καθὼς παρέδοσαν ἡμῖν (1.2), but this ignores the more substantive phrases for the sake of a forced unity with her comparative material.

fulfilled prophecy,[31] inferring the providential dimension of his story through the word πεπληροφορημένων. By further describing his work as 'concerning the words (περὶ λόγων) which you have been taught' (1.4), Luke alludes to the later predominent understanding of the divine word[32] which is preached by Jesus (Luke 5.1; 8.21; 17.28; Acts 10.36) and the apostles (Peter at Acts 4.29,31; 11.1; Philip at 8.14; Paul at 13.5,7,44,46,48; 16.32; 18.11). Together, these phrases indicate Luke's comprehensive interest in the deeds (πραγμάτων) and words (λόγων) of the people in his narrative.

This all-encompassing scope is made explicit in the recapitulatory preface to the second volume[33] in which Luke summarizes the content of his first book as a complete account of 'everything which Jesus did and taught' (Acts 1.1),[34] a phrase reminiscent of the comprehensive scope of universal hellenistic histories.[35] A similar indication of the scope of his work comes at the conclusion of this second volume, where Luke notes that Paul both teaches 'the things concerning the Lord Jesus Christ' and preaches 'the kingdom of God' (28.31).

Luke's interest in the theme of providence can be seen in the way these two phrases are used elsewhere in his work, as well as in the recurrence of other key phrases which point to the importance of this

---

[31] Foakes Jackson and Lake (*Beginnings* 2.496) reject any reference to the fulfilment of scripture, as does Brown ('Prologues' 102–3), but the contrary is argued by N. A. Dahl, 'The Story of Abraham in Luke–Acts', *Studies* (ed. Keck and Martyn) 153, 158 n. 59; Marshall *Luke* 41; Kurz, 'Proof from Prophecy 12; Fitzmyer, *Luke* 1.289, 293; Maddox, *Purpose* 141–2; du Plessis, 'Once More' 263–4; Dillon, 'Preview-ing' 209–12; and see G. Klein, 'Lukas, I, 1–4 als theologische Program', *Zeit und Geschichte: Dankesgabe an Rudolf Bultmann zum 80 Geburtstag* (ed. E. Dinkler; Tübingen: Mohr, 1964) 196–200. The prominent role played by prophecy and fulfilment in Luke–Acts, and the similarities this shares with Deuteronomistic and hellenistic histories, is discussed in chap. 6.

[32] Thus, Marshall, *Historian* 160; Schubert, 'Areopagus Speech' 237 n. 8; du Plessis, 'Once More' 266; Fitzmyer, *Luke* 1.295. On λόγος in Luke–Acts, see O'Toole, *Unity* 86–94; and see Conzelmann's consideration of 'the message', *Theology* 2318–25. Haenchen (*Acts* 49) declares, 'the real subject of Acts is the λόγος τοῦ θεοῦ'.

[33] For such a device in hellenistic histories, see Norden, *Agnostos Theos* 312; Foakes Jackson and Lake, *Beginnings* 2.490. Van Unnik ('Confirmation' 30) com-pares Acts 1.1 with Josephus, CA 1.1–2; see also Didorus Siculus, BH 18.1.6; and the frequent references to the 'previous book' in AJ 5.1; 6.1; 8.1; 9.1; 12.1; 13.1; 14.1; 15.1; 20.1.

[34] περὶ πάντων (Acts 1.1); see also πᾶσιν (Luke 1.3) and πάντων ὧν ἐποίησεν (Acts 10.39); cf. Diodorus Siculus, BH 1.1.3. On the completeness intended by the phrase ποιεῖν τε καὶ διδάσκειν (Acts 1.1), see du Plessis, 'Once More' 269–70; van Unnik, 'Eléments artistiques' 135–6. Cf. Luke 24.19; Acts 7.22.

[35] Cf. Diodorus, BH 1.1.1 and n. 2 above.

theme. 'The things concerning Jesus Christ' (28.31) alludes to the presentation of Jesus by Luke in his Gospel; such material is taught not only by Paul (28.23) but also by Apollos (18.25), Peter (8.12) and the risen Jesus himself (Luke 24.27; cf. 24.44). 'The kingdom of God', preached by Paul (Acts 14.22; 19.8; 20.25; 28.23,31), is prominent in the Gospel as the focus of Jesus' preaching (Luke 4.43).[36] However, although this phrase refers to the eschatological kingdom of Jewish hope in Jesus' preaching, the Pauline sermons in Acts are distinctively different in substance from Jesus' proclamation.[37] What they do have in common is an emphasis on the sovereignty of God over every event of history.[38] This is further signified through the use of a typical Lukan phrase, 'the things that God has done', which refers to the direct divine guidance of both the ministry of Jesus (Luke 8.39; Acts 2.22) and the mission of the early church (Acts 14.27; 15.4,12; 19.11; 21.19). Through these phrases, then, Luke indicates the providential dimension of his story; both 'the things concerning Jesus' and 'the things that God has done' refer to 'the sovereignty (βασιλεία) of God'.

Furthermore, both the apostles (Acts 4.20) and Paul (22.15) describe the content of their preaching as 'the things we have heard and seen'. Luke has used this phrase earlier, in contexts where God's guidance of events is emphasized, to refer to the announcement to the shepherds of the birth of Jesus (Luke 2.20),[39] the healing miracles of Jesus (7.22)[40] and the outpouring of the Spirit on the day of Pentecost (Acts 2.33).[41] It is reasonable to anticipate that the apostolic preaching will conform to this understanding that 'the

[36] Luke summarizes the message of Jesus as τὰ περὶ τῆς βασιλείας τοῦ θεοῦ (Acts 1.3); see also Luke 6.20; 7.28; 8.1,10; 9.2,11,27,60,62; 10.9,11; 11.20; 13.18,20,28,29; 14.15; 16.16; 17.20,21; 18.16,17,24,25,29; 19.11; 21.31; 22.16,18. Haenchen (*Acts* 723) prefers this 'futuristic' sense for Acts 28.23,31.

[37] They are much more like the Petrine speeches of Acts; see the analysis in chapter 3.3.3. Luke has redefined the nature of 'the kingdom of God' in the apostolic preaching, so as to emphasize the providential dimension of God's sovereignty.

[38] On providence as an organizing principle for histories, see n. 4 above. Schulz ('Vorsehung' 114) regards Luke's emphasis on providence as a sign of his 'Historisierung' and 'Kerygmatisierung'.

[39] The phrase summarizes the events of 2.8–14. God's guidance is emphasized by epiphanies (2.9–12, 13–14), the shepherds' words (2.15) and the praise offered to God (2.13, 20).

[40] Jesus himself summarizes his ministry in this phrase, evoking the Isaianic description of God's restorative actions (Isa 26.19; 29.18; 35.5–6; 61.1). The pericope immediately prior to Luke 7.18–23 concludes with the affirmation that through Jesus' healings 'God has visited his people' (7.16).

[41] Peter states that Jesus has poured out 'this which you see and hear'; previously, this outpouring has been declared to be God's action (2.17,18).

things we have heard and seen' refer primarily to God's actions.[42] This is confirmed when Paul uses the phrase in the Jerusalem account of his conversion and call. He was appointed by God (22.14) to bear witness (22.15) in a twofold testimony; 'what you have seen' refers to 'the righteous one' (22.14), God's own agent, whilst 'what you have heard' refers to the 'voice from his mouth' (22.14), God's own words. Through both of these elements Paul gains knowledge of the divine will (22.14). Paul emphasizes this when he takes up the visual element of his commission in his speech before Agrippa. The charge to 'bear witness to the things in which you have seen me and to those in which I will appear to you' (26.16) is a clear declaration that Paul's testimony encompasses God's actions.[43]

Finally, we note that in his retrospective description to the Ephesian elders of his missionary activity, Paul specifies that his message has to do with divine guidance of history, for he preaches 'the Gospel of the grace of God' (20.24) and 'the whole plan of God' (20.27).[44] This latter phrase most directly indicates the providential aspect of the message.[45] Thus, the speeches in Acts provide particularly important evidence for the way in which the events which occurred in the life of Jesus and in the history of the early church together comprise the plan of God.[46]

### 2.3.3 The plan of God in the literary purposes of Luke

Luke undoubtedly believed that God was indeed watching over all events, exercising universal providence. An overview of his whole

[42] The conjunction of seeing and hearing may well have been suggested to Luke by the key scriptural text of Isa 6.9–10, which he uses at Luke 8.10 and Acts 28.25–7, both times with reference to God's activity. For completeness, we note that the phrase is also used by Demetrius the silversmith at Acts 19.26, with reference to Paul's preaching activity in Asia.

[43] The first phrase (εἶδές με) refers to the immediate epiphany of the Lord (26.13); cf. ὤφθην σοι, 26.16); the second phrase (ὀφθήσομαί σοι) refers to the epiphanies of God which are subsequent to Paul's call but which have already been reported by Luke (16.9–10; 18.9; 23.11; there will be another epiphany at 27.23–4). See further in chap. 5.3.3.

[44] These two phrases, along with the reference to 'the kingdom' (20.55), are functionally equivalent, since each refers to the same message, namely 'repentance to God and faith in our Lord Jesus Christ' (20.21). See Schubert, 'Areopagus Speech' 259–60; 'Final Cycle' 4 n. 7.

[45] Note that Apollos preaches 'the way of God' (τὴν ὁδὸν τοῦ θεοῦ) as well as 'the baptism of John' and 'the things concerning Jesus' (18.25–6; cf. τὴν ὁδὸν τοῦ κυρίου 18.26). See Conzelmann, *Theology* 227 n. 1.

[46] The speeches are read as an integrated whole by Schubert ('Areopagus Speech' *passim*) and with particular attention to the wider narrative context by O'Neill (*Theology* 77–83, 87, 94–5; see also Dibelius, *Studies* 152). See further in chap. 3.3.3.

work shows that he generally conveys this assurance through means which are more subtle than direct,[47] as we have noted in the hellenistic-like preface (Luke 1.1–4). However, clear evidence for the prominence of this theme is to be found at crucial points in the narrative where the thematic strands we have already identified are seen to be closely woven together.

### 2.3.3.1 The prologue to the Gospel (Luke 1.5–2.52)

In the extended prologue (Luke 1.5–2.52),[48] written in the style of Jewish scriptural birth accounts, Luke demonstrates quite explicitly how it is that God is at work in this history. These two chapters are replete with incidents and comments which introduce and reinforce the notion that what is to follow takes place under the guidance of God. The theme of divine providence is invoked by means of angelic epiphanies and prophetic oracles, a somewhat veiled allusion to the necessity of events, and direct narrative comments that God is indeed the motivating force and guiding power of these events.[49]

Luke first establishes this theme through a double epiphany of the angel Gabriel, who appears to Zechariah in the temple (1.11), and six months later to Mary in Nazareth (1.26). The initial epiphany establishes the divine origin and purpose of such phenomena, as Gabriel asserts his divine authority to Zechariah: 'I am Gabriel. I stand in the presence of God, and I was sent (ἀπεστάλην) to speak to you' (1.19).[50] In the second epiphany, he assures Mary that 'the Lord is with you' (1.28).

The highly developed parallelism[51] in these two epiphany

---

[47] Dibelius, *Studies* 181.

[48] Following P. S. Minear ('Luke's Use of the Birth Stories', *Studies* (ed. Keck and Martyn 118–19), this section is viewed as a prologue to the whole work. See also Fitzmyer, *Luke* 1.310.

[49] On the importance of interpreting the prologue within the context of the whole Lukan work, see Minear, 'Birth Stories' 111–30; he notes the prominence of 'the overarching purpose of God' at p. 129. For similar comments, see Fitzmyer, *Luke* 309, 315; Danker, *Jesus* 52. This concentration on divine activity in the prologue (1.5–2.52) resembles, albeit on a smaller scale, the similar emphasis in the mythological material of BH Books 1–6 and the ancestral material through the Moses in AJ Books 1–4.

[50] The divine passive (ἀπεστάλην; see Fitzmyer, *Luke* 1.328) is used again at Luke 1.26, and will later be applied to Jesus (4.43, etc.; cf. chap. 3 nn. 95, 102). For the connection between epiphanies and proclamation of a divine message, Pax (*Epiphaneia* 233) cites 2 Tim 1.10–11; Epictetus, *Diss.* 1.29.46; 3.22.23; see also *ibid.*, 188–91.

[51] See Fitzmyer, *Luke* 1.313–21; Brown, *Birth of the Messiah* 251, 292–8.

accounts points to the similar purpose that they play in the overall structure of the story. The former epiphany introduces the prediction that Elizabeth, despite her advanced years (1.18), will conceive a son (1.13), whilst the latter includes the prediction that Mary, despite her virginity (1.27) and lack of husband (1.34), will also bear a son (1.31). Each epiphany includes the standard scriptural annunciation pattern (1.13; 1.31; cf. Gen 16.11; Gen 17.19; Judg 13.3,5; the same pattern is also used in Matt 1.20–1).[52] Both times, Gabriel confirms that God's Holy Spirit will work through the events being announced (1.15; 1.35). Each epiphany concludes with the prospective mother affirming that the conception is indeed an act of God (1.25; 1.38). Through her pregnancy, God has removed Elizabeth's reproach of barrenness (1.25); the pregnancy of Mary indicates that 'with God nothing will be impossible' (1.37). These two epiphanies thus indicate God's providential control.

The third epiphany in the prologue, the appearance to the shepherds of the single angel (2.9) and the choir of heavenly beings (2.13), has a similar function. The oracle from the angelic choir sums up the birth of Jesus as an indication of God's good pleasure (εὐδοκίας, 2.14).[53] This epiphany is the means by which 'the Lord has made known' the news of the birth of Jesus (2.15).

The responses to the first two epiphanies are also paralleled. Mary blossoms into song in a hymn which extols the mighty acts of God in scriptural style (1.47–55)[54] and Zechariah likewise blesses God for his saving deeds (1.68–75).[55] In narrative comments, Luke notes that the birth of John indicates that 'the Lord had shown great mercy' to Elizabeth (1.58) and that 'the hand of the Lord' was with John the Baptist (1.66). These comments cohere with the angelic declaration that Mary's pregnancy indicates to her that 'the Lord is with you' (1.28) and that she has been favoured by God (1.28,30). That same divine favour will remain with her son as he grows (2.40,52).

In the pivotal scene which brings the two women together (1.39–45), the Holy Spirit inspires Elizabeth (1.41) to confirm that

[52] Brown, *Birth of the Messiah* 155–9; Fitzmyer, *Luke*, 1.318, 335.

[53] See Fitzmyer (*Luke* 1.411–2) for this translation; Marshall (*Luke* 112) equates it with the will of God.

[54] God is the subject of all but four verbs, each of which indicates the correct response to be given to God's acts: magnify (Luke 1.46b), rejoice (1.47a), bless (1.48b) and fear (1.50b). See Minear, 'Birth Stories' 116–17; O'Toole, *Unity* 225–60. On the scriptural style of the passage, see Brown, *Birth of the Messiah* 358–60.

[55] God is the subject of every verb except one, which again indicates the correct response to God (λατρεύειν, Luke 1.74). On the scriptural style of the passage, see Brown, *Birth of the Messiah* 386–9.

what is taking place is 'a fulfilment of what was spoken to her from the Lord' (1.45). The same Spirit inspires prophetic outbursts by Zechariah (1.67) and Simeon (2.25,27). Thus, this series of epiphanies is inextricably bound up with an eruption of prophetic activity surrounding the births of John and Jesus. These prophecies amplify the theme of divine guidance, providing deeper insights into the way God will be at work in the story.[56] The oracles uttered in angelic epiphanies and by human prophets establish a series of predictions[57] which are divinely inspired in a manner similar to the way oracles function in Deuteronomic and hellenistic histories.[58]

Some of these predictions receive such fulfilment in very swift order, beginning with the births of John (predicted at 1.13; fulfilled at 1.24, 1.57) and Jesus (predicted at 1.31; fulfilled at 2.6–7, 2.21). The respective names of the children are predicted (John at 1.13; Jesus at 1.31) and fulfilled (John at 1.60;[59] Jesus at 2.21). The shepherds' discovery of the newborn Jesus is likewise 'as it had been told them' (2.20), referring back to the divine oracle (2.15). Thus, within the prologue itself a sequence of divinely given prophetic predictions coming to fulfilment is already established. God is speaking and acting within the story by the time Jesus is born.

Other predictions concern matters whose fulfilment comes later in time. The prophetic status of John (1.76), prophesied by Zechariah under the inspiration of the Spirit (1.67), is subsequently affirmed by Jesus' own words (7.20). The primary role of John, described by Zechariah in the same oracle as being 'to prepare the way' (1.76), is fulfilled in his public ministry (3.3–6).

The status of Jesus also predicted through a series of titles which

---

[56] Compare Josephus' description of contemporary prophecy (chap. 6nn. 59–61) and of false prophecy (chap. 6 n. 62).

[57] On the emphasis on prediction in the prologue, see Schubert, 'Luke 24' 178–9; Minear, 'Birth Stories' 117, 119–20; Johnson, *Possessions* 87; Marshall, *Luke* 49–50, 58, 72–3; Aune, *Prophecy* 146–7. Although the prologue was written after the body of the Gospel (Brown, 'The Annunciation Narratives in the Gospel of Luke', *Perspectives* (ed. Talbert) 126–38), as it stands it forms a comprehensive prediction of ensuing events (Kurz, 'Proof from Prophecy' 150; Fitzmyer, *Luke* 1.306). Nevertheless, commentators generally overlook this function of the prologue in their search for the scriptural antecedents of the oracles.

[58] The divine origin of prophecy is assumed throughout the Deuteronomic history (see especially Deut 18.18). On the divine origin of oracles in hellenistic histories, see chap. 6.1.1.2; in Josephus, see chap. 6.2.1.3. Cf. the Stoic view of the divine origin of prophecy, noted at chap. 6.1.1.2.

[59] The deviation from the common practice of naming the son after the father (1.59) is explained at 1.61–3, where Zechariah concurs with such a deviation. See Marshall, *Luke* 88; Fitzmyer, *Luke* 1.380.

are imbedded within the oracles of Gabriel, Simeon and Anna. Each of these christological titles will be applied to Jesus in the course of the Gospel, thus fulfilling these early predictions. The first word used by Gabriel concerning Jesus is 'great' (μέγας, 1.32); although Jesus rejects the notion of being 'greater' (μείζων) at 22.24–7, he is perceived to be a great (μέγας) prophet (7.16), and his healings reveal the μεγαλειότης of God (9.43). A second prediction is that Jesus will be the son of the Most High (υἱὸς ὑψίστου, 1.32); the title is applied to Jesus at 8.28. In the next oracle, Gabriel uses the more familiar title, son of God (υἱὸς θεοῦ, 1.35), which is the way Jesus is addressed by demons (4.41; 8.28) as well as by the tempter himself (4.3,9). Finally, Gabriel predicts that Jesus will be called holy (ἅγιον, 1.35); the fulfilment of this comes when Jesus is offered for purification.[60] As a firstborn male, he is declared holy (2.23, quoting Exod 12.3). This term is later used of Jesus by demons (Luke 4.34), Peter (Acts 3.14) and the Jerusalem believers (Acts 4.27,30).

Subsequently, the Spirit inspires an unnamed angel to reveal to Simeon that he would see 'the Lord's Christ' (τὸν χριστὸν κυρίου, 2.26); this is immediately fulfilled when Simeon sees Jesus, for he ascribes to him achievements suitable for the Messiah (2.30–2). The same revelation of Jesus as Christ, given to the shepherds (2.11), is explicitly applied to Jesus by the demons (4.41) and Peter (9.20). After the resurrection, it is widely applied to Jesus (24.26,46, and each of the twenty-eight occurrences in Acts). Likewise, the role of Jesus is depicted in terms which are subsequently applied to his work. Gabriel describes him as the Davidic king (1.32) who will have an eternal reign (1.33). Jesus is subsequently acclaimed as king by the crowds who welcome him on his entry into Jerusalem (19.38) and by the inscription over his cross (23.38), reflecting the charge of the Jews (23.2). Paul describes Jesus as 'of the posterity' of King David (Acts 13.23) and is later accused of opposing Caesar by 'saying that there is another king, Jesus' (Acts 17.8). Simeon tells God that, by seeing Jesus, 'my eyes have seen your salvation' (τὸ σωτήριόν σου, Luke 2.30). That Jesus brings such salvation is later affirmed (Luke 19.9; Acts 4.12; 13.26,47; 28.28). Jesus is called saviour by both Peter (Acts 5.31) and Paul (13.23). The significance of Jesus' life in the plan of God is thus established through these prophetic utterances.

The two oracles of Simeon contain predictions which look beyond the immediate events of Jesus' life, for they concern the response of

---

[60] Danker, *Jesus* 37, 62.

Israel to such salvific activity. In his first oracle, Simeon asserts the universality of divine salvation (2.31) and foresees the mission to the Gentiles (2.32a) as well as the glory of Israel (2.32b); the events of Acts will fulfil this prediction comprehensively. Simeon's second oracle is more complex, for he sees Jesus as signifying the future 'fall and rising of many in Israel' (2.34). This oracle is programmatic for the division which will occur in Israel, as first Jesus, then the apostles in Jerusalem, and finally Paul in the Diaspora, each provoke rejection as well as acceptance of Jesus.[61] These oracles of Simeon add to the prophetic declaration of the significance of Jesus. Finally, the necessity motif is alluded to in Simeon's oracle (Luke 2.33–4) concerning 'the salvation which God has prepared' (ὁ ἡτοίμασας, 2.31), which is revealed by Jesus, who is 'set (κεῖται) for the fall and rising of many in Israel' (2.34).[62]

So it is that the prologue establishes without any doubt the way in which God is active in the events that take place. Events subsequent to this prologue are thus introduced and interpreted as taking place under God's guidance. Epiphanies, prophecies, an indication of divine necessity and an insistence on the divine initiative throughout these two chapters indicate that providence is to be a major theme of Luke's story. Through the miraculous events, epiphanies, predictive prophecies and declarations of necessity which will follow throughout the Gospel, Luke will build a case for viewing everything which he narrates as part of the overall plan of God.

Throughout the Gospel, it is not always clear that providence, so forcefully introduced at the start, remains at the forefront of matters. Only occasional narrative remarks in the Gospel indicate the ongoing role of God in the story. When we come to the early chapters of Acts, however, the theme of divine providence comes clearly to the fore. The key phrase of the apostolic speeches, 'the plan of God', becomes the clearest indication of the way Luke regards all the events he narrates as being integral to an overall providential direction of history. Again, miraculous, epiphanic,

---

[61] See Jervell, *Luke* 41–74; Danker, *Jesus* 68; and note the use of ἀντέλεγον at Acts 13.45; 28.19. The prediction by Anna that Jesus is the answer to those who look for the redemption of Israel (2.38) is also expressed on the Emmaus road by two disciples (24.21). Jesus delays the fulfilment of this oracle, for he himself considered that it would only be with the coming of the Son of Man in glory that such redemption would draw near (21.27–8).

[62] Tiede (*Prophecy* 27) notes that in his oracle, along with Luke 2.49, 'the matter of the character and content of this "necessity" is raised, but not yet defined'; the 'pecular usage of the passive voice' indicates divine agency (*ibid.*, 29).

prophetic and inevitable occurrences throughout Acts provide fuller dimensions to this theme, while the missionary speeches develop it most extensively. The overall effect is that of a gradually unfolding exposition of a theme which is always present, but which comes to a clearer, more mature expression in the later parts of the work.[63]

### 2.3.3.2  Paul's apology to Agrippa and Festus (Acts 26.1–29)

A critical moment in the plan of God comes in the conversion of Paul. So important is this moment, that Luke not only reports it at the appropriate place in the narrative (Acts 9.1–19), but twice pauses to have Paul recall the incident in his own words (Acts 22.1–21; 26.1–29). The initial narrative account of this conversion (9.1–19) highlights the role of God in this event through features typical of a call narrative.[64] Paul, the violent opponent of 'the Way' (9.1–2, 13–14),[65] is convinced of the folly of his opposition by a heavenly vision (9.3–5)[66] and is presented with the divine command 'to carry my name before the Gentiles and kings and sons of Israel' (9.15). Confirmation that God has been at work in this event is then given as Paul, the 'chosen instrument' (9.15),[67] regains his sight, is filled with

[63] The fact that so much of the Gospel comprises already existing material means that the distinctively Lukan viewpoint can only be gleaned with certainty from the redactional treatment of these sources, where it accords with features which are to be found in more abundance in Acts. It is especially in the speeches in Acts that Luke's interests are revealed; with hindsight, we can read the Gospel in the light of these interests. See Kurz, 'Proof from Prophecy' 150 esp. n. 2; Johnson, *Writings* 207–11.

[64] All of the features we note are standard elements in scriptural accounts of prophetic calls; see B. J. Hubbard, 'Commissioning Stories in Luke–Acts: A Study of Their Antecedents, Form and Content', *Semeia* 8 (1977) 103–26, and 'The Role of Commissioning Accounts in Acts', *Perspectives on Luke–Acts* (ed. Talbert) 187–98; T. Y. Mullins, 'New Testament Commission Forms, especially in Luke–Acts', *JBL* 95 (1976) 603–14. Especially significant is the similarity of these features to the conversion accounts in 2 Macc 3 and 4 Macc 4; see H. Windisch, 'Die Christus-epiphanie vor Damaskus (Act 9, 22 und 26) und ihre religions-geschichtlichen Parallelen', *ZNW* 31 (1932) 1–23. On the role of the threefold account in Acts, see Schubert, 'Final Cycle' 14–16.

[65] This is intensified in the later accounts of Paul's conversion in Acts 22.4–5 and 26.4–8, 9–12. Cf. 2 Macc 3.4; 4 Macc 4.5–6,10. The strength of such opposition demonstrates the power of God, who is able to effect such a complete turnaround.

[66] The light from heaven on the Damascus road is accompanied by the voice which ends Paul's activity of direct opposition to Jesus (Acts 9.3–5; 22.6–9; 26.13–14,19). cf. the visions of 2 Macc 3.25–6 and 4 Macc 4.10. The vision to Ananias (Acts 9.10–16) serves to emphasize and expand upon the divine origin of the call.

[67] This conversion is thrice described as an act in which God chooses Paul (Acts 9.15; 22.14; 26.16); cf. 2 Macc 3.24,26,30,36,38; 4 Macc 4.9,11,13. At Acts 22.14 this selection is made so that Paul might know the divine will (θέλημα, 'for all

the Holy Spirit (9.17–18) and 'preaches boldly in the name of the Lord' (9.29). All that has taken place is thus placed within the framework of divine guidance.

However, when Luke has Paul recount his conversion later in Acts, the purpose is not just to recall the event, but to interpret it within the overall context of the plan of God. The function of these latter two accounts is clearly signalled as an apologetic defence of Paul's entire career;[68] indeed, the form of both speeches bears strong similarities to the forensic defence speech known in hellenistic literature.[69] The apologetic purpose of the speech in Acts 26 is reflected in Agrippa's ironic comment on Paul's wish 'to make me a Christian' (26.28), which Luke then has Paul broaden to incorporate 'all who hear me this day' (26.29) – and, no doubt, all who would subsequently hear this report of the speech.

When Luke has Paul explain his call to a crowd in Jerusalem (22.1–21), he emphasizes that God chose Paul (προεχειρίσατο, 22.14) to know and declare the divine will (22.14–15). A further epiphany is added (22.17–21) specifically to articulate God's call to the Gentiles (22.21). When Paul recollects his divine commission before Agrippa and Festus (26.1–29), he summarizes his mission in terms which again highlight the providential dimension. By reporting that God chose him (προχειρίσασθαι) as servant and witness (ὑπηρέτην καὶ μάρτυρα, 26.16), Paul evokes the Stoic conception of the wise man who serves God in obedience to his divine commission.[70]

The body of this speech (26.4–23) contains three sections, each of which is significantly expanded from the earlier reports. In the first section (26.4–11), Paul apologetically defends himself against his Jewish accusers by giving more details both of his Pharisaic upbringing (26.4–8; cf. 22.3) and of his opposition to the followers of Jesus

practical purposes a synonym for βουλὴ τοῦ θεοῦ', according to Schubert, 'Final Cycle' 14).

[68] ἀπολογίας appears at Acts 22.1; ἀπολογέω at 26.1, 24. On the apologetic force of the latter speech, see Malherbe, 'Corner' (*passim*). On the use of classical Greek idioms, see Haenchen, *Acts* 691.

[69] See F. Veltman, 'The Defense Speeches of Paul in Acts', pp. 243–56 in *PLA* (ed. Talbert), esp. p. 255.

[70] Epictetus describes the ideal Stoic as a witness (μάρτυρα, *Diss.* 3.24.112,113) who is appointed (κατατεταγμένος, 4.24.114) by God to service (ὑπηρεσίαν, 3.24.114; see also ὑπηρέτης, 3.24.98); likewise his Stoicized version of the ideal Cynic is that of a servant (διάκονον, 3.22.63; ὑπηρέτης, 3.22.82,95) who is a witness (μάρτυς, 3.22.88; see also μαρτυρία, 3.22.86) because of his divine commission (3.22.23, 54, 56, 95). For a full discussion of Epictetus' use of these terms, see J. N. Collins, 'Georgi's "Envoys" in 2 Cor 11.23', *JBL* 93 (1974) 88–96, esp. 92–4.

(26.4–11; cf. 9.1–2; 22.4–5). In the second section (26.12–18), the account of Paul's pivotal experience on the road to Damascus is expanded through a more extensive reporting of God's words. The inevitability of Paul's conversion is emphasized by inserting a report of the divine voice as saying that 'it hurts to kick against the goads' (26.14; cf. 9.4; 22.7), thus echoing a saying found not only in Euripides[71] but elsewhere in Greek literature.[72] The extent of the commission Paul receives from God is likewise much expanded (26.16–18; cf. 9.15–16; 22.14–15), using Stoic terminology as noted above.

Luke uses a series of epiphanies to undergird the theme of divine guidance of Paul. The epiphany on the road to Damascus (26.13–15; par 9.3–5)[73] establishes the divine authority for Paul's task; in the initial narrative account an epiphany to Ananias (ἐν ὁράματι, 9.10) had provided the explicit command to go to Gentiles as well as Israel (9.15), and a further epiphany to Paul (ἐν ὁράματι, 9.12) had ensured that he was duly prepared to receive this divine commission through Ananias. After the second report of his conversion, Paul notes yet a further epiphany, seen in a trance (ἐν ἐκστάσει, 22.17) in the Jerusalem Temple, in which God warns him to leave the city because of the opposition there (22.18) and repeats the divine commission to go to the Gentiles (22.21).

When Paul retells this conversion to Agrippa and Festus, he

---

[71] The saying appears at *Bacch.* 794–5 in somewhat similar circumstances (in connection with the introduction of a new deity). When linked with the similarity between Acts 5.39 and various sayings in Euripides, this led to the theory that Luke was dependent on Euripides for such classical sayings (see the literature listed by Dibelius, *Studies* 188 n. 7; for a discussion of the development of this theory, see Vögeli, 'Lukas und Euripides' 416–28). The saying is also to be found in Euripides at *Frg.* 604 (= Stob. *Flor.* 3.22; see Vögeli, 'Lukas und Euripides' 428 n. 50) and, with textual uncertainty, at *Iph in Taur.* 1396. On the likelihood that someone of Luke's educational level had read Euripides, see Malherbe, *Social Aspects* 43–5.

[72] The authors (collected by Wettstein, *Nov. Test. Graec.* 633; Vögeli, 'Lukas und Euripides' 428 n. 50; see the discussion of J. Munck, *Paul and the Salvation of Mankind* (Richmond: John Knox, 1959) 21–2) include Aeschylus, *Prom.* 324–6; *Ag.* 1624–5; Pindar, *Pyth. Odes* 2.93–6; Philo, *Quod det. pet. ins.* 46; and an inscription noted at *JHS* 8 (1887) 261. The Emperor Julian (*Or.* 8.246B) comments that this saying is well known as a proverb (παροιμία) and formulates it in a particularly Stoic manner. The theory of Luke's literary dependence on Euripides was first disputed by W. G. Kümmel in 1929 (see Vögeli, 'Lukas und Euripides' 428–9); see also Dibelius, *Studies* 188–91 and the more thorough refutations of Vögeli ('Lukas und Euripides' 429–38) and J. Hackett ('Echoes of the Bacchae in the Acts of the Apostles?', *Irish Theological Quarterly* 23 (1956) 218–27, 350–66).

[73] Although each report of this incident states only that Paul saw a 'light from heaven' (9.6; 22.6; 26.13), the event is described as an epiphany of Jesus by Ananias (9.17), Barnabas (9.27) and Paul himself (26.19).

highlights the importance of the vision by which he was commissioned to go to the Gentiles (26.12–18). Paul rests his entire preaching activity in Damascus, Jerusalem and among the Gentiles (26.20) on this epiphany, emphasizing his obedience to 'this heavenly vision' 26.19)[74] as well as establishing this vision as the first of a sequence of divine epiphanies (ὀφθήσομαί σοι, 26.16). Paul's final speech thus reveals the explicitly apologetic function of this pivotal epiphany, which both predicts his missionary activity among the Gentiles[75] and provides the foundation for his self-defence as one guided by God and authorized as God's witness.

The third section of the body of the speech (26.19–23) is virtually a new segment, linking the Damascus road incident both to Paul's general missionary activity (26.19–20) and to the particular reason for his arrest (26.21). The pinnacle of this long apology comes in Paul's justification of the Gentile mission as the fulfilment of prophecy. He describes his own missionary efforts as 'saying nothing but what the prophets and Moses said would come to pass, that the Christ must suffer, and that, by being the first to rise from the dead, he would proclaim light both to the people and to the Gentiles' (26.22–3). In this third, climactic report, Luke makes it quite clear to his hellenistic readers, in their own terms, that Paul's conversion (and the ensuing events) was no surprise, but rather an integral and inevitable part of the plan of God. Thus Luke apologetically defends and justifies Paul's involvement in the Gentile mission and invites his readers to adopt the way of life exemplified by Paul in his conformity to the divine will.

## 2.4 Conclusions

Our analysis of two significant passages (Luke 1–2 and Acts 26) has demonstrated that, at these key points, the various strands we have identified are to be found woven together into a coherent argument. These passages demonstrate the significance of 'the plan of God' in Luke–Acts, and also confirm that this central theme is developed by Luke in a number of related ways. We shall thus proceed, in the next chapter, to trace through the more explicit development of the theme of divine providence, before treating, in subsequent chapters, the strands associated with the theme.

[74] For apologetic uses of this motif, see Plato, *Apol.* 33C; Epictetus, *Diss.* 2.16.44.
[75] Brawley ('Paul in Acts' 1350) notes the similar function of a theophany in Euripides, *Bacch.* 469; see also Pax, *Epiphaneia* 184–5.

Since much of the material in the Gospel is more allusive than definitive, it must be viewed within the context of the whole work; these allusions hint at the theme which blossoms forth in the second volume. As far as this stylistic feature is concerned, Luke's work is more like the histories of Dionysius and Diodorus, where explicit references to providence are relatively scarce, than that of Josephus, who consciously places the theme of providence to the fore at every opportunity.

Nevertheless, when we combine each of the strands identified as related to the plan of God, the result is a comprehensive picture of divine activity in which God's actions stretch from creation to the final judgement and exhibit a consistent intention to guide history in a very specific direction. As far as this substantive matter is concerned, Luke's work is more like that of Josephus, for God oversees and guides the whole range of human history with consistency, rather than simply intervening somewhat haphazardly at particular points in time, as the gods usually do in the histories of Diodorus and Dionysius.

# 3

## PROVIDENCE: GOD AT WORK IN HUMAN HISTORY

Throughout Luke's life of Jesus and the history of the early church, God is depicted as being constantly at work. Luke presents the actions of God in a comprehensive manner, extending throughout the whole span of history, in accord with the consistent divine design and intention. God's actions, as Luke reports them, begin at creation[1] and continue through the history of Israel,[2] the life of Jesus,[3] his resurrection, exaltation and appointment as judge[4] and the growth of the early church.[5] The concentration of divine activity throughout the two volumes is such that we might reasonably speak of God as the subject of the whole story.[6]

This thematic strand in Luke–Acts undoubtedly owes much to the way in which the Hebrews presented their national history in their own scriptures.[7] Although the influence of the Septuagint on Luke is

[1] God created the world (Acts 7.50, quoting Isa 66.2; Acts 4.24 and 14.15, quoting Ps 145.6; Acts 17.24), the nations (17.26a) the seasons and the boundaries of their habitation (17.26b), and the rains and the seasons (14.17).

[2] God made a covenant with the fathers (Acts 3.25; 13.17) and guided Abraham (7.2), Joseph (7.9), Moses (7.35), Saul (13.21) and David (7.46).

[3] Jesus was the promised prophet (Acts 3.22; 7.37), in whose life God was clearly at work (Luke 11.20; Acts 2.22; 10.38).

[4] After his death, God raised Jesus from the dead (Acts 2.24,32; 3.15,26; 4.10; 5.20; 10.40; 13.30,37; 26.8), and he was anointed (10.38), exalted (5.31) and glorified (3.13) by God, who made him Lord and Christ (2.36) and appointed him as judge (10.42; 17.31).

[5] God worked through the deeds of the apostles (Acts 4.19; 5.29,38–9), the growth of the church (2.47; 11.21; 12.24), the mission to the Gentiles (10.34; 11.18; 15.7; 22.14–15; 26.16) and the deeds of Paul (14.27; 15.4,12; 16.10; 19.11; 21.19).

[6] See Nock's review of Dibelius, *Gnomon* 25 (1953) 499; Conzelmann, *Theology* 173; Haenchen, *Acts* 91; Kurz, 'Proof from Prophecy' 8.

[7] For a recent systematic survey of God's sovereignty in the Old Testament, see Carson, *Divine Sovereignty* 24–38. For an examination of this aspect (among others) of Old Testament thought, in the context of ancient Near East historiography, see J. van Seters, *In Search of History: Historiography in the Ancient World and the Origins of Biblical History* (New Haven, Conn.: Yale University Press, 1983). O'Neill (*Theology* 142) notes that the apologetic literature of hellenistic Judaism developed

not to be discounted, in this chapter we will place Luke–Acts within the context of hellenistic historiography, thus enabling us to see how hellenistic readers would have understood this emphasis. As we indicate how Luke's work shares affinities with such literature through his presentation of the divine activity in history, we shall also notice the function which this theme serves in Luke–Acts.

## 3.1 Providence in hellenistic historiography

At various points throughout their histories, both Dionysius and Diodorus advance the proposition that providence is guiding events. Most often this thesis is proposed in direct narrative comments of the authors themselves, although on occasions they have their characters advance the belief in speeches,[8] while Diodorus also notes that the belief in providence was held in ancient societies.[9]

### 3.1.1 Philosophic views of providence

Because of this insistence, by both authors, that there is a divine providence at work in history, it is not surprising to find within the body of their works, direct repudiations of those who hold different views on this matter. Diodorus notes the explanation given for such natural disasters by 'natural scientists [who] make it their endeavour to attribute responsibility in such cases not to divine providence (τὸ θεῖον), but to certain natural circumstances determined by necessary causes (BS 15.48.4), but he prefers to accept the opinion of those who are disposed to venerate the divine power (τὸ θεῖον), '[who] assign certain plausible reasons for the occurrence, alleging that the disaster was occasioned by the anger of the gods (διὰ θεῶν μῆνιν) at those who had committed sacrilege' (BH 15.48.4). Like-

the theme 'that God had manifestly worked in the history of Israel' in much the same way as in Acts.

[8] This belief is discussed most strenuously by Fufetius and Tullus (RA 3.13.3,14.2,16.2; see chap. 4 n. 23); Dionysius also includes it in a speech by Aulus Verginius (10.10.2) and reports it in his summary of a speech by Tullius (4.26.2). The other six uses of πρόνοια in RA occur in narrative. Diodorus uses the term 24 times, of which only four occur in speeches: three brief comments, by Basileia (BH 3.57.5), Orpheus (4.48.7) and Philotas (17.66.7), and in the extended speech of Theodorus (14.67.2). These speeches are all, of course, the creations of the historians themselves; cf. Thucydides 1.22, and the discussion of this issue in relation to Luke–Acts in the literature cited in n. 135 below. On the prominent role of providence in the speeches reported by Josephus, see chap. 3.2.1; in Luke–Acts, chap. 3.3.3.

[9] Egypt (BH 1.70.3), Chaldaea (2.30.1) and Ethiopia (3.5.1); in Greek mythology, see 3.57.5,58.1; 4.43.2,47.1,48.7,51.1; 5.83.4.

wise, Dionysius notes opposition to his views from 'the professors of the atheistic philosophies ... if, indeed, their theories deserve the name of philosophy ... who ridicule all the manifestations of the gods (τὰς ἐπιφανείας τῶν θεῶν) which have taken place among either the Greeks or barbarians ... on the grounds that none of the gods concern themselves in anything relating to mankind' (RA 2.68.1–2). Dionysius himself shares in the belief of 'those who do not absolve the gods from the care of human affairs, but, after looking deeply into history, hold that they are favourable to the good and hostile to the wicked' (RA 2.68.2).[10]

These polemical statements can be understood within the context of the philosophical debate concerning providence in the hellenistic world, which was waged largely between the Epicureans and the Stoics.[11] Although this was an intellectual debate, involving complex arguments which took place in the rarefied atmosphere of ancient academia,[12] its general outline was known to those of some rhetorical training,[13] whilst amongst the general populace some

[10] The same contrast is made at RA 7.68.2 and 8.56.1.

[11] See Cicero, *De nat. deor.* 1.2.3–5; 1.19.51–20.56; 2.29.73–30.75; Plutarch, *De Stoic. repugn.* 1051DE; *Comp arg Stoic.* 1075E; and Diogenes Laertius, *Lives* 7.138–9 (for the Stoics), 10.133 (for the refutation of their claims by Epicurus). For references to the arguments put forward by each school, see van Unnik, 'Attack' 344–5; A. S. Pease, *M. Tvlli Ciceronis De Natvra Deorvm* (2 vols.; Cambridge, Mass.: Harvard University Press, 1955, 1958) 13–14, 125–6, 330–2, 740–1; G. W. Clarke, *The Octavius of Marcus Minucius Felix* (New York: Newman, 1974) 228; and H. Cherniss, *Plutarch's Moralia* vol. 13 part 2 (LCL: Cambridge, Mass.: Harvard University Press, 1976) 492–3, note a.

[12] In addition to the treatises on the subject referred to above (see chap. 1 nn. 70–1), references are made to treatises no longer extant written by Epicurus (Diogenes Laertius, *Lives* 10.28), Chrysippus (*Lives* 7.199), Boethos (*Lives* 7.149), Clitomachus, Philopater, Diogenianus (Eusebius, *Prep. Ev.* 6.8.1), Posidonius (*Lives* 7.149) and Bardesanes (*Prep. Ev.* 6.10.1–48). See W. Gundel, 'Heimarmene', PW VII.2.2624–5. Discussions of providence or Fate are attributed to Heraclitus (*Lives* 9.7), Parmenides (Aetius 1.25.3), Leucippus (Aetius 1.26.2), Democritus (Aetius 1.25.4,26.2), Pythagoras (*Lives* 8.1.27) and Empedocles (Aetius 1.6.1). See the survey by D. Amand, *Fatalisme et liberté dans l'antiquité grecque* (Amsterdam: A. M. Hakkert, 1973) 2–4; and the more detailed discussion of W. Gundel, *Beiträge zur Entwickelungs-geschichte der Begriffe Ananke und Heimarmene* (Giessen: Brühl University, 1914) 9–25.

[13] The handbooks show that the topic of providence was a part of the curriculum of a student of rhetoric. Quintilian notes that *an providentia mundus regatur* was a typical topic for discussion by students (*Instit. Or.* 3.5.6; and see 5.7.35; 7.2.2; 12.2.21). Aelius Theon notes that a suitable topic for debate in the style of a thesis is εἰ θεοὶ προνοοῦνται τοῦ κόσμου (*Progymnasmata* 12, in *Rhetores Graeci*, rec. L. Spengel (3 vols.; Leipzig: Teubner, 1853–6; repr. Frankfurt/Main: Minerva, 1966) II.121), as does Hermogenes (*Progymnasmata* 11, *Rhetores Graeci*, rec. Spengel, II.17). See Clarke, *Octavius* 149; R. M. Grant, *Gods and the One God* (Library of Early Christianity 1; Philadelphia: Westminster, 1986) 49–50.

awareness of the issues involved was also to be found.[14] These polemical remarks against those who refute the role of providence in history certainly further the programmatic aims we have noted in the respective prologues of Dionysius and Diodorus. They can best be understood, however, within this wider context in which the differences of opinion concerning providence, at least in broad terms, between the two main schools of thought, were known to hellenistic historiographers.[15]

### 3.1.2 The apologetic function of providence

This polemical aspect of statements concerning providence is part of the broader apologetic function of the theme in the writings of Dionysius and Diodorus. Apologetic often includes an element of defence against charges which are being levelled and a consequent polemical attack on those who bring such charges; but it can also include the assertion of the validity of one's own views and a more developed exposition of those views.[16] We find these latter aspects

[14] When introducing the topic of providence, Cicero comments that 'there is in fact no subject upon which so much difference of opinion exists, not only among the unlearned (*indocti*) but also among educated men (*De. nat. deor.* 1.2.5). Even his Epicurean opponent, Velleius, admits that the existence of the gods 'is almost universally accepted not only among philosophers but also among the unlearned (*indoctos*)' (*De. nat. deor.* 1.17.44).

[15] Perhaps the most important example of a hellenistic historiographer who was aware of the intricacies of the philosophical debate is Posidonius, whose extensive work (surviving only in assorted fragments quoted by later writers) took as its main theme the providential guidance of events by the gods. The fragments which refer explicitly to Posidonius are collected by L. Edelstein and I. G. Kidd, *Posidonius, I. The Fragments* (Cambridge Classical Texts – Commentaries 13; Cambridge University Press, 1972); a larger collection of allegedly Posidonian fragments is gathered and commented upon by W. Theiler, *Poseidonios: Die Fragmente* (Texte und Kommentare 10/1–2; Berlin/New York: Walter de Gruyter, 1982).

On the dependence of Diodorus on the earlier historical work of Posidonius, contrast J. Malitz, *Die Historien des Poseidonius* (Zetema 79; München: C. H. Beck, 1983) 37–42, and M. Laffranque, *Poseidonios d'Apamée (essai de mise au point)* (Paris: Presses Universitaires de France, 1964) 111. On Diodorus' relation to Stoicism, see G. Busolt, 'Diodors Verhaeltnis zum Stoicismus', *Jahrbücher für Classische Philologie* 139 (1889) 297–315.

On the role of Stoicism as 'an integral part of Roman historiography' by the first century, see P. G. Walsh, *Livy: His Historical Aims and Methods* (Cambridge University Press, 1961) 51; for Livy's awareness of the issues associated with providence, see 51–60; on his critical stance towards Epicureans, see 51 n. 3.

[16] For the literature discussing these aspects of apologetic, see A. J. Malherbe, 'Apologetic and Philosophy in the Second Century', *Restoration Quarterly* 7 (1963) 19 n. 5. For clarity and brevity in the ensuing discussion, reference is made, respectively, to apologetic deference, apologetic polemic, apologetic assertion and apologetic exposition.

of apologetic in the hellenistic historians' use of providence. The further dimension of apologetic protreptic is not found in the historians' works, but is of some importance for Christian writings, including Luke–Acts.[17]

Although Dionysius recognizes 'those who ascribed all human fortunes to divine providence (θείαν πρόνοιαν)' (RA 3.5.1),[18] in practice he accords providence a far narrower role, as is reflected in the claim made by Tullius, that 'the Romans ought to have the leadership of all the Latins ... because they, more than the others, had enjoyed the favour of divine providence (πρόνοια) and in consequence had attained to so great eminence' (RA 4.26.2). In this limiting role of protecting the Romans,[19] providence functions as an apologetic assertion for Dionysius, who attempts to persuade his Greek readers to accept the domination of the Romans and value their history. Closely related to the providence (πρόνοια) of the gods is the goodwill (εὔνοια) of the gods.[20] Again, although Romulus asserts 'the favour (εὔνοια) of the gods, the enjoyment of which gives success to men's every enterprise (RA 2.18.1),[21] this divine goodwill is constantly presented in far narrower terms by Dionysius, as it serves his apologetic purpose of asserting Roman superiority. Invariably he reports it only when it supports the Romans, such as when Minucius declares: 'the greatest assistance of all, and one which in times of danger has never betrayed our hopes, and better too than all human strength combined, is the favour (εὔνοια) of the gods' (RA 8.26.3).[22]

Diodorus knows no such limitation on the range of providence, for he gives a wider scope to its activity, in accordance with the

---

[17] See A. J. Malherbe, 'The Apologetic Theology of the "Preaching of Peter"', *Restoration Quarterly* 13 (1970) 205–23; for the characteristics of protreptic and a representative example, see Malherbe, *Moral Exhortation: A Greco-Roman Sourcebook* (Library of Early Christianity 4; Philadelphia: Westminster, 1986) 122–4. See further in chap. 7 n. 98.

[18] πρόνοια is used eleven times in RA, at 2.63.3; 3.5.1,13.33,14.2,16.2; 4.26.2; 5.7.1,54.1; 10.10.2; 15.3.1; 20.9.2.

[19] Providence designates the protection of Rome at RA 5.7.1,54.1; 10.10.2; 15.3.1.; 20.9.2 (and cf. 2.63.3).

[20] See the use of εὔνοια, nine times in RA, at 2.18.1; 3.14.1,28.9; 4.62.1; 5.10.4; 6.17.3; 7.12.4; 8.26.3; 10.9.4; and note the use of εὐδαιμονίαν (12.14.2) and εὐτύχημα (4.62.1).

[21] See also the comment by Tullus, who ascribes all worthy achievements to the goodwill (εὔνοια) of the gods (RA 3.28.9).

[22] See also RA 6.17.4; 7.12.4; 8.26.3; 10.9.4.

programmatic statement of his preface (BH 1.1.3).[23] He equates the
work of providence with the intervention of the gods, as they save
the Delphic oracle from pillaging by Xerxes (BH 11.14.3–4) and
punish temple robbers in Lacedaemonia (BH 16.58.5–6).[24] Providence thus governs the events of history in order to guide those who
exhibit virtuous behaviour[25] and especially those who perform the
appropriate religious rituals of prayers or sacrifices.[26] In complementary fashion, providence punishes those who rob temples[27]
or behave unjustly.[28] For Diodorus, then providence functions as
apologetic assertion, reinforcing the traditional religious customs,
and apologetic polemic, warning against the abandonment of such
behaviour.

Indeed, Diodorus notes that it is in the interests of society that
'the fear of the gods should be deeply embedded in the hearts of the
people' (BH 34/35.2.47), for the actions of the gods almost inevitably relate to the attitudes held towards them by humans; piety is

[23] For the influence of Posidonius on this prologue, see Busolt, 'Verhältnis'
297–9; Malitz, *Die Historien* p. 413 n. 25, surveying the earlier discussion;
W. Theiler, *Poseidonios* 2.78–80; but cf. A. D. Nock ('Posidonius', *Essays on
Religion and the Ancient World* (2 vols., ed. Z. Stewart; Cambridge, Mass.:
Harvard University Press, 1972) 2.853–76), who argues that Diodorus is the
author because it is 'the proem style of a small man with pretensions' ('Posidonius'
860).
[24] See also 36.13.3 and 38/39.6.1, where the punishment of the gods is considered
to be providential. It may even be that Diodorus accepts the Posidonian view of
providence itself as a god; on providence as a deity in Posidonius, see Laffranque,
*Poseidonius* 340–2; for a suggestion of Posidonian influence at 2.52.1, see Malitz, *Die
Historien* 38; Theiler, *Poseidonios* II.76–7. It should be noted that providence
(πρόνοια) in both authors is considered to be divine, for it is always qualified by
either θεῶν (20 times in BH, 5 time in RA), or δαιμονίων (4 times in BH, 5 times in
RA). In the Loeb translation of Diodorus, τὸ θεῖον and τὸ δαιμόνιον are frequently
translated as 'providence'.
[25] Providence guides the kings of Egypt (BH 1.90.3) and of Ethiopia (3.5.1),
Tennes (5.83.4) and the Syracusans (14.67.2). Events as disparate as the death of
Philip (16.92.2) and the minor action of the servant of Alexander (17.66.7) are guided
by providence.
[26] For their pious deeds, providence saves the Argonauts (BH 4.43.1–2,48.7),
Phrixus and Helle (4.47.1), the ambassadors of Locris (8.32.2), Alexander (17.49.4)
and Ptolemy (17.103.7).
[27] The Phocians in Boeotia (BH 16.58.6), the Cretans in Siphnos (31.45.1) and
Pompeius (36.13.3) when he refused to listen to Battaces' demand for rites of
purification.
[28] The tyrant Dionysius (BH 13.112.2), the children of Agathocles (20.70.1),
Atilius (23.12.1, τὸ θεῖον), and Cinna and Marius, 'the men who had inaugurated a
reign of terror' (38/39.6.1).

rewarded[29] and impiety is punished.[30] This apologetic assertion of divine activity is heightened by Diodorus, who notes that a general such as Marcius, who adheres to the ancestral customs, doing 'nothing not sanctioned by religious usage and the common judgement of mankind' (RA 8.34.3), has the gods as his guides,[31] whilst a leader such as Valerius, who had stood firm with his fellow consuls against paying the 'customary honours' to the gods (RA 9.54.6), is consequently prevented by them from winning a battle (RA 9.55.2).[32] Dionysius comments that even in his own times, 'those who tried to abolish a custom were regarded as having done a thing deserving both the indignation of men and the vengeance (νεμεσητόν) of the gods ... [resulting in] a justifiable retribution by which the perpetrators were reduced from the greatest height of glory they once enjoyed to the lowest depths' (RA 8.80.2).[33] The activities of the gods thus serve the fundamental purpose of justifying and reinforcing the required ritual actions of the Romans (for Dionysius) or of other nations (for Diodorus), and therefore share the apologetic function of providence, asserting the validity of traditional religious customs.

### 3.1.3 Providence, fortune and human affairs

Of the various deities represented in both works, it is the goddess Fortune (τύχη) who seems to play the dominant role as the mis-

---

[29] The gods are described as the συνεργοί of Timoleon (16.66.4, 79.5) and Alexander (17.7.7), and the σίμμαχοι of Philip (16.91.4) and the Romans (28.3.1). They constantly favour Alexander (17.20.3,7,33.1,89.3). Divine favour of pious persons is a prominent theme in Herodotus (see K. H. Waters, *Herodotus the Historian* (London: Croom Helm, 1985) 99); on the significance of reverence for the gods in Livy, see Walsh, *Livy* 48–9.

[30] 'The neglect of the honours of the gods established by the fathers' leads to the defeat of the Carthaginians (BH 20.14.5); earlier, because of their choice of Dionysius, 'the worst enemy of religion', as their commander, the Carthaginians are engaged ἐν τῷ πολέμῳ θεομαχῶμεν (BH 14.69.2, and see 14.77.4, ὑπὸ τῶν θεῶν πολεμούμενοι). The gods also punish those who pillage temples, such as Dionysius (14.69.2), the Phocians (16.56.8), Poleminius (27.4.1–2), Philip (28.7.1), Antiochus (29.15.1) and Alexander (34/35.28.2). See similar examples quoted by the Stoic Balbus in Cicero, *De nat. deor.* 2.3.7–4.12.

[31] ἡγεμόνας, used also at RA 2.69.2. by Tuccia, and 6.73.2 by Lucius Junius, who also uses the verbal form of ἄγω at 6.79.1 and 6.80.4, and see 1.20.1 and ἐνάγω at 11.86.3.

[32] See also RA 1.23.1–4; 8.33.2–4,89.3–4; 9.40.1.

[33] For similar reversals in status, see RA 2.53.2 and 8.52.1.

tress[34] of human affairs.[35] Thus Diodorus deems it appropriate that people humble themselves before Fortune (BH 13.21.4–5) and rest content with whatever decision she makes (BH 34/35.27.1).[36] Dionysius similarly attacks those who accuse[37] Fortune of managing human affairs badly (RA 16.3.4) and defends her as allotting shares of prosperity and adversity to each Roman citizen (RA 3.29.4). In these respects, the goddess Fortune shares the pre-eminent status and apologetic function of providence.[38]

Yet despite the elements so far identified, the sum total of providential activity in Diodorus' history is much less than his programmatic statement concerning the role of providence (BH 1.1.3) leads one to expect.[39] He fails to present history consistently in terms of such an overarching principle of divine activity, for 'human life, as if

---

[34] κυρία, BH 11.11.3. See also 13.24.5, 'one may mention the adages of the wise men of old: "O man, but not high-spirited"; "Know thyself"; "Observe how Fortune is lord of all"'.

[35] Fortune is the strongest of all forces (BH 15.63.2) and is able to bring low the arrogant (13.24.6; 20.13.3; 31.12.1; see also 18.59.6). No human can prevail over Fortune (13.21.5), for the outcome of human actions lies in her hands (26.24.2; but cf. 12.20.2). Drews refers to 'Diodorus' more than 60 references to the power of τύχη' ('Sources' 386 n. 15).

[36] See also BH 20.4.7, and note the comment at 19.42.5 that it is a shameful thing to flee from Fortune. Drews ('Sources' 386 n. 15) notes that 'reverence for τύχη ... is recommended by Diodorus in four philosophical parentheses (18.59.5–6; 20.13.2; 31.12; 34/35.18)'.

[37] The apologetic context has already been set by his use of this same verb κατηγορεῖν relation to Fortune at RA 1.4.2,5.2.

[38] Fortune plays the same role in Dionysius' prologue as providence does in Diodorus' prologue. The clearest equation of the two entities is found in Dionysius' report of the speech of Fufetius (RA 3.14.2), where providence, Fortune and the gods are each in turn declared responsible for the marvellous prodigy which occurred. Diodorus twice depicts providence in terms which are frequently used elsewhere in association with Fortune, namely παράδοξος (BH 4.43.2; 20.70.1–2) and περιπετεία (BH 4.43.2). Busolt ('Verhältnis' 301) cites other passages which show Fortune functioning in the same manner as providence (BH 16.11.1, cf. 14.76.2; 18.53.7, cf. 13.112.2); see Trompf, *Idea* 195; Walsh, *Livy* 56–9.
At BH 29.18.1, Fortune leads to death but providence grants posthumous honours; at RA 6.73.2, Fate leads and Fortune directs affairs. These references may reflect the Stoic view of a universal law which, as τύχη, determines the world, and, as πρόνοια, orders and preserves it; see K. Niederwimmer, *Der Begriff der Freiheit im Neuen Testament* (Berlin: Alfred Töpelmann, 1966) 39–40, who summarizes the detailed argument of S. Eitrem, 'Schicksalsmachte', *Symbolae Osloenses* 13 (1934) 47–64; and see *SVF* 2.966. However, such precise philosophical discriminations are not characteristic of either historian, for they reflect popular, rather than technical, philosophical awareness.

[39] See the criticisms of S. Usher, *The Historians of Greece and Rome* (New York: Taplinger, 1969) 236; and cf. Lucian's criticism of historians who write a dramatic, brilliant introduction, only to follow it with an undistinguished body (*History* 23).

some god were at the helm,[40] moves in a cycle through good and evil alternately for all time. It is not strange (παράδοξον), then, that some one unforeseen event (παράλογον) has taken place, but rather that all that happens is not unexpected (ἀνέλπιστον)' (BH 18.59.6). Accordingly, Diodorus comments that 'in the affairs of men, nothing remains stable, neither the good nor the ill, since Fortune (τύχη), as if of set purpose, keeps all things in constant change (BH 27.15.3)[41] and he persistently notes the capricious nature of Fortune.[42] Likewise for Dionysius, even Rome, whom he considers to have been consistently favoured by Fortune,[43] has been known to have been temporarily opposed by Fortune (RA 3.19.6), who upsets expectations by reversing established principles (RA 8.32.3) and thus earns the reputation of misleading all human calculations (RA 11.12.3).[44]

Such a contradiction in the essential nature of Fortune reveals that, despite their awareness of the philosophical dimensions of the issue, neither Diodorus nor Dionysius was a technical philosopher who used terms with precision and consistency. Rather, they reflect as much the popular conceptions of the fickle goddess Fortune as they do the philosophical notions of a superintending providence. In this regard they are quite different from Posidonius, who quite

---

[40] οἰακιζόμενος. Cf. the common Stoic notion of a god at the helm of history (see chap. 2 n. 13).

[41] Also BH 13.53.2; 20.13.3; 25.5.2; and see 18.59.4–6, concerning 'the incredible fickleness of Fortune ... the inconstancies of human life ... the alternating ebb and flow of fortune'.

[42] Fortune effects changes (μεταβολάς: BH 14.76.1; 17.36.1,3,47.6,66.4; 18.20.1,42.1,59.6; 24.13.1; 26.6.2; 31.12.1,18.3; 32.23.1,24.1; 36.11.2; εὐμεταβολάς: 26.6.2) and reversals (περιπετείας: 8.10.3; 31.18.3; 32.10.5; 34/35.2; ἐναντίας: 30.23.1). The essential nature of Fortune is conveyed through the phrases παράδοξος τῆς τύχης (4.53.4; 12.62.2; 15.33.3; 16.75.1; 17.47.6,59.7; 18.59.4; 20.93.7; 21.11.1; 25.9.1; 31.3.1,10.2; 32.10.5) and παράλογος τῆς τύχης (17.66.2,108.6; 29.8.2; 31.32.1). She is unstable (ἄστατον, 18.67.4; 33.7.1; 34/35.28.3), uncertain (ἄδηλον, 14.20.3; 26.16.1), inconsistent (ἀνωμαλίαν, 20.30.1), inscrutable (χαλεπόν, 31.10.1) and changeable (ἀβεβαιότητος, 37.29.3; 18.60.1). See Sinclair's comment on 'Diodorus' constant addiction to παράδοξος' ('Diodorus Siculus' 41), and note the attribution to Posidonius, by Athenaeus, of the phrase τὸ παράδοξον τῆς τύχης (*Deipn.* 5.212C). See also Strabo, *Geog.* 3.2.9, again quoting Posidonius regarding a 'prodigal fortune' (ἀφθόνου τύχης). For other references in ancient literature, see Trompf, *Idea* 193 n. 63.

[43] 'Fortune alone exalts this commonwealth', RA 10.28.3; see also 1.4.2,5.2,90.1; 2.17.3; 3.20.3,21.10; 4.62.1; 6.15.3; 7.70.4. This was a commonplace in ancient literature (See Trompf, *Idea* 192–4, esp. nn. 61–2), but Diodorus did not subscribe to this view (Trompf, *Idea* 195–6).

[44] Fortune, 'whose whims men can neither foresee nor guard against' (RA 9.25.3), is 'inconstant and quick to change' (ἀβέβαιος and ἀγχίστροφος, 6.19.2), 'uncertain' (ἀτεκμάρτον, 6.21.1) and 'unexpected' (παράλογον, 11.35.2).

firmly distanced himself from the vicissitudes of Fortune.[45] If there is any redeeming feature in the work of Fortune, it is that 'in the inconsistency and irregularity of events, history furnishes a corrective for both the arrogance of the fortunate and the despair of the destitute' (BH 18.59.6).[46] However, most of the occurrences of τύχη must be regarded as simple chance,[47] with no divine forethought implied, and it is this non-technical sense of the term which predominates in both works. The final judgement on the role of providence in these two histories must therefore be that the programmatic goal was worthy, but the pragmatic expression of the idea was lacking in consistency and coherence.

## 3.2 Providence in Josephus

We noted above that Josephus claimed a programmatic role for the motif of providence in the history of the Jewish people which he wrote for the benefit of Roman citizens. The claim which Josephus makes in his preface to this work is largely substantiated throughout

[45] Posidonius' disdain for the fickleness of Fortune is reflected in Seneca's advice to 'live with Chrysippus and Posidonius ... they will bid you be stout of heart and rise superior to threats. The only harbour safe from the seething storms of life is scorn of the future, a firm stand, a readiness to receive Fortune's missiles full in the breast, neither skulking nor turning the back' (*Ep.* 104.22). Compare the criticism by Democritus of Abdera, quoted by Bury (*Historians* 130); and note the warning by Posidonius against complacency in the face of Fortune (Seneca, *Ep.* 113.28). Polybius, although ostensibly dismissing the role of Fortune in history (15.36.1–11), nevertheless himself reports numerous instances of the fickleness of Fortune (see chap. 2 n. 4 and note Rajak, *Josephus* 101); cf. Bomstead, *Governing Ideas* 59–60.

[46] See also BH 13.24.6; 20.13.3; 31.12.1.

[47] Chance (αὐτοματισμός) and Fortune (τύχη) are equated at RA 1.4.2. On occasions, Edward Carey in the Loeb volumes of Dionysius translates 'chance' for τύχη (6.31.3; 7.50.2; 12.20.2), συντυχία (3.70.1) or τυχηρά (7.68.2). τύχη (translated as 'fortune') refers to mere happenstance on many other occasions (2.43.5; 3.23.17; 4.23.1; 5.15.3; 6.47.4; 7.54.4; 19.13.2; etc.) and is similar to the references to μεταβολάς (12.1.3; 13.23.3; 16.70.3; 18.53.1,59.6; 19.53.3; etc.) or περιπετείας (3.31.2,57.8; 4.55.1; 13.33.2; 17.27.7,46.6; 18.21.1,59.5; etc.). What is described by Diodorus as chance (ταὐτόματον) co-operating with the actions of Scipio (BH 31.27.2) is subsequently described as Scipio's τύχη (31.27.4), and again numerous references to τύχη simply refer to happenstance (e.g. 2.2.1; 3.18.1; 13.30.6,41.5,58.1, 102.3,108.6; 17.6.3; 19.7.4; etc.). Note also the extremely common use of the compounds ἀυχία (4.31.2,46.1,50.3; 13.48.3; 14.5.1; 16.61.4; 18.11.4; 19.106.5,108.2; etc.) and εὐτυχία (8.12.11; 9.26.1,33.3; 10.23.1; 11.25.1; 13.52.1; 14.112.1; 17.38.6; etc.) as well as the frequent references to συμφοράς (8.10.3; 13.91.1; 16.61.4,82.2; 17.46.5; 18.21.1,53.4; 20.9.1,15.3,31.1; etc.). For the Stoic equation of chance and Fortune, see *SVF* 2.968, 970 ( = Alexander of Aphrodisias, *De fato* 8); Seneca, *De benef.* 4.8.3. On this subject more generally, see L. H. Martin, 'The Rule of τύχη and Hellenistic Religion', *SBLSPS* 15 (1976) 453–9.

the entire twenty books. The same theme appears in a somewhat different form, with less prominence but with a more blatantly apologetic purpose, in an earlier work he wrote to account for the war between the Jews and Rome of 66–74 CE. In both works, Josephus uses a wide variety of terms to convey the notion of divine providence.[48] These terms are relatively uncommon in his account of the Jewish war, where they refer more often to human foresight[49] or will[50] than to divine providence. Although Josephus occasionally depicts the care of God for the Jews,[51] more often he apologetically asserts that God favours the Romans in their war against the Jews.[52]

Throughout his history of the Jewish people, the saturation of these terms forms a more prominent and distinctive thematic concern.[53] It is particularly in the biblical paraphrase that Josephus develops the notion of divine providence[54] and the will of God.[55] In that section of the work, key terms refer to divine providence, rather

[48] πρόνοια, προνοέω and γνώμη are most common; προμήθεια, etc., κηδεμών, etc., βούλησις, βούλημα, βουλή and προαίρεσις are used frequently. For other terms which convey this notion, see Bretschneider, *Capita theologiae* 25–30; Carson, *Divine Sovereignty* 115–17. For the relation of providence to τύχη, see chap. 3.2.3, and to the various terms for Fate, see chap. 7.1.1, 7.2.2.

[49] πρόνοια is used 24 times in BJ, 12 of these referring to the providence of God; προνοέω is used 9 times in BJ, each time referring to human foresight; κηδεμών and other forms are used 10 times in BJ, of which only 3.387 refers to God's protection (of Josephus); προμήθεια is used once in BJ, for human care.

[50] γνώμη is used 33 times in BJ, only twice referring to the divine will (7.327,358, both in Eleazar's final speech); προαίρεσις refers to human will in all five uses in BJ, whilst βούλησις is not used in this work.

[51] BJ 1.593; 3.28; 4.219; and Josephus himself at 3.391, as we find also at V 15; 301; 425.

[52] BJ 3.144; 4.366,622; 7.82,318; and see 2.457. Cf. 7.453, where the punishment of a Roman is considered providential. God is frequently depicted as the ally (σύμμαχος) of Rome (2.390,391,484; 4.366; 6.41; 7.319). P. Bilde ('The Jewish War According to Josephus', *JSJ* 10 (1979) 199) considers that one of the major theological themes of BJ is that 'the war and the fall of Jerusalem could not but occur in accordance with [God's] plan and will'; likewise, Attridge, 'Josephus' 203–6.

[53] On the centrality of providence in AJ, see Schlatter, *Wie Sprach?* 49; van Unnik, 'Attack' 349, and the earlier literature he cites in n. 33; Attridge, *Interpretation* 67–8, 71–6, 149–50 and 182. Attridge (*ibid.*, 75–6) shows that the providence motif is a central component of the editorial activity of Josephus, since the key term appears only once (Num 23.9) in the source material used by Josephus in his first eleven books. Rajak (*Josephus* 9, 78–9) asserts that Josephus here addresses a Jewish question in a Greek form.

[54] πρόνοια and προνοέω are used 127 times in Books 1–11, as against 62 times in Books 12–20; κηδεμών and other forms are used 8 times in Books 1–11 and only twice in Books 12–20. By contrast, προμήθεια and προμηθέομαι are used only once in Books 1–11, but 11 times in Books 12–20.

[55] βούλησις is used 54 times in Books 1–11, and only ten times in Books 12–20; but προαίρεσις occurs 29 times in in Books 1–11 and 39 times in Books 12–20, whilst γνώμη appears 79 times in Books 1–11 and 107 times in Books 12–20.

than human foresight, much more frequently than in the later section,[56] and other terms are occasionally used to emphasize the providence of God.[57]

### 3.2.1 Providence in speeches

In his *Antiquities*, Josephus reports a number of speeches in which God emphasizes divine providence,[58] as well as speeches by Moses in which God's providence is similarly affirmed.[59] Since he believes that 'no man can defeat the will (γνώμη) of God' (AJ 2.209), Josephus uses examples to encourage his readers not to be like Adam and others who disobeyed the divine will,[60] but rather to follow the examples of Abraham, Sarah and others obedient to God's will.[61]

---

[56] In Books 1–11, 60 occurrences (47%) of πρόνοια προνοέω refer to divine providence; in Books 12–20, 19 occurrences (30%) refer to divine providence. A large majority (78%) of uses of γνώμη in Books 1–11 refer to the divine will; in Books 12–20 only three occurrences refer to the will of God (AJ 15.144; 17.129,240). Forty instances (74%) of βούλησις refer to God in Books 1–11, but only three in Books 12–20 (12.26; 15.383,387). In addition, προμήθεια refers to divine providence twice (4.185; 17.354) as do κηδεμών (7.380; 20.84), κηδεμονία (3.15), βουλή (4.42; 6.38), βούλημα (1.232; 2.304), βουλητός (5.102) and προαίρεσις (4.24,109; 5.116; 8.223).

[57] God is described as the δεσπότης (AJ 1.20; 4.46; 5.93; 11.64,162,230; 18.23) who shows ἐπιστροφή (8.314). Most often God shows εὐμενής (36 times in Books 1–11) which is occasionally linked with providence (AJ 1.225; 2.161; 4.122). The divine activity is conveyed by the verbs ἐπιβλέπω (1.20), κυβερνάω (10.278), τροπεύω (4.21) and ὑπεροράω (6.307; 8.256). See also BJ 3.6; CA 2.160.

[58] In addition to God's first declaration of providence, directed to Adam (AJ 1.46), God asserts that the promise of dominion given to Jacob was made in his providence (AJ 1.283; 2.174); affirms his providential concern for the welfare of Moses and Israel in a speech to Amram (AJ 2.215); for Samson while addressing his mother, the wife of Manoah (AJ 5.277); and for exiles in speeches to Jeremiah (AJ 10.177) and Jaddus (AJ 11.327).

[59] Moses' speeches immediately prior to the Exodus (AJ 2.329,330,332,336; see Attridge, *Interpretation* 76–8); in the wilderness (AJ 3.15; cf. 3.38); at Mount Sinai (AJ 3.99); in the revolt by Korah (AJ 4.47, cf. Korah's fraudulent concern for the public welfare (προνοεῖσθαι), 4.20; see Attridge, *Interpretation* 96–8); and in his final summation of the Law (AJ 4.185; see Attridge, *Interpretation* 90–1). The speeches by Balaam similarly affirm God's providence for Israel (4.114,117,128; cf. 157). On the relative lack of the providence motif in the histories of Diodorus and Dionysius, see above, n. 8.

[60] Adam (AJ 1.47), the people of Babel (1.112) and Sodom (1.223), the brothers of Joseph (2.20,161), the Pharaoh of Egypt (2.283,303,309) and the Egyptians (3.17), the people of Israel (3.16; 4.8; 5.133; 6.143), Balaam (4.110), Balak (4.127), the tribes of Rubel and Manasseh (5.107), Saul (6.137), Solomon (8.208), the friends of Rehoboam (8.216) and all the northern tribes (8.223), Jadon (8.241) and the house of Ahab (9.132,167).

[61] Abraham (AJ 1.157,223,225,232), Sarah (1.216–17; 2.213), Moses (2.223; 3.315; 4.40,185,322), the elders of Israel (4.24,30) and all the people of Israel (4.67;

Both David (AJ 7.95,338,380,385) and Solomon (AJ 8.109)[62] declare the care of God in the provision of the Temple, the latter's speech being the occasion for Josephus to introduce an important dimension of the providence motif, namely that it is made manifest through the fulfilment of prophecy.[63] The prophet Daniel, who is twice saved by the providence of God (AJ 10.214,260), issues prophecies concerning the destruction of the Temple, which gives Josephus occasion for a vigorously apologetic affirmation of God's providence (AJ 10.277–81).

### 3.2.2 Philosophic views of providence

At this point Josephus demonstrates a fully developed apologetic technique; he asserts the theme of providence, expounds it in relation to the fulfilment of prophecies, and polemicizes in an explicitly philosophical fashion against those who 'exclude providence (πρόνοιαν) from human life and refuse to believe that God governs (ἐπιτροπεύειν) its affairs or that the universe is directed (κυβερνᾶσθαι) by a blessed and immortal being' (AJ 10.278).[64] This attack, made in support of the fulfilment of the prophecies, is placed on the lips of Daniel, who encountered enemies who 'did not choose to believe that it was through the deity and his providence (πρόνοιαν) that he [Daniel] had been saved' (AJ 10.260). However, the opponents whom Josephus has in mind are actually the Epicureans of his own time, who are 'very far from holding a true opinion, who declare that God takes no thought (μηδεμίαν εἶναι πρόνοιαν) for human affairs' (AJ 10.280).[65]

Using explicitly philosophical terms and methods,[66] Josephus

---

5.102,116), Balaam's ass (4.109), Eleazar and Joshua (4.185–86), Judah (5.120), David (7.90), Hushai (7.221), Solomon (8.2,4) and Rehoboam (8.218).

[62] On the Stoic aspects in Josephus' portrayal of Solomon in the Temple, see L. H. Feldman, 'Josephus as an Apologist to the Greco-Roman World: His Portrait of Solomon', *Aspects of Religious Propaganda in Judaism and Early Christianity* (ed. E. Schüssler Fiorenza; Notre Dame, Ind.: University of Notre Dame, 1976) 90–1.

[63] See Attridge, *Interpretation* 100–4; and further in chap. 6.2.1.3.

[64] See chap. 2 n. 13 for the Stoic use of διακυβερνάω.

[65] The objection raised by Schlatter (*Wie Sprach?* 50), that 'der Begriff "Epikureer" zum Names für jede unfromme Denkweise dient', is clearly removed by van Unnik's treatment of this passage ('Attack' 345–8).

[66] Van Unnik ('Attack' 351) notes that Josephus here uses the standard Stoic arguments against the Epicureans (cf. Cicero, *De nat. deor.* 1.20.54, 2.29.73–30.75) and echoes Stoic warnings of the disaster that would result if there were no providence (cf. Philo, *De confus. ling.* 1114F). He comments that this passage in Josephus

polemicizes against their notion of the world running automatic-ally,[67] in direct contradiction to his oft-made claim that God provi-dentially cares for the world. The same contrast is asserted in Moses' speech concerning Abiram and Datham, when Moses appeals to God in classic philosophical terms, to 'prove now once again that all is directed by thy providence (σῇ προνοίᾳ) that nothing befalls fortuitously (αὐτομάτως), but that it is thy will (βούλησιν) (AJ 4.47).[68]

At sporadic moments during the period of the second Temple, the providential motif recurs,[69] and examples are provided of those who obeyed God's will[70] and those who disobey God's will (γνώμη), who are described as 'those lacking in virtue' (AJ 17.129). Josephus warns his readers not to let their opinion (γνώμη) obstruct the (προμήθεια) of God (AJ 17.354) and offers an extended account of Izates, a pagan ruler converted to Judaism, who is presented as a particularly attractive example of the benefits to be obtained from adhering to Jewish beliefs. Izates is depicted as under the provi-dential care of God from his birth to his death (AJ 20.18,49,84,91).

Even the final punishment of Israel, the destruction of the Jeru-salem Temple at the hands of the Romans, implies God's provi-dence, for Josephus draws the moral that God 'wished to chasten us by these calamities' (AJ 20.166).[71] Thus, just as Dionysius apologe-tically asserts that providence is protecting Rome, so Josephus in AJ provides a similar apologetic assertion that the work of providence is largely concerned with Israel.[72] His account of the origins and

is 'valuable ... in connection with the history of philosophy at the end of the first century A.D.' On Josephus' philosophical awareness, see Rajak, *Josephus* 35–7.

[67] For the Epicurean belief in the way the gods allow the world to run as an automatism, see Diogenes Laertius, *Lives* 10.133–5; Cicero, *De nat. deor.* 1.19.51–20.56; and Clarke, *Octavius* 268–9. For the Stoic refutation, see Plutarch, *De Stoic. repugn.* 1045B; Cicero, *De nat. deor.* 2.29.73–30.76; and Alexander of Aphrodisias, *De fato* 8. For the Epicurean polemic against Stoic notions of providence, see Cicero, *De nat. deor.* 1.8.18–9.23 and 1.20.52,54.

[68] See van Unnik, 'Attack' 349. Attridge fails to give full weight to the philosophi-cal dimension (see *Interpretation* 100 where he dismisses it curtly and 155 where he explicitly rejects this philosophical dimension).

[69] πρόνοια at AJ 11.169; 12.47,101; 13.163,180,314; 14.391,462; προμήθεια at AJ 17.354; 18.286.

[70] Ptolemy, Aristeas (AJ 12.26); Herod (15.144,383,387).

[71] See Attridge, 'Josephus' 222; and cf. BJ 7.453, where the death of Catullus is presented as proof (τεκμήριον) of the punishment meted out on disobedient people by the providence (προνοίας) of God.

[72] Thus, AJ 2.347–9; 4.47,60. At AJ 4.114, Josephus notes that it is by divine providence that Israel has God as ally (σύμμαχον) and leader (ἡγεμόνα) who gives help (AJ 4.114); notice also the constellation of providential terms at 4.185. God gives

history of the Jewish people, written in the Greek language and directed to the citizens of Rome, thus has a specifically apologetic purpose, namely, to assert the validity of the Jewish faith.

### 3.2.3 Providence, Fortune and human affairs

The prominence of providence is further reflected in the comparatively smaller role accorded to Fortune in the Josephan corpus.[73] In the account of the Jewish war, where τύχη usually signifies the situation or position in life which happens by chance to befall a person,[74] there are some indications of the apologetic point of view, seen also in Dionysius, that Fortune 'has wholly passed over to the Romans' (BJ 3.354).[75] On occasion, however, she may interfere on behalf of the Jews,[76] even if this means that she opposes

Israel help (βοήθεια, 4.114; 5.65,206,216; 6.181; 7.245; 9.14) and has an alliance with Israel (συμμαχία, 1.209; 2.332; 3.45; 8.283; 9.15,55; 10.24; σύμμαχος, 1.229,268; 2.278,334; 3.302; 4.2,114,182,185,296; 5.98; 6.25,189; 9.55; 11.7; 12.285,314; 18.297; see Josephus' speech at BJ 5.377,389,403,489, and 6.99–100. God is the ally of Izates, AJ 20.85,90; but at AJ 9.259 God is not the ally of Hoshea). This alliance is described as occurring by the πρόνοια of God at AJ 4.114,185; BJ 7.318; likewise it is by divine providence that the people of Israel are saved from calamity (AJ 2.332; 4.128; 10.117; 11.279–80), often by miraculous happenings. Nevertheless, Josephus does indicate the wider sphere of God's providence, which watches over Adam (AJ 1.46), the Philistines (6.10), Ptolemy (13.80), Petronius and Gaius (18.39), Agrippa (18.197) and Gaius (19.219); and see BJ 2.457; 3.28,144. Israel's special position is due, not to the covenant made by God, but to her 'virtue and passion for pursuits most noble and pure of crime' (AJ 4.114). On the lack of covenantal theology in Josephus, see Attridge, *Interpretation* 78–83, 87; *contra*, Rajak, *Josephus* 101.

[73] On τύχη in Josephus, see Schlatter, *Wie Sprach?* 55; B. Brüne, *Flavius Josephus und seine Schriften in ihrem Verhältnis zum Judentum, zur griechischen-römischen Welt und zum Christentum* (Wiesbaden: Sändig, 1969) 186–92. Note the cautionary comment of S. J. D. Cohen ('Josephus, Jeremiah and Polybius', *History and Theory* 21 (1982) 372), that 'Josephus' inveterate sloppiness in the use of technical terms precludes any general definition which might apply to all the occurrences of τύχη throughout the Josephus corpus'; similarly, Attridge, 'Josephus' 204 n. 28.
[74] Most occurrences have this standard sense, for example BJ 1.28,45,291,353,390; 2.207,373; 3.24; etc.; see Brüne, *Flavius Josephus* 187–91. τύχη as a divine entity, as we find in Dionysius and Diodorus, is proportionally much less common in Josephus. On the various interpretations of τύχη in BJ, see H. Lindner, *Die Geschichtsauffassung des Flavius Josephus im Bellum Judaicum* (Arbeiten zur Geschichte des antiken Judentums und des Christentums 12; Leiden: Brill, 1972) 89–94.
[75] At BJ 5.367 he equates this with the action of God in giving the rule of ἀρχή to Italy. See also BJ 2.360,387; 3.71,100,106,359; 6.399–400; 7.203. Fortune also guides the Roman leaders Vespasian in 4.40,591,607,622 and Titus in 3.396; 5.46,88; 6.57,63,413. Lindner (*Geschichtsauffassung* 85,88) disputes this interpretation, arguing that 'Die τύχη des Josephus ist offenbarungmässig gebunden' and that 'Der Unterschied zwischen josephischer und griechischer τύχη sollte im Blicke bleiben'.
[76] BJ 4.238,243; 5.78,120–2; 6.14,44; on behalf of Josephus himself in 3.387–91.

the Romans.[77] Accordingly, Josephus gives due recognition to the popular impression of the capricious nature of fortune.[78]

In AJ 1–11 God's consistent providence overshadows the role of Fortune,[79] although in Books 12–20 she appears with increasing frequency. She is still the same fickle Fortune of hellenistic history, who is 'wont to veer now toward one side, now toward the other in human affairs' (AJ 18.267),[80] and whilst to the Romans her undoubted power is not to be ignored (AJ 18.239), for it is 'greater than prudent reflection' (AJ 16.397), to Josephus, Fortune's inconsistency and unpredictability are grounds for repudiating her power.[81] It is divine providence which actually guides history.

### 3.3 God at work in Luke–Acts

Neither the apologetic function of this central theme, nor the philosophic dimension of the issues is immediately apparent in Luke–Acts; these aspects are conveyed through small, often indirect, means.[82]

Our use of 'apologetic' is different from the way in which the term has most often been applied to Luke–Acts, by those who argue that Luke is defending Christianity against political charges and asserting its rightful place as a *religio licita* in the Roman Empire.[83] Our

---

[77] BJ 5.78,122; 7.7.

[78] Fortune 'veers from mood to mood' (BJ 1.374), may unexpectedly 'flit back again to one's side' (4.40), and displays 'spiteful freaks' of fortune (4.243). See also 4.238 and 7.115.

[79] She appears only seven times in the biblical paraphrase, each of these being in the standard pagan sense of one's lot or situation in life (AJ 1.6,8.13; 2.39; 4.266; 11.56,341). Attridge comments that 'τύχη never appears as a cosmic factor in the biblical paraphrase' (*Interpretation* 154 n. 1). In Books 12–20 there are 52 references to τύχη. See Brüne, *Flavius Josephus* 191–2.

[80] At one time Fortune opposes the Jews (AJ 19.29), at another time she assists them (AJ 19.293–4). Josephus comments that 'changes in Fortune are the lot of all men' (AJ 20.61); see also 15.179,374; 17.122; 20.57. Josephus admits that he wrote his history under the persuasions of Epaphroditus, who was 'specially interested in the experiences of history [and] conversant ... with large affairs and varying turns of fortune' (πράγμασι καὶ τύχαις πολυτρόποις, AJ 1.8). Despite these few examples of fickle Fortune, the finished product must have been disappointing to his patron in the light of the pre-eminence of providence shown above.

[81] See AJ 16.397–8. On the equation of Fortune with Fate, see chap. 7 n. 29. Cf. the role of Fortune in Philo, as an agent of God (Wolfson, *Philo* 2.422; Trompf, *Idea* 167–8).

[82] See Cadbury, *Making* 301.

[83] Such an *apologia pro ecclesia* is proposed by Cadbury, *Making* 308–16; B. S. Easton, *The Purpose of Acts* (London: SPCK,1936) 9–17; and Conzelmann, *Theology* 137–49. Maddox (*Purpose* 91–9) severely restricts the apologetic nature of Luke–

focus in treating the apologetic function of providence will be, rather, on the way in which 'the plan of God' is used to assert and expound the central features of the story of Jesus and the early church.[84] Such a conception of apologetic is neither more nor less evident from the text than is the political apologetic. It derives its force from the conjunction of two observations, grounded not in a theological analysis of Luke's aims, but rather in a comparative analysis of his writings.

The first observation is that Jewish apologetic, although ostensibly addressed to 'outsiders', is actually addressed to 'insiders', using categories provided by the 'outsider' for the purpose of reinterpreting the tradition in a new context.[85] Luke's preface indicates that he shares in this task; he is reinterpreting the received tradition concerning Jesus in such a way as to provide 'certainty' for his Christian readers in the wider hellenistic context.[86]

The second observation is that when the providence motif is read comparatively, in this wider context, its apologetic function can be understood.[87] In Christian literature, it is only in the second century that an explicit acknowledgement of the philosophic dimension of providence appears, in the course of apologetic attempts to deal with philosophic criticisms of Christian belief.[88] Justin Martyr,

Acts. Recent reinterpretations of the apologetic motif include the claim for an *apologia pro imperio* made by P. W. Walaskay, *'And so we Came to Rome': the Political Perspective of St Luke* (Cambridge University Press, 1983) and the application of the sociological category of legitimation by P. F. Esler, *Community and Gospel in Luke–Acts: the Social and Political Motivations of Lucan Theology* (Cambridge University Press, 1987) 205–19. On Lukan apologetic in relation to Judaism, see F. F. Bruce, 'Paul's Apologetic and the Purpose of Acts', *BJRL* 69 (1987) 379–93; R. L. Brawley, *Luke–Acts and the Jews: Conflict, Apology and Conciliation* (SBLMS 33; Atlanta: Scholars, 1987).

[84] For the role of exposition in Christian apologetic, see A. Puech, *Les Apologistes grecs du IIe siècle de notre ère* (Paris: Hachette, 1912) 1–18 (esp. 13–14); H. I. Marrou, *A Diognète* (Sources Chrétiennes 33; Paris: Cerf, 1965) 92–5; J. Danielou, *Gospel Message and Hellenistic Culture* (Philadelphia: Westminster, 1973) 7–37 (esp. 20–31); Malherbe, "Preaching for Peter" 205–6. For the relation between apologetic and providence in Luke–Acts, see Johnson, *Writings* 200–4.

[85] See Johnson, *Writings* 74–8.

[86] See Johnson, *Writings* 203–4.

[87] For the link between apologetic and philosophy, see Puech, *Les Apologistes grecs* 7–14; Malherbe, 'Apologetic and Philosophy' *passim*, esp. 27.

[88] See R. L. Wilken, 'The Christians as the Romans (and Greeks) Saw Them', *Jewish and Christian Self-Definition*: vol. 1, *The Shaping of Christianity in the Second and Third Centuries* (ed. E. P. Sanders; Philadelphia: Fortress Press, 1980) 1.107–10. On pagan criticisms of Christianity as a disreputable philosophy, see S. Benko, Pagan Criticisms of Christianity During the First Two Centuries', *ANRW* II.23.2, 1095–7, 1101, 1110; R. L. Wilken, *The Christians as the Romans Saw Them* (New Haven and London: Yale University Press, 1984) 73–83. On Galen's assessment of

whose autobiographical description of his conversion indicates his personal acquaintance with philosophy,[89] presents the Gospel in terms comprehensible to the philosophers.[90] He goes beyond the belief of some philosophers, that 'God takes care of the universe with its genera and species ... but not of me and you, and each individually' (*Dial.* 1.4),[91] when he declares that God 'foreknows that some are to be saved by repentance' (1 *Ap* 28) and justifies this claim by means of proof from prophecy (1 *Ap* 32–53). Athenagoras accuses the poets and philosophers of denying divine providence and claiming that 'this universe is constituted without any definite order, and is driven hither and thither by an irrational chance' (*Leg.* 25).[92] He rejects those who claim that 'there is nothing out of order

Christianity as a philosophy, see Benko, Pagan Criticism' 1098–100; Wilken, *The Christians* 72–3, 79–83, 92–3.

[89] *Dial.* 2–8. For the claim that such a report was a standard literary *topos*, see N. Hyldahl, *Philosophie und Christentum: Eine Interpretation der Einleitung zum Dialog Justins* (Acta Theologica Danica 9; Copenhagen: Prostant apud Munksgaard, 1966); C. Andresen, 'Justin und der mittlere Platonismus', *ZNW* 44 (1953) 157–95; J. C. M. van Winden, 'Le Portrait de la philosophie grecque dans Justin, Dialogue I,4–5', *VC* 31 (1977) 181–90, esp. 187–90; Rajak, *Josephus* 35–7, with literature cited in n. 69; *contra*, L. W. Barnard, 'Justin Martyr in Recent Study', *SJT* 22 (1969) 152–64, esp. 152–6. On this *topos* in Lucian, *Philosophies for Sale*, see Wilken, *The Christians* 74–6.

[90] The most debated aspect is the term λόγος σπερμάτικος in 2 *Ap* 8.3, 13.3–6. See Andresen, 'Platonismus' 170–3; R. Holte, 'Logos Spermatikos: Christianity and Ancient Philosophy according to St Justin's Apologies', *ST* 12 (1958) 109–68; R. A. Norris, *God and World in Early Christian Theology* (New York: Seabury, 1965) 51–5; Barnard, 'Recent Study' 156–61; E. F. Osborn, *Justin Martyr* (Beiträge zur historischen Theologie 47; Tübingen: Mohr, 1973) 140–5.

[91] The distinction is between general providence (the care of the gods for the whole creation) and specific providence (the care of the gods for individuals). General providence was further divided into the providence exercised by the highest god (primary providence) and the providence of intermediary gods (secondary providence). See Ps-Plutarch, *De fato*, and the introduction to the Loeb translation (*Plutarch: Moralia* (Cambridge, Mass.: Harvard University Press, 1959) 307) by P. H. DeLacey and B. Einarson; A. J. Malherbe, 'Athenagoras on the Pagan Poets and Philosophers', *Kyriakon. Festschrift Johannes Quasten* (ed. P. Granfield and J. A. Jungmann; 2 vols.; Münster: Aschendorff, 1970) 1.219–20; A. Dihle, *The Theory of the Will in Classical Antiquity* (Berkeley and Los Angeles: University of California Press, 1982) 103–4; Busolt, 'Verhältnis' 298 n. 1, quoting Cicero, *De nat. deor.* 2.65.164.
On the importance of providence, general and specific, in the Dialogue, see Hyldahl, *Philosophie und Christentum* 100; J. C. M. van Winden, *An Early Christian Philosopher: Justin Martyr's Dialogue with Trypho Chapters One to Nine* (Philosophia Patrum 1; Leiden: Brill, 1971) 36–8. R. Joly (*Christianisme et philosophie: études sur Justin et les apologistes grecs du deuxième siècle* (Brussels: University of Brussels, 1973) 19–23) rightly criticizes van Winden's idea of a uniquely Christian idea of specific providence, and notes that a similar concept is to be found in Dio Chrysostom, Atticus, Nemesius, Epictetus and Plutarch.

[92] L. W. Barnard (*Athenagoras* (Théologie Historique 18; Paris: Beauchesne, 1972) 119) interprets this as an attack on Epicurean philosophy.

or neglected' in the world, since all things have been produced by reason and 'they do not transgress the order prescribed to them' (*Leg.* 25).[93]

This same belief in providence is present in the history which Luke tells, although it is rarely addressed in the same direct manner as we find in the apologists. Nevertheless, there are a substantial number of places at which Luke's awareness of the philosophic issues is apparent.[94] The apologetic function of the theme of providence, although not stated explicitly by Luke, becomes apparent through an analysis of the contexts in which such affirmations are made and the specific issues which are usually associated with this theme.

### 3.3.1 'The things concerning Jesus'

As David Tiede rightly remarks, 'perhaps no New Testament author is more concerned than Luke to testify to the accomplishment of the will of God in history or so caught up in the language of the divine plan and predetermined intention, purpose and necessity.'[95]

In chapter two, we noted how Luke used epiphanies and pre-dictive oracles, as well as direct narrative comments, to establish this concern in the prologue to his Gospel (Luke 1.5–2.52). After this introduction, references to God's guidance of events become less frequent and more fleeting during the ministry of Jesus.[96] A close scrutiny of Luke's editorial activity reveals his propensity to insert subtle indicators of this theme, such as the divine passive,[97] attributions of Jesus' activity to God[98] and sayings of Jesus indicating

[93] See Barnard, *Athenagoras* 118–21, with references to other places where providence is similarly affirmed, in *Leg.* 8.4,8; 19.3; 22.12; 24.3; 25.2; and *De res.* 14.5; 18.1,2; 19.1. For suggestions as to similarities with, and differences from, Christian (and Lukan) uses of the providence motif, see T. F. Torrance, 'Phusikos Kai Theologikos Logos, St Paul and Athenagoras at Athens', *SJT* 41 (1988) 11–26.

[94] See especially our treatment of Acts 4 and 5 (chap. 7, pp. 175–6); 7 (below, pp. 66–8); 17 (below, pp. 71–5); 26 (chap. 7., pp. 174, 177); and the relation of necessity to human freewill (chap. 7, pp. 177–85).

[95] *Prophecy* 33.

[96] This relative sparseness of divine intervention is similar to what we have noticed in the hellenistic histories; although there are numerous references to divine providence, the length of the works means that the final impression is that the assumption of providence becomes explicit only infrequently.

[97] The passive voice of ἀποστέλλω indicates divine intention in Jesus' ministry (Luke 4.43; 9.48; 10.16); it is first applied to Jesus when he reads from the Isaiah scroll in the synagogue of Nazareth (4.18, quoting Isa 61.1). See also Luke 1.19,26 (of Gabriel); 13.34 (of the prophets); Acts 22.1, 26.17 (of Paul); 28.28 (of salvation).

[98] The exorcisms which Jesus performs 'by the finger of God' (Luke 11.20) may be described as 'the things that God has done' (8.39); the healings which he performs are

the scope of God's powers.[99] The other strands we have identified further develop this picture of God's guidance of Jesus' ministry.

In the passion narrative of his Gospel, Luke follows the Markan precedent by omitting any direct reference to divine activity while the details are narrated. Nevertheless, this distinctive Lukan theme may be seen in small redactional touches. The renewed activity of Satan prior to Jesus' betrayal heightens the tension between God and Satan which has been present throughout the ministry of Jesus (22.3,31). Jesus' prayer on the Mount of Olives (22.39–46) emphasizes that what ensues is in accord with God's will (22.42).[100] The last word of Jesus on the cross is not the Markan cry of despair, but a confident declaration of divine mercy (23.46). Despite the terrible turn of events, God's control is acknowledged both by the centurion, who praises God (23.47),[101] and by the second criminal, who exhorts his mocking companion to 'fear God' (23.40).[102]

In the burial scene, Joseph of Arimathaea, who was 'looking for the kingdom of God' (Luke 23.51; par Mark 15.43), is said by Luke to have opposed his fellow council members, for 'he had not consented to their purpose (βουλή) and deed' (Luke 23.51). Luke here seems to hint that the plan (βουλή) of the council stood in opposition to the intentions of God and that the death of Jesus was the pinnacle of opposition to the plan of God.[103] The crucifixion of Jesus, the central character in the story, thus threatens the notion that all events in history occur under the guidance of God.

enabled by 'the power of the Lord' (5.17) and evoke frequent doxologies in praise of God (5.26; 7.16; 13.13; 17.15,18; 18.32). See chap. 4 n. 85.

[99] In pericopes unique to Luke: Luke 11.40; 16.15; 18.7. In pericopes taken from sources: Luke 3.8; 12.5,24,28,30,32; 18.27 (cf. 1.37); 20.38.

[100] The phrasing, 'not my will, but thine, be done', recalls the phrase from the Lord's Prayer which Luke has omitted (Matt 6.10). The scene on the mount also evokes the Lord's Prayer, and the Temptations of Jesus, through the Lukan redaction of the incident as a resistance to temptation (πειρασμόν, 22.40,46; cf. Luke 11.4; 4.2,13); see also chap. 7.3.1.1

[101] ἐδόξαζεν τὸν θεόν, added here by Luke, is one of his favourite phrases. Tiede (*Prophecy* 115) considers that the word of the centurion 'is like an oracle' conveying the divine plan in these events; see also Fitzmyer, *Luke*, 2.1515.

[102] φοβῇ σὺ τὸν θεόν, another favourite Lukan phrase; see Luke 12.5; 18.2,4; Acts 10.2,22,35; 13.1,26; see also Luke 8.25; 9.34; Cf. σέβομαι τὸν θεόν, Acts 16.14; 18.7,13 (see also 13.43,50; 17.4,17).

[103] Such an impression is strengthened by the earlier use of this key term, when Luke comments that the Pharisees and lawyers rejected τὴν βουλὴν τοῦ θεοῦ (Luke 7.30). The death of Jesus is the culmination of their will (23.25) to oppose Jesus (see Luke 5.21,30; 6.2,7,11; 11.53–4; 13.14,17; 14.14; 15.2; 16.14; 18.7; the opponents broaden to include members of the Temple hierarchy in 19.47–8; 20.1,19; 22.2,66; 23.10). See also the comments on 13.31–5 by Johnson, *Possessions* 105 n. 2.

Furthermore, the Hebrew scriptures declare that a person who is hanged on a tree is 'accursed by God' (Deut 21.22–3). This would be a powerful objection to be raised against claims made about Jesus, for the fact was that 'they put him to death by hanging him on a tree' (Acts 10.38).[104] Yet not only in Luke's report of the apostolic preaching, but in other early Christian literature the crucifixion forms an integral part of the message.[105] Although Paul concedes that the cross is cause for offence (1 Cor 1.18), Luke apologetically asserts that this event is part of the plan of God.[106]

This viewpoint is strengthened by the frequent link which Luke makes between the crucifixion and the resurrection of Jesus.[107] The death of Jesus was not the end of the matter; 'God raised him from the dead' is repeated as if it were the inevitable conclusion to the events of the passion.[108] Against the charge that Jesus' death on the cross makes him a common criminal and repudiates the notion that God is in control of history, Luke's presentation of the crucifixion of Jesus forms the very centrepiece of the plan of God. Peter twice refers to the crucifixion of Jesus by invoking the primary terminology of the plan of God (2.23; 4.28) which functions apologetically to explain the event.[109] Thus Luke makes explicit in the apostolic proclamation what was implicit in his Gospel narrative, as he apologetically defends the Gospel against an interpretation of the

---

[104] See also chap. 5 n. 71. For the polemic between Jews and Christians until the middle of the second century, see D. Rokeah, *Jews, Pagans and Christians in Conflict* (Studia Post-Biblica 33. Jerusalem and Leiden: Magnes and Brill, 1982).

[105] See 1 Cor 15.3–4; 1 Thess 1.10; note also 1 Cor 1.23; Phil 2.8; Col 1.20; Eph 2.16; Heb 12.2

[106] Tiede (*Prophecy* 97–9) argues that the cross, a stumbling-block for Jews, remains a problem for Luke. Yet if anything in the early Christian message caused offence, Luke found that it was not the cross but rather the resurrection (Foakes Johnson and Lake, *Beginnings* 4.203). The declaration that God raised Jesus provoked the initial opposition experienced by Peter and John (Act 4.1–2; 5.17). The rebuttal by the Pharisee Gamaliel in Acts 5.34–40 against the claims made by the Sadducees in 5.28,33 indicates that it is the resurrection which is under debate in this instance also. The continuous opposition which Paul encountered on many occasions is due to his preaching of the resurrection (Acts 17.18,32; 23.6–8; 24.21; 25.19; 26.6–8,23–4).

[107] Acts 2.23–4; 3.13–15; 4.10; 5.30; 10.39–40; 13.28–30; 17.3; 26.23.

[108] Acts 2.24; 3.15; 4.10; 5.30; 10.40; 13.30. Talbert ('Promise and Fulfilment' 101) describes it as a sign of 'a providential God'.

[109] Dupont (*Nouvelles études* 68) calls this a 'trait apologétique'. Even the opponents of Jesus (4.27) act under the hand of God (4.28); see Wilckens, *Missionreden* 132.

death of Jesus as in any way being a reversal of the original intentions of God.[110]

### 3.3.2 'The things that God has done'

Events in the early days in Jerusalem likewise take place under the guidance of God. The replacement apostle for Judas is chosen by God (1.24), what happens on the day of Pentecost occurs because of God's initiative (2.17–21)[111] and the healing of the lame man (3.1–10) is an act of God.[112] When charged to cease speaking in the name of Jesus (4.17), Peter insists on the divine necessity of the apostles' actions (4.19, 5.29). Gamaliel then declares that what the apostles are doing is not a human undertaking (5.38), but is truly of God (ἐκ θεοῦ, 5.39), and so he advises the council not to oppose the apostles, for 'you might even be found opposing God' (θεομάχοι, 5.39).[113] Thus the divine impetus for the activity of the apostles is clearly underlined.

In response to the apostolic activity, the number of believers increases; such growth is directly attributable to the guidance of God, for those who are added comprise 'everyone whom the Lord our God calls to him' (2.39). The comment at the end of the day of Pentecost that 'there were added that day about three thousand lives' (2.41), is immediately interpreted in the ensuing summary section (2.43–7) by the note that 'the Lord added to their number

---

[110] Cf. Cosgrove ('Divine ΔΕΙ' 188), who claims that Luke's view of the cross 'expresses paradigmatically God's way of working in history as a providential pattern of reversal'. Further support for our interpretation of the passion is given by the use of proof-from-prophecy on many of the occasions when the passion of Jesus is mentioned, and by the application of the necessity strand to the passion of Jesus (see further in chaps. 6 and 7). Conzelmann (*Theology* 152) correctly infers that the βουλή terminology is taken up by Luke to apply first and foremost to the passion of Jesus; 'from this original purpose the sayings extend to cover past and future'.

[111] The quotation from Joel 2.28–32 described God's actions; by adding the phrase λέγει ὁ θεός (Acts 2.17), Luke specifies that they take place at the instigation of God. See R. F. Zehnle, *Peter's Pentecost Discourse: Tradition and Lukan Reinterpretation in Peter's Speeches of Acts 2 and 3* (SBLMS 15; Nashville: Abingdon 1971) 32.

[112] Note Acts 3.8,9,16; and see chap. 4.3.2.

[113] Haechen (*Acts* 253 n. 2) notes that the move from ἐάν + subjunctive (5.38) to εἰ + indicative (5.39) indicates this work 'was really from God'; see also Flender, *Theologian* 116–17. For opposition to the gods in hellenistic histories, see above, chap. 3.1.2; in Josephus, AJ 14.310; BJ 5.378; CA 1.246,263. See further in chap. 7 nn. 106–8.

day by day those who were being saved' (2.47).[114] Later summary statements also note the divine authorship of this persistent increase in numbers of believers in the dispersed church (9.31), in Antioch (11.21–4) and in Jerusalem where, despite persecution by Herod (12.1–5), 'the word of God grew and multiplied' (12.24) because of God's guidance.

In the middle chapters of Acts, attention turns to another pivotal point of Luke's history, when the spread of the Gospel into the Gentile world is recounted and explained. Since God's plan was originally that the people of Israel were the chosen people (13.17), the Gentile mission raised certain problems. A reader familiar with the Hebrew scriptures might object that such a move away from law-observing Jews, into the pagan world of the Gentiles, contradicts God's original intentions.[115] Such an objection leads Luke to buttress his account of the Gentile mission with apologetic references to scriptural warrants for the undertaking.[116]

A pagan unfamiliar with the differences between Judaism and the emerging faith of Christianity[117] might view the missionary activity of early Christians in the same manner as Jewish proselytism was regarded: as a threat to religious or political stability in the Roman Empire.[118] Thus Christianity was regarded as a supersti-

---

[114] Other summary references to the growth of the church are to be read in the light of this statement (Acts 4.32; 5.14; 6.1,7; 9.31; 11.21; 12.24; 16.5); thus Conzelmann, *Theology* 214–15; Haenchen, *Acts* 189.

[115] On the question of Jewish criticism of early Christian activity among Gentiles, see S. G. Wilson, *The Gentiles and the Gentile Mission in Luke–Acts* (Cambridge University Press, 1973) 174–7; for the necessity of taking into account Jewish objections to Christianity, see Wilken, *The Christians* 116–17; Rokeah, *Conflict (passim)*, esp. 41–50, 61–5.

[116] See further in chapter 6.3.2.2. For the use of this technique by Justin and later Christian apologists, see Wilken, 'The Christians' 120,123.

[117] For evidence that pagans did not distinguish Christianity from Judaism, even in the late second century, see Benko, 'Pagan Criticism' 1076 (on Suetonius, Tacitus and Pliny), 1099 (on Galen), 1106–7 (on Celsus), 1108; Wilken, 'The Christians' 123.

[118] Tacitus rails against Judaism (*Hist.* 5.5.1–5), accusing it of teaching converts to despise the gods, disown their country and dishonour their parents. Juvenal (*Sat.* 14.96–106) depicts Jews as flouting Roman law by being idle on the Sabbath. Seneca's censure of Jewish Sabbath customs (*De superstitione, apud* Augustine, *De civ. dei* 6.11) appears to be a reaction to successful Jewish proselytism; see M. Stern, *Greek and Latin Authors on Jews and Judaism* (3 vols.; Jerusalem: Israel Academy of Sciences and Humanities, 1974–84) 1.186,521. Stern also links with proselytizing activity the remarks of Horace (*Sermones* 1.4.139–43), Valerius Maximus (*Facta et dicta mem.* 1.3.3) and, from later periods, Dio Cassius (*Hist. rom.* 37.17.1; 57.14.1–3,18.5a) and the *Scriptores historiae Augustae* (see Stern, *Authors* 2.511, 515, 517). Rokeah (*Conflict* 42–5, 210) downplays the role of proselytism in Judaism. For direct criticism of Christian proselytism by a pagan, see Origen, *Contra Celsum* 3.55.

tion[119] or a dangerous conspiracy[120] of atheists. Again, Luke's use of proof from prophecy serves to rebut such objections by demonstrating the respectable origins of Christianity[121] and by asserting that its spread throughout the ancient world was in accord with God's providential plan.

A person familiar with the popular depiction of the fickleness and inconstancy of Fortune[122] might dismiss the Gentile mission as merely another example of the changeable nature of yet another deity. Luke refutes this objection in a number of key narrative sections,[123] taking pains to show that God always intended, and directly authorized, this expansion of the mission from Jewish soil into the wider hellenistic world. Thus apologetic defence is turned into exposition of a central feature of the Gospel.

According to Luke's schematic account, the first contact with Gentiles (8.1–40)[124] takes place when the church in Jerusalem is scattered after the first persecution (8.1). In Samaria,[125] Luke notes the divine motivation for Philip's preaching and miraculous deeds, then provides apostolic confirmation of this through Peter and John.[126]

---

[119] Pliny, *Ep.* 10.96; Tacitus, *Ann.* 15.44.2–4; Suetonius, *Nero* 16. See Wilken, 'The Christians' 104–7 and *The Christians* 48–67; Benko, 'Pagan Criticism' 1062–8, 1075–6.

[120] Benko, 'Pagan Criticism' 1109.

[121] In addition to the use of scriptural prophecy, see also Luke's reference to philosophical forebears of Christianity (see below, nn. 156–7, 160, 182, 184).

[122] See above, nn. 41–47.

[123] The Samaritan mission (Acts 8.1–40), the accounts of Paul's call (9.1–19 and pars), the visions to Peter and Cornelius (10.1–11.18) and the apostolic council in Jerusalem (15.1–35). E. Richard ('The Creative Use of Amos by the Author of Acts', *NovT* 24 (1982) 51) notes that the question of the Gentile mission is actually 'an ongoing process from the beginning of Acts to its conclusion' which is addressed in these, and other, passages in Acts (see also 'Divine Purpose' 197–201, esp. 200).

[124] The list of Acts 2.9–11 is intended to refer to Jews and proselytes from these places, rather than to imply that already at Pentecost the Gospel was reaching a widespread audience; see Haenchen, *Acts* 168–71; Wilson, *Gentiles* 122–3. (*Contra*, Hervell, *Luke* 57–8.) By restricting this list to Jews and proselytes (2.10), Luke remains faithful to the programmatic growth predicted by Jesus at 1.8; by noting the ability of the disciples to speak in other languages (2.8), he foreshadows the Gentile mission proper (see Zehnle, *Pentecost Discourse* 119).

[125] Luke regards the Samaritans as 'foreigners' (ἀλλογενής, Luke 17.18) and reflects Jewish–Samaritan tensions (Luke 9.52–3; cf. John 4.9 and 2 Ki 17.24–34,41); see J. Jeremias, 'Σαμαρεία', *TDNT* 7 (1971) 88–94; Strack–Billerbeck I.538–60. This means that the Samaritan mission is the beginning of the Gentile mission; see Conzelmann, *Acts* 60; Haenchen, *Acts* 314; Richard, 'Divine Purpose' 200; *contra* Cadbury, *Book of Acts* 15–16; Wilson, *Gentiles* 171.

[126] They offer 'the gift of God' (τὴν δωρεὰν τοῦ θεοῦ, 8.20) and speak the same 'word of the Lord' (8.25) which Philip has already declared (8.14). See Johnson, *Possessions* 214.

Philip's subsequent encounter with the Ethiopian eunuch also occurs under divine instigation (8.26,29). The role of God is further highlighted in Luke's narrative of Paul's conversion on the road to Damascus (9.1–19), as we noted above in chapter two. The whole cluster of events in Caesarea and Joppa concerning relations between Jews and Gentiles (10.1–11.18) is summarized with the clear affirmation that this is under God's guidance, as the apostles and the brethren in Judaea exclaim, 'then to the Gentiles also God has granted repentance unto life' (11.18).[127]

At the council in Jerusalem (15.1–35), both Peter and Paul emphasize that it was God's decision to expand the mission to include the Gentiles. Paul and Barnabas report on their mission in Asia Minor with the brief note that 'they declared the things that God has done with them' (ὅσα ὁ θεὸς ἐποίησεν μετ' αὐτῶν, 15.4). Peter then refers to the events in Joppa and Caesarea as divinely motivated, when 'God made choice' (15.7) and 'made no distinction' (15.9). Any opposition to the incorporation of the Gentiles is 'making trial of God' (πειράζετε τὸν θεόν, 15.10), for 'God gave them the Holy Spirit' (15.8; cf. 11.17). Barnabas and Paul again report their activity (15.12), this time expanding the catch-phrase (ὅσα ἐποίησεν ὁ θεός) by specifying both the means (signs and wonders) and the recipients (the Gentiles) of God's activity through them.'[128]

To these apostolic claims the voice of James is then added, as he refers to the time 'in the early days' (15.7) when God chose Peter to be the means by which 'God first (καθὼς πρῶτον) visited the Gentiles to take out of them a people for his name (15.14). This was done, says James, in agreement with the scriptural prophecy that the Gentiles would be 'called by [God's] name' (15.17, quoting Amos 9.12). The council, persuaded by apostolic and prophetic witnesses, thus validates the Gentile mission, with the conditions as specified in the decree of Acts 15.23–9. Along with Luke's accounts of Philip's mission, Paul's call and Peter's vision, his report of this council functions as an apologetic exposition of God's intention to spread the Gospel not only to Jews, but also to Gentiles.

[127] 'The dominant role which God plays in chs. 10 and 11' is noted by Wilson, *Gentiles* 177; see also Dibelius, *Studies* 121–2; Haenchen, *Acts* 355, 358–9, 362–3; Wilckens, *Missionsreden* 67; Jervell, *Luke* 57, 65–6; Dupont, *Nouvelles études* 104–5. In his analysis of literary structure ('Ethnocentricity and Salvation History in the Cornelius Episode [Acts 10.1–11.18]', *SBLSPS* 24 (1985) 465–79, esp. 469–74), M. A. Plunkett demonstrates the importance of God's providence in this incident.

[128] For the structural significance of the catch-phrase of 15.4, 12, see Richard, 'Divine Purpose' 190.

The initial mission of Paul and Barnabas to the Gentiles is thus interpreted in terms of God's activity, in both introductory and concluding passages of Luke's account (13.1–14.28). Paul and Barnabas are sent into Asia Minor by the Holy Spirit (13.2,4); when they return to Antioch, they report their mission to the whole church and declare the things that God has done with them' (ὅσα ἐποίησεν ὁ θεὸς μετ᾽ αὐτῶν, 14.27b) and that God had 'opened a door of faith to the Gentiles' (14.27c). Thus the mission in Asia Minor is framed by the divine commissioning and the divine imprimatur.[129] Luke employs the same catchphrase, 'the things that God has done', to describe, in retrospect, the whole of Paul's missionary activity,[130] as he reports to the brethren in Jerusalem (21.19) just prior to his arrest (21.27). This motif thereby interprets the whole of Paul's Gentile mission as an enterprise completely within the providence of God.

The concluding chapters of Acts detail the stages of Paul's journey to Jerusalem, and then to Rome (21.15–28.16). This journey begins after the invocation, 'the will of the Lord be done' (21.14), which stamps it as integral to God's plan for Paul.[131] Paul's recollections of the Damascus road epiphany (22.6–9; 26.13–14) function as reminders of the divine guidance of his life. Explicit indications of this occur again during the sea voyage, when an angel appears to remind Paul of the necessity of his journey and assures him that God will keep safe (κεχάρισταί σοι ὁ θεός, 27.24) all who journey with him.[132] On arrival in Rome, Paul thanks God for a successful journey (28.15), continuing to testify to the sovereignty of God (28.23) and arguing with Jews to show how the prophets both point to Jesus (28.23) and justify the Gentile mission (28.25–8).[133] His final words (28.28) hearken back to the earliest oracles of the Gospel, as the plan of God continues on its course.[134]

---

[129] Likewise, the mission in Macedonia is initiated by the Spirit (16.6,7) and an epiphany (16.9) and takes place because 'God has called us ... to them' (16.1); Haenchen (*Acts* 485) calls all of this 'the mysteriously intervening *providentia specialissima* of God'.

[130] It is also used at Acts 19.11 in relation to the miracles which Paul performed.

[131] Cf. Luke 22.42; and see chap. 7.3.1.1.

[132] The proverb of Acts 27.34 reinforces this assurance. Paul's authoritative words to the centurion and the soldiers (27.31) may be construed as indirect evidence of the divine guidance of this journey, known only to Paul; see Schubert, 'Final Cycle' 8–9. The incident in Malta (28.1–6) dramatizes this divine protection.

[133] Schubert ('Areopagus Speech' 260 n. 18) describes Paul's final words as 'more definitely aligned with the all-embracing βουλὴ τοῦ θεοῦ'. See also 'Final Cycle' 9; Jervell, *Luke* 63.

[134] On Acts 28.28 as a fulfilment of oracles in Luke 1–2, see chap. 6.3.2.2.

### 3.3.3 'The things we have seen and heard'

The speeches in Acts are considered to be a significant indicator of Luke's historiographic method.[135] One of the functions served by the major apostolic missionary speeches of Acts 2–17 is to convey a most complete picture of the plan of God.[136] Both Peter (with John, 4.20) and Paul (22.5) are commissioned to declare 'the things we have seen and heard' and the examples of their speeches in Acts[137] provide ample evidence for the way in which Luke understood the apostolic preaching to be a declaration of God's providential guidance of human affairs. God is the subject of these speeches (2.22; 3.13; 7.2; 10.34; 13.17; 17.24) and their common syntactical construction emphasizes God's guidance as the subject of all the events which are recounted by the speakers.[138]

[135] Cadbury, 'The Speeches in Acts', in Foakes Jackson and Lake, *Beginnings* 5.402–27 (see also 2.13–14,27); Wilckens, *Missionsreden*, T. F. Glasson, 'The Speeches in Acts and Thucydides', *ExpTim* 76 (1964–5) 165; Plümacher, *Lukas* 32–78; G. H. R. Horsley, 'Speeches and Dialogue in Acts', *NTS* 32 (1986) 609–14. Cf. the reservations expressed by Dibelius, 'The Speeches in Acts and Ancient Historiography', *Studies* 138–91 (summarized in Dupont, *Etudes* 47–50); C. F. Evans, 'The Kerygma', *Journal of Theological Studies* 7 (1956) 25–41, and '"Speeches" in Acts', *Mélanges bibliques en hommage au R. P. Beda Rigaux* (ed. A. Descamps and A. de Halleux; Gembloux: Duculot, 1970) 287–302.

[136] Cf. the way Josephus presents the theme of providence in speeches (above, pp. 48–9); contrast this with the relative absence of the theme from the speeches in Dionysius and Diodorus (see above, nn. 8,9). F. G. Downing ('Ethical Pagan Theism and the Speeches in Acts', *NTS* 27 (1981) 544–63) provides a useful comparative analysis of providence in speeches in Josephus and Dionysius, with Luke's use of divine guidance in the speeches of Acts 2, 7 and 13.

[137] We will consider speeches by Peter (Acts 2.14–36; 3.12–26; 10.34–43), and Paul (13.17–41; 17.22–31), as well as that by Stephen (7.2–53), as the major examples of the apostolic preaching. For surveys of scholarship on the speeches, see Foakes Jackson and Lake, *Beginnings* 5.404 n. 2; J. T. Townsend, 'The Speeches in Acts', *Anglican Theological Review* 42 (1960) 150–9; Wilckens, *Missionsreden* 7–31; J. Dupont, 'Les Discours', *Etudes* 41–56, and his response to Wilckens, *Etudes* 133–55; M. B. Dudley, 'The Speeches in Acts', *EvQ* 50 (1978) 147–55.

[138] The common structure of the speeches in Acts is noted by C. H. Dodd, *The Apostolic Preaching and Its Development* (London: Hodder and Stoughton, 1936) 21–30; Dibelius, *Studies* 111, 165; Wilckens, *Missionsreden* 54; E. Schweizer, 'Concerning the Speeches in Acts', *Studies* (ed. Keck and Martyn) 208–16; Dupont, *Etudes* 137–9 and *Nouvelles études* 62 (and further literature in n. 7). Dodd (Apostolic Preaching 33) observes that 'the main burden of the *kerygma* is that ... God has visited and redeemed his people', but does not further develop this point. Had Schweizer noted that even the Christological kerygma is presented in terms of the divine activity, it would have obviated his comments ('Speeches' 214) on the shift from Christological to theological, for the speeches as a whole are fundamentally theo-logical, as our analysis below demonstrates. G. W. H. Lampe ('The Lucan Portrait of Christ', *NTS* 2 (1955–6) 160–75) notes the extent of divine activity in the speeches, but again does not build on this observation. Wilckens (*Missionsreden* 54,

### 3.3.3.1  Peter in Jerusalem

The prologue to the Gospel, as we noted in chapter two, establishes the centrality of the theme of providence for the story which follows. The same function is performed at the start of the second volume by the first major speech reported in Acts, namely, Peter's speech on the Day of Pentecost (Acts 2.14–36). The ostensible occasion for the speech (the manifestation of known human tongues, 2.4–11) provides an opportunity for a thorough exposition of God's activity within history; for this miraculous phenomenon itself is a demonstration of 'the mighty works of God' (τὰ μεγαλεῖα τοῦ θεοῦ, 2.11). Thus Peter begins his speech by explaining what his audience has 'seen and heard' (2.33); a prophetic citation (2.16–21), quoting Joel 2.28–32) establishes that the outpouring of the Spirit is an act of God.[139]

However, Peter does more than interpret this one event to the crowd as a sign of divine providence; for he proceeds to set forth the whole story of Jesus under the general heading of God's providence. The bulk of the sermon thus constitutes a comprehensive presentation of divine superintendence in the life of Jesus.[140] Using a modified form of a typical Lukan expression at the beginning and

85), Zehnle (*Pentecost Discourse* 24) and Dupont (*Nouvelles études* 70–3) note God's dominant role in relation to the crucifixion and resurrection only.

Rajak (*Josephus* 81) comments, 'the texts which will expose Josephus' personal attitudes to us are in speeches'. This is also the case in Acts, for the speeches convey Lukan themes and ideas, not the least of which is this focus on divine activity, whether they are Luke's original composition in the style of hellenistic historians (thus Cadbury, *Beginnings* 5.404–10, 416–20; Dibelius, *Studies* 165–74, 184–5; Townsend, 'Speeches' 150–3, 157–9; Wilckens, *Missionsreden* (*passim*)) or traditions which he has thoroughly redacted (thus Dodd, *Apostolic Preaching* 17–35; Haenchen, *Acts* 186; Dupont, *Nouvelles études* 87; W. W. Gasque, 'The Speeches of Acts: Dibelius Reconsidered', *New Dimensions in New Testament Study* (ed. R. I. Longenecker and M. C. Tenney; Grand Rapids, Mich.: Zondervan, 1974) 232–50).

Against the uniformity of the speeches, see C. F. D. Moule, 'The Christology of Acts', *Studies* (ed. Keck and Martyn) 159–85, esp. 173; M. Wilcox, 'A Foreword to the Study of the Speeches in Acts', *Christianity, Judaism and Other Greco-Roman Cults: Studies for Morton Smith at Sixty* (Studies in Judaism in Late Antiquity 12, 4 parts; ed. J. Neusner; Leiden: Brill, 1975) 1.206–25, esp. 216–18.

[139] God pours out the Spirit (ἐκχέω, 2.17,18) and gives wonders and signs (δώσω, 2.19).

[140] Conzelmann (*Theology* 175–6) proposes a development from a kerygma viewing Christ 'from the standpoint of God's intervention', to the later interest in Jesus 'as a figure in his own right'. Yet even the final stage of that development (namely, in Luke–Acts) keeps the focus on God's guidance of Jesus' life. Conzelmann's deductions concerning Luke's subordinationist Christology are less attuned to Luke's own interests than if he had related this feature to the divine plan and its apologetic function.

end of his proclamation concerning Jesus, Peter establishes the divine sovereignty over Jesus both in his earthly life, in 'the things that God has done through him' (οἷς ἐποίησεν δι' αὐτοῦ ὁ θεός, 2.22), and in his heavenly life, when 'God has made him both Lord and Christ' (ἐποίησεν ὁ θεός, 2.36).[141] Luke also has Peter introduce the primary terminology of the plan of God, here amplified in terms of its predetermined nature (τῇ ὡρισμένῃ βουλῇ καὶ προγνώσει τοῦ θεοῦ, 2.23).[142] When Peter deals directly with Jesus (2.22–4, 32–3, 36) he consistently places Jesus as the object of God's providential activity.[143]

This interpretation is supported by both prophetic and apostolic confirmation. David, a prophet having access to God's intentions (2.30), is quoted twice by Peter (Ps 16.8–11 at Acts 2.25–8, Ps 110.1 at Acts 2.34–5) to show how both the resurrection and the exaltation of Jesus fulfil God's plan. The apostles themselves add further weight to the truth of what Peter says; as witness (2.32) they guarantee the certainty (ασφαλῶς, 2.36) of the interpretation Peter provides.

The same emphasis on God's activity in the life of Jesus is found in Peter's next speech, delivered in Solomon's Portico (3.12–26). The subject of this speech is ὁ θεός (3.13).[144] The healing of the lame man was possible through the power of God (3.12–13),[145] mediated through the name of Jesus (3.16), who suffered as God foretold (3.18),[146] was glorified by God (3.13) and was raised by God

---

[141] For this phrase as the summary of the argument of 2.29–36, see Zehnle, *Pentecost Discourse* 27–8, 69–70. Adams (*Suffering* 55–8) calls it a Lukan 'leitmotif'.

[142] On the cluster of terms used here to express Luke's 'zentrale Vorstellung des göttlichen "Planes"', see Wilckens, *Missionsreden* 124. O'Neill (*Theology* 84) notes 'the strong framework of divine inevitability'; Schubert ('Areopagus Speech' 240) regards ὡρισμένῃ βουλῇ ... τοῦ θεοῦ as the 'basic theme and thesis of Lucan theology' under which this and all following speeches are subsumed. See further in chapter 7.3.1.2.

[143] In these verses, ὁ θεός is the subject of five verbs: ἐποίησεν (2.22), ἀνέστησεν, λύσας (2.24), ἀνέστησεν (2.32), ἐποίησεν (2.36); see Wilckens *Missionsreden* 34–5; Downing, 'Theism' 555. Note also the divine passive of 2.33, and see Conzelmann, *Theology* 175 and the ultimate origin of the Spirit, given by the Father (2.33). Throughout the speech, Jesus is consistently the object in the accusative case (2.22,32,36; see also τοῦτον, 2.23; ὅν 2.24)

[144] On the full title of God in 3.13, see Zehnle, *Pentecost Discourse* 44–6. Again, Jesus is in the accusative throughout (τὸν παῖδα αὐτοῦ (3.13), τὸν ὑγιον καὶ δίκαιον (3.14), τὸν ἀρχηγὸν (3.15), τοῦτον (3.16), χριστόν (3.18,20), ὅν (3.21), τὸν παῖδα (3.26).

[145] See further in chap. 4, pp. 97–8.

[146] Schubert ('Areopagus Speech' 241) notes the threefold emphasis on proof-from-prophecy (3.18,21b,24); Wilckens (*Missionsreden* 43) notes that God's actions in 3.26 fulfil the promises of Deut 18.15 and Gen 22.18.

(3.15,22,26).[147] Peter calls for repentance in his speech (3.19), as he did on the day of Pentecost (2.38), assuring his listeners that the God who guided the life of Jesus will continue to guide those who believe (3.19,26). The life of Jesus is thus in continuity with the spread of the Gospel among 'everyone whom the Lord our God calls to him' (2.39), for the same providential power is at work in each.[148]

### 3.3.3.2  Stephen in Jerusalem

A further dimension of divine providence is conveyed in the speech by Stephen before the Sanhedrin (7.2–53), delivered at the end of the Jerusalem/Judaea section (cf. 1.8) which had been introduced by Peter's two speeches (Acts 2, 3). The subject of this speech is declared at the beginning; it is ὁ θεὸς τῆς δόξης (7.2). Subsequently, God guides Abraham (7.2–8),[149] Joseph (7.9–10)[150] and Moses (7.17–43).[151] Israel's opposition to God's activity is expressed in this latter passage (7.35,39–41,43), but divine guidance resumes throughout the conquest (7.44–5) and the monarchy (7.45). Thus one of the pur-

---

[147] Johnson (*Possessions* 63 n. 1) asserts that ἀναστήσει in Deut 18.15 (Acts 3.22) is an allusion to the resurrection (3.26), against Haenchen, *Acts* 209–10; see also Kurz 'Proof from Prophecy' 19 n. 3. God will also send Jesus (3.20) at 'the times for refreshing [which come] from the presence of the Lord' (3.21). For Peter's emphasis that 'the rejection of Jesus fitted into God's plan', see Johnson, *Possessions* 63–7.

[148] On the common features in Peter's speeches in Acts 2 and 3, see Zehnle, *Pentecost Discourse* 44–60, 71–94, 136–7; on the universal implications of 2.39, see p. 124. Peter's subsequent speech before the Sanhedrin emphasized God's guidance of events (5.29b–32); the subject is ὁ θεὸς τῶν πατέρων ἡμῶν (5.30). See Zehnle, *Pentecost Discourse* 39. Schubert ('Areopagus Speech' 242) notes that the theme of God's plan recurs in 'the most lively parts' of Acts 4 and 5 (4.28; 5.38–9); see also chap. 7.3.1.2.

[149] God is the subject of ὤφθη (7.2), εἶπεν (7.3), μετῴκισεν (7.4), οὐκ ἔδωκεν, ἐπηγγείλατο (7.5), ἐλάλησεν (7.6), κρινῶ, εἶπεν (7.7), ἔδωκεν (7.8). N. A. Dahl ('The Story of Abraham in Luke–Acts', *Studies* (ed. Keck and Martyn) 142–8) notes that it is God's epiphany (7.2) which initiates the events and a divine word (7.6–7) which predicts succeeding events. See also J. Dupont, 'La Structure oratoire du discours d'Etienne', *Bib* 66 (1985) 163–7.

[150] God was with Joseph (7.9); cf. the extensive use of this phrase in the LXX, noted by Johnson, *Possessions* 62 n. 2 (see esp. Gen 39.2). On its polemical function in this speech, see E. Richard, 'The Polemical Character of the Joseph Episode in Acts 7', *JBL* 98 (1979) 260–2. God rescued Joseph from his afflictions when he was in Egypt (7.10), but is then absent from the narrative in 7.11–16; in the Old Testament account of the Joseph cycle, God is similarly almost entirely absent (cf. Gen 40.21–3; 50.20). For Acts 7.9–16 as a fulfilment of the oracle of 7.6, see Dahl, 'Abraham' 144; Dupont, 'La Structure' 164–5.

[151] God is the subject of δίδωσιν (7.25), ὤφθη (7.30), εἶπεν (7.33), εἶδον, ἤκουσα, ἀποστείλω (7.34), ἀπέσταλκεν (7.35), ἀναστήσει (7.37); see Dupont, 'La Structure' 157–9. Dahl ('Abraham' 144) notes that 7.36 fulfils the oracle of 7.7b (ἐξελεύσονται) and 7.35 fulfils the oracle of 7.34 (ἀποστείλω).

poses of the history of Israel which Stephen tells is to declare the conviction that God has been at work throughout this history.[152]

However, the climax of Stephen's speech comes in his attack on the Temple, with his assertion that the Most High does not live in houses made by human hands (7.48).[153] This leads inevitably to the eruption of the conflict that had been simmering throughout the speech, as his listeners become enraged (7.54) and stone Stephen (7.58).[154] Yet in contrast to a notion of a capricious overseer such as Fortune, the God of Israel exercises a consistent providential guidance in the events of human history, even when his people consistently reject his purposes.[155]

Stephen charges that the faithlessness of Israel's idolatrous conduct (7.39–43) persists in the Jerusalem Temple (7.47–50). The original Jewish audience would have heard here an echo of a prophetic text (Isa 66.1); for Luke's hellenistic readers, there is a direct resonance with a hellenistic saying, for the prohibition on building the Temple would reflect the well-known saying of the Stoic Zeno[156]

[152] Kee (*Miracle* 196–7) interprets the speech in the context of Acts' 'encompassing framework of divinely shaped history' and contends that 'the point is clear: *God is in control of history* [his emphasis]'. Likewise, see Schubert, 'Areopagus Speech' 243; Marshall, *Acts* 131–2; O'Neill, *Theology* 81; E. Richard, *Acts 6:1–8:4: The Author's Method of Composition* (SBLDS 41; Missoula, Mont.: Scholars Press, 1978) 265, 330–2; J. Killgallen, *The Stephen Speech: A Literary and Redactional Study of Acts 7,2–53* (AnBib 67; Rome: Biblical Institute Press, 1976) 24–6. On features of this speech which are common to other speeches in Acts, see Schubert, 'Areopagus Speech' 241–2; Townsend, 'Speeches' 155; Downing, 'Theism' 556–7.
[153] This relates back directly to the charge which provoked Stephen's speech (6.13); on the links between the speech and the Lukan narrative, see Killgallen, *Stephen Speech* 119; Richard, *Composition* 219–24, 229–42, 287–93, 315–17; *contra*, Dibelius, *Studies* 167; Haenchen, *Acts* 286–8; Evans, 'Kerygma' 32–3; Wilson, *Gentiles* 132. On the appropriateness of speeches to their contexts in hellenistic histories, see Rajak, *Josephus* 80–1 (with bibliography).
[154] Wilson, *Gentiles* 137–8, notes that this episode forms a climax to the 'opposition' motif which runs throughout chapters 1–5; see also Killgallen, *Stephen Speech* 111–13; Richard, *Composition* 313–15; Downing, 'Theism' 560. O'Neill (*Theology* 83) characterizes the speech as 'an attack on the Jews rather than a measured defence'.
[155] Stephen speaks of the way in which Israel had previously opposed God's designated leader, rejecting Moses (7.27,35,39), offering a sacrifice to the idolatrous golden calf (7.41), and persecuting and killing the prophets (7.52); see Dibelius, *Studies* 167. On the polemical nature of the speech, see Richard, *Composition* 319–24 and 'Joseph Episode' (*passim*).
[156] Diogenes Laertius, *Lives* 7.33; Plutarch, *De Stoic. repug.* 1034B; Clement of Alexandria, *Strom.* 5.11; Origen, *Contra Celsum* 1.5. For other references, see Geffcken, *Zwei Griechische Apologeten* (Leipzig and Berlin: B. G. Teubner, 1907) xx–xxiv; L. Ramaroson, 'Contre les "temples faits de mains d'homme"', *RPLHA* 43 (1969) 231 n. 1, with a comparison of wording in the various sources at p. 235.

and possibly also Plato's strictures on temples.[157] Stephen's own dictum, that God 'does not dwell in temples made by hands' (ἐν χειροποιήτοις, 7.48), also has scriptural overtones[158] but likewise resonates with the criticism of idols and temples found throughout the hellenistic world.[159] The Stoic use of this criticism is significant, for often an attack on idols is associated with an affirmation of providence.[160] Thus Stephen could well have been understood by Luke's readers to be implying that his accusers, by succumbing to idolatry, have given up on the God of providence.[161] His Jewish-prophetic polemic against idolatry has become a hellenistic-apologetic assertion of divine providence.

### 3.3.3.3 Peter in Caesarea

Peter's speech in Caesarea (10.34–43) stands within the Samaritan section, the turning point between Judaea and 'the end of the earth' (cf. 1.8). In this sermon, Peter summarizes the view of Jesus which he has presented in his earlier speeches, emphasizing that God has

[157] Plato, *Leg.* 955E–956B; Cicero, *De leg.* 2.18.45; Clement of Alexandria, *Strom.* 5.11; Eusebius, *Prep. Evang.* 3.18; for other references, see Ramaroson, 'Temples' 217–30.

[158] See Haenchen, *Acts* 285 n. 3; B. Gaertner, *The Areopagus Speech and Natural Revelation* (Uppsala: Gleerup, 1955) 211–14; Richard, *Composition* 133.

[159] Simon (*St Stephen* 87) calls this phrase 'the technical term' for ancient descriptions of idols and temples. See Euripides, *Frag.* 968, quoted by Clement of Alexandria, *Strom.* 5.11; Ps.-Heraclitus, *Ep.* 4; Cicero, *De verr.* 2.5.187; Ramaroson, 'Temples' 221–3; H. W. Attridge, *First Century Cynicism in the Epistles of Heraclitus* (HTS 29; Missoula, Mont.: Scholars Press, 1976) 23 (quoting an Egyptian sherd). For more extensive examples of this type of this type of criticism, see Dio Chrysostom, *Or.* 12 (see the discussion below, chap. 3.3.3.5); Plutarch, *Isis et Os.* 382C; Cicero, *De nat. deor.* 1.36.101; Lucian, *Jupp trag.* 7; Clement of Alexandria, *Strom.* 5.11 (quoting Euripides, Plato, Acts 17, Zeno and the Hebrew prophets).

[160] Gärtner (*Areopagus Speech* 203–5) correctly traces a 'duality in the Stoic attitude' to idols; however, this observation should not be used to dismiss the hellenistic evidence, but rather to refine one's perspective on the issue. On the Stoic *rapprochement* with popular forms of idol worship, see A. J. Malherbe, 'Pseudo Heraclitus Epistle 4: The Divinization of the Wise Man', *Jahrbuch für Antike und Christentum* 21 (1978) 46. For the development of the Cynic criticism, see Attridge, *Cynicism* 16–17, and for the radical Stoic appropriation of this criticism in the first centuries BCE and CE, see Attridge, *Cynicism* 18–23. The significant ancient texts include Cicero, *De nat. deor.* 1.27.77; Dio Chrysostom, *Or.* 12.27–38; Epictetus, *Diss.* 2.8.11–14; Plutarch, *De superstit.* 167D; Ps.-Heraclitus, *Ep.* 4; Seneca, *Ep.* 41.1–3; 95.47. Jewish appropriation of the criticism is found in Philo, *Ad Gaium* 290, and Wis 13.10–14.11 (note the explicitly Stoic terms at 14.1–4; see chap. 2 n. 13).

[161] On the link between worship of images and the nature of the gods, see Malherbe, 'Pseudo Heraclitus' 53. Stephen's view is representative of what Attridge (*Cynicism* 22) calls 'a type of piety widespread in the period of the early Roman Empire'.

acted consistently in the life of Jesus. The title of the sermon (10.34) declares God as the primary theological and syntactical subject of the speech; the basic theme of the speech is the universal scope of God's saving activity (οὐκ ἔστιν προσωπολήμπτης ὁ θεός, 10.34)[162] which comes through Jesus Christ, the universal Lord (10.36). In addressing the admission of the Gentiles into the faith (ἐν παντὶ ἔθνει, 10.35), Peter sets forth the desired response to God's actions.[163] By fearing God and doing good (10.35) the Gentiles are declared acceptable to God, and thus Peter is able to 'go to uncircumcised men and eat with them' (11.3; see also 10.25).

The following period (10.36–7) develops this subject by referring to the word which God sent to Israel, through Jesus, in all of Judaea. That word is then expounded in two subsequent periods in which ὁ θεός remains the subject. The ministry of Jesus (10.38) comprises two divine actions: God anointed Jesus; God was with him as he went about doing good and healing people. After the ministry of Jesus, God continues to be at work in him (10.40), raising Jesus and making himself manifest. Both sets of divine actions are supported by the testimony of Peter and the apostles (10.39,41). Connecting the two sets of divine actions, each attested by apostolic witness, is the curt statement of 10.39b, 'they put him to death by hanging him on a tree', the only reference in this speech to the opposition encountered by Jesus.[164]

Peter then moves to an implied change of subject, from God to Jesus, although God's activity remains in focus with a reference to God's ordaining (ὡρισμένος) of Jesus as judge (10.42).[165] The universal scope of the message is reaffirmed as Peter asserts that Jesus is judge over all, 'the living and the dead' (10.42), and that forgiveness of sins is available to 'every one (πάντα) who believes in

---

[162] J. M. Bassler ('Luke and Paul on Impartiality', *Bib* 66 (1985) 546–52) notes the explicitly Greco-Roman notions of universalism which lie behind this statement of divine impartiality; see also Bassler, *Divine Impartiality: Paul and a Theological Axiom* (SBLDS 59; Chico, Calif.: Scholars Press, 1979) 105–9, 176–8. Schulz ('Vorsehung' 111) correctly relates this saying to the divine will and providence, but incorrectly limits it to 'dem Schicksalszwang' of 'die hellenistisch-römische Antike' alone. Only the Old Testament background is discussed by Haenchen, *Acts* 351 n. 4, and Dupont, *Nouvelles études* 320–1.

[163] Healings and sermons often end with a doxological comment to demonstrate the desired response; see chap. 4 n. 85.

[164] For Jewish opposition to Jesus as integral to God's plan, see O'Neill, *Theology*, 83–8.

[165] It is Jesus who commands the apostles to preach to the people (Israel) and to bear witness to this appointment (10.42). For Jesus as judge, see 17.31; and cf. 2.33,36; 3.13; 5.31.

him' (10.43). The thrust of universal providence inherent in the title
has been realized in the sermon.[166]

### 3.3.3.4 Paul in Antioch of Pisidia

Paul's sermon in Antioch of Pisidia (13.17–41) stands at the beginning of his preaching 'to the uttermost parts of the earth' (13.47; cf.
1.8). Here he draws together two of the dimensions of providence
seen in earlier speeches. Again, the subject is stated at the beginning,
as ὁ θεὸς τοῦ λαοῦ τούτου Ἰσραήλ (13.17), whose actions
encompass both Israel (13.17–22) and Jesus (13.23–41). The syntactical structure of Paul's summary of Israel's history emphasizes the
constancy of God's care for Israel; nine of the ten indicative verbs
refer to God's actions regarding Israel,[167] as do all three participles.[168] The climax of Israel's history is David, who does God's will
(θελήματα, 13.22). David is the pivotal point for turning from
Israel's history to the story of Jesus, for he functions as a reliable
prophetic witness to the gospel proclamation, which itself is a
fulfilment of God's promise (13.23,32). Paul, like Peter, presents the
things concerning Jesus in terms of a consistent divine activity.[169]

By contrast to Stephen's speech, the 'opposition' motif is omitted
from the section dealing with the history of Israel,[170] for this is
reserved for the trial and crucifixion of Jesus (13.27–9). Paul thus
contrasts an Israel which was faithful to God's constant care

---

[166] Schubert's claim ('Areopagus Speech' 244) that 10.36–43 'has little to do with
the Cornelius-situation' ignores these factors; so also Dibelius, *Studies* 111, 119, 162.
[167] ἐξελέξατο, ὕψωσεν, ἐξήγαγεν (13.17), ἐτροποφόρησεν (13.18), κατεκληρο-
νόμησεν (13.19), ἔδωκεν (13.20), ἔδωκεν (13.21), ἤγειρεν, εἶπεν (13.22). The tenth
indicative verb, ᾐτήσαντο (13.21), refers to Israel's request for a king.
[168] καθελών (13.19), μεταστήσας, μαρτυρήσας (13.22).
[169] God is the subject of seven verbs: ἤγαγεν (13.23), ἤγειρεν (13.30), ἐκπεπλ-
ήρωκεν, γεγέννηκα (13.33), δώσω (13.34), ἤγειρεν (13.37), ἐργάζομαι (13.41); cf.
the divine passive of 13.26; see Wilckens, *Missionsreden* 54. Schulz ('Vorsehung'
109–10) calls this speech 'einen programmatischen Einblick in die lukanische Kon-
zeption der Vorsehungsgeschichte', expressing hellenistic predestination rather than
Jewish election ideas; but this draws the distinction far too sharply. For the similarities with Acts 13, see Schubert, 'Areopagus Speech' 245–6.
[170] Maddox (*Purpose* 52–3) links the speeches of Acts 7 and 13 with the common
Old Testament technique of recounting Israel's history in the form of a song or
speech, but notes that 'whereas these other examples finish with a promise of
celebration of God's salvation, [Acts 7] builds up to a climax of condemnation'.
Schubert ('Areopagus Speech' 245) is incorrect when he dismisses 13.17–19a as 'a
short and apt summary of the main part of the Stephen speech'; Vielhauer makes the
same mistake ('Paulinisms' 44). On the differences and similarities, see Richard,
*Composition* 257–8, 266.

(13.17–22) with an Israel which opposed God's provision of a Saviour in Jesus (13.27–8). The history of Israel serves as a *praeparatio evangelica* which should have alerted the inhabitants of Israel to the way God would work through Jesus, for the crucifixion and burial of Jesus fulfil the words of the prophets (13.27,29) and the resurrection and incorruptibility of Jesus fulfil the prophetic words of David (13.33,35), who himself 'had served the plan of God (τῇ τοῦ θεοῦ βουλῇ) in his own generation' (13.36). Thus the consistent care of God for Israel (13.17–22) is in continuity with the provision of a Saviour (13.23) who offers forgiveness of sins to all (πᾶς) who believe (13.38–9); all of this together comprises the divine plan. Again, the providential motif is central to this speech.[171]

### 3.3.3.5 Paul in Athens

The last of Paul's missionary speeches which Luke reports is that given on the Areopagus in Athens (17.22–31).[172] Its significance for geographical and religious reasons has often been noted,[173] but its literary significance has not been equally appreciated.[174] The speech serves as a programmatic example of Paul's universal preaching to the Gentiles, expanding the scope of God's activity to encompass the whole of human history.[175] The main thrust of the speech has frequently been seen to be the polemic against a false understanding of God, who does not dwell in shrines made by human hands (17.25), who is not far from each one of us (17.27) and who may not be thought of as an image (17.29). Yet this polemic is furthered by a positive presentation of God's actions, and although the motif of

[171] On its apologetic purpose, in common with the other missionary speeches, see Evans, 'Speeches' 294–5.

[172] Paul's speech in Lystra (14.15–17) is frequently linked with the Areopagus speech; again the speech centres around God (θεὸν ζῶντα) who is the subject of 14.15b–17.

[173] On Athens as the centre of Greek culture and religion, see Dibelius, *Studies* 79–80, and Dupont, *The Salvation of the Gentiles: Essays on the Acts of the Apostles* (New York: Paulist, 1979) 30. For the ancient references to Athens, see Haenchen, *Acts* 520 n. 6.

[174] Schubert comments that when Paul, in the next extended speech of his which Luke reports, declares to the Ephesian elders, in 'the most thematic occurrence of all', that he has proclaimed 'the whole counsel of God' (20.27), it is clear that 'the unfolding of the plan of God found its culmination in the preceding speech, the Areopagus speech' ('Areopagus Speech' 260).

[175] Conzelmann (*Theology* 17) notes the universal scope of this speech, but interprets it with his distinctive theological aim ('the twofold structure of eschatology is replaced by the threefold structure of historical perspective') rather than relating it to the other speeches of Acts.

providence is never directly stated by Paul, it forms an important theme in his Areopagus speech.[176] By placing Paul in direct dialogue with Stoic and Epicurean philosophers, for whom the matter of providence was hotly debated,[177] Luke directly relates his speech to the broader philosophical debates concerning providence.[178]

Paul quotes the Stoic poet Aratus (17.28, quoting *Phaenom.* 5)[179] and asserts the common Stoic notion of human kinship with God.[180] Norden[181] comments that the phrase καί γε οὐ μακράν (17.27) is similar to that found in Dio Chrysostom's Olympic Oration, ἅτε γὰρ οὐ μακράν (*Or.* 12.28); in fact, many of the statements which Paul makes are paralleled in Dio's oration, for they were widespread philosophical traditions commonly used by Stoics to assert divine providence.[182] Thus, Paul notes that God is creator (Acts 17.24; cf.

[176] Previous investigations of the Areopagus speech have failed to notice the importance of the providence motif in this speech, with the exception of M. Pohlenz, 'Paulus und die Stoa' (*ZNW* 42 (1949) 92. Schubert ('Areopagus' 249) declares 'the true God – this is the all-dominating theme spelled out in the speech itself'. Grant (*Gods* 50–1) links Paul's attack on idols with his use of the rhetorical *topos* concerning providence (see above, n. 13). A recent investigation of this aspect of the speech is made by D. L. Balch, 'The Areopagus Speech, An Appeal to the Stoic Historian Posidonius against Later Stoics and the Epicureans', *Greeks, Romans and Christians: Essays in Honor of Abraham J. Malherbe* (ed. D. L. Balch, E. Ferguson and W. A. Meeks; Minneapolis: Fortress Press, 1990), 52–99.

[177] See above, n. 11.

[178] C. K. Barrett ('Paul's Speech on the Areopagus', *New Testament Christianity for Africa and the World* (ed. M. E. Glasswell and E. W. Fashole-Luke; London: SPCK, 1974) 72) argues that Luke specifically had in mind the Stoics and Epicureans because they were most concerned with the subject matter of Paul's speech, including providence. Gaertner (*Areopagus Speech* 176–7) notes the antithetical views of these two schools concerning providence; Flender (*Theologian* 67) concludes that 'the content of Paul's sermon is summed up by his audience, the Epicurean and Stoic philosophers'. Conzelmann's assertion that Luke 'takes no account whatsoever of the particular teachings of either' ('Address' 219) is curiously inaccurate. For a more general survey of hellenistic elements in the speech, see Flender, *Theologian* 68.

[179] See K. Lake, 'Your Own Poets', in Foakes Jackson and Lake *Beginnings* 5.246–51; Haenchen, *Acts* 525; R. Renehan, 'Classical Greek Quotations in the New Testament', *The Heritage of the Early Church: Essays in Honour of G. V. Florovsky* (Orientalia Christiana Analecta 195; ed. D. Neiman and M. Schatkin; Rome: Pont. Institut. Studiorum Orientalium, 1973) 40. Renehan dismisses the alleged quotation from Cleanthes (*art. cit.* 37–40; see also Dibelius' retraction of his earlier view regarding a quotation of Epimenides, at *Studies* 187 n. 84). Dibelius (*Studies* 51 n. 76) notes that the plural τινες can apply to one author only; see also Renehan, 'Classical Greek Quotations' 40–2.

[180] See Dio Chrysostom, *Or.* 12.27,39,43,44,61; Seneca, *Ep.* 41.1.–2; 120.14; Epictetus, *Diss.* 2.8.11–12; Minucius Felix, *Oct.* 32.7–9; further references in Clarke, *Octavius* 345 n. 545, 346 nn. 546,549.

[181] *Agnostos Theos* 18–19.

[182] A detailed analysis of these and other parallels is made by Balch, 'Areopagus Speech' 72–9; note also the parallels to *Or.* 12 adduced by Theiler, *Poseidonios*

*Or.* 12.29, 37) and lord of all (Acts 17.24; cf. *Or.* 12.27,34) who gives life (Acts 17.25; cf. *Or.* 12.74) and breath (Acts 17.25; cf. *Or.* 12.30), making every nation from one (Acts 17.24; cf. *Or.* 12.29) and establishing the seasons (Acts 17.26; cf. *Or.* 12.32). The polemic against idols (17.24) is yet another component of this collection of traditions, functioning (as we have seen already in Stephen's speech, 7.48) as a defence of providence.[183] Paul here utilizes the widespread Stoic connection between affirmations of providence and attacks on the worship of images, as he addresses the philosophers.[184]

The focus on the providence of God is further conveyed through the syntax of the speech. The analysis of Paul Schubert[185] demonstrates the centrality of God's actions in the speech. The first period (17.24–5) establishes God as the primary subject of the speech, both through the relationship between God and humanity and through

2.275–87. On affinities with Stoic thought in Paul's speech, see Dibelius, *Studies* 29–34,43, 47–9; H. Conzelmann, 'The Address of Paul on the Areopagus', *Studies* (ed. Keck and Martyn) 221–4; Cadbury, *Book of Acts* 45–6; W. Eltester, 'Gott und die Natur in der Areopagrede', *Studien* (ed. Eltester) 206–10; Barrett, 'Paul's Speech' 12–4. These parallels, however, are set within a wide context which relies upon Old Testament concepts of God as creator and judge, thereby indicating that the Stoic content is modified in its nature. The most likely explanation is that such concepts had been mediated to Luke through hellenistic Judaism, in which efforts to shape the message to Greek thought had already been undertaken. See W. Nauck, 'Die Tradition und Komposition der Areopagrede', *ZThK* 53 (1956) 11–52; Conzelmann, 'Address' 221,224, 225–6.

[183] See above, n. 160. Haenchen (*Acts* 522–3) notes the way the charge of idolatry (17.24c) is immediately swept aside by the affirmation of God's providence (17.25b).

[184] This connection is found also in Dio Chrysostom. *Or.* 12, where the Stoic arguments in favour of providence (12.27–35) culminate in the polemic against the Epicureans, especially their worship of the image of Pleasure (12.36–7). See further references in n. 160 above; on this aspect of Acts 17, see Conzelmann, 'Address' 221; Grant, *Gods* 50–1. Another way in which the Stoics rebutted the worship of images was to insist that 'the whole world is the temple of the gods' (Seneca, *De benef.* 7.7.3; see also Dio Chrysostom, *Or.* 12.34; Philo, *Spec. leg.* 1.66; Ps-Heraclitus, *Ep.* 4); see the discussion of Attridge, *Cynicism* 19–23. This bears some similarities to the line of thought in Acts 17.27b–29.

[185] We follow Schubert's syntactical analysis in 'Areopagus Speech' 249–52, sharpening his observations concerning the central and dominant role of God throughout the speech. With the exception of the placement of verse 27c, this analysis based on syntax agrees with that based on hellenistic rhetoric, found in D. Zweck, 'The Exordium of the Areopagus Speech, Acts 17.22,23', *NTS* 35 (1989) 94–103.

On the links between this speech and those antecedent to it in Acts, see Schubert, 'Areopagus Speech' 253–9. Jervell is inaccurate when he rejects this speech as 'not characteristic of Luke's theology' (*Luke* 202 n. 24) and 'a foreign body within Acts' (*The Unknown Paul: Essays on Luke–Acts and Early Christian History* (Minneapolis, Minn.: Augsburg, 1984) 17).

God's activity in human history.[186] God's actions are the focus of the first half of the second period (17.26–7),[187] God's relationship to humanity of the second half of this period.[188] In the third and fourth periods (17.28–9), although humanity ('we') becomes the subject, 'the exception is only syntactical, not material, for verses 28–9 deal just as much (from the point of view of Luke) with the proper relationship between God and men as do the others'.[189] The fifth period (17.30–1) returns syntactically to the primary subject, ὁ θεός, and thematically to the actions of God in history.[190] The scope of God's activity thus encompasses the whole of history, from creation to judgement, from first breath to resurrection, with individual and cosmic dimensions, focussed on the central figure of the appointed man, Jesus.[191]

The scene in Athens is constructed by Luke so as to highlight the positive response of one segment, at least, of Paul's audience (17.34), although in characteristic Lukan manner there is a division amongst the listeners,[192] for some reserve their judgement for the moment, whilst others mock Paul outright (17.32). Paul's declaration of divine providence thus serves an apologetic function,[193] as he

[186] ὁ θεός governs not only the parallel pair of negated indicative verbs (οὐκ ... κατοικεῖ and θεραπεύεται) but also the pair of present participles (ὑπάρχων and προσδεόμενος) and the pair of aorist participles (ὁ ποιήσας and αὐτὸς διδούς).

[187] In verse 26, the aorist indicative (ἐποίησεν) and the aorist participle (ὁρίσας) both depend on the initial subject of verse 24, namely ὁ θεός. Schubert ('Areopagus Speech' 260) notes the close association of ὁρίζω with the thematic term βουλή.

[188] τὸν θεόν (v. 27) is the object of both ζητεῖν and εὕροιεν.

[189] Schubert, 'Areopagus Speech' 250; likewise, see Zweck, 'Areopagus Speech' 97, 99.

[190] God is the subject of three principal verbs; God commands repentance because God has established the day of judgement and has chosen a man. In addition, three participles further describe the actions of God, who overlooks the times of ignorance, gives assurance to all, and has raised the chosen man from the dead.

[191] Schubert ('Areopagus Speech' 261) notes 'it covers, in good order and balance, everything from creation to consummation, via the resurrection of Christ'. A detailed explanation of the ministry and passion of Jesus is missing from the Areopagus speech because it has already been given in earlier speeches; on this literary technique of interruption, see Foakes Jackson and Lake, *Beginnings* 5.425–6;l Dibelius, *Studies* 60–1; Horsley, 'Speeches' 610–11.

[192] Paul's speeches in synagogues inevitably ended with a division among the listeners. In those cases, however, as well as those Jews who believed (Acts 9.21, 13.12,48, 14.4, 17.4,12, 18.8, 19.9b), there were Jews who were openly hostile towards Paul (9.23, 13.50, 14.2, 17.8,10, 18.6, 19.9a).

[193] The apologetic dimension of Paul's activities is a consistent feature in Luke's portrayal of his preaching amongst Gentiles (Acts 22.1, 24.10, 25.8, 26.1,24). Haenchen (*Acts* 624, 654) regards it as the central emphasis of these chapters, but he views this apology only as political, addressed to the Romans (*Acts* 40–1, 403). For the apologetic function of Paul's Areopagus speech, see O'Neill, *Theology* 160–71;

defends the Gospel in the face of objections that he is a σπερμολόγος (17.18)[194] who preaches a mere novelty (17.19).[195] Luke here presents Paul as a philosopher[196] who, in contrast to the Athenians' own insatiable desire for novelties (17.21), proclaims an authentically ancient message which is rooted in the Stoic tradition of divine providence.[197]

### 3.3.3.6 Paul in Miletus

Paul delivers a farewell speech to the Ephesian elders while he is in Miletus (20.18–35). Although this is not a missionary speech, it provides a retrospective view of Paul's missionary activity (20.18,21, 25b–27, 31–5). As we have noted above, Paul summarizes his preaching among Jews and Gentiles (20.21) as a testimony to the grace of God (20.24) and boldly declares, 'I did not shrink from declaring to you the whole plan of God' (πᾶσαν τὴν βουλὴν τοῦ θεοῦ, 20.27). This serves as a climactic summary of the foregoing preaching of providence by Paul and the apostles.[198]

There are a number of reasons for the prominence of this theme in the speeches in Acts. (1) The speeches are constructed by Luke himself, reflecting and addressing tendencies and issues which were

Flender, *Theologian* 66–72; with particular attention to the philosophical context of Acts 17, see A. J. Malherbe ('"Not in a Corner": Early Christian Apologetic in Acts 26.26', *Second Century* 5 (1985–6) 193–210), who concludes that Luke has Paul present his message 'in a manner reminiscent of the apologists' ('Corner' 199).

[194] For the derogatory sense of this term, see Dio Chrysostom, *Or.* 32.9; Norden, *Agnostos Theos* 333; Malherbe, 'Corner' 198 and n. 25.

[195] On the suspect nature of such innovation, see Malherbe, 'Corner' 197–9 and the literature cited in n. 29; on the value accorded to antiquity in the ancient world, see Cicero, *De nat. deor.* 3.2.5–6; Tacitus, *Hist.* 5.5 (on Judaism); Minucius Felix, *Oct.* 6.1–3; Origen, *Contra Celsum* 5.25; Julian, *Contra Gal.* 238D; Clarke, *Octavius* 189–90, 195; Wilken, *The Christians* 50–2; Benko, 'Pagan Criticism' 1106 (esp. n. 814); Esler, *Community and Gospel* 214–17.

[196] For the allusions to Socrates in Luke's presentation of Paul, see Foakes Jackson and Lake, *Beginnings* 4.212; Plümacher, *Lukas* 19,97–8; Malherbe, 'Corner' 198 n. 26.

[197] Malherbe ('Corner' 199) observes 'a subtle turning of the tables: the pagan philosophers who question the apostle do not themselves hold to the legitimate tradition; it is Paul who does'. Balch ('Areopagus Speech' 71) notes that 'against the "recent" defense of images by Stoics like Dio [Chrysostom], Acts pictures Paul as presenting the ancient, authentic philosophical opinion and practice'. Thus apologetic exposition becomes polemic. See above, nn. 160, 184.

[198] See Schubert, 'Areopagus' 260. If 'the grace of God' is 'a specifically Pauline catchword' (Haenchen, *Acts* 592), then 'the plan of God' is a characteristically Lukan catchword for the apostolic preaching. We have noted above (chap. 2.3.3.2) that Paul's later speeches continue to include this element of divine providence; see also chap. 7.3.1.2.

most important in Luke's own time and place. The theme of providence is, as we have seen, most important for Luke. (2) The speakers add their apostolic authority to the expression of this theme, enabling Luke to call upon them as support for his argument, at least as far as his Christian readers are concerned. (3) The clearest philosophical articulations of the theme come from those best suited to know of the Greek positions on providence, namely, Stephen the Hellenist and Paul the apostle to the Gentiles. (4) The claim that the life and passion of Jesus was guided by God stands as the basis for Luke's presentation of the mission to the Gentiles as an integral part of the plan of God. What is declared in the speeches is consistent with what the speakers are doing in their own lives. (5) The apologetic function of the theme can be demonstrated through the speeches; the speakers defend their actions and beliefs in the face of opposition and rejection. This dimension is further developed in Paul's apologetic speeches in Acts 22–6.

### 3.4 Conclusions

The theme of the plan of God plays an important role in Luke–Acts. The author refers to God's guidance of events from the very beginning of the Gospel through to the end of Acts. At key points in the narrative, such divine control is emphasized; however, Luke intends throughout to convey the message that God's guidance is comprehensive in scope and consistent in nature, underlying all the reported events.

There is a clear literary development of this theme: hints concerning divine providence are found in the preface to the work; clear, albeit brief, statements are included in the Gospel; the early chapters of Acts provide more extensive and explicit indications of God's guidance; the course of events in the later sections of Acts is frequently interpreted in this way. The series of missionary speeches in Acts 2–17 provides the most thorough expression of the plan of God, as it includes Israel, Jesus, the church and the final judgement.

Two particular events are emphasized as occurring within the plan of God: the crucifixion of Jesus and the mission to the Gentiles. Both events might be construed as involving a change of course in that original divine plan; thus Luke carefully presents each event as integral to God's purposes. The crucifixion is defended by the use of providential terminology; the mission is introduced as divinely intended. This theme thus functions apologetically to defend Christian beliefs and attack other views, as well as to assert and expound these two crucial aspects of Christian history and belief. Luke exhibits an awareness of the philosophic dimension of this providential theme. This is displayed most clearly in the speeches in which Stephen and Paul attack idolatry by using themes of divine providence which were commonly part of rhetorical techniques to attack idolatry in the hellenistic world. Such a philosophic awareness is not, however, consistently prominent throughout the work.

Our analysis of the extent, use, purpose and background of this theme reveals similarities at each point with the way providence appears as a factor in hellenistic histories. Luke, like Josephus, Diodorus and Dionysius, is probably aware of the philosophic issues only in broad terms. More important in Luke–Acts is the literary skill shown in Luke's use of the theme of the plan of God for his own apologetic purposes of expounding the history of Jesus and the church and defending the passion of Jesus and the Gentile mission in the face of attacks on them. The scope and nature of the plan of God exceeds, however, the role of providence in the histories of Diodorus and Dionysius, being more like the all-encompassing providence found in Josephus' history of the Jewish people.

In the ensuing chapters, further analysis of the related strands we have identified will clarify the ways in which this comparative analysis is legitimate and useful for an interpretation of Luke–Acts. Chapters four, five and six will treat, in turn, the ways in which Luke reinforces the plan of God by means of portents which declare how God is at work, dreams and visions which convey the divine will, and prophecies which come to fulfilment, thereby indicating God's faithfulness to the plan which has been declared from of old.

# 4

## PORTENTS: SIGNS OF DIVINE ACTION IN HUMAN HISTORY

Luke attests to God's providential oversight by certain 'miraculous' means. He refers to the signs and wonders which God performs[1] and reports a number of healings which Jesus is able to perform because 'God was with him' (Acts 10.38).[2] This function of emphasizing God's ongoing guidance of history by portentous events shares certain similarities with the way such events are presented in hellenistic histories. Nevertheless, such phenomena are critically evaluated by Diodorus, Dionysius and Josephus, as well as by Luke, who reports that both Jesus and Paul cast out demons which attempt to hinder or oppose the agents of God's plan.[3] Luke thus uses this 'miraculous' domain to confirm his presentation of God's providential guidance and to show how such events play a significant role in the plan of God.

### 4.1 Portents in hellenistic historiography

#### 4.1.1 Signs sent by the gods

The hellenistic historians we have considered demonstrate the popular acceptance of the role of divine interventions in human history. Both Dionysius of Halicarnassus and Diodorus Siculus report many such portentous occurrences, which were popularly considered to have been signs from the gods indicating their will. The science of divination arose as a means of interpreting the

---

[1] God performs signs and wonders through Jesus (Acts 2.22) and the apostles (Acts 2.19; 6.8; 8.6; 14.3; 15.12).

[2] The Lukan reports of Jesus' healings emphasize that they were the workings of God (Luke 7.16; 8.56; 9.43; 13.13,17; 17.15; 18.43), as do the reports of the apostles' healings (Acts 2.47; 3.7–9; 4.30; 5.12; 9.41; 13.6–12; 14.8–18; 19.8–12; 20.7–12; 28.6–10).

[3] Luke 4.33–7; 6.18; 7.21; 8.2,26–39; 9.37–43; 11.14–26; 13.32; Acts 13.9–11; 16.16–18; 19.12.

significance of such omens,[4] which Cicero divided into two main categories (*alterum artis est, alterum naturae, De div.* 1.6.11)[5] in order to make sense of the bewildering range of ways in which the gods were believed to have been communicating.

Certain 'artificial' means of communication were used by the gods, such as birds, dice, sacrificial entrails, thunder and lightning, earthquakes, the stars, or portentous events such as unnatural births or involuntary movements. Dionysius describes the 'terrible portents sent by the gods' (τὰ θεῖα δείματα) during the eighteenth Olympiad: 'flashes shooting out of the sky and outbursts of fire ... the rumblings of the earth and its continual tremblings ... the spectres ... flitting through the air ... voices that disturbed men's minds' (RA 10.2.3), culminating in a heavy snowstorm of pieces of flesh which lay on the ground for a long time without rotting. All except the last phenomenon 'were found to have occurred in times past as well, to either a greater or a lesser degree' (RA 10.2.3). He provides numerous examples of these and other types of portents as one way that the will of the gods was to be known.

Thus Dionysius readily equates a favourable omen (οἰωνός) of a lightning flash, given in the process of appointing a magistrate, with 'the will of the gods' (τὸ βούλημα τοῦ θεοῦ, RA 2.6.3), concluding that the magistrate (in this case, the first magistrate, Romulus) had thereby received 'the sanction of heaven' (τὰ παρὰ τοῦ δαιμονίου βέβαια, RA 2.6.1). Indeed, all the important stages in the life of Romulus are marked by a number of omens, each of which indicates the favour within which he is held by the gods.[6] Further omens

---

[4] Cicero (*De div.* 1.1.1) defines *divinatio* as 'the foresight and knowledge of future events', and claims that the etymological root of *divinatio* (*divi*, 'gods') indicates the divine origin of this foresight. For other definitions of divination, see *De div.* 2.63.130; *SVF* 2.1190.

[5] See also *De div.* 1.18.34. On the philosophical basis for this distinction, see E. Bevan, *Sibyls and Seers: a Survey of some Ancient Theories of Inspiration* (London: George Allen and Unwin, 1928) 129–34. For evidence of the antiquity of this division and alternative divisions provided in antiquity, see A. S. Pease (ed.), *M. Tvlli Ciceronis De Divinatione Libri Dvo* (originally in *University of Illinois Studies in Language and Literature* 6 (1920) 159–500 (book I), 8 (1923) 153–474 (book II); reprinted in 2 vols., Darmstadt: Wissenschaftliche Buchgesellschaft (1973)) I.70–71. Cicero's division of divination forms the basis for our discussion, treating 'artificial' divination in this chapter and 'natural' divination in the next two chapters. In practice, as A. D. Nock ('Religious Attitudes of the Ancient Greeks', *Essays on Religion and the Ancient World* (2 vols.; ed. Z. Stewart; Cambridge, Mass.: Harvard University Press, 1972) 538–39) demonstrates, adequate interpretation of 'artificial' signs inevitably required recourse to some 'natural' medium as well.

[6] Omens appear at his birth (RA 1.77.2), his competition with Remus (1.84.1–4), his appointment to the magistracy of Rome (2.4.1,6.4) and his death (2.56.6). On this

signify the favour or displeasure of the gods at various times in the history of Rome, usually in relation to the religious practices of the people.[7]

Similarly, Diodorus emphasizes the divine origin of portentous happenings. He introduces his account of the death of Alexander by recounting occurrences of 'many strange portents and signs' (οἰωνῶν καὶ σημείων) which the soothsayers interpreted to Alexander as being the means by which 'heaven (τὸ θεῖον) began to foretell his death' (BH 17.116.1). Elsewhere Diodorus gives frequent indication of his belief that the gods give signals through omens.[8] Again, the religious practices of the people are related to the signal conveyed by the omen.[9]

### 4.1.2  Signs of divine providence

There can be no denying the entertainment value of reporting such happenings; indeed, historians had long recounted amazing events for precisely this purpose.[10] On the other hand, such an approach came under scrutiny from those who criticized the alleged divine status of portents.[11] Dionysius indicates his awareness of such criticism when, after recounting the numerous omens (visions, voices, unnatural births, oracles, divine frenzies and a pestilence) which occurred in Rome in the time of Titus Latinius (RA 7.68.1), he notes that 'although some thought these occurred according to

phenomenon in ancient literature, see L. Bieler, *Theios Aner: Das Bild des 'Göttlichen Menschen' in Spätantike und Frühchristentum* (2 vols.; Wien: Oskar Höfels, 1935–6, reprinted Darmstadt: Wissenschaftliche Buchgesellschaft, 1967) 2.110–11. For Dionysius' guarded acceptance of some of these omens, see R. M. Grant, *Miracle and Natural Law in Graeco-Roman and Early Christian Thought* (Amsterdam: North Holland, 1952) 55–6.

[7]  The gods act favourably when religious practices are properly observed (RA 3.36.1,47.1–3.48.1,70.2–3; 6.17.3; 7.3.2–4.2; note also 6.6.2). However, twice the gods signify their approval of changes instigated in Rome (4.40.1; 10.2.2–6). Failure to adhere to traditional religious customs evokes the displeasure of the gods towards the Pelasgians (BH 1.23.1–24.1), Tulli Hostili (3.35.2–36.3), Marci (8.89.4–5; 9.40.1) and Gnaei Manli (9.6.4).

[8]  He uses the term σημαίνειν in conjunction with an act of the gods at BH 2.25.5–8; 4.9.2; 5.7.11; 15.50.2; 16.56.8; 17.10.6–12,17.6,41.5,114.5,116.1; 19.103.5; 20.5.5,7.3,11.5; 22.13.3; 36.2.1. At 15.53.4 the σημεῖα are claimed to be of god, but are in fact false omens.

[9]  Divine favour is shown to the Delphians at BH 22.9.5; divine displeasure is indicated as a result of the sacking of a temple by the Phocians (16.56.8) and the Cretans (31.45.1).

[10]  Grant, *Miracle* 61–77.

[11]  See the examples collected by Grant, *Miracle* 41–60, esp. 50–8 from the hellenistic era.

the will of the god (κατὰ θεοῦ γνώμην) . . . others held that nothing occurred as a work of god (θεοῦ ἔργον) but that both these and all other human events were due to chance (τύχημα) (RA 7.68.2).

Dionysius had already declared his position in his account of Romulus' appointment as magistrate after the favourable omen (RA 2.6.1–3) with the note that he felt obliged to tell this story on account of 'the contempt of the divine power (ὑπὲρ τῆς εἰς τὸ δαιμόνιον ὀλιγωρίας) that prevails today' (RA 2.6.4). His accounts of omens as divine signs are to be read in the light of this polemical statement.[12]

Likewise, Diodorus firmly admonishes 'those who adopt a sceptical attitude (ἀπίστως) towards histories because they recount what is astonishing (παράδοξον)' (BH 3.30.4),[13] and his presentations of omens and divination consistently emphasize their divine dimension. Although some would claim that anticipating victory in a battle on the basis of which birds were seen flying by (BH 20.11.3–4) was reliance on an 'inane device' (BH 20.11.5), Diodorus considers this to be a legitimate way by which Athena signalled victory to Agathocles (τὸ θεῖον προσημαίνει, BH 20.11.5).[14]

Those who deny the divine origin of such portents are never specified by either historian; however, evidence from the ancient world indicates an ongoing discussion amongst the historians on the value of portentous happenings.[15] This variety of positions is due to

---

[12] Grant, however, considers that Dionysius is trying 'to steer a middle course between piety and scepticism' (*Miracle* 55).

[13] On the basis of Diodorus' discussion of mythology in BH 4.8, Grant considers that Diodorus reflects the custom of his day 'to question the reliability of strange stories of divine or semi-divine power' (*Miracle* 54); for this moderately sceptical attitude, see Nock, 'Religious Attitudes' 541–2. H. C. Kee notes, in passing, that when he presents his aretalogy of Isis, Diodorus asserts her powers whilst 'anticipating a skeptical response from his readers' (*Miracle* 126).

[14] For a Stoic defence of divination by birds, see Cicero, *De div.* 1.53.120. In his discussion of the 'flaming beam' which appeared in the heavens to warn the Lacedaemonians of their final defeat (BH 15.50.2), Diodorus refers to opponents who 'ascribed the origin of the torch to natural causes, voicing the opinion that such apparitions occur of necessity' (BH 15.50.3). For a Stoic defence of divination by the stars, see Cicero, *De div.* 1.67.130.

[15] Polybius explicitly criticizes Timaeus for his constant use of 'dreams, prodigies and unlikely stories', which he calls 'ignoble superstitions and old wives' tales' (*Hist.* 12.24.5, trans. Walbank); but Grant comments that 'it was almost a convention of Greek historical writing to claim that one's predecessors are uncritical and credulous', and cites examples from Theopompus, Timaeus, Polybius, Cicero, Strabo and Aelian (*Miracle* 50, and see 52 for further concerning Polybius). Herodotus did not shy away from reporting extravagant miraculous events; see J. Hart, *Herodotus and Greek History* (London: Croom Helm, 1982) 33, 43–4; Waters, *Herodotus* 1, 97, 106–10. A. H. McDonald ('Herodotus on the Miraculous', *Miracles* (ed. Moule) 87)

the varied influence of rhetorical criticism, which not only emphasized the entertainment value of miraculous tales, but also developed a critical awareness of the educative value of such stories.[16]

   The popularity of artificial divination is attested as a widespread
popular belief well before the first century,[17] but in philosophical
circles the basis of divination was related to one's attitude concerning providence; thus Quintilian relates the interpretations of
omens to 'the endless disputes between the adherents of the Stoics
and the Epicureans, as to whether the world is governed by providence' (*Instit. or.* 5.7.35). Cicero's brother, Quintus, expresses the
Stoic belief that artificial divination is based on 'the clear and
unimpeachable records signed and sealed by the hand of Time' (*De
div.* 1.40.88)[18] and draws directly on Posidonius, who declared that
'the vital principle of divination' must be traced to God, Fate and
Nature (*De div.* 1.55.125).[19] Cicero notes that Cleanthes argued

argues that Herodotus took a more moderate position; for indications of his critical
acumen, see H. Remus, *Pagan–Christian Conflict over Miracle in the Second Century*
(Patristic Monograph Series 10; Cambridge, Mass.: Philadelphia Patristic Foundation, 1983) 189–90; for similar indications in Livy, see Walsh, *Livy* 47–8 (and 48
n. 1 on Herodotus), 62–3. Thucydides showed the most restraint (Bury, *Historians*
129). Cadbury, Foakes Jackson and Lake ('The Greek and Jewish Traditions of
Writing History', *Beginnings* 2.11) note the willingness of Dionysius 'to record the
most extravagant legends of early Rome'.

   [16] In one of his rhetorical works, Dionysius of Halicarnassus criticizes accounts of
historians prior to Thucydides as containing 'silly tales' (*On Thucydides* 5). Lucian
polemicizes against mere entertainment in *How to Write History* 9–13, 61, 63. See
Grant's comments on the role played by rhetoric in shaping a critical attitude to the
miraculous (*Miracle* 47, 58–60, and see 50–6 for hellenistic historians and wonder
stories). On the relation between rhetoric and divination, see F. Guillaumont, *Philosophie et augure: recherches sur la théorie cicéronienne de la divination* (Collection
Latomus 184; Bruxelles: Revue d'études Latines, 1984) 17–42.

   [17] See W. Burkert, *Greek Religion* (Cambridge, Mass.: Harvard University Press,
1985) 111–14 on the origins of the various forms; J. D. Mikalson, *Athenian Popular
Religion* (Chapel Hill: University of North Carolina, 1983) 39–52 on the fourth
century BCE; R. Flacelière, *Greek Oracles* (New York: Norton, 1961) 1–19 on
classical and hellenistic times; M. P. Nilsson, *Greek Folk Religion* (New York:
Harper, 1961) 125–7 on the role of omens in warfare.

   [18] See also *De div.* 1.49.109. Quintus provides an extensive catalogue of the
phenomena of artificial divination, citing examples which were widely known in the
first century BCE (*De div.* 1.33.72–49.109). See also Minucius Felix, *Oct.* 7.1–6;
Nock, 'Religious Attitudes' 867–8. Philodemus notes that the Stoics regarded divination as worthy of honour (*SVF* 3.2.72, p. 228). For the Stoic defence of divination,
see *De div.* 1.3.6,33.72; Diogenes Laertius, *Lives* 7.149.

   [19] For the equivalence of these three terms, see chap. 7 nn. 10,12; but Cicero
himself states that the three terms refer to distinct entities (*De div.* 2.11.27); see also
Nock, 'Posidonius' 867; Grant, *Miracle* 22–3. For Cicero's use of Posidonian arguments throughout Book 1 of *De div.*, see Pease, *De Divinatione* 22–4; W. A. Falconer,
*Cicero* (LCL, vol. 20; Cambridge, Mass.: Harvard University Press, 1923) 216–19; on

that the gods exist on the basis of 'the awe inspired by lightning, storms, rain, snow, hail, floods [and many more examples], all of which alarming portents have suggested to mankind the idea of the existence of some celestial and divine power' (*De nat. deor.* 2.5.13–14),[20] but Cicero himself propounds the more sceptical view of the academy, as he rejects Posidonius' views on omens as *absurda* (*De fato* 3.5) and provides his own extensive catalogue of omens, whose portentous powers he refutes one by one (*De div.* 2.12.28–47.99).[21]

Hellenistic historians in general showed their awareness of the philosophic views concerning such phenomena.[22] Dionysius reflects a Stoic perspective when he directly attributed such portentous occurrences to the workings of providence on two occasions, in the speeches of Fufetius and Tullus concerning the two sets of triplets who are providentially opposed in battle (RA 3.14.1–16.3)[23] and on the occasion of the adverse wind which stopped the ships of Pyrrhus, which occurred because of 'the just providence' (ἡ δικαία πρόνοια, RA 20.9.2). Diodorus also reflects a Stoic view of the providential nature of portents when two storms intervene to rescue the Delphic oracle and Alexander's army.[24] Two seemingly insignificant remarks made by humans, perceived by those who heard them as portentous, are likewise described by Diodorus as sent by provi-

variations in his own view throughout his writings, see Pease, *De Divinatione* 11; Guillaumont, *Philosophie et augure* 123–69, esp. 137–40, 165–9.

[20] See also *De div.* 1.52.118,53.120; 2.15.35.

[21] See also Panaetius' rejection of divination at Cicero, *Acad.* 2.33.107; Diogenes Laertius, *Lives* 7.149; and for similar arguments against omens employed by later Christian writers, see Minucius Felix, *Oct.* 26.1–6; Origen, *Contra Celsum* 8.45.

[22] See Grant, *Miracle* 41–7, 51–3.

[23] The 'good omen' (οἰωνοῦ ἀγαθοῦ, RA 3.13.4) that they were born to twin sisters on the very same day is described as θαυμαστής (3.13.3,14.1,15.1) and παράδοξον (3.13.3). When the twins meet in battle, the encounter is described by Dionysius not only as θαυμαστής (3.22.10) and παράδοξος (3.22.1), but as an act of Fortune (τύχη, 3.19.6,20.3,21.1). Yet their birth is no mere caprice of Fortune (τύχη), as is claimed by both Fufetius (3.14.3) and Tullus (3.15.1), as well as by the Alban triplets (3.17.4); rather, this is an act of God (3.13.4,14.1) which shows the divine favour (θεία εὐεργεσία, 3.14.1) and indeed the divine providence, as is recognised by both Fufetius (θεία πρόνοια, 3.13.3, and τὴν τοῦ δαιμονίου πρόνοιαν, 3.14.2) and by Tullus (θείαν πρόνοιαν, 3.16.2).

[24] The storm of thunder and lightning which stopped Xerxes' army from destroying the oracle of Apollo occurred by δαιμονίᾳ τινὶ προνοίᾳ (BH 11.14.4); the rainstorm which rescued Alexander and his army in the middle of the desert was welcomed as having been due to the action of θεῶν προνοία (17.49.4). On the Stoic relation of such natural phenomena to divine providence, see Cicero, *De nat. deor.* 2.5.14. For an Epicurean polemic against such omens, see Lucretius, *De rerum natura* 6.43–79, 379–422, and note also the refutation of Posidonius' view that omens reveal destiny in Cicero, *De fato* 3.5–6.

dence (BH 16.92.2; 17.66.7).[25] The providential nature of portents, generally assumed by Diodorus, is thus stated explicitly on these occasions.[26]

## 4.2 Portents in Josephus

The people of Israel certainly knew of the practices of the various types of diviners in the cultures which surrounded them,[27] and although certain aspects of this divination were complete anathema to the Hebrew faith, the constant struggle to purge these elements from Israel herself indicates that there never was a 'pure' Hebrew society in which divination was completely eschewed.[28] Yet every important strand of the tradition witnesses to the efforts to rid Israel of practices associated with divination of omens, and the strength and frequency of these condemnations is evidence for the extent to which such practices were to be found in Israel.[29]

---

[25] At the marriage of Cleopatra and Alexander, a casual remark by Olympias to Philip 'seemed like an omen sent by providence' (ὥσπερ θείᾳ τινὶ προνοίᾳ διεσήμαινε τὸ δαιμόνιον, BH 16.92.2), whilst the remark of Philotas regarding an action of the king's slave was made 'by the divine providence and will' (δαίμονός τινος προνοίᾳ καὶ βουλήσει, BH 17.66.7).

[26] In one other place Diodorus contrasts the providence of God and omens, when he notes that the Locrian ambassadors accepted the aid offered by the Lacedaemonians, 'whether under the guidance of the providence of God (προνοίᾳ θεοῦ) or because they took the reply as an omen (οἰωνισάμενοι)' (BH 8.32.2).

[27] The Hebrew scriptures indicate a knowledge of the Babylonian customs of 'artificial' divination (Num 23.1–6; Ezek 21.21–3). Other references are made to the use of omens by Ben-hadad's son (1 Kings 21(20).33), divination by the Philistines (1 Sam 6.2), sorcery by the Assyrians (Nah 3.4) and the Canaanites (Wis 12.4), magic by the Egyptians (Wis 17.7) and astrology by the Babylonians (Isa 47.13).

[28] The priests supervised divination by the Urim and Thummim (Exod 28.30; Num 27.21; Deut 33.8; 1 Sam 14.41–2) and the ephod (1 Sam 23.9–12; 30.7–8). Some of the prophets are said to have 'divined for money' (Mic 3.11), whilst Saul's famous enquiry of the witch of Endor (1 Sam 28.8–14) is told, although his death is attributed to the fact of this divinatory enquiry (1 Chron 10.13). Manasseh is roundly condemned as having practised all manner of divination (2 Kings 21.6, par 2 Chron 33.6), whilst Isaiah laments that 'the land is filled as at the beginning with divinations' (Isa 2.6). See D. E. Aune, *Prophecy in Early Christianity and the Ancient Mediterranean World* (Grand Rapids, Mich.: Erdmans, 1983) 82–3; J. Blenkinsopp, 'Prophecy and Priesthood in Josephus', *JJS* 25 (1974) 253–4.

[29] The Deuteronomic tradition contains the comprehensive ban on various 'abominable practices' of divination (Deut 18.9–12); the priestly tradition contains a similarly broad condemnation of various types of 'artificial' divination (Lev 19.26,31; 20.6,27). The prophets condemn μαντεία (Isa 44.25; Jer 14.14; 34(27).9; 36(29).8; Ezek 12.24; 13.6–10,23; 21.21–9; 22.28; Micah 3.5–7; Zech 10.2), οἰωνός (Jer 14.14 and 34(27).9), ἐγγαστριμύθους (Isa 8.19 and 44.25) and φαρμακεία (Isa 47.9–14; Jer 34(27).9; Micah 5.12; Mal 3.5). Even the wisdom tradition describes both μαντεία and οἰωνός as 'vain' at Wis 31(34).5.

However, a number of miraculous events were declared to be clear signs of God's guidance and protection of Israel. Certain of the former prophets (notably Elijah and Elisha) performed miraculous deeds,[30] but language which highlights the miraculous dimension is used most frequently in conjunction with the key event of all of Jewish history, namely the Exodus from Egypt, which is described as a sign and a wonder,[31] a paradox[32] and a manifestation of God.[33]

Josephus follows the Septuagint in affirming that the signal event of the Exodus, that surprising miracle, was a clear manifestation of God's activity. Subsequent events throughout the history of the Jewish people are similarly presented as miraculous occurrences[34] by the use of a cluster of related terms.[35] Such events are consistently linked with divine providence,[36] thereby providing clear examples of how God's will is to be known and obeyed (cf. AJ 1.14).

---

[30] See J. P. Ross, 'Some Notes on Miracle in the Old Testament', *Miracles* (ed. Moule) 43–60; B. Lindars, 'Elijah, Elisha and the Gospel Miracles', *Miracles* (ed. Moule) 61–79. Ross concludes that the purpose of retelling such miraculous events was, 'for the Israelite, then, [that] mighty works were the clearest and purest evidence of God' ('Notes' 54). For similar conclusions about omens in Mesopotamian texts, see van Seters, *In Search of History* 55–6, 77–9, 91.

[31] The words σημεῖα καὶ τέρατα are applied to the plagues in Egypt (Exod 7.3,9, 11.9–10; σημεῖα appears alone at Exod 8.23; 10.1,2; 11.9) but most often to the Exodus itself (Deut 4.34; 6.22; 7.19; 11.3; 26.8; 29.3; 34.11; Neh 9.10; Ps 77(78).43; 104(105).27; 134(135).9; Jer 39(32).20–1; Bar 2.11; σημεῖα appears alone at Num 14.11,22; and τέρατα alone at Exod 15.11; Wis 19.8). K. H. Rengstorf ('σημεῖον', TDNT 7 (1964) 221) notes 'the formula σημεῖα καὶ τέρατα ... seems to be reserved for God's wonders in the days of Moses'.

[32] The Exodus shows forth the wonder (παράδοξον) of God's actions (Exod 8.22(18); 9.4; 11.7; Deut 28.59; Wis 16.17; 19.5).

[33] The Exodus is described as ἐπιφάνεια (τοῦ θεοῦ) at 2 Sam 7.23 and 3 Macc 6.4.

[34] On miracles in Josephus, see G. Delling, 'Josephus und das Wunderbare', *NovT* 2 (1958) 291–309; G. McRae, 'Miracle in "The Antiquities" of Josephus', *Miracles* (ed. Moule) 127–47; H. R. Moehring, 'Rationalization of Miracles in the Writings of Flavius Josephus', *Studia Evangelica* 11 (1973) 376–83; and O. Betz, 'Das Problem des Wunders bei Flavius Josephus im Vergleich zum Wunderproblem bei den Rabbinen und in Johannesevangelium', *Josephus-Studien: Untersuchungen zu Josephus, die antiken Judentum und die Neuen Testament: Otto Michel zum 70. Geburtstag gewidmet* (ed. O. Betz, K. Haacker and M. Hengel; Göttingen: Vandenhoeck und Ruprecht, 1974) 25–34.

[35] σημεῖα, τέρατα, παράλογοι, παράδοξοι and ἐπιφάνεια. On these terms in Josephus, see McRae, 'Miracle' 142–7.

[36] McRae writes of the 'consistent emphasis on the πρόνοια θεοῦ as the *raison d'être* of miracles' ('Josephus' 139; see esp. 132–6); note also Delling, 'Wunderbare' 303–6.

#### 4.2.1  Signs and wonders

The common Septuagintal pairing of signs and wonders (σημεῖα καὶ τέρατα) appears only twice in the writings of Josephus,[37] but he uses these terms individually throughout his biblical paraphrase to refer to various actions of God. Signs of the divine will[38] come through angelic messengers,[39] miraculous events,[40] thunderstorms[41] and the words of prophets.[42] God exhorts Moses 'to use miracles (σημείοις) to convince all men "that thou art sent by me and doest all at my command"' (AJ 2.274), and when he does perform such σημεῖα his fellow Hebrews are convinced that 'God was caring for their safety' (θεοῦ προνοουμένου, AJ 2.280).

The theophanies of the burning bush (AJ 2.265) and on Mount Sinai (AJ 4.43) are both described as divine portents,[43] whilst in his account of the Jewish War Josephus reports various portents which warn of God's anger (BJ 1.378; 4.287–8). Those portents (τέρατα) which occur immediately before the fall of Jerusalem are also called signs (σημεῖα) which are 'plain warnings of God' (τῶν τοῦ θεοῦ κηρυγμάτων, 6.288), and if one reflects on them, 'one will find that God has a care for men, and by all kinds of premonitory signs shows (τὸν μὲν θεὸν ἀνθρώπων κηδόμενον καὶ παντοίως προσημαίνοντα)

---

[37] BJ 1.28 concerning the signs before the destruction of Jerusalem, and AJ 20.168 (where they are linked with providence) concerning the false signs claimed by impostors; see also AJ 10.28. On σημεῖα and τέρατα in the literature of the time, see K. Berger, 'Hellenistisch-heidnische Prodigien und die Verzeichen in der jüdischen und christlichen Apokalyptik', *ANRW* II.23.2, 1428–69; Rengstorf, 'σημεῖον' 206–7.

[38] σημεῖον is used 80 times by Josephus, divided almost equally throughout AJ 1–11 (29 times), AJ 12–20 (27 times) and BJ (24 times). The divine origin of these signs is noted eight times in AJ 1–11 and twice in BJ. Rengstorf ('σημεῖον' 224) notes that 'the word is ... a term for the means by which God as the One who reveals Himself in history shows (σημαίνει) what He wills and does'. σημαίνω is used 139 times by Josephus, and God is the subject of this verb only eleven times, all in AJ 1–11. Schlatter (*Wie Sprach?* 52) comments that 'gebraucht er σημαίνειν [etc]. von der Gottes Willen'.

[39] To Sarah (AJ 1.198) and to Jacob (1.333).

[40] The burning bush (AJ 2.276), the miracles of Moses (2.280,283), the sparing of the spies (5.12), the altar which broke and dripped fat (8.232), the turning back of the sun by ten degrees (10.29) and the finger writing on the wall (10.238).

[41] Supporting Samuel (AJ 6.91–3), opposing Philistines (6.27).

[42] Samuel (AJ 6.50), Micaiah (8.405) and Jeremiah (10.124,180); cf. the false prophet Sedekias (8.409). On the link between prophecy and signs, see chap. 6 n. 68.

[43] τέρας appears four times in AJ and eight times in BJ, of which two occurrences in AJ and four occurrences in BJ refer to the divine origin of the portents. Rengstorf ('σημεῖον' 225) defines the divine reference of the term thus: 'when He works a τέρας, this is not important as such, but as a σημεῖον it denotes God's presence and thus points to God'; but cf. his subsequent redefinition (Rengstorf, 'τέρας', *TDNT* 8 (1972) 114–15, 121–3) emphasizing the 'theological reference' of τέρας.

His people the way of salvation' (BJ 6.310).[44] The function of such signs and wonders, then, is to declare the divine will and encourage obedience to God.

#### 4.2.2 Surprises and miracles

Events which seem to be unbelievable or astonishing are consistently ascribed to the activity of God, and thus 'the sacred scriptures recount surprising reversals' (παράλογοι περιπέτειαι, AJ 1.13). The Exodus, miraculous (παράδοξον, AJ 2.345,347; 3.1,14)[45] and surprising (παράλογον, AJ 2.339,345; 3.18), took place in accordance with God's will.[46] The preservation of the Hebrews in spite of all the calamities and surprises (παράλογα, AJ 4.127) which they encountered through their history was guaranteed because of God's providence (πρόνοια τῷ θεῷ, AJ 4.128) and will (βούλησιν τοῦ θεοῦ, AJ 4.127). Later, in the words which he attributes to Hezekiah, Josephus defends his retelling of such events; 'things that are beyond belief (τὰ παράλογα) and surpass our hopes are made credible by acts of a like nature' (AJ 10.28).

G. McRae notes Josephus' 'sparing use of the word παράδοξον ... which was common in hellenistic Judaism'.[47] Nevertheless, it is prominent enough to warrant attention, and it reveals Josephus' inherent tendency to attribute events of such wondrous nature to the intentions and actions of God.[48] Accordingly, Moses is associ-

---

[44] See S. V. McCasland, 'Portents in Josephus and in the Gospels', *JBL* 51 (1932) 323–35, and the bibliography in K. Berger, 'Prodigien' 1457. Kee (*Miracle* 174–83) relates this passage to the Roman histories in which portents signify divine destiny; Rajak (*Josephus* 91) notes that Josephus uses 'the claims of popular superstition' to demonstrate that 'God does care for man'.

[45] The Exodus is described as a παράδοξον six times in the Septuagint (see above, n. 32).

[46] The Hebrews left Egypt κατὰ τὴν σὴν βούλησιν (AJ 2.335); the separation of the sea is depicted as ἐπιφάνειαν τοῦ θεοῦ (AJ 2.339); the passage of the Israelites through the Red Sea led them διὰ θείας ὁδοῦ (AJ 2.339); and the destruction of the Egyptians occurred παρὰ τὴν τοῦ θεοῦ γνώμην (AJ 3.17). On the link between providence and miracles, firmly asserted in Moses' speech prior to the crossing of the Red Sea (AJ 2.330–33), see Attridge, *Interpretation* 78.

[47] McRae, 'Miracle' 143. The word appears 29 times in the biblical paraphrase but in the LXX παραδοξάζειν is used four times, in the Pentateuch only, each time in connection with the Exodus, whilst παράδοξος appears only in books of the hellenistic era. In AJ 12–20, the noun is used a further eleven times. Cf. the common use of παράδοξος in connection with τύχη in the hellenistic histories (chap. 3, pp. 45–6).

[48] Of the 40 occurrences in AJ, 25 explicitly refer to the divine origin of the παράδοξος, and 22 of these are to be found in the biblical paraphrase.

ated with a string of 'paradoxical' events of divine origin,[49] whilst subsequent events in the biblical paraphrase are described as παρα- δόξα caused by God.[50] In the remainder of the *Antiquitates* three similar events are recorded as being divinely sent surprises.[51]

Josephus explicitly and persistently links such surprising events (παράδοξα) with divine providence. God tells Amram that he 'watches over (προνοούμενον) the common welfare of you all' (AJ 2.215), including Moses' being 'reared in marvellous wise' (2.216), and so the 'marvellous gifts' (2.285) exhibited by Moses in Egypt 'proceed from God's providence (θεοῦ πρόνοιαν) and power (2.286). Likewise the 'marvellous prodigy' of water gushing forth from the rock at Rephidim is a 'gift from God' which demonstrates to Israel 'God's care (θεοῦ πρόνοιαν) for their welfare' (3.38)f. When the companions of Daniel 'miraculously escaped death' Jose- phus notes that they were 'saved by divine providence' (θείᾳ προνοίᾳ, 10.214).[52] Such phenomena thus underline the consistent provi- dential care exercised by God.

On occasion, Josephus concludes his report of a miraculous event with a 'rationalist' formula, 'on these matters everyone is welcome to his own opinion'.[53] H. St J. Thackeray suggested that this phrase indicated Josephus' non-committal attitude towards miracles,[54] but this places too much weight on a traditional historiographical con- vention which has formal, but not substantial, significance.[55] That

[49] The birth of Moses in Egypt (AJ 2.215–6), his miraculous salvation in Egypt (2.223), the burning bush (2.267), his magical powers (2.285), the plague of blood (2.295), the passage through the Red Sea (2.339), the provision of manna at Elim (3.30) and water at Rephidim (3.38).

[50] The conquest of Jericho (AJ 5.28), Saul's escape from David (6.291), the workmanship of the Temple (8.130), the victory of Jehoshaphat over the Ammonites (9.14), Ben-hadad's vision of the chariots encircling Elisha (9.60), all the deeds of Elisha (9.128), Hezekiah's deliverance from the Assyrians (10.24) and his subsequent recovery from illness (10.28), the rescue of Daniel's companions from the fire (10.214), the writing on the wall seen by Belshazzar (10.238) and all the happenings of Daniel's life (10.267,277).

[51] AJ 13.282; 14.455; 15.379; cf. 17.330. The inauthentic *Testimonium Flavianum* depicts Jesus, the Messiah, as one who performed παράδοξα (AJ 18.63).

[52] See also the linking of the Exodus with the will of God (AJ 2.347; 3.17) and the explanation of a miracle concerning Herod in terms of the goodwill of God (εὔνοια, AJ 14.455).

[53] AJ 1.108; 2.348; 3.81; 4.158; 10.281; 17.354; and without reference to miracles at AJ 3.268,322; 8.262; 19.108; see also BJ 5.257 (and cf. AJ 19.196).

[54] *Josephus the Man and the Historian* (New York: Jewish Institute of Religion Press, 1929) 57.

[55] Lucian notes that this should be a feature of hellenistic history (*History* 60). Avenarius (*Lukians Schrift* 163–4) cites a number of instances from Dio Cassius, Arrian, Tacitus, Josephus, Dionysius, Diodorus, Thucydides and Herodotus; to

Josephus himself has a strong opinion on the matters he reports,[56] even as he allows his readers to form their own opinions, can be seen from his use of the same formula after his claim that 'our constitution was established by God himself, through the agency of Moses and of his merits' (AJ 3.322). Furthermore, his use of the phrase at the conclusion of his strongly argued support of divine providence in connection with the prophecies of Daniel (AJ 10.281) in no way undermines his belief in such miraculous events.[57] Like signs and wonders, surprises and miracles confirm and convey divine providence.

### 4.3 Portents and the plan of God in Luke–Acts

Luke's account of Jesus and the early church is replete with instances of divine intervention by miraculous means, seen in the various signs and wonders to which Luke refers and in the healings and exorcisms in which the divine power works through certain individuals. Earlier critical investigations of these miracles explored their form critically in relation to contemporary accounts of miracles.[58] More recently, when the miracles have been viewed in relation to the redaction-critical interest in Luke's theological perspective, they have been seen as furthering Luke's missionary purpose[59]

which should be added Herodotus 5.45; Diodorus Siculus BH 2.14.4; 4.26.3,47.6; Pliny, *Hist. nat.* 9.18 (cited by Delling, 'Wunderbare' 305 n. 1). Grant, in surprising ignorance of the general custom, considers the use of such a phrase by Dionysius to be an 'abandonment of critical historiography' (*Miracle* 55). McRae's assessment of Josephus' use of the phrase is accurate: 'it must be regarded as a superficial gesture of courtesy to the pagan readers who cannot accept the interpretation of the author ... Josephus ... is not expressing personal scepticism' (McRae, 'Miracle' 140–1). See also Cohen, *Josephus* 39 n. 61; Aune, *New Testament* 82, 109.

[56] Rajak (*Josephus* 79) notes that 'Josephus is the kind of author who likes to make his opinions explicit at frequent intervals', and cites BJ 1.9 in support.

[57] The phrase is also associated with Josephus' characteristic claim for divine providence at AJ 17.354. Dealing with evidence other than this 'rationalist' formula, Moehring argues that 'although he insists that miracles are, in the last analysis, performed by the providence of God', Josephus sometimes rationalizes miracles in order to distance God from such events and 'gain the respect of his educated Gentile readers for the sacred traditions of his people' ('Rationalization' 381).

[58] For the Gospel accounts, see the survey of F. Neirynck, 'The Miracle Stories in the Acts of the Apostles: An Introduction', *Actes des Apôtres* (ed. J. Kremer) 188–202; for the application of form criticism to Acts, see Dibelius, *Studies* 11–25.

[59] For redaction-critical studies of the miracles in Luke, see Neirynck, 'Miracle Stories' 202–5. For their relation to Luke's missionary purpose, see A. Fridrichsen, *The Problem of Miracle in Primitive Christianity* (Minneapolis: Augsburg, 1972) 61–3, 77–84; Conzelmann, *Theology* 190–3; A. Richardson, *The Miracle-Stories of the Gospels* (New York: Harper Bros., 1942) 108–14; G. W. H. Lampe, 'Miracles in

or as attesting to Jesus' Messianic status.[60] Some interpreters have drawn the conclusion 'that miracles point to God is clear in Luke',[61] but have failed to develop this useful perspective.[62] Our approach will be to show that Luke interprets the miracles as visible manifestations of God's activity which demonstrate the outworking of the plan of God in human history. In just the same way as we have seen in the hellenistic historians, such portents are proof of divine providence.[63]

### 4.3.1 Wonders and signs which God did through Jesus

A typical Lukan description of divine intervention in history is the phrase 'signs and wonders'. In Peter's first public proclamation about Jesus, on the day of Pentecost (Acts 2.22–36), he emphasizes the divine guidance of Jesus' life. By describing the deeds which Jesus performed before he was crucified as 'mighty works and wonders and signs' (δυνάμεσι καὶ τέρασι καὶ σημείοις, 2.22)[64] Peter draws upon a conventional Deuteronomic appellation for miracles[65] which is equally comprehensible to readers familiar with

the Acts of the Apostles', *Miracles* (ed. Moule) 165, 171, 174; P. J. Achtemeier, 'The Lucan Perspective on the Miracles of Jesus: A Preliminary Sketch', *JBL* 94 (1975) 553–62. For a different redactional approach to the miracles, emphasizing their symbolic importance, see D. Hamm, 'Acts 3,1–10: The Healing of the Temple Beggar as Lucan Theology', *Bib* 67 (1986) 305–19.

[60] Richardson, *Miracle-Stories*; and see the apologetically dogmatic treatment of R. L. Hamblin, 'Miracles in the Book of Acts', *South Western Journal of Theology* 17 (1974) 19–34, esp. 20.

[61] Achtemeier, 'Lucan Perspective' 561; see also Grant, *Miracle* 168–71; Lampe, 'Miracles' 166.

[62] Achtemeier ('Lucan Perspective' 562) unfortunately concludes that 'few if any of the themes normally identified as characteristically Lucan emerge from Luke's telling of the miracles'.

[63] Van Unnik ('Eléments artistiques' 134) includes 'prodigies and divine interventions' as one signal of Luke's historiographical method.

[64] In what follows we develop Rengstorf's description of 2.22 as an 'interpretative key' ('σημεῖον' 242).

[65] See above, n. 31. Luke has inserted the second member of the phrase, σημεῖα, into the prophecy of Joel (2.28–32) which Peter has just quoted (Acts 2.16–21), with two important results: (1) this introduces the Deuteronomistic phrase into the prophecy of Joel in the reverse order which Peter uses (2.22; also 6.8); (2) this enables Peter to depict Jesus as part of the fulfilment of this prophecy in his description of 2.22. See R. J. Dillon, 'The Prophecy of Christ and His Witnesses According to the Discourses of Acts', *NTS* 32 (1986) 545–7. Berger ('Prodigien' 1436–8) adduces parallels which indicate that Luke has assimilated this quotation to a hellenistic understanding of portents.

hellenistic historiography.[66] Luke combines this with δύναμις, one of his favourite expressions for such deeds.[67] The source and origin of these deeds is explained in another typically Lukan phrase; they are deeds 'which God did through him [Jesus] in your midst' (οἷς ἐποίησεν δὶ αὐτοῦ ὁ θεός, 2.22).[68] The purpose of these deeds is also set forth, for by doing such things Jesus was 'attested to you by God' (2.22). Thus the first apostolic proclamation of Jesus' ministry begins with his miraculous deeds and places them in continuity with what we have shown to be the main theme of the speech. The 'definite plan and foreknowledge of God' (2.23) was thus evident not only in Jesus' passion, but also in all the events of his life.

In his sermon at Caesarea (10.34–43), Peter again emphasizes divine guidance in the life of Jesus, the one whom God anointed (10.38), raised (10.40) and ordained (10.42). Peter again interprets the miraculous deeds wrought by Jesus as divinely motivated and enabled, placing them into continuity with his main theme, namely, God's overarching providence. Here, however, Peter uses a phrase more closely attuned to the way Jesus is presented in the Gospel: 'he went about doing good[69] and healing all that were oppressed by the devil, for God was with him' (10.38). Throughout Luke's Gospel, as in each of the synoptic Gospels, the signs and wonders which are reported are, in the vast majority of cases, healings[70] or

---

[66] See chap. 4.1.1. M. Whittaker ('"Signs and Wonders": The Pagan Background', *Studia Evangelica* 5 (1968) 155–8) claims that 'Luke may have used the phrase because of its frequent occurrence in the Septuagint, but perhaps he realized that neither word alone would have been wholly convincing to a pagan reader' (*ibid.*, 158).

[67] δύναμις is used by Luke in a special relation to both exorcisms and healings (see below, nn. 76,84). Conzelmann (*Theology* 182, esp. n. 4) shows that, for Luke, 'δυνάμις stands for miraculous power and for miracle itself'; similarly, C. K. Barrett concludes: 'δυνάμις is frequently used in the Synoptic Gospels to describe the mighty activity of God' (*The Holy Spirit and the Gospel Tradition* (London: SPCK, 1947) 78).

[68] On Luke's use of the phrase, 'what God has done', see chap. 2.3.2; 3.3.2; note Johnson, *Possessions* 61. Haenchen's remark, 'that God is the true author of the miracles corresponds to the Jewish outlook' (*Acts* 180 n. 7) introduces the false cultural dichotomy noted in chap. 1.2.3; this is equally credible as a hellenistic viewpoint.

[69] εὐεργέται is used only once in the Gospel (Luke 22.25), referring to pagan rulers. Nevertheless, the concept is important for Luke's presentation of Jesus, as is noted by Fridrichsen (*Problem of Miracle* 65–7) and demonstrated by F. W. Danker (*Luke* (Proclamation Commentaries; Philadelphia: Fortress Press, 1976) 6–17; *Benefactor* 324, 342); see also D. J. Lull, 'The Servant-Benefactor as a Model of Greatness (Luke 22:24–30)', *NovT* 28 (1986) 289–305.

[70] Jesus heals at Luke 4.38–9,40; 5.12–16,17–26; 6.6–11,17; 7.1–10,11–17,21; 8.2,41–56; 9.1,11; 19.9; 13.10–13,32; 14.2–6; 17.12–19; 18.35–42; 22.51.

exorcisms[71] which Jesus performs. The contrast with the preponderance of nature miracles in the historians is notable. Luke makes use
of two such nature miracles known to him from his sources (the
calming of the storm, Luke 8.23–7; the feeding of the 5,000, Luke
9.10–17), but omits others.[72] Thus the focus is on the way Jesus casts
out demons and heals the sick.[73] Luke alone explicitly makes the
further point that Jesus' exorcizing and healing (13.32) are linked
with God's destiny for him in Jerusalem (13.33). Although the
Gospel assumes the divine origin of such powers, the focus is on the
way they validate Jesus as the chosen agent for carrying out the
divine plan.

### 4.3.1.1 Exorcisms and healings

Many exorcisms which Luke reports are performed 'in the name of
Jesus',[74] but in his redaction of exorcism pericopes Luke is
especially concerned to note that such authority[75] and power[76] is of
divine origin. The exorcism of the Gerasene demoniac demonstrates
'what God has done' (8.39),[77] that of the epileptic child shows 'the
majesty of God' (9.43),[78] and the exorcism of the woman possessed

---

[71] Jesus exorcizes at Luke 4.33–7,41; 6.18; 8.2,26–33; 9.1,37–43,49–50; 10.17;
11.14,17–20; 13.16.

[72] Luke omits Jesus walking on the water (Mark 6.45–52), the feeding of the 4,000
(Mark 8.1–10) and the withering of the fig-tree (Mark 11.20–5); but he adds the
miraculous draught of fish to the call of the first disciples (Luke 5.1–11, cf. Mark
1.16–20).

[73] Luke depicts both aspects in individual pericopes (exorcism, 4.33–7; healing,
4.38–9) and in a summary statement (4.40–1).

[74] Luke 9.49 par Mark 9.38; Luke 10.17, cf. Mark 16.17.

[75] ἐξουσία enables exorcisms at Luke 4.36; 9.1; 10.19; it is defined as a divine
authority at 5.24. See Barrett, *Holy Spirit* 82; W. Förster, 'ἐξουσία', *TDNT* 2 (1964)
566–7.

[76] Luke notes that δύναμις is the basis for exorcisms by adding it to pericopes
where Mark has only ἐξουσία (Luke 4.36, cf. Mark 1.27; Luke 9.1, cf. Mark 6.7); at
Luke 6.19 he adds δύναμις where there is no reference to authority or power at Mark
3.10. For the use of δύναμις to convey God's activity, see Richardson, *Miracle-
Stories* 5–19; Grundmann, 'δύναμαι/δύναμις', *TDNT* 2 (1964) 301–3, 306 (and cf.
286–8 on the role of δύναμις as the expression of divine power in Stoic philosophy).

[77] This is the first occurrence of this characteristically Lukan phrase; by a slight
modification of his Markan source (Mark 5.19), Luke removes the ambiguity of ὁ
κύριος and clarifies that it was undoubtedly ὁ θεός at work in this exorcism. See
F. W. Danker, *Jesus and the New Age* (Philadelphia: Fortress Press, 1988) 184.

[78] τῷ μεγαλειότητι τοῦ θεοῦ, added to Mark 9.27; Schubert ('Luke 24' 182) calls
this 'a kind of key sentence' which links the exorcism to Luke's proof-from-prophecy
scheme.

for eighteen years is an example of 'the glorious things (τοῖς ἐνδό-
ξοις) that were done by him' (13.17).[79]

The most extensive and polemical discussion of exorcism (11.14–
26)[80] comes immediately after another exorcism, reported only
briefly (11.14). Jesus is accused of casting out demons by Beelzebul
(11.15,18b); he replies by placing himself in clear opposition to
Beelzebul. He refutes the accusation in a series of statements worked
together by Luke: a direct repudiation (11.17–18), a setting forth of
the alternatives (11.19–20), a parable highlighting the conflict
(11.21–23) and a concluding story concerning the exorcized spirit
(11.24–26).[81]

Jesus directly repudiates the notion that he would be working
against Beelzebul (equated with Satan)[82] if he were actually intend-
ing to co-operate with him (11.17–18). The parable of the strong
man (11.21–3) signifies that Beelzebul, the 'strong one', has been
overcome by Jesus, the 'stronger one' (cf. 3.16), thereby clarifying
the opposition (11.23). The saying about the exorcized spirit who
returns with seven more spirits (11.24–6) further indicates Jesus'
firm opposition to the work of Beelzebul.

The alternative interpretations of Jesus's power to exorcize are
placed side by side in two conditional sentences (11.19–20). To
heighten the significance of these sentences, the accusation (11.15) is
repeated (11.18b). The first possibility, that Jesus co-operates with
Beelzebul (11.19), had already been ruled out (11.17–18). Thus, it is
in the second sentence that Jesus offers the basis for his powers of
exorcism, expressed indirectly in the conditional construction, 'if it
is by the finger of God that I cast out demons, then the kingdom of

[79] This pericope is unique to Luke. ἔνδοξος indicates divine activity (G. Kittel,
'ἔνδοξος', *TDNT* 2 (1964) 254; Marshall, *Luke* 599); its root, δόξα, is closely linked
with the divine activity, for in the Septuagint it usually translates כבוד, 'the divine
glory which reveals the nature of God in creation and in His acts' (Kittel, 'δόξα',
*TDNT* 2 (1964) 244); see Luke 2.9; 9.26; 17.18; Acts 7.2; 12.23. On παράδοξα, see
below, n. 86.
[80] On the polemical nature of this discussion, see Fridrichsen, *Problem of Miracle*
74–5, 102–10.
[81] Both Mark and Q provide potential source material for this section of Luke.
Marshall (*Luke* 471) argues persuasively that, whereas Matthew attempted to con-
flate the two sources, Luke largely follows Q. Significant Lukan redactional features
occur at Luke 11.16, 18b, 21–2.
[82] Luke 10.18; 13.16 are both unique to Luke. In 11.18, Luke explicitly equates
Satan with Beelzebul. The parable of 11.21–2 makes clear that Satan has been
defeated (Marshall, *Luke* 477).

God has come upon you' (11.20).[83] That God enables and oversees
the exorcisms performed by Jesus is thus firmly stated in this claim,
which is central to the whole passage. Such activity reveals Jesus as
the agent selected by God.

Likewise, the fact that God is at work in the healings performed
by Jesus is evident throughout the Gospel. Luke signifies this in a
number of ways in his redaction of the pericope of the healing of the
paralytic (5.17–26). The power by which Jesus heals is the δύναμις
κυρίου (5.17).[84] The response of the healed man is thus to praise
God (5.25), not merely to thank Jesus; the same response from the
crowd (5.26)[85] underlines the fact that God is at work in this event.
The description of the healing as one of the παράδοξα of Jesus
evokes the familiar terminology applied to the activity of the
goddess Τύχη in hellenistic histories,[86] interpreting such an occurrence to hellenistic readers as a manifestation of divine power.[87]

[83] Luke replaces Jesus' early proclamation of the nearness of the kingdom (Luke
4.14–15, cf. Mark 1.15) with a less imminent message (Luke 4.43). However, Jesus
commands the 70(72) to proclaim, 'the kingdom of God has come near to you' (10.9,
cf. 10.11) and later informs the Pharisees that 'the kingdom of God is in the midst of
you' (17.21). It is clear that Luke retains some notion of a realized kingdom, since the
construction is that of 'εἰ with the indicative of reality' (BDF 372, classifying Luke
11.18 thus); see the literature cited by Marshall, *Luke* 476; Fitzmyer, *Luke* 1.267;
2.848–9, 922. The topic of eschatology in Luke–Acts has been much debated; see the
schematic summary of Fitzmyer (*Luke* 1.231–5) and the more detailed discussions of
Wilson (*Gentiles* 59–87) and E. Franklin (*Christ the Lord: A Study in the Purpose and
Theology of Luke–Acts* (Philadelphia: Westminster, 1975) 9–47).
[84] For δύναμις as a description of miracles in hellenistic contexts, see Grundmann, 'δύναμαι/δύναμις' 289, esp. n. 23. Marshall (*Luke* 212) notes, 'κύριος used
without the article means God'; see also C. H. Talbert, *Literary Patterns, Theological
Themes and the Genre of Luke–Acts* (Missoula, Mont.: Scholars Press, 1974) 19. Luke
also adds δύναμις to his reports of healings at 6.19; 8.46; cf. 9.1–2.
[85] Luke finds this response already in his source (Mark 2.12); he strengthens the
point by developing the response of the onlookers into a threefold doxology (Luke
5.26). This same reaction to healings is found often in the Gospel (7.16; 13.13;
17.15,18; 18.43, all unique to Luke; cf. 2.20; 24.53) and in Acts (4.21; 11.18; 13.48;
21.20). Such a mood of praise has already been set in the prologue; see Luke
1.46–8,58,63; 2.12,14,18,20,28,33–4,38. Van Unnik ('Remarks' 11) indicates that this
technique was common in hellenistic histories, but provides no specific references;
Barrett (*Holy Spirit* 57) refers to Philostratus, *Vit. Ap.* 4.20.
[86] See chap. 3.1.3; on the use of the term in other ancient accounts of healing, see
A. Oepke, 'ἰάομαι', *TDNT* 3 (1965) 206. The word is not used by any other New
Testament writer; at Luke 13.17 ἔνδοξα is applied to the healing of the infirm
woman.
[87] Thus in contrast to the widespread and popular identification of the workings of
Fortune as 'paradoxical', attested by the historiographical sources which we have
examined, Luke understands the healings of Jesus to be consistent indications of the
way in which God is acting in his life. See also Oepke, 'ἰάομαι' 211–13.

Subsequent healings are thus to be interpreted in the light of this programmatic occurrence.[88]

### 4.3.1.2 Signs and the sign

On occasions in Luke's Gospel, however, Jesus has appeared unwilling to allow his actions to be interpreted as signs which indicate God's activity in his life. Despite his obvious reputation as one who performed signs (Luke 23.8)[89] and mighty works (19.37),[90] Luke notes Jesus' adverse reactions to this view. Those who seek from him a sign from heaven are said to be testing him (11.16)[91] and it is an evil generation which seeks a sign (11.29). Jesus insists that 'the kingdom of God is not coming with signs to be observed' (17.20); even if this were the case, and the signs were as clear and obvious as flashes of lightning (17.24),[92] their meaning would not be apparent to the soothsayers who 'do not know how to interpret the present time' (12.56). Thus Jesus refuses to perform a sign on the cross, when the taunting soldiers dare him to save himself (23.39); all that he has offered is the curious statement that 'no sign shall be given except the sign of Jonah' (11.29).

When some of his listeners urgently request a sign to indicate when his prediction of the destruction of the Jerusalem Temple will come about (21.7), Jesus again warns against seeking such signs (21.8) and postpones until the very end (21.9) the time of the signs of earthly distress (21.11) and cosmic upheaval (21.25).[93] Only the

---

[88] Thus, Kee, *Miracle* 205.

[89] Luke alone notes that Herod was glad to see Jesus because 'he was hoping to see some sign (τι σημεῖον) done by him'.

[90] Luke alone notes that the crowd's acclamation of Jesus as he enters Jerusalem is 'for all the mighty works that they had seen'. See also Luke 10.13–15, where Jesus acknowledges that he has done 'mighty works' in Chorazin, Bethsaida and Capernaum.

[91] At Luke 4.2–13 it is the devil who tests, and at 22.40–6 such testing runs contrary to the will of God. See also 10.25 and 22.28; cf. Acts 15.10. Marshall (*Luke* 473) suggests that the request for a sign was because 'exorcisms, it is implied, were inadequate as a proof of divine authorization'. However, Jesus' reply indicates that 'to ask for a special sign now was to deny the activity of God in all that Jesus had hitherto done' (Barrett, *Holy Spirit* 90). On the polemic here, see Fridrichsen, *Problem of Miracle* 76–7.

[92] Marshall, *Luke* 660–1; *contra*, Conzelmann, *Theology* 124; Fitzmyer, *Luke* 2.1170; Danker, *Luke* 33, who emphasize its suddenness.

[93] Luke redacts Mark's eschatological discourse so as to provide a more precise timetable by means of certain phrases (21.6,9,12,20,24,28); see Conzelmann, *Theology* 126–7; Fitzmyer, *Luke* 2.1327, 1388. The signs fall into the latter phases of this timetable (Berger, 'Prodigien' 1436 n. 26). Marshall (*Luke* 765–6) notes that,

capture of Jerusalem itself is indirectly allowed to function as a sign (21.20), but after this there will still be much more to happen before the end will come.[94]

The explanation for Jesus' apparent refusal to perform any sign lies in the prologue to the Gospel, where it is twice declared that Jesus himself is a sign (σημεῖον, 2.12.34).[95] The belief that Jesus will perform signs which point to some event of significance external to himself is misguided, for it is Jesus himself who is the sign. To examine his actions with the expectation that they will illuminate the significance of other events is to read the equation in reverse order. What is required, rather, is to read Jesus as the sign of divine providence; it is by examining everything that Jesus did that one can make sense of God's plan and purpose. So when Peter declares that Jesus is 'a man attested to you by God' (Acts 2.22) he is stating that Jesus is first of all a sign of who God is and what God does. Likewise Simeon has declared that Jesus signifies God's intentions to bring the Gospel to the Gentiles, even at the cost of dividing Israel (Luke 2.34–5).[96]

Thus, to ask Jesus for a sign which interprets other events is futile, for the only true sign is Jesus, who allows one to interpret events as they fit within the plan of God. The only sign which Jesus will give is 'the sign of Jonah' (11.29–30), alluding to his own resurrection,[97] yet even so, 'something greater than Jonah is here' (11.32). Even at the moment of death, Jesus remains a sign of divine providence, as is attested by the centurion who 'glorified God' (24.47).[98] This has been the function of the 'wonders and signs' performed by Jesus during his lifetime; his own comments, in situations of dispute,

although such signs are 'typical of apocalyptic', Luke's redaction makes the point 'that such phenomena are not apocalyptic signs of the End'. For similar examples in hellenistic literature, see Berger, 'Prodigien' 1437 n. 28.

[94] The distress will last 'until the times of the Gentiles are fulfilled' (Luke 21.24). Luke's redaction (in the Western text) of the Joel citation at Acts 2.17 also shows his view that such signs belong to the end of time; he adds ἐν ταῖς ἐσχάταις ἡμέραις to Joel 2.28 (see Berger, 'Prodigien' 1438).

[95] For the Septuagintal formulation used in 2.12, see Rengstorf, 'σημεῖον' 231 n. 213; Marshall (*Luke* 110) notes that 'God confirms what he is about to do by the sign'.

[96] On the apologetic force of Simeon's oracle, against those who reject Jesus as God's sign, see Rengstorf, 'σημεῖον' 238–9; Marshall, *Luke* 22; Fitzmyer, *Luke* 1.430.

[97] J. Jeremias, ''Ιωνᾶς', *TDNT* 3 (1965) 409; for a survey of alternative interpretations, see Marshall, *Luke* 482–5.

[98] The 'signs' of darkness and the tearing of the Temple curtain (23.44–5) indicate the temporary absence of God's reign (Fitzmyer, *Luke* 2.1514); cf. the opposite function of signs in hellenistic histories (see above, n. 6 and chap. 4.2.1). For a comparison between Jesus and Romulus, see Trompf, *Idea* 151–2.

provide a foundation for his apologetic claim that God is at work through these miracles.[99]

### 4.3.2 Wonders and signs done through the Apostles

The many reports of wonders and signs which follow in the first half of Acts are thus to be read in this light. These phenomena are integrally related to the proclamation about Jesus and the performance of miracles in his name. Since Jesus is central to God's preordained plan, the recurrence of such signs function as reminders that the divine providence which was evident in the life of Jesus continues to watch over events in the early church. The wonders and signs performed by each of the major figures in Acts 1–15 thus attest to continuing divine activity in the early church.[100]

This continuity is indicated in the summary references to the wonders and signs performed by all the apostles (Acts 2.43; 5.12) and by Stephen (6.8) and to the powerful deeds performed by Paul (19.11),[101] for they are acts of healing and exorcism (5.15–16; 19.12), the same type of wondrous deeds which Jesus performed. When Luke reports the details of four instances of wonders and signs being performed,[102] he invariably relates the general terms (τέρατα καὶ σημεῖα)[103] to particular instances of healing or exorcism. In each case, he also apologetically emphasizes the continuity by specifying that the miracles were done 'in the name of Jesus' or that they signify God's activity.[104]

The healing of the lame man performed by Peter and John at the Beautiful Gate of the Temple (3.1–10) stands as a reminder of the nature and function of miracles performed by the apostles; they are the same as those performed by Jesus in essential features. Although the divine nature of the healing is immediately recognized by both

---

[99] For the apologetic use of Jesus' miracles in early second-century literature, see Wilken, *The Christians* 99–100.

[100] See Rengstorf, 'σημεῖον' 240, for signs as pointers to God.

[101] On the programmatic role of 19.11 for Luke's description of Paul, see R. L. Brawley, 'Paul in Acts: Lucan Apology and Conciliation', *Luke–Acts: New Perspectives* (ed. Talbert) 137.

[102] The healing of the lame man (Acts 3.1–4.22); the prayer of the believers (4.23–31); the encounter with Simon in Samaria (8.4–21); missionary work of Barnabas and Paul in Iconium (14.1–7; 15.12).

[103] Luke uses this order at Acts 2.19,22,43, 6.8, possibly to conform to the version of Exod 7.3 which Stephen quotes at Acts 7.36. The distinction in emphasis which is seen in the varying orders by Rengstorf ('τέρας' 125) is overly subtle.

[104] Rengstorf ('σημεῖον' 242, esp. nn. 292, 294) notes also the preponderance of divine passives in association with signs.

the healed man (3.8) and the onlookers (3.9–10), others are astounded (ἔκθαμβοι, 3.11; θαυμάζετε, 3.12) and seem, to assume that it was the apostles' own power or piety (3.12) which enabled them to do this.

Peter's speech to the people (3.12–26) begins as an apologetic defence of his actions. He turns the emphasis away from the disciples' 'power or piety' (3.12) to the originator of their power and the object of their piety, namely, God (3.13), who thus becomes the subject of the whole speech. This particular healing is set into the context of God's overall providence. It is God who has raised (3.15) and glorified (3.13) Jesus; it was in the name of this Jesus (3.16; cf. 3.6) that the healing occurred. As he continues his speech, Peter deals not with the healing, but with the relationship between God and Jesus, through the theme of prophecy. What has happened in Jesus is fulfilment of God's intentions which were signalled by all the prophets (3.18) from of old (3.21), in Moses (3.22–3) and from Samuel onwards (3.24). The conclusion of the speech reinforces the basic answer to the initial question: God sent Jesus to the people to bless them (3.26). Thus, the healing which took place was a very specific indication of God's providential care for humanity.

The dialogue which ensues within the Sanhedrin develops the same theme. When the priests wish to know 'by what power or by what name did you do this?' (4.7), Peter again replies that they healed 'by the name of Jesus Christ of Nazareth' (4.10; cf. 4.12), who is again identified as the one whom 'God raised' (4.10). Thus, this good deed (εὐεργεσία, 4.9)[105] is recognized as a sign (σημεῖον, 4.16, 22) of the divine activity in the apostles (4.21).[106] In these two scenes of debate, Luke has rebutted objections and asserted that the apostles' deed was divinely authorized.[107]

The prayer of the believers (4.24–30) which follows immediately after the release of Peter and John from custody (4.23) further confirms this aspect of the apostolic behaviour. Such signs and wonders as do occur are healings performed 'in the name of your

---

[105] Cf. Acts 10.38, where the cognate verb describes Jesus' activity. See Danker, *Luke* 15.

[106] Luke's final comment on the healing is overly ambitious, for it is clear from the ensuing events (Acts 5.17–40) that the priests and Sadducees were not included in 'all people' (πάντες) who recognized God at work in this healing (4.21).

[107] This healing stands as a paradigm for the subsequent healings by Peter in Jerusalem (5.15–16), Lydda (9.33–5) and Joppa (9.36–42); and by Paul in Lystra (14.8–10), Ephesus (19.11), Troas (20.7–12) and Malta (28.8,9); see Johnson, *Possessions* 193–4, 196; Adams, 'Suffering' 80.

holy servant Jesus' (4.30). Luke here links these deeds very closely with the plan of God; the hand of God which enables these healings (4.30) is the same divine hand which effected the predestined plan (4.28) of the passion of Jesus (4.27). This characteristically Lukan phrase[108] evokes the common Septuagintal anthropomorphism for 'God's action in history'[109] which Luke will later repeat in connection with God's blinding of Bar-Jesus (13.11) as well as the growth of the church in Antioch (11.21) and the very creation of the world by God (7.50, quoting Isa 66.2).

Again in this passage, the assertion of divine providence through the apostles' healings is made within an apologetic context. The 'hand and plan' of God was active, in the past, in response to plotting against Jesus (4.25b–27); the performance of signs and wonders is now a fitting rebuke to the threats uttered by the Jerusalem council (4.29a), matching with actions the words which God enables the apostles to speak (4.29b).[110] The shaking which follows the prayer, linked with the renewed filling by the Holy Spirit (4.31), further underlines God's providential presence.[111]

Just as God's hand guided the events of Jesus' passion in the past (4.25–8), so God's hand even now (καὶ τὰ νῦν, 4.29)[112] guides events in Jerusalem, including the apostolic signs and wonders (4.29–31). This is to be expected of the God whose providence encompasses not only 'the heaven and the earth and the sea', but also 'everything (πάντα) in them' (4.24).[113] This comprehensive scope of divine providence thus assures the continuity of God's actions through the passion of Jesus and in the deeds of the apostles.

A third incident involving the performance of miraculous deeds described as signs leads to a further assertion of God's activity through such phenomena. The 'signs and great miracles' (σημεῖα καὶ

---

[108] See Luke 1.66; Acts 4.28,30; 7.50; 11.21; 13.11; for other New Testament uses, see E. Lohse, 'χείρ', *TDNT* 9 (1974) 431.

[109] Lohse, 'χείρ' 427; see also Rengstorf, 'τέρας' 125. The hand of God is linked with the divine plan and purpose at Isa 14.24–7.

[110] The boldness (παρρησία) of the apostles is enabled by God; see also Acts 4.31; 14.3; Adams, 'Suffering' 69–74. At 4.13, the παρρησία of Peter and John is attributed to the fact that 'they had been with Jesus'. This term described the method commonly used by the ideal philosophical speaker; see Dio Chrysostom, *Or.* 32.11; 35.1–2.

[111] Foakes Jackson and Lake, *Beginnings* 4.47; Haenchen (*Acts* 229) calls this 'a vivid device which he dared to borrow from pagan religion'.

[112] The phrase is found in the New Testament only in Acts, each time as a transition from recalling past deeds to declaring present actions; see 5.38; 20.32; 27.22 (cf. 17.30).

[113] The invocation of the prayer evokes the fourth commandment (Exod 20.11); see also Ps 146.6; Acts 14.15; and cf. Acts 17.24.

δυνάμεις μεγάλας, 8.13) performed by Philip, which are specified as exorcisms and healings (8.7), are contrasted with the magic of Simon,[114] who was popularly regarded as 'that power of God which is called Great' (8.10).[115] Peter's polemic is apologetic, as he reveals the falsity of this popular view; Simon is 'in the gall of bitterness and in the bond in iniquity' (8.23). In place of this impiety, Peter and John offer 'the gift of God' (8.20) and speak the same 'word of the Lord' (8.25) which Philip has already declared (8.14). Their power is the real one, for it comes from the Holy Spirit (8.19), whence Philip's power also came.[116]

The fourth full report of apostolic signs and wonders occurs in Iconium, where Barnabas and Paul were 'speaking boldly for the Lord, who bore witness to the word of his grace, granting signs and wonders (σημεῖα καὶ τέρατα) to be done by their hands' (14.3). These deeds thus serve as testimony which authenticates the preaching of Barnabas and Paul.[117] Luke immediately gives an example of such signs and wonders, in the healing of the cripple in Lystra (14.8–10).[118] In contrast to the misinterpretation of this event by the crowds (14.11–13), Barnabas and Paul emphasize that they are able to heal only because they are so enabled by the God whose providence encompasses all creation (14.15; cf. 4.24).[119] In their report to the Jerusalem council (15.12), Paul and Barnabas recall such signs

---

[114] For the common view that Luke was attacking popular magical customs, see A. D. Nock, 'Paul and the Magus', Beginnings (ed. Foakes Jackson and Lake) 5.188; Grundmann, 'δύναμαι/δύναμις' 302–3; Fridrichsen, Problem of Miracle 62–3, 85–9; Kee, Miracle 214–15; Haenchen, Acts 308. Against this, J. M. Hull (Hellenistic Magic and the Synoptic Tradition (SBT 2/28; Naperville, Ill.: Alec R. Allenson, 1974) 105–8) argues that Luke in fact represents 'the tradition penetrated by magic' and D. E. Aune ('Magic in Early Christianity', ANRW II.23.2, 1507–57) traces magical motifs and techniques in early Christian literature, including Luke–Acts. However, Achtemeier ('Lukan Perspective' 556–9) demonstrates that the evidence is capable of being interpreted in either way. For a thorough criticism of Hull, see Sanders and Davies, Synoptic Gospels 278–83; for a comprehensive study of magic in Luke–Acts, see S. R. Garrett, The Demise of the Devil (Philadelphia: Fortress Press, 1989).

[115] For τοῦ θεοῦ as a Lukan addition to the divine title, see Foakes Jackson and Lake, Beginnings 4.91; Haenchen, Acts 303.

[116] Philip is one of the 'seven men of good repute' who are 'full of the Spirit and of wisdom' (6.3).

[117] They are παρρησιαζόμενοι (14.3), an activity whose divine origin has already been established (see above, n. 110). For the parallels between 14.3 and 5.12, see Haenchen, Acts 420.

[118] This miracle 'is not an isolated event, an exceptional case, but a link in a long chain' (Haenchen, Acts 423). On parallels with 3.2–8, see Foakes Jackson and Lake Beginnings 4.163.

[119] For 'the living God' as a polemic against idols, see 1 Thess 1.9; Foakes Jackson and Lake (Beginnings 4.166) refer also to Acts 17.25,28.

and wonders (σημεῖα καὶ τέρατα), note their divine origin (ὅσα ἐποίησεν ὁ θεός) and explain that their purpose within the plan of God was to bring the Gospel to the Gentiles through them (ἐν τοῖς ἔθνεσιν δι αὐτῶν). These deeds continue to show God at work in history.

The same insight is found when Luke reports exorcisms performed by Paul. The power which enables him to cast out demons is recognized by the Philippian slave girl: 'these men are servants of the Most High God' (16.17). However, such divinely bestowed powers are not able to be replicated simply by repeating a formula (19.13,15), as is demonstrated in the comic picture of the defeat and scattering of the seven Jewish exorcists in Ephesus (19.16). Evoking magical formulas (13.8) is futile, for the process of exorcism is a battle in which the lines are clearly drawn between the devil and the Spirit-filled agents of God (13.9–10) and in which 'the hand of the Lord' inevitably brings victory (13.11). Exorcism is thus a clear manifestation of the divine superintendence of events.

Thus, each of the major apostolic figures acts in conformity with the way Peter understands Jesus to have acted, performing signs and wonders[120] which attest to God's involvement in, and oversight of, their deeds and words. Such miraculous activity attests to one of Luke's central affirmations, namely that the story of Jesus and the early church is one of the continuity of God's plan, demonstrating God's ongoing guidance of human history. These portents are proof of such divine providence.

## 4.4 Conclusions

Luke reports numerous miraculous occurrences, in which healings, exorcisms or unspecified signs and wonders are performed. Such phenomena are common in various types of literature of the hellenistic period. A comparison of the types and functions of these portentous events in Luke–Acts and hellenistic histories reveals both similarities and differences.

Both Diodorus and Dionysius reflect the common viewpoint that portents are signs sent from the gods, at times presenting a Stoic-like justification for this claim. Josephus relates portentous events most particularly to his overarching interest in divine providence. Luke

---

[120] There are other incidents in Acts, including some nature miracles, which, although not explicitly designated as such, might be regarded as signs or wonders; see 5.19; 9.8; 12.7,10; 13.11; 16.26; 19.11; 28.3–5.

also reflects this connection, often indicating the divine origin and purpose of such events. Luke's theocentric outlook is further demonstrated by his depiction of portents as proof of divine providence.

Each of the major writers we have examined displays a critical perspective on portents. Such events are recounted not solely for entertainment value, but as illustrations of divine guidance. In the context of hellenistic historiography, Luke shows a restrained use of portents, which normally are focussed on the role of Jesus, or an apostle, as divine agent, and thus are invariably related to his interest in divine guidance. His reports of exorcisms especially reveal the opposition to the plan of God.

Luke's single most important contribution in this matter is his presentation of Jesus as the supreme sign of God's acting in history. All other signs are to be measured by what Jesus has shown and spoken about God. Thus, as well as this theocentric outlook, Luke offers a theological perspective on portents. The function of the signs and wonders is consistently apologetic, in the service of the major thesis concerning divine providence. As Jesus, Paul and the apostles each defend their miraculous activity in the face of opposition, they insist that such deeds are enabled and directed by God. Furthermore, the presence of signs and wonders in the early church is an assertion of continuity with the life of Jesus, all of which points to the ongoing providence of God.

# 5

## EPIPHANIES: INSPIRED INDICATIONS OF THE PLAN OF GOD

At strategic places throughout his work, Luke reports epiphanies in which God, or a divine agent, appears and guides the course of events. Such epiphanies occur at the beginning of Jesus' life and his ministry[1] as well as in various places in the history of the early church.[2] In addition, the final chapter of the Gospel includes reports of three epiphanies of Jesus and angelic figures.[3] Each of these incidents is strategically related to the course of events in Luke's history, for such epiphanies indicate the intentions of God with regard to the direction in which history proceeds. This function of asserting the divine will and guiding human actions is similar to the role played by such phenomena in hellenistic histories, especially the significance attached to dreams as indicators of the gods' desires.

### 5.1 Epiphanies in hellenistic historiography

#### 5.1.1 Philosophic views of divination and providence

In the previous chapter, we noted the relationship between divination and providence which was part of Stoic belief in the ancient world, paying particular attention to divination by 'artificial' means. Our attention now turns to those 'natural' means of divination which, in Stoic belief, provided still further evidence for the existence of the gods and their providential guidance of events.[4] The

[1] Luke 1.11–22,26–38; 2.9–15; 3.22; 9.30–2; 22.43.
[2] In Jerusalem (Acts 2.3; 5.19–20; 12.7–11,23; 22.17–21; 23.11); on the road to Damascus (9.3–6; 22.6–8; 26.13–18); in Joppa (10.3–7,10–16; 11.5–10), Caesarea (10.30–2; 11.13–14), Troas (16.9–10) and Corinth (18.9); and on board ship near Crete (27.23–4).
[3] At the tomb (Luke 24.4–7), on the road to Emmaus (24.15–31) and in Jerusalem (24.36–49); see also Acts 1.3,9–11.
[4] Cicero, *De nat. deor.* 1.20.55; 2.5.13. A detailed elaboration is given in *De nat. deor.* 2.3.7–4.12; see the comments by Pease, *De Natvra Deorvm* 342; Nock, 'Religious Attitudes', *ERAW* 2.535 n. 6. For a survey of the varieties of epiphanies in

Stoic Lucilius Balbus proposed that divination 'affords the very strongest proof that man's welfare is studied by divine providence' (*De nat. deor.* 2.65.162), arguing that 'this power or art or instinct[5] therefore has clearly been bestowed by the immortal gods on man, and on no other creature, for the ascertainment of future events' (*De nat. deor.* 2.65.163). This opinion was not universally held, however, for 'nothing provokes the ridicule of Epicurus so much as the art of prophecy' (*De nat. deor.* 2.65.162).[6]

Evidence that the Stoics also argued in the opposite direction, from the existence of the gods to the validity of divination, is to be found in the syllogism (as stated by Cicero's Stoic brother Quintus) that 'if the kinds of divination which we have inherited from our forefathers and now practise are trustworthy, then there are gods and, conversely, if there are gods, then there are men who have the power of divination' (*De div.* 1.5.9).[7] Again, this position was opposed by the Epicureans, whose rejection of providence logically required them also to reject divination.[8]

In his discussion of divination, Cicero provides for two basic types of 'natural' divination: *somniorum aut vaticinationum praedictione* (*De div.* 1.6.12), each of which is justified by the Stoics on the basis of their belief in providence.[9] Tertullian notes that 'the Stoics

ancient Greek literature, see E. Pax, *Epiphaneia; ein religions-geschichtlicher Beitrag zur biblischen Theologie* (Münchener Theologische Studien 10; München: Karl Zink, 1955) 15–19.

[5] Pease (*De Natvra Deorvm* 966) suggests that these three terms, although presented as co-ordinates, should be read as a whole (*vis*, the power of divination) and its parts (*ars*, artificial divination, and *natura*, natural divination). Cf. *De div.* 1.6.11–12, where the twofold division is quite clear; and see chap. 4 n. 5.

[6] See also Diogenes Laertius, *Lives* 10.135. Origen (*Contra Celsum* 4.88) notes this dispute without naming the parties. For the Stoic use of epiphanies 'im Dienste antiepikureischer Tendenzen', see Pax, *Epiphaneia* 47–8.

[7] For the use of this argument in other literature, see Pease, *De Divinatione* 69. This syllogism was supported by a series of five steps in the argument, which is presented by Quintus (*De div.* 1.38.82–3) and repeated by Cicero (2.49.101–2), before being refuted by Cicero himself (2.49.103–6). See also *De div.* 2.17–41; *De nat. deor.* 1.20.55; *De leg.* 2.3.32–3.

[8] On the differences of opinion concerning divination amongst the classical philosophers, see Quintilian, *Instit. or.* 5.7.35; Cicero, *De div.* 1.3.5–7, and his comments on the opposition expressed by Xenophanes (1.40.87), Epicurus (1.3.5,49.109; 2.17.40) and Carneades (1.4.7,49.109). See Pease, *De Divinatione* 55 (on Epicurus) and 64 (on Carneades); for a survey of philosophic views on dreams, see J. S. Hanson, 'Dreams and Visions in the Graeco-Roman World and Early Christianity', *ANRW* II.23.2, 1399–400. For the importance of the debate between Carneades and Chrysippus in subsequent Greek literature, see Amand, *Fatalisme* (*passim*).

[9] The same division is also drawn at *De div.* 1.18.34. The latter type, frenzied (i.e. inspired) prophecy, will be treated in the following chapter.

are very fond of saying that God, in his most watchful providence
(*providentissimum*) over every institution, gave us dreams amongst
other preservatives of the arts and sciences of divination, as the
especial support of the natural oracle' (*De anima* 46).[10] Cicero
records Chrysippus' definition of dreams as 'visions sent by the
gods' (*De div*. 2.63.130) and Posidonius' three explanations of the
divine origin of dreams (*De div*. 1.30.64).[11] Chalcidius comments
likewise that the Stoics regarded dreams as *instrumentibus divinis
potestatibus* (*ad Tim*. 251 = SVF 2.1198) and Quintus claims that
two instances 'which are so often recounted by Stoic writers' of
dreams which accurately foretold the future[12] are proofs that
dreams are divinely inspired (*divinitus*, *De div*. 1.28.57). Such a
belief is rebutted by Cicero himself, as he disputes the doctrine of
συμπάθεια (*De div*. 2.69.142) which sees a connection between
dreams and the laws of nature (*De div*. 2.70.144).[13]

### 5.1.2 Divination by dreams or visions

Towards the end of a bitter speech opposing the return of the exiled
Marcius, Dionysius has the Roman consul Minucius advance the
sceptical proposition that 'the gods have not given it to any mortal
creature to possess sure knowledge of future events' (RA 8.27.1).[14]
Nevertheless, popular belief was that it was quite possible for
humans to possess such prophetic powers, and hellenistic histories

[10] For the popularity of this view in antiquity, see E. R. Dodds, *The Greeks and the
Irrational* (Sather Classical Lectures 25; Berkeley and Los Angeles: University of
California Press, 1951) 107–10, 118–20. Pax (*Epiphaneia* 83) notes that, for the
Greeks, 'Gotteserkenntnis weniger sache des Denkens als des Sehens ist'.
[11] (1) The soul's kinship with the gods (cf. Acts 17.28–9); (2) the doctrine of
demons; (3) direct conversation with the gods. For other references to these beliefs,
see Pease, *De Divinatione* 208–9.
[12] The dream about Simonides (*De div*. 1.27.56) and that of the two Arcadians (*De
div*. 1.27.57). Chrysippus assembled a large catalogue of dreams (*De div*. 1.20.39), one
of which is the oft-repeated dream about an egg (*De div*. 2.65.134 = *SVF* 2.1201; see
also SVF 2.1202–3; Pease, *De Divinatione* 562–3).
[13] See also *De div*. 2.60.124,71.147; *De nat. deor*. 3.39.93; and Cicero's own comment on the egg dream: 'obscure messages by means of dreams are utterly inconsistent with the dignity of gods' (*De div*. 2.65.134).
[14] A similar scepticism regarding the possibility of predicting the future is
expressed at RA 13.6.4; 19.13.2; and *On Thuc*. 40. Cf. the epitome of Epicurus: 'no
means of predicting the future really exists, and if it did, we must regard whatever
happens according to it as nothing to us' (Diogenes Laertius, *Lives* 10.135). On the
Epicurean scorn of dreams, see Cicero, *De div*. 1.30.62,39.87.

regularly included examples of those who predict the future on the basis of dreams or visions[15] which they experience.[16]

At the end of his account of the dream which was seen by Publius and Marcus Tarquinius (RA 5.54.1), Dionysius indicates his motive for including such a phenomenon in his history. Whereas another historian would have given only a bare outline of the course of events concerning the conspiracy, Dionysius tells all the details to show the causes, means, motives and instances of divine intervention (RA 5.56.1). Visions or auditions thus function as a means of declaring divine providence, in both its positive and negative forms:[17] they signify both the favour of the gods[18] and the displeasure of the gods with those who have violated the customs of religion[19] or the rules of battle.[20]

Indeed, most of the dreams reported by Dionysius play an important role in the progress of events. The founding of Alba Longa occurred in accordance with the vision (or voice) which instructed

[15] Hanson ('Dreams and Visions' 1409) notes 'the rather rigid modern distinction between the terms dream (a sleeping phenomenon) and vision (a waking phenomenon) is not paralleled in antiquity'. On the development of the terminology for dreams, see A. H. M. Kessells, *Studies on the Dream in Greek Literature* 174–225; Hanson, 'Dreams and Visions' 1407–9.

[16] Recent investigators have noted the predictive nature of dreams in classical Greek literature; see Kessels, *Studies on the Dream* 152 on Homer; R. C. A. van Lieshout, *Greeks on Dreams* (Utrecht: HES, 1980) 116–18 on Plato, 136–7 on various authors. In hellenistic times, examples of accurate predictions in dreams were widespread and popular; see the collection of examples retold by Quintus (*De div.* 1.20.39–30.65). From the time of the Empire we have the *Oneirocritica* of Artemidorus and Aelius Aristides' discussion of the various typologies of dreams; see C. A. Behr, *Aelius Aristides and the Sacred Tales* (Amsterdam: A. M. Hakkert, 1968) 171–95; Pease, *De Divinatione* 161 with further literature cited; Dodds, *Irrational* 106–8, 110–15, and *Pagan and Christian in an Age of Anxiety: Some Aspects of Religious Experience from Marcus Aurelius to Constantine* (Cambridge University Press, 1965) 39–45; cf. Hanson, 'Dreams and Visions' 1401.

[17] For examples of this in a cross-section of ancient literature, see Brawley, 'Paul in Acts' 138; on the divine nature of dreams, see van Lieshout, *Greeks on Dreams* 34–8, 116–18, 131–2, 136–7, 204–6; Kessells, *Studies on the Dream* 153–5; Dodds, *Irrational* 107–10. Polybius offers a most insightful comment on the ready acceptance of such phenomena; Scipio managed to persuade his men 'to face perilous enterprises' by instilling in them the belief that his projects were divinely inspired (*Hist.* 10.2.12), namely by referring to 'dreams and omens' (*Hist.* 10.2.9). In fact, as Polybius wryly comments, 'everything he did was done with calculation and foresight' (*Hist.* 10.2.13). A similar use of a vision is attributed to Eumenes by Diodorus (BH 18.60.4; see Eumenes' rise to power in 18.61.2–63.6).

[18] Twice to Aeneas (RA 1.56.3–5, 1.57.4), to Faunus (5.16.3) and to the Roman reformers (10.2.2).

[19] Titus Latinius at RA 7.68.3–6; see also 8.89.4–5.

[20] Pyrrhus, RA 20.12.1–2, who had plundered the temple of Persephone in Locris (10.9.1–2).

Aeneas (RA 1.66.1, referring back to 1.56.3–5),[21] whilst the treaty between the Trojans and the original Greek inhabitants of the area (RA 1.59.1,60.2) was drawn up because of a vision seen by Aeneas (RA 1.57.4). The introduction of democratic reforms into Rome in 459 BCE (10.3.3–6) occurred as a result of visions, portents and oracles (RA 10.2.1–5).[22] The apologetic programme outlined by Dionysius in his introduction[23] is developed extensively in his report of the first sedition (RA 7.66.1), when he reports a number of Roman rituals (RA 7.70.1–72.18) which prove that 'the founders of Rome are not barbarians, but Greeks' (RA 7.72.18).[24] The validity of these rituals is underscored by the recurring dream of Titus Latinius (RA 7.68.1–2). Dreams or visions thus occupy strategic places, when they appear in Dionysius' history.

In the early 'mythological' section (Books 1–5) of the history of Diodorus, where they are relatively more frequent, dreams are again related to providence: six visions indicate divine favour[25] whilst three convey the dissatisfaction of the gods.[26] In subsequent books, eight more dreams are recounted, four indicating divine displeasure[27] whilst three convey positive messages from the gods.[28]

Most significant in Diodorus' work are his reports of manifestations of gods in which future events are signalled in advance.[29] Three such incidents occur as a result of divine providence: two stars appear over the heads of the Dioscori, signalling that Orpheus is rescued by θεῶν προνοίᾳ (BH 4.43.1–2),[30] Glaucus the sea god

[21] See also BH 7.5.5–7, where the vision has a similar function.

[22] The occurrence of dreams in association with omens or oracles is common; see also RA 1.56.3–5 and 1.55.1–5,67.1; 1.57.4 and 1.59.4; 7.68.1–2 and 7.68.3–6; 8.89.4 and 8.89.5; 20.9.1 and 20.12.1–2.

[23] See chap. 2.1

[24] See also RA 7.70.1,72.4; and note his comments at 1.90.2.

[25] Osiris to Semele (BH 1.23.4–5), Hephaestus to the father of Sesoosis, (1.53.9), Cybele to Myrira (3.55.8), the two stars of the Samothracian deities to Orpheus (4.43.2) and to Corybantes (5.49.6), and Memithea who appears in a dream to heal the suffering and restore the diseased (5.63.2).

[26] The god of Thebes to Sabaco (BH 1.65.5–6), the Fates to Althaea (4.34.6) and Dionysius to Theseus (5.51.4).

[27] A dream of Aeneas (BH 7.5.5), a dream of the Athenian general Thrasybulus (13.97.6–7), Apollo to one of the Tyrians (17.41.7) and dreams of Philip (29.25.1).

[28] A dream of Alexander (BH 17.103.7–8), a wondrous dream of Eumenes (18.60.4) and a dream of Seleucus (19.90.3–4).

[29] See BH 1.53.9, fulfilled at 1.55.1–2; 4.34.6, fulfilled at 4.34.7; 4.43.2, fulfilled immediately; 4.48.6–7, fulfilled at 4.49.2; 13.97.6–7, fulfilled at 13.99.3–6; 17.103.7, fulfilled immediately; 19.40.4, fulfilled at 19.91.1–92.5.

[30] On the Stoic use of astrological phenomena to prove divine providence, see Cicero, *De nat. deor.* 2.5.15; 2.40.101–44.114. For Posidonius' enthusiasm for this proof, see Pease, *De Natvra Deorvm* 631.

appears to Heracles and the Argonauts by θεῶν προνοίᾳ (BH
4.48.6–7),[31] and the vision of a snake which Alexander saw in his
sleep is attributed by some εἰς θεῶν πρόνοιαν (BH 17.103.7). These
incidents make explicit what underlies the use of epiphanies by these
two historians, namely the Stoic position, as presented by Quintus,
that 'the human soul has an inherent power of presaging or fore-
knowing infused into it from without, and made a part of it by the
will of God' (Cicero, *De div.* 1.31.66).[32] Such epiphanies signify
divine providence.

### 5.2 Epiphanies in Josephus

#### 5.2.1 A critical appraisal of divination

In one of his discussions of Essene prophecy,[33] Josephus praises the
powers of Manaemus, the Essene diviner (μάντις), who 'had from
God a foreknowledge (πρόγνωσιν) of the future' (AJ 15.373),
and defends his reporting of such things, however incredible (παράδοξα), on the basis that such men (the Essenes) had been 'vouch-
safed knowledge of divine things' (AJ 15.379). Indeed, Josephus
himself had such a power of divination (μάντις), which was not a
fabrication made out of fear, but was genuinely divine (θείας, BJ
4.625).[34]

Yet although his basic position shows affinities with the Stoic
view of divination, Josephus does not uncritically accept every
instance of divination. He criticizes the divinatory activity of
Balaam (AJ 4.108–57) and the witch of Endor (AJ 6.220),[35]

[31] Balbus summarizes the Stoic position concerning epiphanies: 'often has the
apparition of a divine form compelled anyone that it is not either feeble-minded or
impious to admit the real presence of the gods' (Cicero, *De nat. deor.* 2.2.6). On
similarly worded attacks made on Epicureans, see Pease, *De Divinatione* 55, 419; *De
Natvra Deorvm* 381–3.

[32] See also Cicero, *De fato* 15.33; *De nat. deor.* 2.65.163; *SVF* 2.1190. For the
Epicurean criticism of inspiration, see Pease, *De Natvra Deorvm* 280–1, and note the
parody of this view at *De nat. deor.* 1.24.66 and the comments of Pease, *De Natvra
Deorvm* 362. Walsh (*Livy* 53) notes the Stoic belief in '*fata* as Gottesprüche, divine
communications made through oracles, dreams, prodigies, divination, and augury'.

[33] Three Essene prophets are noted as having made accurate predictions: Judas
(BJ 1.78–80, par AJ 13.311–13), Simon (BJ 2.112–13, par AJ 17.345–8) and Manaemus (AJ 15.373–9).

[34] For Josephus' view of himself as an inspired interpreter of dreams, see Aune,
*Prophecy* 139–44.

[35] Josephus condemns divination such as that practised by the witch of Endor
(ἐγγαστριμύθους, AJ 6.327–30; cf. 1 Sam 28.7–25) and the mother of Joram
(φαρμακόν, AJ 9.118; cf. 2 Kings 9.18; but cf. his defence of his companions when

heightening the conflict between 'Balaam, the best diviner (μάντις) of his day' (AJ 4.109) and God. It is God's will (γνώμην, AJ 4.110; βούλησιν, 4.121) and providence (πρόνοια, AJ 4.117,128,157) that has overcome whatever pretensions Balaam had to foreknowledge of God's intentions.[36]

The negative view of the Septuagint concerning magicians (μάγοι) in the court of Nebuchadnezzar is repeated by Josephus,[37] yet such a negative perspective on magic is rejected when he recounts the deeds performed by Moses during the plague in Egypt. When the Pharaoh accused Moses of being an evil fraud who was 'trying to impose on him by juggleries and magic' (τερατουργίαις καὶ μαγείαις, AJ 2.284), Moses replied by comparing himself to the Egyptian magicians, saying 'my deeds far surpass their magic and their art, as things divine (τὰ θεῖα) are remote from what is human ... [for] it is from no witchcraft (γοητείαν) or deception of true judgement, but from God's providential power (θεοῦ πρόνοιαν καὶ δύναμιν) that my miracles proceed' (AJ 2.286).[38]

### 5.2.2 Dreams and divine providence

Josephus is consistently positive in his treatment of 'natural' divination. Divine epiphanies,[39] found occasionally in the Septuagint,

they are wrongfully accused of sorcery, V 149–50). He applies this scriptural view beyond the biblical paraphrase, when he further condemns divination by omens (οἰώνισμα, AJ 18.212–18; cf. the charge placed against Jeremiah, of being a prophet who used divination, οἰωνιζομένου, at AJ 10.90), and in other works when he condemns the use of lots (κλῃδών, BJ 1.45; 3.123; 6.3,307–9; but note his use of lots in the cave at Jotapata (BJ 3.388–91) and the comments on the flight of birds (ὀρνιθεύω, CA 1.202). See Brüne's survey, *Flavius Josephus* 129–43.

[36] In like fashion Josephus condemns pagan divination at CA 1.201–4 (quoting Hecataeus) and CA 1.256–9 (quoting Manethos). For similar criticisms of divination in the pagan literature, see Clarke, *Octavius* 309.

[37] AJ 10.195,198,216,234–6. He adds negative pictures of magicians (μάγος, AJ 11.31 and 20.192 in some MSS), and consistently depicts various imposters of his day as magicians (γόης, AJ 20.97,160,167,188; BJ 2.261–4,565; 4.85; 5.317; V 40).

[38] See Delling, 'Wunderbare' 297; Betz, 'Wunders' 26. W. A. Meeks (*The Prophet–King: Moses Traditions and the Johannine Christology* (NT Suppl. 14; Leiden: Brill, 1967) 139) comments that 'this passage illustrates also the reserve which Josephus displays towards Moses' miracles, which could have been expanded, as in Artapanus, to depict Moses as a virtual μάγος'.

[39] Five of the 15 occurrences of ἐπιφάνεια in AJ refer to divine appearances. For the cognates, see Schlatter, *Wie Sprach?* 52; Pax, *Epiphaneia* 151–2. McRae considers the word to be 'the most interesting term for miracle in the *Antiquities* – and the one that best fits Josephus' understanding of it' ('Josephus' 144). On the development of the meaning of the word ἐπιφάνεια, see McRae, 'Miracle' 145–7, and note also Delling, 'Wunderbare' 307–8.

appear more often in his history.[40] An angel of God appears to
Balaam to announce the will of God (γνώμην τοῦ θεοῦ, AJ 4.110)[41]
and to the wife of Manoah to foreshadow the birth of her son
according to divine providence (κατὰ θεοῦ πρόνοιαν, AJ 5.277),
thereby underscoring the relation between such visions and God's
providence which oversees Israel.

Josephus recounts numerous dreams positively,[42] frequently
emphasizing the fact that God works through dreams[43] and presenting dreams as a legitimate prophetic activity.[44] Reports of dreams
are not extraneous to his history, for 'they provide instances ...
of the way in which God's providence (προμήθεια) embraces the
affairs of men' (AJ 17.354). In particular, he appropriates and
develops the scriptural depictions of the ability to interpret dreams
shown by Joseph and Daniel, both of whom are positively contrasted with pagan interpreters.[45]

[40] For the use of ἐπιφάνεια in the Septuagint, see Pax, *Epiphaneia* 159–70. Four
times Josephus describes an event as a divine epiphany; ἡ ἐπιφάνεια τοῦ θεοῦ is used
of the parting of the Red Sea (AJ 2.339), the cloud in the wilderness (3.310), the
dedication of the Temple by Solomon (8.119) and the vision of the chariots which
surrounded Elisha (9.60). God is manifested to various Israelites; ὁ θεὸς (επι) φανείς
to Abraham (1.191), twice in a dream to Solomon (8.22,125 and to the prophets
Jadon (8.240), Ahijah (8.268) and Elijah (9.20).

[41] The appearance to Jadon is also described as occurring in accordance with
God's will (τὴν τοῦ θεοῦ βούλησιν, AJ 8.241).

[42] He reports dreams which he found in his scriptural source (AJ 1.208,313–14,
279,341; 2.11–16,75,176,200; 5.219; 10.195,200,234) and adds a further dream to
Amram (2.217) and many more after his biblical paraphrase has ended (12.112;
13.322; 14.451, par BJ 1.328; 17.166; 17.345, par BJ 2.112; 17.353, par BJ 2.114).
Oepke notes that Josephus' 'post-canonical history is richly adorned by dreams'
('ὄναρ' 233). He interprets as dreams the scriptural epiphanies to Jacob (AJ 2.176),
Ehud (5.193), Nathan (7.147) and to Solomon at Gabaon (8.22) and in the Temple
(8.125). See Brüne, *Flavius Josephus* 34–5.

[43] This is stated in the dreams to Abimelech (AJ 1.208), Jacob (1.331–3,341–2),
Amram (2.209,217), Moses (2.275), Ehud (5.193), the Midianite (5.215), Manoah
(5.284, and his wife at 5.273), Saul (6.334–6), Nathan (7.147), Solomon (8.106,125,
196), the Syrians (9.55), Jaddus (11.327–8), Alexander (11.334–5) and Hyrcanus
(13.322).

[44] Dreams are seen by the prophets Saul (AJ 6.334) and Daniel (10.234–9), and by
Josephus, who regards himself as a prophet (BJ 3.351; V 208–10; cf. AJ 2.77; and see
Rajak, *Josephus* 169–72. On the greater attention paid to dreams in the Slavonic text
of the *Jewish War*, see Thackeray, *Josephus* 150.

[45] In contrast to the Egyptian magicians and wise men who are unable to interpret
Pharaoh's dream (Gen. 41.8), Joseph explains to the Egyptians that God is the source
of his ability (Gen 41.16). Judah recognizes that he is able to divine only with God's
approval (Gen 44.16). Similarly, Daniel's ability to interpret dreams is a gift of God
(Dan 1.17; 2.18–23; 5.24–8) which is contrasted with the interpretive inability of the
assembled magicians, enchanters, sorcerers, Chaldaeans and astrologers (Dan 2.2;
5.7–8). See Brüne, *Flavius Josephus* 132–3.

Joseph's ability to interpret dreams is depicted by Josephus not only in terms appropriate both to the Hellenistic wise man[46] and the Pharisaic teacher,[47] but especially as a gift from God.[48] Significantly, Josephus has introduced the Joseph cycle with the comment that, when Joseph totally committed his cause to God, 'of his providence (προνοίας) he had proof forthwith' (AJ 2.60) through his accurate interpretation of dreams. Daniel, who possessed the same gift, is directly contrasted with the Chaldaeans and Magi and soothsayers who are unable to interpret Nebuchadnezzar's dream (AJ 10.197–8,217,234–6).[49] Although he is able to interpret the dream, it is because of intense and sustained prayer to God (AJ 10.198,199,201), and so he entreats the king not to attribute this to his skill or greater effort, but to God who answered his prayer (AJ 10.203).

Josephus ends his account of Nebuchadnezzar's two dreams with what seems like an embarrassed statement that he is constrained to report such incidents because of the nature of his enterprise of 'translating the books of the Hebrews into the Greek tongue, promising to repeat their contents without adding anything of my own to the narrative or omitting anything therefrom' (AJ 10.218).[50]

Nevertheless, as he proceeds with the remainder of the story of Daniel, it is clear where his sympathies really lie, for he ends Book 10 with his strongest statement in support of the legitimacy of such divinatory activity.[51] The fulfilment of Daniel's prophetic vision

[46] He exhibits qualities of excellence and extreme sagacity (AJ 2.80), discernment and wisdom (2.87), and amazing intelligence (2.91). On Josephus' hellenizations of biblical figures, see Feldman, 'Apologist', esp. endnote 3.

[47] His ability to interpret dreams is described by the term ἐξήγησις (2.69,75,77, 93), which Josephus elsewhere applies only to interpreters of the Law (AJ 1.12; 11.192; 18.15; cf. ἐξηγεῖσθαι, BJ 1.649; AJ 18.81).

[48] The divine origin of this ability is acknowledged by Judah (AJ 2.145, 146, 153).

[49] This repeats the negative view of the Chaldaeans found in his scriptural source. Josephus himself has a more positive view of the Chaldaeans, who first taught Daniel to interpret dreams (AJ 10.187,194). Earlier in his history he had noted that the Chaldaeans taught Abraham arithmetic and astronomy (AJ 1.157–8, 167–8), and in another work he praised them for their excellence in history (CA 1 (*passim*), 2.1) and their hospitality to Jews (CA 1.171, and see AJ 1.151).

[50] A similar phrase has been used in connection with miracles at AJ 9.46,208,214, and is to be found as a programmatic statement at 1.17 (and see 2.347; 4.196; CA 1.42). See McRae ('Miracle' 138–9); Montgomery, 'Religion' 291–2; Feldman, 'Hellenizations' 336–9, and 'Apologist' 93 n. 4; Cohen, *Josephus* 24–33; and the more extensive tretment by W. C. van Unnik, 'Die Formel "nichts wegnehmen, nichts hinzufügen" bei Josephus', *Flavius Josephus als historischer Schriftsteller* 26–40, esp. 34–5 concerning AJ 10.218. By contrast to AJ 10.218, Josephus criticizes pagan accounts which include dreams to excess (CA 1.293–303).

[51] See also AJ 10.266–8, justifying his report of things that happened to Daniel 'in a marvellously fortunate way (παράδοξος) as to one of the great prophets', on the

concerning the four great kingdoms is a clear sign of divine providence (πρόνοιαν, AJ 10.278,280) and an argument against the claim
that 'the world goes on by some automatism' (AJ 10.280).[52] Dream
interpretation, and the foretelling of the future through dreams, is a
legitimate prophetic activity which is inspired by God and is made
possible by divine providence.

### 5.3 Epiphanies in Luke–Acts

Howard Kee aptly summarizes the function of epiphanies in Luke's
history: 'God demonstrates his approbation of each new stage in the
cosmic process of redemption by a divine manifestation.'[53] Many of
these epiphanies relate closely to the Gentile mission, while the
others occur in connection with key moments in the life of Jesus.
Broadly speaking, the function of these epiphanies is either to
confirm God's guidance of events (especially in epiphanies which
include oracles of consolation) or to predict the future course of the
plan of God and to guide those who see the epiphanies in their
immediate actions.[54]

### 5.3.1 The life of Jesus

As we have noted, the prologue to the Gospel (Luke 1.5–2.52)
establishes the significance of God's activity in Luke–Acts, as
angelic epiphanies and Spirit-inspired oracles introduce the divine
dimension of Luke's story in a most Jewish fashion. A fundamental
hope for Israel is consistently affirmed,[55] the language and forms

basis that 'Daniel spoke with God', foretold the exact time of fulfilment of his
prophecies, and brought good tidings rather than disastrous news.

[52] See Delling, 'Wunderbare' 300–1; and note also 309 n. 1, where he proposes that
the affirmation of providence in AJ 6.9–10 likewise indicates 'das Josephus hier gegen
eine rationalistiche Erklärung polemisiert'. See also chap. 3.2.2.

[53] *Miracle* 210; see his survey of epiphanies, 208–10, and note also the survey of
the whole New Testament in Pax, *Epiphaneia* 171–4.

[54] Hanson notes that in ancient literature, 'dream-visions are not merely decora-
tive, but function to direct or redirect the movement of the narrative' (Dreams and
Visions' 1413); further, 'the dream-visions provide the motivation for the actions of
the main actors in Acts, clearly showing how the author has made use of this form in
his literary work' ('Dreams and Visions' 1422).

[55] Luke 1.16,33,54–5,68–78; 2.25,30–2,38; see Minear, 'Birth Stories' 116. Cf. the
saying at 2.34–5 concerning division in Israel. Only by ignoring these opening
chapters is Conzelmann able to claim that 'the Eschaton and judgement do not seem
to come within the range of Scriptural prophecy' (*Theology* 161). See the criticisms by
Minear, 'Birth Stories' 120–5.

clearly imitate the Septuagint,[56] and direct quotations are made from the Law[57] as well as the Prophets.[58] Yet although the epiphanies and oracles are reminiscent of traditional scriptural incidents,[59] these portentous occurrences need not be comprehensible solely within such a Jewish tradition. The epiphanies of Gabriel (1.11; 1.26) and an unnamed angel with an accompanying multitude (2.13) emphasize the divine initiative in a manner akin to the way in which epiphanies are regarded as indications of divine providence in the hellenistic historians whom we have considered.[60] The predictions which accompany this series of epiphanies further strengthen the impression of divine activity in these early events.

Luke narrates further epiphanies at strategic places in the life of Jesus,[61] two of which are accompanied by an oracle in which the divine voice conveys approval of Jesus. Luke uses these epiphanies and oracles to assure his readers that Jesus' life is in accord with the plan of God. The appearance of the Holy Spirit at the baptism of Jesus (3.22) conveys God's commissioning and proleptic approval of Jesus' ministry; this is made explicit in the heavenly oracle of commendation accompanying the epiphany: 'you are my beloved Son, in whom I am well pleased' (3.22b).[62] The occasion is clearly an act of God (Acts 10.38). The epiphany of the transfigured Jesus[63] signifies that his departure (ἔξοδον) to Jerusalem (9.31) will occur as part of God's plan for Jesus. This is emphasized by the repetition of the oracle heard at the baptism by a 'voice from the cloud' (9.35).

[56] P. Benoit, 'L'Enfance de Jean-Baptiste selon Luc', *NTS* 3 (1956–7) 171–6, 1833–4 (language), 176–80 (forms); Dahl, 'Abraham' 149–50, 156 n. 45; R. E. Brown, *The Birth of the Messiah* (Garden City, N.Y.: Doubleday, 1977) 319–28, 357–65, 384–92, 456–60; Fitzmyer, *Luke* 1.315–16.

[57] Lev 12.2–4 at Luke 2.22; Exod 13.2 at Luke 2.23; Lev 5.11 at Luke 2.24. See also the general references to 'the Law' at Luke 2.21,27,39,42.

[58] Isa 40.3 at Luke 1.76; Isa 49.6 et al. at Luke 2.22.

[59] Marshall, *Luke* 49–50; especially the birth of Samuel (1 Sam 2–3), for which see Minear, 'Birth Stories' 116; Brown, *Birth of the Messiah* 268–9; Trompf, *Idea* 145; Tiede, *Prophecy* 23–5.

[60] See RA 7.68.2; BH 4.48.6–7; on Josephus, see above, chap. 5.2.2. Thus, Trompf, *Idea* 150 (esp. n. 157). Schultz. ('Vorsehung' 114) calls epiphanies 'den technischen Mitteln der hellenistisch-römischen Historiographie'.

[61] At Jesus' baptism, transfiguration and agony on the mount. Conzelmann (*Theology* 180) notes how these three scenes are assimilated to one another; cf. Pax, *Epiphaneia* 253. On the similar role of portents in Roman histories, see chap. 4 n. 6; Kee, *Miracle* 174–83.

[62] Fitzmyer (*Luke* 1.481) regards this announcement as 'the main purpose' of Luke's report of the baptism.

[63] The incident is reported with typical epiphany language; the appearance of Jesus is altered so that Peter and John 'saw his glory' (9.32), as he stands alongside earlier prophets, Moses and Elijah, who are also 'seen in glory' (9.31).

The epiphany of an angel on the Mount of Olives (22.43) as Jesus agonizes over his imminent death, emphasizes that 'this cup' is indeed the will of God (22.42). These three epiphanies in the life of Jesus point towards the climax of the Gospel, confirming the fact that the passion of Jesus is part of God's plan.

### 5.3.2 The appearances of the risen Jesus

The closing chapter of Luke's Gospel returns to the concentration on epiphanies with which the Gospel began. At the empty tomb, the women 'had seen a vision of angels' (ὀπτασίαν ἀγγέλων ἑωρακέναι, 24.23)[64] in which they had learned of the next stage in the plan of God; after Jesus' betrayal and crucifixion, there comes his resurrection (24.7). The primary concern of the remainder of the chapter is to establish the resurrection of Jesus by reporting his appearances.[65] For dramatic and literary reasons, the first such appearance, on the road to Emmaus, is only gradually unveiled.[66] Subsequent appearances are described in traditional epiphany terminology, both in the Gospel[67] and in summary recollection at Acts 1.3.

Luke's purpose in reporting these appearances is quite clear: the risen Jesus enables the disciples to recognize the plan of God which he himself had already declared, and which the ancient prophets had predicted. The epiphany on the Emmaus road resolves the ignorance displayed by the disciples concerning God's plan for Jesus, when, at their lament that the women in the tomb saw angels but not Jesus (24.23–4), Jesus erupts into anger at their slowness to believe and explains to them how the predictions of Moses and the prophets (24.27) point to God's plan for himself. This epiphany of Jesus, at first not recognized (24.16),[68] is eventually understood because of

[64] Their appearance 'in dazzling apparel' (Luke 24.4) recalls the transfigured Jesus, whose 'raiment became dazzling white' (9.29).

[65] Kurz, 'Proof from Prophecy' 152–3.

[66] For the importance of the recognition theme in the early church's resurrection accounts, see C. H. Dodd, 'The Appearances of the Risen Christ: An Essay in Form-Criticism of the Gospels', *Studies in the Gospels* (ed. Nineham) 9–20, 34; see esp. 14 concerning the centrality of recognition in the Emmaus pericope.

[67] Jesus appeared to Simon Peter (Luke 24.34), and stood in the midst of the Jerusalem gathering (24.36), exhorting them to see him (24.39). Pax (*Epiphaneia* 172) classifies these appearances as Christophanies, a subtype of epiphanies.

[68] Words of the γνω-root are significant at Luke 1.4; 2.15,17; 24.16,31; Acts 1.7; 2.14; 4.10; 13.38; 28.28. For the ignornce of the disciples, see Luke 9.45; 18.34; 24.16, 25,45. The number of passives which occur in these verses is notable, suggesting that the divine intention was to keep the disciples ignorant until the appropriate time,

the exposition of these prophecies (24.31–2).[69] The epiphany in Jerusalem likewise demonstrates that the events of the previous week were predicted by the prophets and foreshadowed by Jesus (24.44).[70] The final chapter of the Gospel thus asserts the continuance of the divine plan.

The apologetic purpose of these epiphanies, implied through the emphasis on recognition, is more clearly articulated in the apostolic speeches. A Jewish objection, that the crucifixion of Jesus on the tree makes him 'accursed by God' (Deut 21.22–3), is reflected in the speeches of Peter (Acts 5.30; 10.40) and Paul (Acts 13.29).[71] However, in each case, such an objection is immediately rebutted by an affirmation of God's providential activity in the resurrection (5.30; 10.40; 13.30) and appearances of Jesus (ἐμφανῆ, 10.40; ὤφθη, 13.31). Such a response to Jesus' death is not accidental, but a deliberate action resulting from God's original intention.[72] Thus Luke reports the epiphanies of Jesus in order to rebut attacks from a Jewish perspective, and he links them with the central motif of providence which functions apologetically in defence of the passion of Jesus.

In his appearance to the disciples in Jerusalem, Jesus expands the scope of God's plan to encompass further events beyond his passion (24.47–9).[73] This emphasis on what is yet to occur is seen also in the report of Jesus' ascension, 'the day when he was taken up'

namely after the resurrection. For the way the ignorance motif emphasizes the necessity of the passion, see Conzelmann, *Theology* 90–3.

[69] Although it is the blessing and breaking of bread which finally enables the two disciples to recognize him (24.31,35), it is the interpretation of scripture which, with the benefit of hindsight, is acknowledged to be the turning point (24.32). See Talbert, *Literary Patterns* 22, and further in chap. 6.3.11.

[70] This epiphany also serves to overcome the fear of those gathered together in Jerusalem (24.36), as Jesus placates their anxiety that they were seeing a spirit (24.37) by proving his corporeal nature (24.39–40). See Schubert, 'Luke 24' 172; Conzelmann, *Theology* 203 n. 5.

[71] For the use of Deut 21.22–3 in 'early Jewish polemic against acceptance of a Crucified One as Messiah', see M. Wilcox, '"Upon the Tree": Deut 21.22–3 in the New Testament', *JBL* 96 (1977) 86. Wilcox emphasizes the Christological use of this scripture text in the New Testament (see 86–90; on Acts 13.28–9, see 91–3).

[72] Peter declares that Jesus is ordained by God (10.42) and appears to those chosen by God (10.41); God exalts him as Leader and Saviour (5.31). Paul interprets the resurrection as fulfilment of prophecy (13.33–5) in accord with God's plan (13.36). See Wilcox, '"Upon the Tree"' 89–90.

[73] The function of epiphanies in Luke 24.13–49 is thus, in part, the same as epiphanies in 1.8–38, namely to allow an authority figure to appear and make predictions whose fulfilment will be subsequently reported. The epiphanies in Luke 24 point forward to the whole of Acts, with the added emphasis that already many of the predictions have been fulfilled in the events narrated thus far.

(ἀνελήμφθη, Acts 1.2,11).[74] This final epiphany of Jesus[75] is immediately followed by a further epiphany of two men in 'white robes' who shift the focus of attention from the departure of Jesus to his future coming 'in the same way as you saw him go into heaven' (1.11). The sequence of epiphanic events is thus not closed; the two men predict that there will be further epiphanies from heaven, the place of divine disclosure.[76] Consequently, as epiphanies do occur in Acts, they continue to function apologetically, confirming and predicting the divine guidance of events as the Gospel is preached among the Gentiles.

### 5.3.3 The mission to the Gentiles

This apologetic function of epiphanies is especially evident in the middle chapters of Acts, where the mission to the Gentiles both begins and is validated. The epiphany to Paul on the Damascus road (9.1–19), as we have noted, establishes God's role in converting Paul and sending him on his mission to Israel and the Gentiles. The epiphanies to Cornelius in Caesarea (10.1–8) and to Peter in Joppa (10.9–16) authorize Peter's table fellowship with Gentiles and reinforce God's intentions concerning the Gentile mission. Each of these epiphanies is so significant that Luke repeats them with elaborations which amplify the role they play in the plan of God.[77]

The structure of Acts 10.1–11.18 highlights the pivotal role of the epiphanies in the story. There are four scenes in this section of Acts; at the centre of each scene stands an epiphany by which God guides the events narrated. In the first scene, in Caesarea (10.1–8), the impetus for the sequence of events here described comes from what Cornelius sees in a vision (ἐν ὁράματι, 10.3). Although his first reaction is to misunderstand and show terror (10.4), Cornelius is faithful to his reputation of devotion to God (10.2) and does as he has been commanded (10.7–8).

A tension in the narrative is set up in the second scene, in Joppa (10.9–23), by the vision (ὅραμα, 10.17,19) which Peter sees whilst in

---

[74] For this reading of Acts 1.2, against the Western ἐντειλάμενος, see Haenchen, *Acts* 138 n. 8. Cf. Flender (*Theologian* 33–5) who argues that ἀνελήμφθη refers to the ongoing exhaltation of Jesus, not just his ascension.

[75] Note the twofold reference to the visual element in Acts 1.9.

[76] The word is used three times in Acts 1.11, thereby placing special emphasis on the place from which the divine revelation will come; see Haenchen, *Acts* 150 n. 8.

[77] For an analysis of the repetitions of 9.1–19 at 22.1–21 and 26.1–29, see above, chap. 2.3.3.2.

a trance (ἔκστασις, 10.10). He is commanded, three times, to abandon the Jewish food laws and eat what has hitherto been regarded as unclean (10.13–16). Peter's initial reaction of perplexity is further intensified by the arrival of the men sent by Cornelius (10.17). The way to resolve this tension is indicated by the Spirit (10.19–20); Peter obediently invites the men in as guests to share his table and then sets out with them to meet with Cornelius in Caesarea (10.23).

That both of these epiphanies are unquestionably communications from God is emphasized within the narrative. The instructions to Cornelius, to send to Joppa and bring Peter back to Caesarea, come from a messenger of God (10.3).[78] This external indication of the divine origin of this epiphany is paralleled by the internal indicators found within the vision seen by Peter. The object seen in this vision comes from heaven, the place of divine revelation, whence it descends (10.11) and to which it returns (10.16). The vision contains within itself its own interpretation as a divine directive to overlook the distinctions of food laws (10.15). This is validated by the command of another divine messenger, the Spirit (10.19–20). Thus, the two short opening scenes have established that what will take place is undoubtedly under God's guidance.

The third scene, in Caesarea (10.24–48), brings together the two main characters and works out the resolution pointed towards in the first two scenes. Once again, the scene commences with misunderstanding as Cornelius inappropriately kneels in worship (10.25) before Peter corrects him (10.26). After a passing reference to the vision he saw, Peter focusses on the main point, that he has come on God's command (10.28, repeating the phrase of 10.15). For his part, Cornelius rehearses in full his experience of seeing a vision (10.30–3), alluding to the divine origin of his vision.[79] This retelling underlines the divine initiative in arranging this meeting. Cornelius concludes by acknowledging that Peter speaks as commanded by the Lord (10.33).

The sermon which follows is an exposition of God's providence, not only through Jesus[80] but in the offering of this good news to 'every one' (10.43) 'in every nation' (10.35) as a sign of God's

---

[78] The instructions are later described as having been revealed (ἐχρηματίσθη, 10.22) by a divine messenger.

[79] The description of the 'bright apparel' of the messenger (10.30) evokes other divine messengers; cf. Luke 9.29; 24.4; Acts 1.10.

[80] See my analysis above, chap. 3.3.3.3.

impartiality (10.34). The title of the sermon, 'God shows no partia-
lity' (οὐκ ἔστιν προσωπολήμπτης ὁ θεός, 10.34), develops the
theme of Peter's vision in which 'God has shown me that I should
not call any man common or unclean' (10.28). This intervention by
God would seem (to a Torah-observing Jew of the day) to run
contrary to his traditional religious beliefs. This also is quite different from the way the gods were understood to intervene in favour of
the *status quo* in hellenistic histories.[81] Nevertheless, Luke emphasizes that God's present actions are in complete accord with the
'traditional' intentions of the divine will. Table fellowship amongst
Jews and Gentiles is consistent with God's intentions right
throughout the life of Jesus.

The fourth scene, in Jerusalem (11.1–18) recapitulates all the
events thus far reported. This time, it is Peter's vision which is the
focal point, for he is required to justify his actions in the face of
criticisms made over his actions (11.2–3). The account of the vision
which he gives (11.5–10) closely follows the initial narrative version
(10.9–16). He retains the emphasis on heaven as the place where the
vision originated (11.5 par 10.11) and to which it returned (11.10 par
10.16) and adds a further comment on the heavenly origin of the
voice (11.9; cf. 10.15) which issues the divine command to eat with
Gentiles (11.9 par 10.15). Just as the vision to Cornelius has been
repeated in scene three, so the vision to Peter is repeated in scene
four. The pivotal role of both of these epiphanies is undergirded
through repetition.

Peter then summarizes the subsidiary message he received from
the Holy Spirit (11.12; cf. 10.19–20), as well as the vision seen by
Cornelius (11.13–14; cf. 10.3–6; 10.29–32) and the further action of
the Spirit's falling on the Gentiles (11.15 par 10.44). Thus, the point
is made once again, in summary form, that by means of these
visions, God has authorized table fellowship with the Gentiles and
the start of the Gentile mission. Any objection to this course of
action must be interpreted as attempting to 'withstand God' (11.17).
The conclusion to this whole section (placed on the lips of the
Jerusalem leaders) is unambiguous; God has authorized the Gentile
mission (11.18). It is through these epiphanies that the next stage in
the plan of God has been made known.

The course of this Gentile mission, as Luke presents it through
the activities of Paul, is guided by further divine interventions

[81] See above, chap. 3.1.2

through epiphanies. In a vision which appears at night in Troas, a man invites Paul to help the Macedonians (16.9), leading Paul and his companions to conclude that this is a divine initiative (16.10).[82] Later, the Lord himself appears to Paul in Jerusalem to confirm that he will testify in Rome (23.11) and an angel of God reassures Paul aboard ship that he will indeed stand before Caesar (27.23–4). Both of these epiphanies indicate the continuing divine guidance of Paul's life, despite the difficulties he is experiencing (imprisonment in Jerusalem; under guard, without food, and caught in a storm on the ship). As befits these difficult circumstances, the form of the messages given in these epiphanies is that of a classic Jewish assurance oracle, beginning with an explicit charge not to fear.[83] These epiphanies thus function both to indicate the overarching, universal providential guidance of events and to assure the immediate, specific assistance of God to Paul in his difficulties.[84]

This consolatory function of epiphanies has been evidenced earlier in Acts, especially in contexts of adversity or opposition. In Jerusalem, an angel of the Lord appears at night (5.19) to Peter and John, releasing them from their imprisonment by the priestly hierarchy (5.17–18) and encouraging them to continue their public preaching (5.20). Despite the opposition this engenders from the council (5.33), they are not afraid to suffer dishonour (5.41) because of the way God has vindicated them. During the persecution by Herod (12.1), an angel of the Lord appears at night (12.6) to release Peter from prison (12.7–11) in order that he might encourage the believers (12.17).[85] The subsequent activity of an angel of God who

---

[82] Compare this event especially with Josephus, AJ 17.354. Schulz ('Vorsehung' 115) calls this pericope 'die geradezu klassische Belegstelle für den indiskutablen Eingriff der Gottesvorsehung'.

[83] Acts 27.24 begins μὴ φοβοῦ, an assurance common in Lukan epiphany oracles (Luke 1.13,20; 2.10; Acts 18.9) and in sayings of Jesus (Luke 5.10; 8.50; 12.4,7,32); cf. the oracles of Matt 1.20; 28.5,10. Marshall (Luke 56) claims that the phrase 'is almost an indicator of the divine presence'. Acts 23.11 begins θάρσει, an assurance not found elsewhere in Luke's work but commonly attributed to Jesus (Mark 6.50 par Matt 14.27; Mark 10.49; Matt 9.2,22; John 16.33). On the assurance oracle in Acts, see Aune, *Prophecy* 266–8. Cf. the way visions encourage humans at RA 5.16.3; BH 5.49.6,63.2; 17.103.7–8.

[84] Aune (*Prophecy* 268) concludes that the assurance oracles 'underscore that the growth and development of early Christianity was a divinely superintended phenomenon'.

[85] See also 16.26–34. For the ancient view that 'divine sanction stands behind miraculous release from prison', see Brawley, 'Paul in Acts' 137; Haenchen, *Acts* 383. Foakes Jackson and Lake (*Beginnings* 5.135, 196) refer to other literature in which this theme appears; on the weakness of the claim that Luke took this theme from Euripides, see *Beginnings* 5.196–7 and the literature cited in chap. 2 n. 72.

kills Herod (12.23) confirms the divine intention to strengthen and encourage the Jerusalem church as it grows and multiplies (12.24). These epiphanies, associated with dramatic actions, demonstrate the providence of God, who intervenes directly into history to save his servants.

In Corinth, the oracle spoken by the Lord in a night vision (18.9) to Paul takes the form of an assurance (μὴ φοβοῦ), encouraging him to continue his testimony amidst opposition from some of the Jews (18.6) and confirming that God will preserve his life (18.10; cf. 27.24,34). Subsequent events demonstrate how God continually rescues Paul from harm and ensures that this special witness will be able to continue to declare God's providential guidance of history.[86]

### 5.4 Conclusions

A comparative analysis of the major texts demonstrates the common use of epiphanies (visions and dreams) in hellenistic histories. In each author, this phenomenon is employed in order to signify divine providence, and is often asserted at critical moments in the narrative. In Luke–Acts, such epiphanies function in two ways. (1) They confirm divine providence. God's guidance of events is manifested in such epiphanies; often the figure in the dream or vision will explicitly declare this fact, in the form of an assurance oracle. (2) They predict the course of future events. In the life of Jesus, such epiphanies signify how God will be at work in Jesus' life and especially in his passion. In the time of the early church, oracles spoken in dreams and visions look forward to the fact of the Gentile mission itself and to the various developments which take place in that mission. The reader is thus invited to interpret the whole sequence of epiphanies in both volumes as a means of expounding and defending the role of the plan of God.

---

[86] The vision reported by Stephen (7.55–6) stands apart from the other epiphanies in Acts; Aune (*Prophecy* 270) suggests that it functions 'as a visionary announcement of judgement'. It is thus a declaration of God's universal providence at the end of time, as well as a demonstration of God's specific providential care for Stephen (Aune, *ibid.*, 319–20).

# 6

## PROPHECY: FORETELLING AND
## FULFILLING THE PLAN OF GOD

A frequent emphasis throughout Luke's two volumes is on the way in which certain events, especially the passion of Jesus and the mission to the Gentiles, fulfil the words of the prophets. The story Luke tells is the outworking of these prophecies in human history, in accordance with the plan of God. Such a view of prophecy assumes three things: its predictive nature, the certainty of its being fulfilled and the fundamental assurance of divine guidance which guarantees this. Luke provides a number of instances of predictive prophecies whose fulfilment is possible[1] because God is guiding history.

Although central to Luke's presentation of the plan of God, this perspective is not unique to Luke, for he shares a common view of the nature and function of prophecy. The same three characteristics also appear in the scriptures of the Hebrews, most prominently in the Deuteronomic history, and it has been claimed that these similarities, among others, mean that the Septuagint was actually the primary influence upon Luke's manner of presenting the story of Jesus and the early church.[2] Nevertheless, this view that prophecy entails the utterance of divinely given predictions which come to fulfilment, is not unique to the Deuteronomistic history, for it is widespread throughout the hellenistic world and is to be found in the hellenistic histories which, as we have already seen, reflect other dimensions of Luke–Acts.[3]

---

[1] The fulfilment motif is conveyed in the use of the verbs πληρόω (Luke 4.21; 9.31; 21.24; 22.16; 24.44; Acts 1.16; 2.28; 3.18; 12.25; 13.25,27,52; 14.26; 19.21) and τελέω, (Luke 12.50; 18.31; 22.37).

[2] D. Schmidt, 'The Historiography of Acts: Deuteronomistic or Hellenistic?', *SBLSPS* 24 (1985) 417–27; W. S. Kurz, 'Luke–Acts and Historiography in the Greek Bible', *SBLSPS* 19 (1980) 296 n. 1; Tiede *Prophecy* 74–6.

[3] D. Balch ('Acts as Hellenistic Historiography', *SBLSPS* 24 (1985) 429–32) argues that hellenistic historiography is just as valid as the Deuteronomic history as a background for Luke–Acts. He refers explicitly to promise and fulfilment on 431–2.

### 6.1 Prophetic activity in hellenistic history

The schematic analysis of divination propounded by the philoso-phers[4] places oracles as a subdivision of one type of divination. In practice, however, the role played by oracles in popular religious and political life was far more substantial than such a categorization might imply.[5] The pervasive impact of predictions uttered by all manner of prophetic figures is reflected in the histories of Dionysius and Diodorus as they depict the way guidance was sought from official prophets at cultic sites, individual prophetic figures and written collections of oracles attributed to ancient mythical seers.[6] The popular view in antiquity was that all such oracular pronounce-ments were inspired by the gods'[7]

The emphasis in each historian varies in accordance with their subject matter. Since Dionysius reports the history of Rome, the Sibylline Oracles receive most attention, for they were very sig-nificant for the Romans. He also notes the importance of the Delphic oracle, which figures even more prominently in Diodorus' history because of its key role in political affairs throughout the classical period. Yet the function of oracles in both histories is the same; they serve to advance the story-line, giving structure to the narrative.[8] Both writers also agree with the popular view that predictive prophecies are made possible by the gods.

---

[4]  For a succinct summary, see Cicero, *De div.* 1.18.34.

[5]  See esp. Nilsson, *Greek Folk Religion* 121–39 (on the popular impact) and *Cults, Myths, Oracles and Politics in Ancient Greece* (Gleerup: Lund, 1951) 123–42 (on the political role); Nock, 'Religious Attitudes' 539 n. 22.

[6]  For these types of oracular activity, see Flacelière, *Greek Oracles* 25–32; Burkert, *Greek Religion* 114–18; Mikalson, *Athenian Popular Religion* 40–1; Aune, *Prophecy* 23–48; cf. Dodds, *Pagan and Christian* 53–7.

[7]  The gullibility of the populace with regard to oracles is attested by Polybius (*Hist.* 10.2.11): 'Lycurgus made his own scheme [for the constitution of Sparta] more acceptable and more easily believed in by invoking the oracles of the Pythia in support of projects due to himself.' Nock ('Religious Attitudes' 534–5 n. 2) comes to a similar conclusion regarding Philip's use of the Delphic oracle 'with an eye on public opinion', but allows that such invention of oracles was generally acceptable (*ibid.*, 540, 544–5). Cf. the more sceptical view of oracles held within the Academy and articulated by Cicero himself in *De div.* 2.44.112.

[8]  Cf. the way an oracle in Herodotus is 'not merely a literary device for brightening his narrative, but a real framework to his history' (H. W. Parke and D. E. W. Wormell, *The Delphic Oracle* (2 vols.; Oxford: Blackwell, 1961) 2.vii); and the function of an oracle in Greek mythology as 'first cause or *deus ex machina* which closes the story' (*ibid.*, 2.xx). For examples, see Aune, *Prophecy* 401 n. 11; Talbert, 'Promise and Fulfilment' 97, 103 n. 18.

## 6.1.1 Oracles delivered at Delphi and other sites

### *6.1.1.1 Predictions and their fulfilment*

The oracle at Delphi occupies an important place in many of the events which Diodorus relates,[9] because of its long-standing prominence in political strategy[10] and the role it is claimed to have played in the colonization of many areas of Greek settlement.[11] The oracle at Ammon in Libya is prominent in Diodorus' account of Alexander,[12] who consults it concerning the extent of his reign and is favoured with the prediction that he will rule the whole world.[13] Dionysius likewise notes the Roman interest in a variety of oracles, mentioning the oracles of Dodona (RA 1.18.2,19.3,51.1,55.4), Delphi (RA 1.49.3; 4.69.2–4; 12.10.2; 19.1.3) and other places.[14] Both authors acknowledge the predictive capacities of oracles.[15]

A gnomic saying preserved from the fragments of Book 10 of Diodorus' history declares that 'the successful turn of events (τὸ ἀποτέλεσμα) constitutes a sufficient proof of what has been

---

[9] Especially in the Greek myths related in Books 4 and 5, and in some of the fragments preserved in Books 7–15. The collections in 8.21–30 and 9.31–6 concern oracles almost exclusively. The most extensive narrative concerning the Delphic oracle, in Book 16, tells of the capture of the area by a number of Phocian leaders. On the Delphic oracle in Diodorus, see Parke and Wormell, *Delphic Oracle* 2.vii–ix.

[10] BH 4.37.1; 11.14.3; 15.13.1; 16.14–60,78.3; and 38/39.7.1 are instances where the oracle was pillaged for political purposes. The words of the oracle are used to political advantage at 9.32.1 and 16.27.1, and its importance for the Lacedaemonians is noted at 16.57.4 and 7.12.1–8. More generally, see Flacelière, *Greek Oracles* 60–72. Polybius provides a realistic insight into the manipulation of the Delphic oracle for political gain at *Histories* 10.2.11.

[11] In accordance with its predictions, settlements are made at Sardinia (BH 4.29.1; 5.15.1), Thebes in Boeotia (5.49.2), Carpathos (5.54.4), Rhodes (5.59.5), Lesbos (5.81.6), Croton (8.17.1–2), Sicily (8.23.1), Rhegium (8.23.2), Cyrene (8.29.1–2), Thurium (12.10.5; 12.35.3) and Phares (15.13.4). Settlements are made in accord with other oracles at Alba Longa (7.5.4–6) and Fair Shore of Sicily (12.8.2). On such 'foundation oracles', see Cicero, *De div.* 1.1.3; Pease, *De Divinatione* 45; Parke and Wormell, *Delphic Oracle* 2.xix–xx.

[12] Of the fifteen references to Ammon, nine are connected with Alexander.

[13] BH 17.51.1–4, and 17.93.4, where it is linked with the Delphic oracle. The same oracle is extorted from the oracle under trickery by Philomelus the Phocian (16.27.1); Parke and Wormell (*Delphic Oracle* 1.231 n. 21) adjudge the latter to be the authentic incident, forming a basis for the 'fictitious anecdote concerning Alexander the Great'.

[14] Dionysius refers to χρησμούς (RA 1.14.5,24.1; 2.19.3; 7.68.1; 12.16.1; 19.2.1), θέσφατα (1.40.2; 4.4.2; 10.14.2) and a λόγιον (19.2.1).

[15] Although the prefix προ- does not refer to foreseeing the future (E. Fascher, *Prophetes: eine sprach- und religions-geschichtliche Untersuchung* (Giessen: Alfred Töpelmann, 1927) 6; H. Kraemer, 'προφήτης', *TDNT* 6 (1968) 795), the predictive nature of prophecy in the Greek-speaking world was never in doubt (Aune, *Prophecy* 56; cf. Kraemer, *ibid.*, 783–4); see esp. Plato, *Phaed.* 244A–B.

predicted' (BH 10.19.4). The fulfilment of oracular predictions is a persistent theme in both authors, who use a variety of means to depict this.[16] At times Dionysius will simply note the prediction of a person, and later report how it came to pass, without further comment,[17] but on occasion he explicitly interprets an event as being the fulfilment of an oracular prophecy, through the use of the formulaic phrase, 'the oracle had its fulfilment'.[18]

The successful occurrence of what the Delphic oracle has predicted is emphasized by Diodorus in various ways. Frequently he reports events with a prior statement of what it was that the oracle predicted,[19] and on occasion he describes events as having taken place 'in accordance with the oracle'.[20] The efficacy of the oracle is noted in the polemical comment of the Spartan elder, who notes that since seers are often unable to foresee the future, the oracle at Delphi should be consulted (BH 8.8.1). Diodorus makes his most explicit references to the fulfilment of the words of the oracle in formulaic statements containing the verb τελέω.[21]

[16] For similar examples in other literature, along with a Stoic justification for this belief, see Plutarch, De Pyth. orac. 399B–E.

[17] For example, the wife of Tarquinius knew from many oracles that Tullius would become king, so she helped him attain the crown (RA 4.4.2); Valerius utters dire prophecies of what is to come (6.43.2) and they subsequently occur (6.46.1); the prediction of future evils by Appius Claudius (6.88.3) comes to pass in the plebeian uprising (7.15.2–3); and Veturia notes that her early predictions of the defeat of Marcius are subsequently vindicated (8.52.1).

[18] The phrase is most common in the first book; it refers to the fulfilment of oracles given to the Pelasgians (τέλος ἔχειν, RA 1.19.2, and τέλος ἕξειν, 1.24.1), and to oracles given at Dodona (τέλος ἔχοι, 1.55.3, and τέλος ἔχειν, 1.56.1–2). The same phrase designates the fulfilment of the oracle to Artemedes of Chalcis (τέλος ἔχειν, 19.2.1) and of the omen of a thunderbolt (τέλος ἔχῃ, 9.12.2).

[19] The twelve labours of Heracles, predicted at BH 4.10.7, take place in 4.11–26; his immortality, predicted at the same time, is noted at 4.38.3–5 and 4.53.7. Likewise for the story of Oedipus (4.64.1, fulfilled at 4.64.2), the victory of the Epigoni (4.66.1, fulfilled at 4.66.4), Clazomenae's rule over Leuce (15.18.2, fulfilled at 15.18.4), the death of Philip (16.91.2–3, repeated at 16.92.4, fulfilled at 16.94.1–4) and the domination of Carthage and Sicily by Agathocles (19.2.3, fulfilled in the remainder of Books 19 and 20).

[20] Predictions of the Delphic oracle come to pass κατὰ τὸν χρησμόν (BH 4.64.4,67.4; 5.15.1,49.2,59.4; 12.58.6,77.1; 13.108.4; 15.13.4, 49.2); the same phrase applies to the fulfilment of other oracles at 2.14.3; 15.49.3; and 15.74.4. The phrase κατὰ τὸ λόγιον is used of Delphi at 4.65.2–3 and 5.54.4, whilst the colonization of Lesbos is said to have occurred κατά τι πυθόχρηστον (5.81.6). Nock ('Religious Attitudes' 538), notes, '"and this came true" … is part of the pattern of popular stories' about oracles in antiquity. Chrysippus is said to have made a collection of numerous Delphic oracular responses, 'attested in every instance by abundant proof' (Cicero, De div. 1.19.37; 2.56.115; see also 1.3.6, and Pease, De Divinatione 60–1). For the criticisms of this collection, see Cicero, De div. 2.56.115–18.

[21] The formula appears eleven times, in various forms, in connection with the Delphic oracle: τετελέσθαι τὸν χρησμόν (BH 2.27.2; 20.26.2), τὸ λόγιον τετελέσθαι

The origin of the oracle at Ammon is narrated (BH 3.73.3–8) in order to show that its predictions are fulfilled,[22] while Diodorus also records the way events bore out the truth of predictions made by the oracle of Dodona (BH 15.72.3) and various unnamed oracles.[23] Each of these oracular pronouncements, then, find their fulfilment in events of history and occupy important places in the histories which Diodorus and Dionysius report. Such fulfilments serve an apologetic purpose, justifying the events which take place by means of the authority of the venerable oracles of Delphi or elsewhere.

### 6.1.1.2 Divinely inspired predictions

Such consistency in fulfilment is attributed by Dionysius to the divine origin of oracles,[24] in accord with the Stoic view that 'men capable of correctly interpreting all these signs of the future[25] seem to approach very near to the divine spirit of the gods whose wills they interpret' (*De div.* 1.18.34).[26]

Diodorus likewise reflects the view that the gods communicate through oracles[27] and that they foretell the future by this

(4./3.6), προρρήσει τελεσθῆναι (19.55.9), συνετελέσθη (19.2.9), οὗ τελεσθέντος (19.84.5), ὁ δὲ προαισθόμενος τὸ μέλλον τελεῖσθαι (37.12.3) and τὸ ἀποτέλεσμα (4.30.4 and 10.9.4 as quoted above). The cognate noun is also applied to the fulfilment of an oracle at Branchidae (τὸ τέλος ἔσεσθαι, 19.90.3) and the compound verb to the fulfilment of the prophecy of Demetrius of Phalerum (συντελεσθῆναι, 31.10.2). Notice also the phrases τοῖς χρησμοῖς ἀκολούθως (4.38.5) and ἀκόλουθον ἔσχε (37.9.1).

[22] The immortality of Dionysus, predicted at BH 3.73.3, is fulfilled at 3.73.5.

[23] The oracle of Cronus concerning Zeus at BH 5.70.1 is fulfilled at 5.71.1; the oracle to Aeneas concerning the founding of the city at 7.5.4 is fulfilled at 7.5.6; the Fair Shore colony is founded in accordance with an oracle at 12.8.2; and the prediction of the assassination of the king of Abae by the oracle of Apollo in Cilicia at 32.10.2 is fulfilled at 32.10.8.

[24] See, for Delphi, RA 4.69.2–4; 12.10.2; for Dodona, 1.19.3.

[25] Quintus has just specified the instances of Bakis, Epimenides and Sibyl as examples of prophets who are *divinitus*. The wider context is a discussion of all types of natural divination.

[26] See also Cicero, *De fato* 15.33; Minucius Felix, *Oct.* 7.6; Origen, *Contra Celsum* 7.7; 8.45. On the 'divine soul from which the human soul is sprung', see Cicero, *De div.* 1.32.70; Plutarch, *De Pyth. orac.* 404BC,F; *De defac. orac.* 432A; 433D; and chap. 5 n. 32.

[27] Diodorus explicitly describes oracles as given by the gods, by relating the words θεός and χρησμός in various ways. See χρησμὸν ὑπὸ θεῶν (BH 12.8.2), τις θεοῦ χρησμός (37.9.1), θεῖόν τινα χρησμόν (15.33.2), χρῆσαι τὸν θεόν (20.26.1), ἔχρησεν ὁ θεός (4.30.4,73.2), τοῦ θεοῦ χρήσαντος (4.29.1), and κεχρηματικέναι τοὺς θεούς (3.6.2); on Delphi, see Fascher, *Prophetes* 34. Cf. Plutarch, *De defac. orac.* 413E: 'prophecy is something created by a god'. For a discussion of this aspect of the Stoic theory of oracles, see R. Flacelière, *Plutarque: sur la disparition des oracles* (Annales de l'Université de Lyon 3.14; Paris: Les Belles Lettres, 1947) 43–6.

means.[28] Thus the discovery of the oracular powers of the chasm at Delphi, with its emphasis on the inspiration conveyed by the place,[29] is strategically recalled in the midst of the narrative of the Phocian attempts to recapture control of the shrine (BH 16.1.1–60.1).[30] The moral of this battle is clear; those who pillage the temple are guilty of sin against the gods.[31] Yet for all his virtue in liberating the oracle from the Phocians, Philip is rewarded only with the prediction of his death, given in a most ambiguous (but nevertheless accurate) form.[32] This fundamental aspect of oracles, namely their divinely inspired origin, thus explains the fact that their predictions are consistently fulfilled in the events of history. Conversely, the completion of what was foretold is indicative of the way in which the gods convey to humans their foreknowledge of history. Oracles are thus related to divine providence.

### 6.1.2 Oracles written in the Sibylline collections

Dionysius includes further examples of 'natural' divinatory activity in the consultation of the Sibylline oracles, which were guarded by the Romans more carefully than any others, and consulted often

[28] This is said of the gods in general at BH 3.65.4,73.1; 4.9.4,48.6,84.4; 5.7.7; 6.6.3; and of specific gods at 4.82.1 (Apollo) and 18.1.2 (Hector). At 19.90.3 it is said that the gods make predictions (πρόρρησις). See also 31.10.1.

[29] BH 16.26.1–6. When the oracular chasm is discovered by goats, they behave like those inspired (ἐνθουσιάζουσι) and the goatherd begins to foretell the future (προλέγειν). Diodorus describes it as 'the prophecy-giving shrine of the earth', see Pease, De Divinatione 161; cf. Flacelière, Greek Oracles 43–7. Explicit mention of its divine origin is made by Dionysius, using the formula noted above, at BH 4.29.1,30.4,73.2; 15.33.2; see also Plutarch, De Pyth. orac. 397BC; 406D,F; 409C; and for a summary of Plutarch's views on the oracle, see Nock, 'Religious Attitudes' 535–7. For the popular view of the Pythia's inspiration, see Dodds, Irrational 70–4; for the Stoic theory derived from this view, see Cicero, De div. 1.36.79.

[30] See Parke and Wormell, Delphic Oracle 1.222–31.

[31] Opposition to the pronouncements of Delphi is described as ἀσεβείας (BH 16.64.2), ἠσεβήκατε (16.57.3) and ἐξαμαρτάνειν (16.57.2); see Parke and Wormell, Delphic Oracle 1.225. For pagan criticisms of the Delphic oracle, see Cicero, De div. 1.19.37–8; 2.56.116–18; Plutarch, De Pyth. orac. 402B–D; De defac. orac. (passim), esp. 409E–414E. See Parke and Wormell, Delphic Oracle 1.283–91; other references are given by Clarke, Octavius 310–11; Pease, De Divinatione 160.

[32] BH 16.91.2–94.4. The ambiguous oracle, misinterpreted by Philip (16.91.2), actually predicts his death (16.91.3), which occurs as foretold (16.94.1–4). On the ambiguity of oracular language, see Pease, De Divinatione 187, 537–58; cf. Josephus, BJ 6.312–15 and the comments by Kurz, 'Proof from Prophecy' 143–4. After the death of Philip, the oracle recedes from prominence in Diodorus' history; only six further references are made to it (17.10.3; 19.2.3; 22.9.1; 31.11.1; 34/35.13.1; 38/39.7.1).

(RA 4.62.5) for guidance to Rome on many occasions throughout her history.[33] On one occasion he explicitly notes the fulfilment of a prediction made by the Sibyl (14.11.4).[34]

The Sibylline oracles are regarded as having a divine origin by both Dionysius[35] and Diodorus who explains that 'to be inspired (ἐνθεάζειν) in one's own tongue is expressed by σιβυλλαίνειν' (BH 4.66.6).[36] Since prophetic utterances share with portentous occurrences the common function of revealing the will of the gods, the Sibylline oracle is at times related to omens, as when 'both the Sibylline oracles and the portents sent by heaven (τὰ ἐκ τοῦ δαιμονίου φανέντα)' foretold the civil dissension in Rome under Gaius Claudius (RA 10.9.1).[37] Dionysius notes, however, the superiority of oracles to omens; when the soothsayers are unable to interpret the meaning of an omen, a satisfactory interpretation is provided by the Sibylline oracles (RA 10.2.5).[38]

### 6.1.3 Oracles delivered by other individuals

Dionysius reports other instances in which people foresee what is to come (RA 6.70.1; 7.22.3; 7.42.5; 9.53.7) and foretell the future (RA 1.53.5; 6.88.3; 7.49.4). He attributes to divine inspiration the predictive ability of people such as Themis of Arcadia (RA 1.31.1,3), certain women in Rome (RA 7.68.1) and the augur Nevius Attius (RA 3.71.5), each of whom exemplifies the divine gift of prophetic insight.

---

[33] The Sibylline oracles are consulted and obeyed at RA 3.67.3; 6.17.3; 8.37.3; 10.2.5,9.1; 12.9.1; 14.11.1; see also Cicero, *De div.* 1.2.4; 2.54.110. These oracles attest to the sacred nature of Italy (1.34.5) and to the arrival of Aeneas and the Trojans in Italy (1.49.3). Dionysius tells of how Tarquinius came to acquire them for Rome (4.62.1–4), laments the destruction of many of them in the temple fire of 83 BCE (4.62.4), and warns of the existence of inauthentic interpolations which do not adhere to the acrostic scheme of the genuine oracles (4.62.4; see also Cicero, *De div.* 2.54.111–12). For the role of the Sibylline oracles in the Roman *collegia*, see Nock, 'Religious Attitudes' 546–7.

[34] ἐπιτελῆ ποιῆσαι τὰ μαντεύματα refers to the Sibyl's prediction recorded at RA 14.11.1.

[35] RA 1.34.5; 8.37.3; 10.9.1. On this view in general, see J. J. Collins, 'Sibylline Oracles', *The Old Testament Pseudepigrapha* (ed. J. H. Charlesworth; 2 vols.; Garden City, N.Y.: Doubleday, 1983) 1.320.

[36] See Pease, *De Divinatione* 50–1; Flacelière, *Sur la disparition* 46. For the Stoic acceptance of this aetiology, see Cicero, *De div.* 1.36.79; Plutarch, *De Pyth. orac.* 398C–E; for an Epicurean criticism, see Plutarch, *De Pyth. orac.* 398F–399A.

[37] See also RA 8.37.3; 12.9.1; 14.11.1; on the Delphic oracle, see 4.69.3.

[38] The same point is made in connection with the explanation of the Tyrrhenian seer (RA 12.11.1–3), which is in accord with the Delphic oracle (12.10.2).

Diodorus also notes individuals who exhibit an inspired ability to predict events (BH 15.33.2; 16.92.3). The ironic comment of Demetrius of Phalerum concerning the rise and fall of the Macedonians, that fifty years earlier nobody would have thought that these world rulers would be supplanted by the Persians, even 'if some god had foretold the future', is recognized with hindsight to have been 'an utterance of more than human inspiration' (BH 31.10.1–2). The basic principle, then, is that 'only the gods foresee the future' (BH 8.8.1).[39]

The most extensive example of fulfilled prophecy comes when God introduces the death of Alexander with a reference to Pythagoras' belief that the immortality of souls allowed them to 'foreknow the future at that moment in death when they are departing from the bodies' (BH 18.1.1).[40] Alexander's own presentiment of his imminent death and its violent aftermath (BH 18.1.4) thus forms a prophecy whose fulfilment is worked out in the ensuing events of Book 18. It is the clearest example of the commonly accepted view that 'indications of the future were a proof of Providence'.[41]

Thus, the histories which Diodorus and Dionysius write are marked by numerous acknowledgements of the divine guidance of human affairs by means of inspired oracular pronouncements. Many of the events which they narrate occur in accordance with these oracles and are thus defended and authorized as being the fulfilment of such prophetic activity. Diodorus reports a larger number of instances and exhibits a greater interest in oracles and prophecies than does Diodorus; nevertheless, both writers indicate the significant role of such phenomena within hellenistic historiography. Scepticism concerning the possibility of knowing the

---

[39] Some astrologers are able to predict the future – for instance, the Thebans (BH 1.50.2), Athyrtis (1.53.8), the Chaldaeans (2.29.1,31.2; 15.50.3; 17.112.4,116.4; 19.55.8), the Indians (2.40.3), Uranus (3.56.4) and Athenion the astrologer (36.5.4). However, only once (2.30.1–2) does Diodorus explain this as being due to any god-given ability. Other than this, Diodorus rarely reports that those who foresee (προοράω) the future do so without divine assistance. By contrast, the divine element is inevitably emphasized in the verbs for foretelling (προλέγω, προεῖπον, προ-γινώσκω, προδηλόω) which we have already noted, as well as in the noun προρρήσις (which usually refers to astrological predictions).

[40] The belief was widely held beyond the neo-Pythagoreans, however; Diodorus notes it again at BH 37.19.3, and the Stoic Quintus declares this to be his belief (Cicero, De div. 1.30.63) as well as that of Posidonius (1.30.64–5,67.129–30). For examples of this commonplace in other literature, see Aune, Prophecy 397 n. 50, 435 n. 226. Cf. Josephus' comments on a similar belief held by the Indians (BJ 7.353).

[41] Nock, 'Religious Attitudes' 535 n. 6, referring to Aelian, VH 2.31 and secondary literature.

future[42] is eliminated by the many specific examples of predictions which come to fulfilment, thus providing concrete proofs for the view that divine providence is guiding history.

## 6.2 Prophetic activity in Josephus

Josephus demonstrates how a basically Jewish perspective on prophecy can be presented in a thoroughly hellenistic manner without damage to either point of view. This is possible because of the fundamental similarities in the nature of prophetic activity held by Jewish and Greek writers; the divine dimension of 'natural' divination is recognized by both Jewish and Greek writers.[43] The Deuteronomic evaluation of the prophet as a messenger of God, whose authority is validated by the fulfilment of his prophecies, dominates the Hebrew scriptures. In each generation a Mosaic prophet is raised up by God, who guides the prophet in his utterances (Deut 18.18). The false prophet, who tries to show divine authority by giving a sign or wonder (Deut 13.1–2) in imitation of Moses (Deut 34.11), actually teaches rebellion against God (Deut 13.5), and can be recognized by the lack of fulfilment of his prophecies (Deut 18.22).[44]

Examples of fulfilled prophetic oracles are variously noted in scripture: (1) by the verb πληρωθῆναι,[45] (2) by a standardized oracle predicting the end of three royal dynasties,[46] along with the formulaic notice of its fulfilment,[47] (3) by other uses of this formula with

---

[42] See chap. 5 n. 14.

[43] The Israelite equivalent to divination by oracles is prophecy (see Num 12.6; A. Oepke, 'ὄναρ', *TDNT* 5 (1967) 230; Aune, *Prophecy* 82–3; cf. Kraemer, 'προφήτης' 790).

[44] A similar argument is advanced by Plutarch. *De Pyth. orac.* 406F–407C. The Deuteronomistic supporters of the Israelite prophets refrain from criticizing divination in principle, although they do warn of the possible abuses to which such prophetic activities are liable (Deut 13.1–5; Isa 65.2–4; Jer 23.25–32; 34(27).9–10; 36(29).8–9; Zech 10.2; Mic 3.5–7). Sirach equates dreams with divinations and soothsayings (Sir 31(34).5) and advises, 'unless they are sent from the Most High as a visitation, do not give your mind to them' (Sir 31(34).6). See further in Aune, *Prophecy* 87–8.

[45] See 1 Kings 2.27; 1 Kings 8.15,24 (par 2 Chr 6.4,15); 2 Chron 36.1–2 (par 2 Esdras 1.1); 1 Macc 2.55; Dan 4.30.

[46] 'I will utterly sweep away the house of NNN ... anyone belonging to NNN who dies in the city the dogs shall eat; and anyone who dies in the open country the birds of the air shall eat.' The oracle is given by Achias concerning Jeroboam (1 Kings 14.10–11), Jehu concerning Baasha (1 Kings 16.3–4), Elijah concerning Ahab and Jezebel (1 Kings 21.21–4 and 2 Kings 9.7–9).

[47] 'According to the word of the Lord, which he spoke by his servant NNN'; see 1 Kings 15.29; 16.12; 22.38; 2 Kings 9.36.

the same formula[48] or with slight variations on the pattern.[49] It is said of the prophecies of both Samuel (1 Sam 3.19) and Elijah (2 Kings 10.10) that their words do not 'fall to the ground', that is, they find their fulfilment in events of history.[50] The capacity for fulfilment inherent in a true prophecy thus assumes that the activity of the prophet is essentially a predictive activity. As God declares through Deutero-Isaiah, 'so shall my word be, whatever shall proceed out of my mouth, it shall by no means turn back, until all the things which I willed shall have been accomplished' (Isa 55.11). Such fulfilled prophecies thus function as demonstrations of divine guidance in the events of history.[51]

### 6.2.1 Prophetic predictions and their fulfilment

The same characteristics of oracles in the hellenistic historians appear with regard to prophecy in the historical work of Josephus:[52] a true prophecy is predictive; it is inevitably fulfilled and it is therefore divinely given.

#### 6.2.1.1 Prophetic predictions

In his redaction of scriptural stories concerning prophecy, Josephus makes its implicitly predictive nature quite explicit. The prophetic ability to foretell the future is conveyed by various προ- verbs, such as προλέγω, προέρω and προεῖπον,[53] which describe the activities

[48] κατὰ τὸ ῥῆμα κυρίου, at 2 Kings 1.17; 14.25; 24.13.
[49] See 2 Kings 15.12; 17.23; 24.2; 2 Chron 29.25; 36.5; 1 Esdras 8.82 par Ezra 9.11. Tobit 14.5.
[50] Likewise the promise made by God at Josh 1.1–9 is fulfilled through the events narrated in the book, so that 'not one of all the good promises which the Lord had made to the house of Israel had failed; all came to pass' (Josh 21.43(45)).
[51] Van Seters (*In Search of History* 269–75) recognizes this as a major theme in the Deuteronomist's account of David's rise to power. For the same function of prophecies in Mesopotamian literature, see *ibid.*, 96–9.
[52] On prophecy in Josephus, see Fascher, *Prophetes* 161–4; O. Michel, 'Spätjudisches Prophetentum', *Neutestamentliche Studien* (ed. Eltester) 60–6; J. Blenkinsopp 'Prophecy and Priesthood in Josephus', *JJS* 25 (1974) 239–62; G. Delling, 'Die biblische Prophetie bei Josephus', *Josephus Studien* (ed. Betz et al.) 109–21; W. C van Unnik, 'Prophetie bei Josephus', *Flavius Josephus als historischen Schriftstelle;* 41–54; D. E. Aune, 'The Use of προφήτης in Josephus', *JBL* 101 (1982) 419–21 S. J. D. Cohen, 'Josephus, Jeremiah and Polybius', *History and Theory* 21 (1982 366–81; G. L. Johnson, 'Josephus: Heir Apparent to the Prophetic Tradition' *SBLSPS* 22 (1983) 337–46; L. H. Feldman, 'Prophets and Prophecy in Josephus' *JTS* 41 (1990) 386–422.
[53] These verbs of foretelling are not used in the Septuagint. Foreknowledge i ascribed to God (Jub 9.6, 11.19; Ps 138(139).3) and to Wisdom (Wis 19.2) but no

of various 'former prophets'[54] and each of the four major 'latter prophets',[55] as well as some of the 'minor prophets',[56] and even of the prototype of Israelite prophecy, Moses himself.[57] Beyond the biblical paraphrase, the same terms are used to describe the prophetic activity of other individuals,[58] as well as the Essenes,[59] the Pharisees[60] and Josephus himself.[61] These terms are conspicuously

directly to any human person. For the predictive nature of prophecy in Josephus, see Aune, *Prophecy* 153; Feldman, 'Prophets' 394–7, 400, 407–11.

[54] Balaam (προγινώσκω at AJ 4.121, προλέγω and προεῖπον at 4.125), Eli (προαπαγγέλλω and προγινώσκω at 5.358), Samuel (προδηλόω at 6.39, προεῖπον at 6.39,49,57 and 7.27, προερέω at 6.44,66,344, προλέγω at 6.322, πρόρρησις at 6.43, and προγινώσκω at 6.348), Elijah (προλέγω at 8.322, προεῖπον at 8.319,407; 9.26,27,107,124,127; πρόρρησιω at 9.120), Elisha (προερέω at 9.1,74, προεῖπον at 9.175,179,183, προοράω at 9.90), Ahijah (προεῖπον at 8.207,267), Jadon (προερέω at 8.232,235,244, προεῖπον at 8.233, πρόγνωσις at 8.234), Jehu (προεῖπον at 8.299, προερέω at 8.302), Michaiah (προεῖπον at 8.389,403,417, προερέω at 8.412,417) and the false prophets who opposed him (προερέω at 8.404), Zechariah (προλέγω at 9.169) and various unnamed prophets (προλέγω at 9.168,195,265,281; 10.60,268; προεῖπον at 11.4, προκαταγγέλλω at 10.67 and προαποφθέγγομαι at 17.170, and see BJ 4.387 and 6.109). See Blenkinsopp, 'Prophecy' 242–3; Delling, 'Prophetie' 111–14.

[55] Isaiah (προλέγω at AJ 9.265; 10.13,14,33; and see BJ 7.432), Jeremiah (προλέγω at AJ 10.89,92,118, προερέω at 10.96, προεῖπον at 10.141, προθεσπίζω and προκηρύσσω at 10.79), Ezekiel (προεῖπον at 10.141), and Daniel (προεῖπον at 10.217, προλέγω and πρόρρησις at 10.268, προερέω at 10.280). See Blenkinsopp, 'Prophecy' 243–6; van Unnik, 'Prophetie' 52–3; Delling, 'Prophetie' 115–18.

[56] Jonah (προεῖπον at 9.139), Nahum (προερέω at 9.242), Micah (προλέγω at 10.92) and Haggai and Zechariah (προλέγω at 11.96). See van Unnik, 'Prophetie' 51; Delling, 'Prophetie' 114.

[57] προεῖπον at AJ 2.293,329; 3.38; 4.312; 5.40,69,90,96; 7.91; 8.192; πρόρρησις at 4.303. On Moses as a prophet in Josephus, see Meeks, *Prophet–King* 137–42. προεῖπον is also used of David (8.109–10) and Jacob (2.194). προλέγω is used of the high priest at 7.72.

[58] Judas Maccabeus (προλέγω at AJ 12.342) and a number of pagans, such as Salome (προγινώσκω at 16.214), the German prophet (πρόγνωσις and προαγόρευσις at 18.199, προεῖπον at 18.202), Tiberius (προγινώσκω at 18.218), Gaius (προλεύω at 19.31) and his wife Caesarea (προαγορεύω at 19.195,197). See also CA 1.232 (πρόγνωσις) and the criticisms of the seer's πρόρρησις at CA 1.256.

[59] προαγόρευσις at BJ 2.159, πρόγνωσις of Manaemus at AJ 15.373, and for Judas the Essene, see AJ 13.311–12 (προλέγω and προεῖπον) and BJ 1.78 (προαπάγγελμα). See Fascher, *Prophetes* 161; Michel, 'Prophetentum' 60–1; Blenkinsopp, 'Prophecy' 258–9; O. Betz, *Offenbarung und Schriftforschung in der Qumram-Sekte* (WUNT 6; Tübingen: J. C. B. Mohr, 1960) 99–105.

[60] προλέγω and πρόγνωσις at AJ 17.43, and the πρόρρησις of Pollon at AJ 17.45. See Blenkinsopp, 'Prophecy' 257–8.

[61] Josephus never describes himself as a prophet, but does depict his activity in prophetic fashion.

absent from the reports of false prophets who appeared during Josephus' own time.[62]

In discussing Ahab's death, Josephus admonishes his readers to 'realize that nothing is more beneficial than prophecy (προφητείας) and the foreknowledge (προγνώσεως) which it gives, for in this way God enables us to know what to guard against' (AJ 8.418). Thus, when the altar at Bethel broke in two and the fat of the sacrificial victims dripped to the ground, as Jadon had prophesied, Josephus asserts that Jeroboam realized that 'the man was telling the truth and possessed divine foreknowledge' (θείαν πρόγνωσιν, AJ 8.234). So, too, when he notes the good tidings brought through Daniel's prophecies, Josephus comments that 'through the auspiciousness of his predictions (προλεγομένων) he attracted the goodwill of all . . . and at the same time won their esteem for his divine power' (θειότητος, AJ 10.268). In his brief encomium of John Hyrcanus, Josephus describes him as 'accounted by God worthy of three of the greatest privileges, the rule of the nation, the office of high-priest, and the gift of prophecy; for the Deity (τὸ θεῖον) was with him and enabled him to foresee and foretell[63] the future' (AJ 13.299–300).

### 6.2.1.2 Fulfilment of prophecy

Prophecy contains an inexorable quality, which Josephus emphasizes as he concludes his report of the fall of Jerusalem. Noting the inevitability of the prophecies made by Jeremiah and Ezekiel concerning this event, he draws his familiar moral from the inability of the royal courtiers to perceive this fact:

> these things, then, which we have related should make it sufficiently clear to those who do not know, how varied and manifold is the nature of God and how those things which

[62] A Samaritan (AJ 18.85–7), an Egyptian (AJ 20.168–72 par BJ 2.261–3) and an unnamed Palestinian (BJ 6.285–6) are described as ψευδοπροφῆται. Theudas (AJ 20.97–9), the same Egyptian (BJ 2.261–3) and other unnamed Palestinians (AJ 20.167–8 par BJ 2.259, AJ 20.188) are labelled γόητες. See Fascher, Prophetes 162–4 P. W. Barnett, 'The Jewish Sign Prophets – A.D. 40–70 – Their Intentions and Origin', NTS 27 (1981) 679–97; Blenkinsopp, 'Prophecy' 259–61. On false prophets in biblical times, see Schlatter, Theologie 221–3; Michel, 'Prophetentum' 61–3 Delling, 'Prophetie' 119–20; J. Reiling, 'The Use of ψευδοπροφήτης in the Septuagint, Philo and Josephus', NovT 13 (1971) 155.

[63] The translation quoted here, that by Marcus in the Loeb Classical Library unaccountably downplays the saturation of predictive terms. The Greek reads τὴν τῶν μελλόντων πρόγνωσιν παρεῖχεν αὐτῷ τε εἰδέναι καὶ προλέγειν οὕτως προεῖδέν τε καὶ προφήτευσεν.

he foretells must come to pass (ἅ τε δεῖ γενέσθαι προ-λέγει), duly take place at the appointed hour, and should also make clear the ignorance and disbelief of those men, by which they were prevented from foreseeing any of these future events and, when they were delivered over to disaster, were taken off their guard, so that any attempt to escape from it was impossible for them.     (AJ 10.142)

Thus Josephus expands and intensifies the note of fulfilment which is to be found, on occasion, in various parts of the biblical material (notably within the Deuteronomic history), using a variety of formulas to attest to this aspect of prophecy.

The standard Deuteronomistic oracle predicting the end of the royal dynasties in Israel, and the similarly standardized note of its fulfilment, which we noted above, is reported on each occasion by Josephus, although without the repetitive pattern of his source. Further prophetic oracles whose predictions duly come to pass are noted in the Deuteronomic history by means of similar formulas, and Josephus reports almost all of these,[64] but again without following the pattern of his source. Indeed, Josephus himself uses a variety of phrases to note the way events occurred 'in accordance with the prophecy'[65] or 'just as the prophet foretold'.[66] On seven occasions the word τέλος is applied to pronouncements of prophets which occur as predicted.[67] Josephus thus makes it clear that

---

[64] He omits 2 Kings 15.12 and the details of the sacking of the Temple in 2 Kings 24.13. He does note the fulfilment of the prophecies of 2 Kings 1.17 (AJ 9.27); 2 Kings 14.25 (AJ 9.207); 2 Kings 17.23 (AJ 9.281); 2 Kings 24.2 (AJ 10.96); and see 2 Chron 29.25 (AJ 9.269). On the fulfilment of prophecies in Josephus, see Delling, 'Prophetie' 112–14.

[65] κατὰ τὴν προφητείαν appears 13 times in AJ (6.57,136; 7.214; 8.110,289,309; 9.85,175,185; 10.35,107,280; 12.322) as well as at BJ 4.387; κατὰ τὴν πρόρρησιν AJ 9.120; cf. 4.303.

[66] καθὼς προεῖπεν ὁ προφήτης is used at AJ 8.233; 9.27,107,129; 10.141,217. Similar phrases used include καθὼς εἶπεν ὁ προφήτης (8.273), προεφήτευσεν (6.261,336), ὡς προεφήτευσεν (9.207), προφητεύσαντος (9.86,242) and τὰ ὑπὸ [NNN] προειρημένα (9.74,103,242; 10.280). Cf. the notes of fulfilled prophecies which record the name of the prophet but also note that God spoke through them (Eli at 6.261, Elijah at 9.129, Isaiah at 10.33, Jeremiah at 10.126,178, Ezekiel and Jeremiah at 11.96), or which simply ascribe the prophecy directly to God (8.289, 9.145).

[67] The noun is used with the verb λαμβάνω in connection with Balaam's predictions of future calamities (AJ 4.125), Achias' prediction of the divided kingdom (8.218) and his forecasting of the death of Ahab (8.409), Elisha's oracle concerning an abundance of food in the midst of a famine (9.73) and Jadon's prophecy of Josiah's reforms (10.67). Josephus also uses the phrases παρελθεῖν εἰς τέλος of David (7.373)

'whatever happens to us, whether for good or ill, comes about in accordance with their prophecies' (κατά τὴν ἐκείνων προφητείαν, AJ 10.35). Such fulfilment of prophecy functions to interpret the events which have occurred in an apologetic fashion, as authentic indications of the divine will.

### 6.2.1.3 Prophecy and providence

This third feature of prophecy, its divine quality, is frequently asserted by Josephus. Even foreign rulers acknowledge such: Benhadad notes that 'the Deity (τὸ θεῖον) was so evidently present' with Elisha (AJ 9.60) and Cyrus 'wondered at the divine power (τὸ θεῖον ὁρμή), in the words of Isaiah (AJ 11.6). The ability of the prophets to perform signs[68] is a clear indication of their divine capacities, as is the inspiration (ἔνθεος) of Elijah (AJ 8.346) and Elisha (AJ 9.35). However, the most characteristic expression of the divine power which energizes prophecy is provided when Josephus links prophecy with his distinctive notion of divine providence, such as in his final comments on the prophecies of Daniel:

> it therefore seems to me, in view of the things foretold (προειρημένοις) by Daniel, that they are very far from holding a true opinion who declare that God takes no thought (πρόνοιαν) for human affairs. For if it were the case that the world goes on by some automatism (αὐτοματισμῷ), we should not have seen all these things happen in accordance with his prophecy (κατὰ τὴν ἐκείνου προφητείαν).          (AJ 10.280)

Josephus thus notes both Daniel's ability to foretell the future (10.267) and the accuracy of his predictions (10.269), with the result that the prophecies are fulfilled.[69] These aspects of prophecy, which we have seen to be central to the hellenistic understanding of history, and which are prominent elsewhere in Josephus' writings, are here

and ἀπὸ τοῦ τέλους of Daniel (10.268). The noun is also used at AJ 2.73; 3.189 and 7.275, and BJ 4.386–7 with the sense of fulfilment. Cf. ἐπιτελῆ at AJ 8.110.

[68] σημεῖα are performed by Jadon at Bethel (AJ 8.236,244), Elijah on Mount Carmel (8.347) and Isaiah in Jerusalem (10.28–9); see Betz, 'Wunders' 29–30. Elijah performed θαυμαστὰ καὶ παράδοξα as a result of the divine power (δύναμιν θείαν) which he had (9.182–3). By means of thunder, lightning and hail God signifies the truth of Samuel's prophecy (AJ 6.92).

[69] Josephus suggests that it is valuable to read the book of Daniel because in it one can 'learn of the hidden things which are to come' (AJ 10.210). See also 10.277.

drawn into close proximity with providence. The fundamental argument of this passage is that the fulfilment of Daniel's prophecies is a proof of the existence of divine providence.[70]

The same cluster of features appears in Josephus' summary of Solomon's exhortations at the dedication of the Temple, when he

> made clear the power and providence of God (τοῦ θεοῦ τὴν δύναμιν καὶ τὴν πρόνοιαν) in that most of the future events which he had revealed to David, his father, had actually come to pass (καθὼς ἀποβέβηκεν), and the rest would come about, and how God ... had foretold (προείποι) what he was to be called and that none but he should build Him a temple ... and now that they saw the fulfilment (ἐπιτελῆ) of these things in accordance with David's prophecy (κατὰ τὴν ἐκείνου προφητείαν), he asked them to praise God.
>
> (AJ 8.109–10)

Josephus makes the same point, somewhat less compactly, but nevertheless with the same emphatic force, in his retelling of the story of Balaam. This pagan seer has acquired a certain fame because of his ability to foretell the future (AJ 4.105),[71] but these abilities of Balaam do not come from human abilities, for 'wholly impotent are those who pretend to foreknowledge of human affairs (οἱ προγινώσκειν περὶ τῶν ἀνθρωπίνων), drawn from their own breasts, as to refrain from speaking that which the deity suggests (τὸ θεῖον λέγειν), and to violate His will (βούλησιν)' (AJ 4.121).[72] Further, it is clear to Josephus that Balaam's prophecies did indeed come true, and thus 'from all these prophecies having received the fulfilment (τέλος) which he predicted (προεῖπε) one may infer what the future also has in store' (AJ 4.125). Finally, the theme of divine

[70] For the connection between prophecy and providence in Josephus, see van Unnik, 'Prophetie' 54 and 'Attack' 342–3; Talbert, 'Promise and Fulfilment' 98; Attridge, 'Josephus' 223–4; Delling, 'Prophetie' 119; Feldman, 'Prophets' 393. The link is expressed by Plutarch at *De defec. orac.* 413A; 423C; 435E; *De Pyth. orac.* 402E; and see also chapter 5.2.2 concerning dreams. Van Unnik ('Attack 347–8) notes that the argument at AJ 10.278–80 is the same as that proposed by the Stoic Cleanthes, who in his discussion of divination claimed that because humans are able to have foreknowledge of future events the gods must exist (see Cicero, *De nat. deor.* 2.5.13).

[71] He predicts to Balak that the Hebrews shall occupy the land (AJ 4.115) and that there will be calamities for kings and cities yet unheard of (AJ 4.125).

[72] Although he is never labelled a prophet, Balaam is nevertheless controlled by the divine spirit (τὸ τοῦ θεοῦ πνεῦμα, AJ 4.118,119) and makes inspired utterances (ἐπεθείαζεν, 4.118). The divine origin of Balaam's prophecies is noted frequently (AJ 4.105,107,108,109,110,111,114,117,121 and 124).

providence is associated with the prophecies, for the providence of God which is given to Israel (πρόνοιαν, AJ 4.114,117) forms the basis for Balaam's predictions of Israelite prosperity.[73]

The predictive ability of a number of prophets is related to the will of God, which both motivates some prophecies[74] and is the content of other prophecies.[75] The same connection between prophetic activity and providence can be seen in Josephus' use of the verb χρηματίζω, which is infrequent in the Septuagint,[76] but is applied by Josephus, in his biblical paraphrase, to divine oracles given to Moses (AJ 3.212), Joshua (AJ 5.42) and Daniel (AJ 10.13).[77] Later, he describes the task of the priest in these terms when he reports Azariah's prophecy that there would be 'no true prophet ... nor any priest to give righteous judgement' (τὰ δίκαια χρηματίζων, AJ 8.296) because of disobedience to the will (βούλησιν) of God (AJ 8.295). Likewise Jaddus the high priest, after God had spoken oracularly (ἐχρημάτισεν) to him in a dream, announced the revelation (τὸ χρηματισθέν) that his people would be kept safe by the providence (προνοουμένου) of God (AJ 11.327–8).[78]

Thus the connections which Josephus draws between predictive prophecies, their fulfilment in history and the providence of God are firm and frequent. The relation of prophecy to providence is always assumed and often expressed in the writings of Josephus. In this he reflects an unquestioningly Septuagintal theme, but in such a way

[73] The other example of a pagan prophet who emphasizes the relation between his predictive ability and divine providence is the German prisoner who foretells future blessings for his fellow prisoner Agrippa. The German warns Agrippa, 'you will hardly credit the statement that interprets Divine Providence (τοῦ θείου τὴν πρόνοιαν) as designing your deliverance from your present difficulty' (AJ 18.197), but then proceeds 'to set forth clearly what the gods foretell' (τὴν προαγόρευσιν τῶν θεῶν, 18.199).

[74] Prophecies occur κατὰ τὴν τοῦ θεοῦ βούλησιν at AJ 5.120; 8.218,328. The death of the prophet Jadon also occurs in accordance with the will of God (8.241), because he succumbs to the invitation of the false prophet at Bethel (8.239). The will of God, here opposed to false prophecy, is clearly linked with true prophecy.

[75] See ὁ θεὸς βούλεται (AJ 8.207); κατὰ βούλησιν θεοῦ (8.295,389). Isaiah tells Cyrus that God has told him 'it is my will (βούλομαι) that Cyrus ... shall build my temple' (11.5). The near sacrifice of Isaac, which takes place κατὰ τὴν τοῦ θεοῦ βούλησιν (1.223) and ἐκ τῆς ἐκείνου προνοίας (1.225), is described by Josephus as occurring because of a prophecy (πρόρρησις) of God (1.225).

[76] It is used of divine oracles to Jeremiah only at Jer 32(35).30; 33(26).2; 36(29).3; 37(30).2; see also Job 40.3(8). Elijah uses it, mockingly, of Baal at 1 Kings 18.27.

[77] He also notes that an oracle convinced the Samaritans to worship the Most High God (AJ 9.289) and that the sacred scriptures contain an oracle which was to apply to Vespasian (BJ 6.312).

[78] Cf. Saul's rebuke of Abimelech for delivering oracles (ἐχρημάτιζες, AJ 6.255), the only negative use of this term.

that it is eminently comprehensible to hellenistic readers. Indeed, Josephus' own view of prophecy points to Deuteronomistic and hellenistic historiographical features which are both to be found in his work, and highlights the way in which prophetic activity was widely understood to be an expression of divine providence in human history.

### 6.3 Fulfilled prophecy and the plan of God in Luke–Acts

In this context of consensus with regard to the relation of prophecy to providence, certain aspects of prophecy and fulfilment in Luke–Acts can be seen to be yet a further expression of the theme of the plan of God. Luke signals his interest in the theme of fulfilled prophecy in the preface to the Gospel, where he describes the content of his work as 'the things which have been accomplished among us' (περὶ τῶν πεπληροφορημένων, Luke 1.1), and towards the end of the Gospel, where the risen Jesus explains how 'everything written about me in the law of Moses and the prophets and the psalms must be fulfilled' (Luke 24.44).[79] The opening chapters of Acts not only look forward to coming events[80] but also indicate the ongoing fulfilment of scripture (Acts 1.16–20; 2.16–21). The end of Acts depicts Israel's refusal to believe by quoting a prophecy from the scriptures of Israel (Isa 6.9–10), which is now deemed to have been fulfilled (Acts 28.25–8). Thus, the beginning and ending of each volume point to the importance of fulfilled prophecies in Luke's literary and theological purposes.[81]

Indeed, by stressing the prophetic role of a number of characters in his story, Luke makes it clear that prophecy is a significant, ongoing phenomenon. In addition to references to the prophets of Israelite history,[82] there are a number of people who are depicted as prophets, beginning with Zechariah (Luke 1.67), Elizabeth (Luke

---

[79] Schulz ('Vorsehung' 115) comments, 'Tora, Propheten und Psalmen sind der Mund der Providentia, der Prognosis.'

[80] Jesus repeats his prediction concerning 'the promise of the Father' (Acts 1.4; cf. Luke 24.49) and prophesies the course of the testimony which will follow from the gift of the Spirit (Acts 1.8). The programmatic significance of such prophetic statements is noted by Dibelius, *Studies* 193–4; Johnson, *Possessions* 16–18. On Acts 1.8, see the literature cited by Johnson (*ibid.*, 7 n. 4).

[81] Commenting on the threefold scheme of God's plan, Conzelmann (*Theology* 150) declares: 'it is prophecy in particular that creates the continuity'. Johnson (*Possessions* 17–18) emphasizes the role of Luke 1–2 and Acts 28 especially.

[82] Luke 1.70; 3.4; 4.17,22; 6.23; 10.24; 11.47,49,50; 13.28,33–4; 16.16,29,31; 18.31; 24.21,27,44; see Jervell, 'The Center of Scripture in Luke', *Unknown Paul* 122–37.

1.41), Anna (Luke 2.36) and John the Baptist (Luke 1.76; 7.26,28; 20.6; Acts 13.24). Jesus is called a prophet by Jewish crowds (Luke 7.16; 9.8,19)[83] and by Cleopas (Luke 24.19), although some cast doubt on his prophetic powers (Luke 7.39; 22.64).[84] Twice he is presented as fulfilling the prediction concerning 'a prophet like Moses' (Deut 18.15,18, quoted at Acts 3.22–3; 7.37).[85] Verification of this claim comes through the ultimate fulfilment of a number of predictions made by Jesus.[86]

In addition to predictive abilities, Luke sees that another prophetic mark was suffering persecution and murder (Luke 6.22–3; 11.47,49; Acts 7.52). That Jesus was treated in the same way thus further characterizes him as a prophet (Luke 4.24; 13.33,34).[87] This same persecution was experienced by the Jerusalem community of believers (Acts 8.1–3; 9.1–2; 11.19); Luke especially notes that this community included a number of prophets.[88] One of a number of Jerusalem prophets who come to Antioch (11.27) is Agabus, who predicts the famine which occurred under Claudius (11.28); two others are Judas, called Barsabbas, and Silas (15.32), one of Paul's two main travelling companions (see 15.40–18.5). In all, Luke mentions twelve Christian prophets by name and infers the existence of many more.[89] Paul, by contrast, is never explicitly described as a

---

[83] See Fascher, *Prophetes* 176–7; Aune, *Prophecy* 124,127,154,158–69.

[84] It is clear, however, that the real false prophets are those referred to at Luke 6.26, Acts 13.6 and alluded to at Luke 17.23; 21.8. Note also the pseudo-prophetic figures of Theudas (Acts 5.36), Judas (Acts 5.37) and the Egyptian (Acts 21.38).

[85] See Johnson, *Possessions* 60–9, 91–103; Aune, *Prophecy* 155.

[86] See Aune, *Prophecy* 171–87; and above, chap. 2.3.3.1. Many of Jesus' predictions come from Luke's Markan source (Luke 9.22,44; 18.17,29–30,31–3; 19.30; 21.6–33; 22.10–12,21,34,69) and his sayings source (Q) (Luke 10.14,15; 11.30; 13.28–9,35; 17.23–4,26–7,34–7). Luke has added others unique to his Gospel (Luke 5.10; 15.7; 17.22,25,28–30; 19.43–4; 21.34–5; 22.15–18; 23.29–30,43).

[87] See Aune, *Prophecy* 157–9; cf. the reservations of Moule, 'Christology' 162. Ticde (*Prophecy* 47) suggests that Luke 4.16–30 'represents a Christian response to the charge that Jesus was a false prophet'; see also J. A. Sanders, 'From Isaiah 61 to Luke 4', *Christianity, Judaism and Other Greco-Roman Cults: Studies for Morton Smith at Sixty* (Studies in Judaism in Late Antiquity 12, 4 parts; ed. J. Neusner; Leiden: Brill, 1975) 1.99.

[88] On prophets in the early Christian communities, see Aune, *Prophecy* 263–6. In addition to sounding the theme of prophecy at Acts 2.17–18, Luke also depicts as prophetic the first martyr Stephen, whose long speech (7.2–53) can be regarded as a prophetic condemnation of contemporary religion, grounded in a covenantal understanding of Israel's relationship to God (7.8,32). On the proof-from-prophecy motif in Stephen's speech, see Dahl, 'Abraham' 142–8. Likewise, the prayer of the Jerusalem believers (4.24–30) can be viewed as a petition for the prophetic phenomena of bold speech (4.29) and signs and wonders (4.30).

[89] Aune, *Prophecy* 191.

prophet. He is, however, often to be found in prophetic company[90] and is thus regarded as a prophet by association rather than by acclamation during his missionary activity.[91]

Thus, prophetic figures play a significant role throughout Luke's two-volume work. This is more than just adopting a paradigm of scriptural prophecy, for Luke has these figures carry out an important role in the ongoing story of God's plan. The fulfilment of scripture and the realization of spoken oracles take Luke's narrative beyond a typology of fulfilling individual predictions, and move in the direction of a promise-fulfilment schema. In this context, everything that occurs is seen to be part of an overall pattern in which God's promises continue to come to fruition throughout the story. Such written prophecies and spoken predictions can be understood within the hellenistic context of predictions uttered by prophets at oracular shrines under divine inspiration, as well as in the light of written collections of oracles which are consulted for guidance in understanding events.[92] However, they especially serve the larger apologetic purposes of Luke in relation to two key issues. The fulfilment of prophecies reveals God's age-old intentions concerning both the passion of Jesus and the mission to the Gentiles.

## 6.3.1 Predictions concerning the passion of Jesus

### 6.3.1.1 Predictions spoken by Jesus

Our examinations of the preface and the prologue to the Gospel have demonstrated how the fulfilment of prophecy is set forth as a major theme in Luke–Acts from the very beginning. It is already very clear, by the start of the public ministry of Jesus, that because some predictions have already been fulfilled, other predictions, yet

---

[90] He journeys with Silas (Acts 15.40); in Ephesus he enables a dozen disciples to engage in prophetic activity (19.6–7); in Caesarea he stays with Philip, whose four daughters also prophesied (21.9).

[91] Johnson (*Possessions* 59) deduces that the various 'Men of the Spirit' in Acts are 'portrayed deliberately as Prophets' by literary means if not by explicit titles. Minear ('Birth Stories' 120) includes Paul among his list of prophets in Luke–Acts; see also Aune, *Prophecy* 422 n. 2. Certain aspects of Paul's activities in Acts 13.1–19.20 have prophetic overtones: he is commissioned by the Spirit (13.2,4); he interprets the history of Israel covenantally (13.17,22); he condemns infidelity in Israel (13.46); he performs signs (14.3,8–10; 15.12; 19.12; see also 20.7–12; 28.3–5,8–9).

[92] See above, chapter 6.1.1 to 6.1.3. For the predictive nature of prophecies in Acts, see Fascher, *Prophetes* 169–70; G. Friedrich, 'προφήτης', *TDNT* 6 (1968) 832–3; Aune, *Prophecy* 264.

unfulfilled or still to be noted, will in turn be accomplished. So, when Jesus reads from the scroll of Isaiah (61.1–2) and then announces that this writing has been fulfilled (πεπλήρωται, 4.21), Theophilus and all who read or hear this story (unlike the surprised audience in the synagogue) are completely prepared for his bold claim, for the extended prologue has already introduced him most thoroughly to the motif of divinely inspired predictions which are now coming to fulfilment. Indeed, this declaration of the fulfilment of prophecy applies not only to this specific incident in Nazareth, but has a programmatic significance,[93] for it refers to the whole of Jesus's life, which is presented as a fulfilment of prophecies, both ancient and contemporary.[94] This is most strikingly so with regard to the passion of Jesus.

Already in his Markan source, Luke has at hand the important triple prediction of the suffering, death and resurrection of the Son of Man (Mark 8.31–3; 9.30–2; 10.32–4), which depicts Jesus as a prophet making predictions which come to fulfilment. Luke edits this triple prediction[95] to emphasize both the predictive capacities of Jesus and, especially, the clarity of fulfilment of these prophecies.

Jesus' passion predictions are related by Luke to the crucial journey of Luke 9–19 (which we consider in more detail in the next chapter). The first prediction (9.22)[96] precedes the Transfiguration (9.28–36), with its announcement of Jesus' journey (9.31), and the healing of the possessed boy, which Luke presents as a mighty act of God (9.43). Before Jesus decides to set out towards Jerusalem (9.51), his prediction is repeated in summary form (9.44); its significance is emphasized by the contrast with the disciples' lack of understanding.[97] During the journey, allusions to this prediction

[93] This is widely recognized; see Tiede, *Prophecy* 19–23, 34–9; Sanders, 'From Isaiah 61' 80; Marshall, *Luke* 177–8.

[94] See especially Luke 7.22; 19.46; 20.17; 22.37.

[95] On Luke's use of the Markan triple prediction, see Wilckens, *Missionsreden* 116–17; Marshall, *Luke* 367–71, 392–4, 689–91. On the literary function of the triple prediction in Luke, see Aune, *Prophecy* 178. Danker (*Jesus* 302) argues for a series of six passion predictions.

[96] Luke finds in his source a dominical saying in which the motif of necessity already governs the four elements of the prediction: 'the Son of Man must (δεῖ) suffer ... be rejected ... be killed ... be raised' (Mark 8.31); see Marshall, *Luke* 369–71.

[97] This is expressed in three distinct clauses, 'they did not understand ... it was concealed from them ... they were afraid to ask' (9.45); then exemplified in two incidents in which Jesus corrects their false understandings of greatness (9.46–8) and exorcism (9.49–50); see Marshall, *Luke* 394–5; Fitzmyer, *Luke* 1.813.

recur (11.30[?]; 12.50; 13.33; 17.25).[98] As the journey draws near to its end, Jesus repeats his prediction in full (18.31–3). Here Luke again highlights its significance by repeating the disciples' ignorance (18.34),[99] adding a reference to the scriptural prophecies[100] and emphasizing that 'everything will be accomplished' (τελεσθήσεται πάντα, 18.31). By the time Jesus enters Jerusalem, his predictive capacities have been made quite clear.

In the subsequent passion narrative, each element of Jesus's prediction comes to pass, vindicating his prophetic powers.[101] He is delivered[102] to men who seize him with their hands.[103] He is rejected by the Jewish leaders[104] and delivered to the Gentiles.[105] His suffering is depicted at various points in the passion narrative; most notably, Luke thrice repeats that he is mocked.[106] In accord with his own predictions, he is also scourged[107] and treated shamefully[108] (but not spat upon),[109] and so his death takes place as predicted.[110]

The final chapter of the Gospel contains three main scenes, each

---

[98] Tiede (*Prophecy* 72) comments that 'the divine purposes ... are disclosed only by oblique allusions that the reader may spot in retrospect of their accomplishment'.

[99] 'They understood nothing ... this saying was hid from them ... they did not grasp what was said', Luke 18.34; cf. 9.45. Tiede (*Prophecy* 32) considers the ignorance motif, already introduced at 2.49–50, to be 'a literary technique for alerting the reader that as the narrative unfolds, the divine plan will be disclosed in greater detail'; see also *Prophecy* 84–6.

[100] This gives greater authority to the predictions, for they are seen to be an integral part of divine revelation. Precisely what ancient prophecies Luke has in mind, however, remains a mystery (see Tiede, *Prophecy* 100–1); by contrast, the contemporary oracles of Jesus are reported in detail.

[101] Talbert ('Promise and Fulfilment' 99) interprets this and other fulfilments as a legitimation of Jesus' authority; likewise, see Danker, *Jesus* 266.

[102] παραδίδοσθαι of 9.44 is used of Judas at 22.4,6,21,22,48.

[103] χεῖρας of 9.44 is used of the band who arrests Jesus at 22.53.

[104] The three terms of 9.22 (πρεσβυτέρων, ἀρχιερέων, γραμματέων) recur at 22.66; the first term is joined with στρατηγούς at 22.52; the latter two terms are also used at 23.10.

[105] Predicted at 18.32, fulfilled (under Pilate) at 23.1–25.

[106] The prediction of 18.32 is fulfilled at 22.63 (by the men holding Jesus in the high priest's house), 23.11 (by Herod and his soldiers, who dress him lavishly) and 23.36 (by the soldiers, who offer him vinegar on the cross).

[107] Predicted at Luke 18.33, fulfilled at 22.63.

[108] Predicted at Luke 18.32, fulfilled at 22.47–53 (betrayed by a friend); 22.54–62 (denied by Peter); 22.63–5 (mockingly ordered to 'prophesy'); 23.11 (dressed contemptuously); 23.18–25 (replaced by Barabbas); 23.34 (lots are cast for his garments); 23.39 (one criminal rails at him).

[109] The prediction of Luke 18.32 is not fulfilled in Luke (cf. Mark 14.65; 15.19; both omitted by Luke).

[110] This prediction (9.22; 13.31; 18.33; and see 20.14,15 in the parable of the wicked tenants) is fulfilled at 23.46.

of which revolves around the fulfilment of prophecy.[111] In the first scene, at the empty tomb (24.1–12), the two men in dazzling apparel repeat the predictions once more (24.7). With the benefit of hindsight, they give still more specificity to the words of Jesus.[112] Yet the narrative turns away from an instantaneous resolution. Luke had the opportunity to recount the immediate fulfilment of the last item of the prediction (resurrection on the third day). Instead, he notes that the women's report to the disciples is dismissed as 'an idle tale' (24.11). This sets up a contrary thread running through the last chapter of the Gospel: the fulfilment of predictions must now be declared in the face of misunderstanding and opposition even from within the group of Jesus's own disciples.[113]

The irony of this situation is heightened by Luke in the two scenes which follow. In the second scene (24.13–32), the passion prediction is repeated (24.20). To the travellers on the road to Emmaus, however, it appears that the last part of the prediction – resurrection on the third day – is unfulfilled (24.21). Thus, it is precisely as the decisive vindication of the prophetic powers of Jesus is at last made manifest that his followers are unable to recognize him as such. Although the travellers describe Jesus as 'a prophet mighty in deed and word before God' (24.19), they are unable to recognize him as such (24.16). Even when he interprets the fulfilment of what 'Moses and all the prophets' predicted in 'all the scriptures' (24.26–7), they do not recognize him (24.31).[114] It is only with hindsight, after the breaking of bread (24.30,35), that they understand that it was the interpretation of prophecy which provided the key to identifying Jesus (24.32).

In the third scene of this chapter (24.33–53),[115] the motif of misunderstanding continues. 'The eleven and those who were with them' in Jerusalem (24.33) receive the travellers' message, but even

[111] Schubert ('Luke 24' 172–7) demonstrates that the climax of each of the three pericopes in Luke 24 is the proof-from-prophecy concerning Jesus' passion and resurrection, in a steadily ascending manner, culminating in 24.44; see also Fitzmyer, *Luke* 2.1540, 1558.

[112] The Son of man is to be delivered into the hands of men who are described as 'sinful', and the means of death is identified as crucifixion. See Marshall, *Luke* 371, 886. Fitzmyer (*Luke* 2.1542–3) notes that only in Luke's account of the empty tomb is there any reference to such a prediction.

[113] We have seen this conjunction of prophecy and misunderstanding at Luke 9.44–5; 18.31–4; cf. 22.37; see also Danker, *Luke* 391.

[114] Fitzmyer (*Luke* 2.1563) notes 'the dramatic concealment used by Luke to build up suspense'.

[115] Although a composite of various sources, verses 36–53 function as one scene (Fitzmyer, *Luke* 2.1572).

when Jesus himself appears, they are 'startled and frightened' (24.37), 'troubled and questioning' (24.38). After Jesus speaks to them, they still 'disbelieved for joy and wondered' (24.41). Yet the Gospel ends on a vastly different note: the believers are blessed by Jesus (24.50,51), they show 'great joy' (24.52) and they bless God in temple worship (24.53). This breakthrough comes as a result of the final and most extensive exposition of fulfilled prophecy (24.44–7). Jesus asserts the comprehensive nature of the fulfilment he had brought about, encompassing not only his own words, but also all major parts of scripture (24.44). Once again he asserts the necessity of his suffering and resurrection (24.46),[116] thus bringing the first volume to a resolution. What has taken place has all been in accord with what God has intended, declared and decreed necessary. Jesus then moves on to indicate that the programme of the second volume also springs out of the fulfilment of prophecy (24.47–9).[117] In this concluding statement, the Lukan Jesus thus links his own prophetic oracles with the ancient Israelite prophecies, which together have been fulfilled by his passion and resurrection in Jerusalem. The Gospel ends with a resolution brought about by means of the fulfilment of prophecy.

### 6.3.1.2 *Prophecies written in the scriptures*

This second strand of prophecies, those written in scripture, which relate to Jesus' passion, appears on occasions throughout Luke's Gospel. Luke notes that the ἔξοδον[118] of Jesus was to be fulfilled (πληροῦν) at Jerusalem (9.31), and that in this city 'everything that is written of the Son of Man by the prophets will be accomplished' (τελεσθήσεται, 18.31).[119] In material found only in Luke, Jesus looks forward to his passion, figuratively described as a baptism

---

[116] Jervell (*Unknown Paul* 135–6) rightly notes that the content of all of Luke's references to scripture is the suffering and resurrection of Christ; see also Moule, 'Christology' 168.

[117] 'It is written' governs three infinitives; two are concerned with the passion (παθεῖν and ἀναστῆναι), the third with the mission to the Gentiles (κηρυχθῆναι).

[118] Whilst this word has clear scriptural overtones, it also has a role in Greek tragedy which is generally overlooked: the final scene of a tragedy was described as an ἔξοδος (see Tiede, *Prophecy* 149 n. 16). Although Tiede considers Jesus' exodus as quite different (*ibid.*, 104), he later (*ibid.*, 114–16) notes certain similarities between Luke's passion narrative and Greek tragedy.

[119] Luke has added these references to fulfilment respectively to the sayings source (Luke 9.31, cf. Matt 17.3) and to the Markan source (18.31, cf. Mark 10.33). See also Luke 22.16 on eschatological fulfilment, a saying unique to Luke.

which is yet to be accomplished (τελεσθῇ, 12.50), and quotes Isaiah 53.12, emphasizing that 'this scripture must be fulfilled (δεῖ τελε-σθῆναι) in me ... for what is written about me has its fulfilment' (τέλος ἔχει, 22.37).[120]

It is after the resurrection, however, that this motif is most prominent, beginning with the words of the risen Jesus himself (24.44) and continuing throughout the second volume.[121] Recourse to the prophecies of Hebrew scripture is found in contexts where early Christians are engaged in debate or dispute with Jews, both in Jerusalem and throughout the Diaspora. It has been suggested that, by focussing on this aspect of the Gentile mission, Luke is addressing problems current in his own time, and offering a solution in the words of Peter and Paul.[122] Thus, problems associated with the passion of Jesus are resolved by recourse to the scriptures.[123]

In speeches in which, as we have seen, divine providence is asserted, the fulfilment of prophecy in the passion of Jesus is integral to the apologetic argument.[124] Peter proclaims that the suffering of Christ was foretold by God 'through the mouth of all the prophets' and is thus fulfilled (ἐπλήρωσεν) in Jesus' passion (Acts 3.18).[125] The inspired David also spoke God's message concerning the opposition encountered by 'the Lord and his anointed' (4.25–6)[126] which came to pass in the rejection of Jesus in Jerusalem (4.27). Luke quotes a selection from Isaiah 53 concerning the humiliation of the servant

---

[120] For different nuances between the verb and noun in this verse, see Fitzmyer, *Luke* 2.1433. Schulz ('Vorsehung' 115) calls this verse, with its linking of necessity and fulfilment, 'die Kardinalstelle für die lukanische Umformung der Schriftzitatfor-mel'. See also Wilckens, *Missionsreden* 139–43.

[121] Jesus' own use of scripture thus sets out 'the principle of exegesis which is later frequently employed in the Acts of the Apostles' (Conzelmann, *Theology* 157). Fitzmyer (*Luke* 2.1583) collates scriptural references to the Messiah which may be pertinent, but issues a warning against becoming more specific than Luke himself does (*ibid.*, 2.1567).

[122] For a brief sketch of such a context, see Wilson, *Gentiles* 248–9; see further, Esler, *Community and Gospel* 220–3.

[123] See chap. 5, p. 115. Rokeah (*Conflict* 93) comments that 'even the Christians admitted that these events were of such a character as to be inconceivable in connection with a Messiah and a God had they not been foreseen by the prophets'.

[124] On the apologetic function of such prophecies, see Cadbury, *Making* 304; Kurz, 'Proof from Prophecy' 149–54, 174–84; Johnson, *Writings* 205.

[125] On the prophecy–fulfilment theme in Peter's speech, see Dahl, 'Abraham' 149; for the rhetorical form of the proof at 3.18, see Kurz, 'Proof from Prophecy' 121–2; on divine providence in the speech, see chap. 3.3.3.1. Haenchen (*Acts* 207–8) paraphrases thus: 'so by God's will it had to come to pass'. Later, Peter draws upon Psalm 118.22 (Acts 4.11), which he sees fulfilled in Jesus' death and resurrection (4.10).

[126] The Lord's anointed (Acts 4.26, quoting Ps 2.2) is explicitly identified as Jesus, whom God anointed (4.27). On providence in this prayer, see chap. 4.3.2.

(8.32–3) and applies this to Jesus (8.34–5). Paul likewise states that by condemning Jesus, the people of Jerusalem and their leaders fulfilled (ἐπλήρωσαν) 'the utterances of the prophets which are read every sabbath' (13.27); after his death, 'when they had fulfilled (ἐτέλεσαν) all that was written of him, they took him down from the tree' (13.29).[127] The prophetic basis for Paul's preaching of the passion and resurrection of Jesus is asserted in Thessalonica (17.2) and Beroea (17.11); at the climax of his speech before Agrippa, Paul apologetically asserts that he preaches 'nothing but what the prophets and Moses said would come to pass (μελλόντων γίνεσθαι) – that the Christ must suffer . . . and be the first to rise from the dead' (26.23).[128]

Furthermore, within the speeches asserting God's providence, the motif of fulfilled prophecy applies beyond the death and resurrection of Jesus, addressing questions concerning the present status of Jesus. In his speech on the day of Pentecost, when Peter insists that David, 'being a prophet,[129] foresaw and spoke of the resurrection of the Christ', he claims that David also foresaw the incorruptibility of the risen Jesus (2.30–1) and his exaltation to the right hand of God (2.32–5).[130] In Paul's speech in Antioch of Pisidia, he echoes Peter's words from Pentecost when he asserts that the prophets foresaw Jesus' resurrection (13.30–3) and incorruptibility (13.34–7).[131] Peter also indicates that Jesus, 'the one ordained by God' to be judge (10.42), is the one to whom 'all the prophets bear witness' (10.43), and the return of 'the Christ appointed for you, Jesus' (3.20), will take place at 'the time for establishing all that God spoke by the mouth of his holy prophets from of old' (3.21).[132] God's plan for

---

[127] On the prophecy–fulfilment theme in Paul's Antioch speech, see Dahl, 'Abraham' 148–9; on divine providence, see chap. 3.3.3.4.

[128] This declaration of fulfilled prophecy is reminiscent of Jesus' final affirmation at Luke 24.44–9, for it both asserts past fulfilment and anticipates future events. Paul emphasizes the veracity of the prophets shortly after this, at Acts 26.27.

[129] David establishes the prophetic office within the cultic group of musicians according to 1 Chr 25.1–6. On David as a prophet, see Haenchen, *Acts* 182; Jervell, *Unknown Paul* 126–7 and nn. 26–9; on David as 'the center of scripture' for Luke, see *ibid.*, 129.

[130] Peter quotes Psalm 16.8–11 at Acts 2.25–8 and Psalm 110.1 at Acts 2.34–5. On providence in this speech, see chap. 3.3.3.1.

[131] Paul quotes Isa 55.3 at Acts 13.33, Psalm 16.10 at Acts 13.35 and Psalm 2.7 at Acts 13.3. See further in E. Schweizer, 'The Concept of the Davidic "Son of God" in Acts and its Old Testament Background', *Studies* (ed. Keck and Martyn) 186–93; Wilckens, *Missionsreden* 141; on providence in this speech, see chap. 3.3.3.4.

[132] The return of Jesus is also predicted in the epiphany at Acts 1.11. For ἀποκαταστάσεως as 'the establishment of what was predicted', see Foakes Jackson and Lake, *Beginnings* 4.38; Haenchen, *Acts* 208; Kurz, 'Proof from Prophecy 48–9.

Jesus, was predicted by the prophets and fulfilled by events, stretches beyond his death on the cross to encompass this heavenly dimension; the thread of fulfilment of prophecy throughout these speeches thus reinforces the apologetic assertion of God's providence in the life of Jesus.

This fulfilment motif is certainly comprehensible within the framework of the Deuteronomic history, but again it is equally befitting to the way in which hellenistic histories are structured in terms of the fulfilment of oracular predictions. For Luke, these fulfilled prophecies reveal the divine will[133] and function as apologetic defence against Jewish objections to the role accorded to Jesus. Nevertheless, although such a use of prophecy shares formal similarities with the role played by oracles in the hellenistic histories, there is a subtle difference. The oracles are in accord with the traditional religion, whereas the interpretation of the scriptural prophecies in Luke–Acts is a direct challenge to the status quo of the Jewish faith. This issue arises with particular reference to the Gentile mission.

### 6.3.2  Predictions concerning the mission to the Gentiles

#### 6.3.2.1  Predictions spoken by Jesus

The final words of Jesus in the Gospel (Luke 24.44–7) predict, in broad terms, the course of events in Acts; in reverse order, he refers ahead of time to the coming of the Spirit,[134] testimony to the Gospel of Jerusalem,[135] and preaching to all nations.[136] In the prologue to Acts, Jesus recalls this prediction, beginning with the promise of the Spirit (Acts 1.4,8a) and continuing with a more schematized prophecy (1.8) establishing the geographical outline of what ensues in Acts.[137]

An earlier, more extensive, prophecy of Jesus also serves as an

Conzelmann, with his oft-repeated assertion that 'according to Luke, prophecy reaches as far as Christ, but not to the Eschaton' (*Theology* 113; see also 131 n. 2, 161), has overlooked Acts 1.11; 3.20–1; and the prophecies in Luke 1–2.

  [133]  Schubert, 'Luke 24' 186; 'Final Cycle' 1–2; Tiede, *Prophecy* 124.
  [134]  Luke 24.49, fulfilled at Acts 2.1–21.
  [135]  Luke 24.47–8, fulfilled at Acts 2.22–8.1a; 21.17–20. The phrase belongs with verse 48, as the textual witnesses in Nestlé–Aland verify.
  [136]  Luke 24.47, fulfilled from Acts 1.8 onwards.
  [137]  Jerusalem and all Judaea (Acts 2.22–8.1a), Samaria (8.1b–40), to the ends of the earth (9.1–28.31). Cf. the similar programmatic role of Alexander's prophecy at BH 18.1.4 (see p. 128 above).

advance glimpse of certain events in Acts. A section of Jesus' 'eschatological discourse' is edited by Luke so that it refers directly to the activity of testifying to the Gospel in the face of opposition and persecution[138] which is so characteristic of Acts.[139] Luke's use of the Markan warning (Mark 13.9a) about being delivered to synagogues (Luke 21.12b) anticipates the opposition experienced by the apostles,[140] as does the reference to imprisonment.[141] The introductory statement, 'they will lay their hands on you and persecute you' (21.12a) also looks forward to events in Acts,[142] as does the prediction of being 'brought before kings and governors for my name's sake' (21.12b).[143]

Jesus' statement concerning the necessity to testify and the associated consolation concerning what words to say (Mark 13.10–11) are thoroughly reworked by Luke (21.13–15), and again the characteristic Lukan vocabulary points forward to events recorded in Acts. In place of the Markan command to preach the Gospel (Mark 13.10), the Lukan Jesus predicts a giving of testimony (μαρτύριον, Luke 21.13).[144] The consoling declaration that the Holy Spirit will speak at that hour of trial (Mark 13.11) becomes yet another Lukan depiction of events in Acts, with the admonition 'not to meditate beforehand how to answer' (ἀπολογηθῆναι, Luke 21.14)[145] and the

[138] On the temporal indications which Luke has added to this discourse, see chap. 4 n. 93. Luke 21.12 explicitly places the ensuing events before the final cosmic signs (21.8–11, 25–8) and the destruction of the Temple (21.5–7, 20–4).

[139] This link is noted by Johnson (*Possessions* 16–17) and Marshall (*Luke* 767), and developed by Neyrey (*Passion* 84–8).

[140] See the opposition in the synagogues to Stephen at Acts 6.9 and Paul at Acts 13.43–50; 14.1–2; 17.1–5; 18.4–6; 19.8–9. παραδίδωμι is used at Acts 8.3; 12.4; 21.11; 22.4; 27.1; 28.17.

[141] Acts reports a number of imprisonments: Peter and John (Acts 5.19); Peter (12.4–5); Paul and Silas (16.23); and followers of 'the Way' at the hands of Saul (8.3; 22.4; 26.10).

[142] Note the arrests of Peter and John (Acts 4.3; 5.18), some of the Jerusalem church (12.1) and Paul (21.27); a similar phrase is used of Jesus at Luke 22.51,53. The phrase is found in the Septuagint at 1 Sam 21.6, etc.; see Marshall, *Luke* 767. διώκω is used of Saul's activity against the followers of 'the Way' (Acts 9.4–5; 22.4,7–8; 26.11,14–15); the same word describes persecution of the prophets at Luke 11.49 and Acts 7.52.

[143] Some Jerusalem believers are brought before King Herod (Acts 12.1); Paul is arraigned before King Agrippa (25.13–26.30) and the two governors, Felix (23.24–24.10) and Festus (26.30).

[144] μαρτύριον is Luke's characteristic term for the activity of the apostles (Acts 4.33) and of Paul (22.18; 23.11; 26.22); see also μάρτυρες at 1.22; 2.32; 3.15; 5.32; 10.39,41; 13.31; 22.15,20; 26.16. See H. Strathmann, 'μάρτυς', *TDNT* 4 (1967) 489, 492–4, 504; Fitzmyer, *Luke* 1.243.

[145] Cf. Luke 12.11. ἀπολογέω is used of Paul at Acts 22.1; 24.10; 25.8,16; 26.1,2,24.

assurance that Jesus[146] will provide 'a mouth[147] and wisdom[148] which none of your adversaries will be able to withstand[149] or contradict'[150] (Luke 21.15).

The prediction of family betrayal (Mark 13.12) is again shortened by Luke so as to allow him to add material concerning opposition from 'kinsmen and friends' (Luke 21.16a),[151] who will put 'some of you' to death (Luke 21.16b).[152] The prediction of universal hatred (Mark 13.13a) is retained verbatim by Luke (Luke 21.17), but he completely modifies the assurance of salvation (Mark 13.13b) by inserting a prediction of safekeeping (21.18)[153] and an exhortation to endurance (21.19).[154]

Thus the opposition and suffering encountered by the early believers can be understood in the light of these predictions by Jesus. Even the martyrdoms of early leaders of the movement (Acts 7.60; 12.2) do not undercut its vitality; indeed, these and many other acts of opposition take place as fulfilment of the predictions of Jesus, demonstrating the outworking of the plan of God as it has been announced by the prophet Jesus and as it comes to fruition in history.[155]

---

[146] At Mark 13.11 it is the Holy Spirit who will provide the words to speak; Luke alters the saying here because he has already used a form of it closer to his source at Luke 12.12.

[147] Note the speeches which come forth from the mouth of Peter (Acts 10.34) and Paul (15.7; 22.14). The believers in Jerusalem receive 'boldness of speech' from God at Acts 4.29,31.

[148] Wisdom is granted to the seven in Jerusalem (Acts 6.3) and to Stephen (6.10). cf. Apollos, Acts 18.24.

[149] οὐκ ἀντιστῆναι is used of the members of the synagogues who oppose Stephen (Acts 6.10). Elymas vainly seeks to withstand Paul and Barnabas (Acts 13.8).

[150] οὐδὲν ἀντειπεῖν is used of the Jewish leaders who witness Peter's healing of the lame man (Acts 4.14). The Jews contradict Paul at Acts 13.45; 28.19,22.

[151] The reflection here is of Jesus' sayings concerning his true family (Luke 8.21 11.27–8) and of the betrayal of Jesus by Judas, who greets Jesus with a kiss (Luke 22.48).

[152] Some of the believers are indeed put to death; see Acts 7.54–60 (Stephen) and 12.1–2 (James); thus, Fitzmyer, *Luke* 2.1340.

[153] Conzelmann (*Theology* 129–30) says 'it speaks of the general providence of God'. See also Luke 12.7; Acts 27.24; cf. 1 Sam 14.45; 2 Sam 14.11; 1 Kings 1.52. On the proverbial nature of this saying, see Marshall, *Luke* 769–70.

[154] Endurance is exhorted at Luke 8.15. For gaining one's life, see Luke 9.24 17.33; Acts 15.26; 20.24; 27.22. On the hortatory nature of Luke 21.12–19, see Fitzmyer, *Luke* 1339; Marshall, *Luke* 754; Conzelmann, *Theology* 128, 131.

[155] The context of the whole discourse underscores the notion that God's providence continues despite the coming of signs which evoke despair; this is especially the case with regard to the destruction of the Temple (see Fitzmeyer, *Luke* 2.1344). The discourse ends with assertions of divine providence in an epiphany (21.27), redemption (21.28) and God's sovereignty (21.31; cf. 21.36).

### 6.3.2.2 Prophecies written in the scriptures

Luke twice sounds the note of fulfilment of scripture in his introduction to Acts, when he reports the death of Judas (1.16–20a, quoting Ps 69.25) and his replacement by Matthias (1.20b–26, quoting Ps 109.8b). The note of fulfilled prophecy is especially prominent in those parts of Acts which detail the mission to the Gentiles and once again it functions apologetically. Jewish criticisms of the Gentile mission undoubtedly focussed on the apparent abandonment of the Law by early Jewish–Christian missionaries and the consequent illegitimacy of the Christian faith.[156] Against such criticisms, Luke reports how the Christians defended these activities by recourse to the Hebrew scriptures. Once more, his presentation of history undoubtedly speaks to the present concerns of his own time,[157] as a string of prophetic citations is adduced in apologetic defence and exposition of the Gentile mission. In like manner, appeal to scriptural prophecies functions as a defence against pagan criticisms that Christianity is but a mere novelty.[158]

Peter initially alludes to prophetic justification for such a mission in his Pentecost speech (2.16–21, quoting Joel 2.28–32). After God leads Peter to preach to the Gentiles (10.1–11.18) and Barnabas and Paul to work extensively among the Gentiles (13.2–14.28), the Apostolic Council in Jerusalem validates their activities, in part because James argues that the prophets agree (συμφωνοῦσιν, 15.15) with what they have done. Quoting a string of prophetic texts (15.15–17), citing Jer 12.15; Amos 9.11–12; Isa 45.21), James shows the Gentile mission to be a valid part of God's plan,[159] since it is in

---

[156] See Jervell, *Luke* 174–7; Wilson, *Gentiles* 248–9.

[157] For this aspect of Luke–Acts, see Jervell, *Luke* 174, 177; Wilson, *Gentiles* 232–3, 255, 265–7.

[158] Esler (*Community and Gospel* 65–70, 214–19) notes the political ramifications of criticisms of novelty. For such criticisms in later pagan writers, see Justin Martyr, *Dial.* 10; Lucian, *Peregrinus* 38; Galen, *De puls. diff.* 3.3; Origen, *Contra Celsum* 2.1,4; 3.14; 5.33,65; 7.18; Wilken, 'The Christians' 104, 119–23 and *The Christians* 112–17, 121–5; Benko, 'Pagan Criticism' 1106–7, 1109. For the use of proof-from-prophecy by Christian apologists in response to these criticisms, see Wilken, 'The Christians' 120–3; Rokeah, *Conflict* 92; for subsequent pagan attacks on the practice, see Wilken, *The Christians* 137–43, 179–84, and 'Pagan Criticism of Christianity: Greek Religion and Christian Faith', *Early Christian Literature and the Classical Intellectual Tradition, in honorem R. M. Grant* (Théologie Historique 54; ed. W. R. Schödel and R. L. Wilken; Paris: Beauchesne, 1979) 117–34.

[159] The prophecies again concern what God will do; five of the seven verbs have κύριος as their subject. Tiede (*Prophecy* 91) notes that this quotation is made 'to deal not so much with the matter of the Gentiles per se ... [as] to demonstrate that [this] fits with God's plan'. Likewise, Conzelmann, *Theology* 212; Wilson, *Gentiles* 224–5.

complete accord with the will of God as revealed by a number of prophets.

Paul himself interprets his work among the Gentiles as a fulfilment of prophecy, thereby (he believes) legitimating his activity from a Jewish standpoint. To conclude the first detailed report of his preaching, Luke has Paul quote a prophetic warning against those who refuse to acknowledge God's deeds in their own time (13.40–1, quoting Hab 1.5). The very lack of faith which Habakkuk had predicted immediately occurs in Antioch of Pisidia, when some of the Jews contradict and revile Paul (ἀντέλεγον ... βλασφημοῦντες, 13.45), leading to the first of three explicit rejections of the Jews in favour of the Gentiles (13.46). Paul immediately justifies turning to the Gentiles with another prophetic citation (13.47, quoting Isa 49.6).[160] A similar incident in Corinth, when some of the Jews oppose and revile Paul (ἀντιτασσομένων ... βλασφημούντων, 18.6) evokes a prophetic-like protest from Paul,[161] who utters a curse with prophetic overtones.[162] The Gentile mission is yet again under-girded by reference to prophecy at the climax of Paul's apology to Agrippa (26.22–3).

The amount of space devoted to Paul's apologetic defence of his call and missionary activity probably reflects Luke's own context in which churches founded by Paul are being attacked by means of criticisms of Paul's activity.[163] Yet his defence of Paul is bound up with his defence of the whole Gentile mission in response to criticisms that Christianity was a new religion.[164] The constant recourse to scriptural prophecies asserts Christianity's faithfulness to its Jewish origins and is intimately related to the apologetic exposition of the Gentile mission through the theme of divine providence.

Paul's last reported words in Rome represent a final affirmation of the prophetic basis for his activities among the Gentiles; he quotes Isaiah 6.9–10, concerning Israel's inability to listen to the work of

[160] Thus, 'even the obstinacy of the covenant people has been foretold by the prophets and by Jesus' (Dahl, 'Abraham' 151, and see 157 n. 53 for other passages).
[161] 'He shook out his garments' (Acts 18.6a); cf. Acts 13.51; Luke 9.5; 10.11; but H. J. Cadbury ('Dust and Garments', *Beginnings* (ed. Foakes Jackson and Lake) 5.269–77) is sceptical of any prophetic origin for the phrase. Nevertheless, as Haenchen (*Acts* 535) notes, Paul's words interpret the action symbolically.
[162] 'Your blood be upon your heads' (Acts 18.6b) evokes Ezek 33.4–6; for rabbinic parallels, see Str–B 1.1033.
[163] See Jervell, *Luke* 176–7.
[164] See n. 158 above; and chap. 3 n. 195.

God.[165] In interpreting this prophecy, Paul not only summarizes the oft-repeated prophecies about bringing the Gospel to the Gentiles, but also reflects the fulfilment of the earliest oracles in the Gospel;[166] he asserts with certainty[167] that the 'salvation of God[168] has been sent[169] to the Gentiles,[170] for they will listen'.[171] (28.28). Thus Luke's work ends with the fulfilment of the predictions with which it began.

### 6.3.2.3 Predictions spoken by Paul

We have noted above that Luke places Paul in the company of prophets. It is only in his farewell speech (20.18–35) at the end of his missionary journeys that Paul's predictive prophetic ability is directly revealed for the first time. Not only does he look back on his past activity (20.18–21,25–7,31–5), but he also predicts what his future will hold (20.22–5) and what will happen to his followers (20.28–30). The latter prediction lies beyond the scope of Luke's two volumes,[172] but the fulfilment of each of the five elements of the former prediction forms the basis for the immediately ensuing events. The first three elements of this prediction are amplified by Agabus (21.10–11), who has already been introduced by Luke as a prophet whose predictive ability can be trusted (11.27–8). The final two elements of Paul's prediction come to pass rather swiftly in the next chapter.

Paul is most confident of his prediction that he is going to Jerusalem (20.22a); despite a warning against this from the disciples

---

[165] The Jews in Rome are in disagreement (ἀσύμφωνοι, 28.25) with regard to the Gospel, in contrast to their ancient prophets, who agree (συμφωνοῦσιν, 15.15) on God's activity amongst the house of Israel (15.16) and the Gentiles (15.17). For the debate on whether this represents a final rejection of the Jews, see Haenchen, 'Source Material' 278; Jervell, *Luke* 91–2; Wilson, *Gentiles* 226–33; Tiede, *Prophecy* 121–2; Brawley, 'Paul in Acts' 129–34.

[166] Brown, *Birth of the Messiah* 459–60. On the parallels between Luke 24 and Acts 28, see Schubert, 'Luke 24' 185; Talbert, *Literary Themes* 22. For Acts 28 as a fulfilment of 1.8, see Wilson, *Gentiles* 236–7.

[167] γνωστόν, cf. Luke 1.18; γινώσκω, 1.34; ἐγνώρισεν, 2.15; and note the purpose expressed at Luke 1.4, ἵνα ἐπιγνῷς τὴν ἀσφάλειαν. γνωστόν is also used at Acts 2.14; 4.10; 13.38.

[168] Cf. Luke 1.47,69,71,77; 2.11,30.

[169] Cf. Luke 1.19,26; and see chap. 3 n. 97.

[170] Cf. Luke 2.31–2.

[171] Cf. Luke 1.41,58,66; 2.18,20,47; in each case those who listen respond with praise or amazement at what they hear.

[172] On the use of the prophetic 'I know' in 20.29–30, see Aune, *Prophecy* 320. Brawley ('Paul in Acts' 140) argues that the prophecy reveals something of Luke's own situation; see also Esler, *Community and Gospel* 19,26.

in Tyre (21.4), a further prophecy from Agabus reinforces Paul's prediction that he will be in Jerusalem (21.11) and strengthens his resolve to make the journey (21.13). The prophecy is thus fulfilled in short order (21.15–17). Paul is less confident that he knows what will happen to him in Jerusalem (20.22b), except that he will be imprisoned and afflicted there, as he will be 'in every city' (20.23). Agabus clarifies this uncertainty when he predicts that the Jews will 'deliver'[173] him into the hands of the Gentiles' (21.11); this, too, occurs almost immediately (21.33) and Paul remains in Roman custody 'in every city' as he predicted.[174]

Agabus confirms the third element of Paul's prophecy, telling Paul by deed and by word that he would indeed be bound in Jerusalem (21.11); within ten days of his arrival, Paul is bound with two chains (21.33).[175] He remains bound in other cities, just as he had predicted (20.23).[176] The fourth element of his prediction is expressed as a hope that he might accomplish his course and testify to the Gospel (20.24); this is fulfilled not only as he testifies before Jewish and Gentile authorities[177] but also while he is in Rome.[178]

The final element of his prediction, that he will no longer see the elders of Ephesus (20.25), is noted by Luke as the part of the speech which made the most impact on the audience (20.38). The certainty of this parting is underscored by similar scenes in Tyre (21.5) and Caesarea (21.12–13), the latter ending with the affirmation that this is the will of the Lord (21.14). Luke gives no further indication that anything to the contrary takes place. Thus, the prophecies of Paul (20.22–5), made in accordance with his understanding of the plan of God (20.27), are fulfilled.

---

[173] Agabus uses the verb παραδώσουσιν, evoking memories of Jesus' betrayal (see above, n. 140).

[174] In Jerusalem (Acts 21.30–6), Caesarea (23.35; 24.23,27) and Rome (28.16).

[175] For the prophetic nature of Agabus' symbolic act, see Foakes Jackson and Lake, *Beginnings* 4.268; Haenchen, *Acts* 602. Fulfilment comes when the tribune orders Paul to be bound (Acts 21.33), thereby fulfilling the prediction which the Spirit gave to Paul (20.32) and Agabus (21.11); see also 22.29. Although it is not the Jews who bind Paul, they do cause his detention (21.27–33; 22.30); see Foakes Jackson and Lake, *Beginnings* 4.268.

[176] In Caesarea, Paul is bound for two years (Acts 24.27); in Rome, he remains under guard (28.16) for a further two years (28.30), albeit with considerable freedom (28.31).

[177] Verbs from the stem μαρτυρ- are used at Acts 23.11, referring to his speech before the Jerusalem Sanhedrin (22.1–21), and 26.22, referring to his speech before Agrippa and Festus (26.2–23). Paul reminds each authority that this is his divine calling (22.15,18; 26.16).

[178] Acts 28.23,31; the vision of 23.11 again asserts that this is part of God's plan for Paul.

A final depiction of Paul's predictive powers occurs during the sea voyage to Rome, when the slow progress from Myra to Fair Havens makes further sailing dangerous (27.5–9). Paul foresees the danger, predicting the loss of cargo, ship and lives (27.10). The first element of this prediction is fulfilled in a storm off Cauda (27.18),[179] when the loss of lives also seems inevitable (27.20). At this point, Paul repeats the second element of his prophecy, that the ship will be lost (27.22), whilst asserting that the third element will not take place. He justifies this change of mind by reporting the epiphany by which he is assured that no lives will be lost (27.23–4),[180] whilst reinforcing the fact that the ship will be lost (27.26). This duly takes place off Malta when the ship is stuck on a shoal (27.41); the revised third element is also fulfilled, for 'all escaped to land' (27.44).[181] Paul is spared, and travels on 'to the end of the earth', arriving in Rome in accord with the plan of God as it has been revealed by prophecies ancient and modern.

Thus, Luke's history of Jesus and the church is driven by the fulfilment of prophecies. This is similar to the role played by oracles in hellenistic histories, although with a difference of intensity: the place of prophecies in Luke–Acts is far more significant, the number of examples cited by Luke is far greater, the presence of this phenomenon is more concentrated. Such prophecies thus structure the narrative and show how events occurred in accordance with the plan of God which had been declared as of old and was constantly reiterated during the very fulfilment of these events. Any claim that what happened to Jesus or among the Gentiles was a betrayal of the Jewish faith, is apologetically countered by Luke through this motif of fulfilled prophecy. The events he reports are indeed willed by God.

### 6.4 Conclusions

The phenomenon of oracles was a common feature of historiographical works in the ancient world. Our survey of hellenistic and

---

[179] Curiously, the cargo is again jettisoned at Acts 27.38, which Haenchen (*Acts* 704 n. 2) believes to be the actual event; 27.18 alludes to Jonah 1.5, removal of grain only. Foakes Jackson and Lake (*Beginnings* 4.333, 337) read the verses in opposite fashion (27.18 = cargo, 27.38 = grain).

[180] See above, n. 153, on the saying; chap. 5.3.3. on the epiphany.

[181] For shipwreck as divine retribution, see G. B. Miles and G. W. Trompf, 'Luke and Antiphon: The Theology of Acts 27–28 in the Light of Pagan Beliefs about

Jewish works reveals a commonly held understanding of the nature of oracles, or prophecies, which we have summarized in three features: oracles are predictive; they come to fulfilment; and they are divinely inspired. Such oracles could be associated with a particular religious site, be contained within written collections, or be delivered by individuals with predictive abilities.

Josephus, who is important evidence for the conjunction of Jewish and hellenistic viewpoints, explicitly relates the fulfilment of prophecy to divine providence. His major apology on behalf of providence occurs in association with the fulfilment of the prophecies of Daniel. Within the historiographical genre, oracles or prophecies play a significant literary role, for they often introduce key aspects of the narrative and provide divine validation for religious customs or for important individuals in the historical account.

Each of these aspects of oracles is to be found in Luke–Acts. Prophecy, in Luke's understanding, includes both the written scriptures of the Hebrew people (particularly, but not exclusively, those books designated as 'The Prophets') and the spoken predictions of Jesus and a substantial number of the early Christians. Such examples of prophecy as he reports demonstrate that prophecy is predictive and that the fulfilment of a prophecy indicates its divine origin.

Prophecies play a strategic role in the narrative of each volume of Luke's history; this is evident from the prologue, in which oracles delivered by angels and by humans predict, in general and in specific ways, the course of events to follow. The two crucial events of Luke's history, namely the passion of Jesus and the mission to the Gentiles, are each authorized and guided by prophecies given in both written and oral forms. Both written and oral predictions, concerning both passion and mission, are drawn together by the Lukan Jesus in the final scene of the Gospel. Thus, the plan of God is able to be discerned by means of an interpretation of the written prophecies and by careful attention to the spoken predictions which are reported throughout both volumes. These ancient prophecies are especially adduced as support for God's plan in the speeches in Acts in which divine providence is asserted. Thus any claim that these central components of the Christian faith (as Luke presents it) are not founded in antiquity and are therefore not part of the divine plan, is to be firmly repudiated. Such prophecies reinforce the apologetic assertion of the plan of God.

Divine Retribution', *HTR* 69 (1976) 260–4. Brawley ('Paul in Acts' 136) notes the main pagan references; in Acts 27, therefore, 'survival reveals God's approbation'.

# 7

## FATE: THE NECESSITY OF THE PLAN OF GOD

Luke highlights the inner necessity inherent in the plan of God as it works itself out in the life of Jesus and the growth of the early church. This necessity, expressed in a variety of verbs,[1] governs the life of Jesus as well as the apostolic mission. Certain sayings of the apostles also indicate the inevitability of the course of events.[2] However, alongside this insistent emphasis on the necessity of the plan of God, there are frequent moments emphasizing both the possibility of opposing God's purposes[3] and the dimensions of human co-operation with the plan of God. Amongst others, both Jesus and Paul play significant roles in the plan of God, not merely as human pawns of an arbitrary divine necessity, but as key figures in implementing that plan.[4] The explicitly philosophical issue of the relation of such human free-will to divine necessity thus requires investigation with regard to Luke's overall conception of the plan of God.

### 7.1 Fate and free-will in hellenistic historiography

Complementary notions of a predominating, deterministic Fate (μοῖρα) and of a fickle, cantankerous Fortune (τύχη) are found throughout the popular Greek literature of antiquity.[5] Alongside

---

[1] δεῖ, μέλλω, ὁρίζω, and various προ-compounds.
[2] Acts 4.19–20; 5.29,39; 11.17; 15.10; 26.14.
[3] Luke 7.30; 23.51; Acts 2.23; 3.14–15; 5.39; 7.52; 11.17; 13.45–6; 15.10; 16.19–24; 17.5–7; 19.23–41; 23.12–15.
[4] For example, Luke 9.51; 22.42; 23.46; Acts 18.21; 19.21; 21.14.
[5] See L. H. Martin, 'The Rule of τύχη and Hellenistic Religion', *SBLSPS* 10 (1976) 453–9; Gundel, *Beiträge* 30–41; Schulz, 'Vorsehung' 111–12. An example of the predominance of Fortune in the hellenistic age is to be found in the *Metamorphoses* of Lucius Apuleius; Lucian of Samosata testifies to the pervasiveness of belief in Fate in his satirical work, *Zeus Catechized* (see Amand, *Fatalisme* 12–15). Each of these second-century works reflects widespread and long held popular religious attitudes. For the more technical philosophical discussion, see the treatises

the role which Dionysius and Diodorus accord to Fortune, each acknowledges a view of Fate somewhat akin to the Stoic conception of universal Fate.[6]

### 7.1.1 Fate in Dionysius of Halicarnassus

Dionysius recognizes Fate[7] as formidable (δεινή, RA 8.26.6) and inexorable (ἄφυκτον, RA 13.1.2), unable to be changed (RA 4.60.4) or conquered (RA 4.63.3); it is the one thing of which all human nature stands in dread (RA 9.8.1), for it is stronger than human nature (RA 5.64.3).[8] By watching over human affairs (ἐπισκοπεῖν, RA 11.27.1) and compelling human actions,[9] Fate is able to render people brave beyond all expectation (RA 6.19.3) and to control even the end of human life (RA 3.5.2; 5.8.6,15.2; 10.45.4). Since it has been enacted from the beginning of time (RA 8.34.1), Fate works in conjunction with Nature (RA 3.5.2),[10] implementing the laws of Nature which are necessary (ἀναγκαῖον, RA 3.11.1), inviolable (ἀκινήτους, RA 8.23.3) and universal (ἄπασι κοινός, RA 1.5.2).

on Fate (see chap. 1 nn. 70–1; chap. 3 n. 12) and the commentaries of Alexander of Aphrodisias (*De fato*, early third century) and Calcidius (*In Timaeum*, early fourth century).

6 For the Stoics, 'all things happen by Fate' (Cicero, *De fato* 15.33), which 'is defined as an endless chain of causation, whereby things are, or as the reason or formula by which the world goes on' (Diogenes Laertius, *Lives* 7.149; for other definitions of Fate, see Aulus Gellius, *Noct. Att.* 7.2.1–3; Pease, *De Natvra Deorvm* 339, 1000). For references to the Stoic views on Fate, see *SVF* 1.172–7 for Zeno; 1.527,548–51 for Cleanthes; 2.912–1007 (p. 249) for Chrysippus; 3.3.35 (p. 249) for Antipater. For an overview of Stoic views, see Gundel, 'Heimarmene' PW VII.2.2627–32; Amand, *Fatalisme* 8–11; Gundel, *Beiträge* 61–74; Pohlenz, *Die Stoa: Geschichte einer geistigen Bewegung* (2 vols; Göttingen: Vandenhoeck und Ruprecht, 1949) 1.98–106; A. A. Long, 'Freedom and Determinism in the Stoic Theory of Human Action', *Problems in Stoicism* (London: Athlone, 1971) 176–80; J. B. Gould, *The Philosophy of Chrysippus* (Albany: State University of New York, 1970) 137–52.

7 Various terms for Fate appear in Dionysius' history, namely πεπρωμένη (8 times), χρεία (8 times) and μοῖρα (6 times). ἀνάγκη (approx. 70 times) usually has the sense of compulsion or necessity, without specifically referring to a divine entity.

8 An example is given at RA 20.12.2, where Pyrrhus is unable to defeat πεπρωμένη. Cf. Lucian's quotation of two Homeric proverbs concerning the universal extent of Fate's dominion over humanity (*Apology* 8, citing *Iliad* 6.488 and 20.128; see also *Zeus Catechized* 1); and see the examples in Livy, cited by Walsh, *Livy* 53–5.

9 βιάζω at RA 1.58.3; 6.47.2; 16.1.3; 19.15.16; καταστάντες at 2.72.3.

10 On the Stoic equation of nature with Fate, see *SVF* 1.176; Plutarch, *De Stoic. repugn.* 1050AB; Diogenes Laertius, *Lives* 7.148; Seneca, *Nat. quaest.* 2.45.1–2; *De benef.* 4.7.1–2,8.3; Theiler, *Poseidonios* F382ab (with his commentary at 2.308–10); G. F. Moore, 'Fate and Free Will in the Jewish Philosophies according to Josephus', *HTR* 22 (1929) 376. See also Cicero, *De nat deor.* 2.22.57–8, for Zeno's equation of nature with providence.

Fate may be revealed by dreams (RA 5.54.1; 20.12.2), portents
(RA 4.2.2,60.4,63.3; 16.1.3) or oracles (RA 4.4.2,69.3)[11] and could
thus be regarded as a divine force.[12] The gods may implement Fate
(RA 3.6.4; 4.83.5; 6.73.2; 7.44.2), be asked concerning Fate (RA
4.70.1), or command what has been fated (RA 19.3.1); yet such is the
power of Fate (ἀνάγκης) that it is 'the one thing to which even the
gods yield' (RA 6.54.2).[13] However, the logical result of this view of
Fate is a strict determinism in which, as Lucian (*Zeus Catechized* 18)
characterizes it, 'we men do nothing of our own accord (ἕκοντες)
but only at the behest of some inevitable necessity (ἀνάγκῃ ἀφύκτῳ)'.
This is not at all what Dionysius believes, and he avoids such a result
by distinguishing Fate from providence; whilst providence is bene-
ficent towards the Romans, Fate does not produce pleasing results
and is depicted as being of minimal worth.

On one occasion, Dionysius equates Fate with providence,[14]
when he reveals that the conspiracy led by Publius and Marcus
Tarquinius was brought to light by divine providence (θεία
πρόνοια). This took place when, through fearful visions in their
dreams, they 'were forced by the compulsion of heaven (ὑπὸ θείας
ἀνάγκης) to reveal it' (RA 5.54.1). However, Dionysius also
presents providence and Fate as distinctly different ways of
explaining the tragic death of Cliulius.[15] Some attributed it to
'Nature's stern law and Fate (ἡ τῆς φύσεως ἀνάγκη καὶ τὸ χρεών),
when once he had finished the destined course (τὴν ὀφειλομένην
μοῖραν) which is marked out (πέπρωται) for everyone that is born'
(RA 3.5.2), but Dionysius offers two alternative views,[16] 'of those

---

[11] On the relation of divination to Fate, see Cicero, *De div*. 1.56.125–8; *De nat.
deor*. 1.20.55; Pease, *De Divinatione* 69; Gould, *Philosophy* 144–5.

[12] This was held by the Stoic Zeno (Diogenes Laertius, *Lives* 7.1350); the Stoics
often equated Fate with Zeus (Seneca, *De benef*. 4.7.2; *Nat quaest*. 2.45.2; Augustine,
*Civi. Dei* 5.8; see also Minucius Felix, *Oct*. 11.6).

[13] So also Livy, *Hist*. 9.2.15,4.16; see also Walsh, *Livy* 55.

[14] The same equation was made by the Stoics Chrysippus (*SVF* 2.913, 928–33;
Plutarch, *De Stoic. repugn*. 1050AB; Calcidius, *In Timaeum* 144b and Posidonius
(Cicero, *De div*. 1.55.125; Gundel, 'Heimarmene', PW VII.2.2634–5, and *Beiträge*
73; *contra*, Pease, *De Divinatione* 320); see also Seneca, *Nat. quaest*. 2.45.1–2.

[15] Similarly, the Stoic Cleanthes distinguished providence from Fate (Cicero, *De
fato* 14; Alexander of Aphrodisias *De fato* 10; Calcidius, *In Timaeum* 144b); see
Amand, *Fatalisme* 7–8; Gundel, *Beiträge* 63–4.

[16] The Stoic position on Fate came under criticism from 'the authors of other
views and of other schools of philosophy' (Aulus Gellius, *Noct. Att*. 7.2.5). For the
most extensive survey of the discussion in Greek literature from Plato and Aristotle
through to the end of antiquity, see Amand, *Fatalisme* (*passim*). Gundel (*Beiträge*
5–60) provides more details regarding the centuries prior to the Hellenistic period; see
also 'Heimarmene', PW VII.2.2622–45; F. Sandbach, *The Stoics* (London: Chatto

who said that his death was due to human agency (the treachery of his fellow citizens or his own suicide) and those who ascribed all human fortunes to divine providence [and] said that this death had been due to the anger of the gods' (RA 3.5.1).

The overall thrust of Dionysius' history of Rome is, as we have seen, in favour of the view that history is guided by providence and a somewhat flexible Fortune, rather than by an unyielding Fate. Although he appears to be reticent to offer his judgement on this case (in the manner of hellenistic historiography in general),[17] it is clear that his discussion of Cliulius' death is intended to reject the popular view of the power of Fate.

This negative attitude towards Fate is revealed in various ways by Dionysius. When Aeneas explains to the Latins why his soldiers plundered them to excess, he begs them to realize 'that we did it, not out of wantonness (ὕβρει), but constrained by necessity (ὑπ' ἀνάγκης ταῦτα βιασθέντες), and everything that is involuntary (τὸ ἀκούσιον) deserves forgiveness' (RA 1.58.3).[18]

However, Dionysius does not show such forgiveness towards Fate, for instead he reveals the unhappy results of its influence. It was Fate which evoked the hatred of the people towards the first Roman divorcee, Spurius Carvilius (RA 2.25.7), reduced the Athenians to 'dire and cruel calamities' (RA 11.1.3) and led the tribunes into contempt (RA 7.49.1). It is this same Fate which is equated with deception (RA 6.20.1) and contrasted with reason (RA 7.42.5). In the account of the building of the temple on the Capitoline Hill (RA 4.60–1), the polemic against the abuse of divination also contains a

and Windus, 1975) 103–6; Dihle, *Theory of the Will* 99–107.

Carneades was an early critic of Chrysippus, refusing to accept the deterministic basis of the latter's thought (Amand, *Fatalisme* 29–68). Although no extant work by Carneades remains, Amand makes an attempt to reconstruct the 'argument antifatalistique' of Carneades by a synthesis of scattered references to his views (*Fatalisme* 571–86). Many followers of Epicurus, who objected to the exaltation of Fate by the Stoics (Diogenes Laertius, *Lives* 10.133), engaged in polemic against the Stoics in this matter (Cicero, *De nat. deor.* 1.20.55; see Gundel, *Beiträge* 81–2; Amand, *Fatalisme* 116–34, concerning Oenomaeus of Gadara, Diogenes of Oenoanda and Diogenianus). From within the Academy, opposition was also forthcoming; two writings of Cicero (*De fato, De div.*) pit Stoic and Academic opponents against each other, while in *De nat. deor.* the Academician Cotta refutes both Stoic and Epicurean views. Sextus Empiricus also exemplifies this sceptical perspective (*Against the Mathematicians* 9.111–14; see Amand, *Fatalisme* 76; Gundel, *Beiträge* 83–4).

17 See chap. 4 n. 53; chap. 5 n. 50.
18 This latter phrase is proverbial; in his Loeb translation (vol. 1, p. 194 n. 1) E. Carey notes its use at Thucydides 3.40.1; 4.98.6; Aristotle, *Eth. Nic.* 3.1.1; and Plato, *Phaedrus* 233C.

warning that the simplistic claim that 'Fate (τὸ χρεών) cannot be changed' (RA 4.60.4) is also liable to gross abuse.[19]

The proverb which Vetura quotes to her son Marcius that 'a voluntary agreement (σύνβασις κατὰ τὸν ἑκούσιον) between friends is more secure than concessions extorted by necessity (ὑπ' ἀνάγκης)' (RA 8.48.9) demonstrates that, for Diodorus, actions performed under constraint are less favourably viewed than choices which are freely made.[20] Although the Stoics had attempted to come to grips with this latter problem of Fate and free-will at an early stage in their development of the notion of Fate,[21] the preference for free-will espoused by Dionysius does not reflect any technical awareness of these philosophical debates.[22]

## 7.1.2 Fate in Diodorus Siculus

Diodorus acknowledges the popular view that 'nothing is stronger than Fate' (BH 15.63.2),[23] and reports that 'Alexander railed at those who argued away the power of Fate' (BH 17.116.5).[24] Fate is a divine power,[25] which works through omens (BH 15 80.3; 17.116.1–7) or oracles (BH 4.31.5, 5.59.1; 15.74.3–4)[26] and is quite

---

[19] Both the soothsayer and the ambassadors of Tarquinius believe in an unalterable Fate. The soothsayer tries his hardest to manipulate events so that Fate will cause a result favourable to him; the ambassadors, although they steadfastly hold to the truth, almost demonstrate the problems with a belief in a deterministic Fate which is, in reality, subject to human interpretation and manipulation.

[20] See also the contrast between ἀνάγκη on the one hand, and εὐνοίας and κρίσιν on the other, at RA 7.49.1; and the rejection of ἀνάγκη and τὸ χρεών at 9.6.7.

[21] See the discussion of ancient sources below, chap. 7.2.1. For the modern discussion of this aspect of Stoic belief, see J. M. Rist, 'Fate and Necessity', *Stoic Philosophy* (Cambridge University Press, 1969) 112–32; A. A. Long, 'Freedom and Determinism', *Problems in Stoicism* 173–99 and 'Stoic Determinism and Alexander of Aphrodisias De Fato (i–xiv)', *Archiv für Geschichte der Philosophie* 52 (1970) 247–68; M. E. Reesor, 'Necessity and Fate in Stoic Philosophy', *The Stoics* (ed. J. M. Rist; Berkeley: University of California Press, 1978) 187–202, and in the same volume, C. Stough, 'Stoic Determinism and Moral Responsibility', 203–23; Sandbach, *The Stoics* 101–8; and Gould, *Philosophy* 148–52.

[22] The issues are more clearly addressed by Josephus; see below, chap. 7.2.1.

[23] The terms used for Fate by Diodorus include πεπρωμένη ten times, χρεία seven times, μοῖρα twice and οἶτος once. ἀνάγκη is used over 40 times, rarely with any specific reference to Fate as a divine entity.

[24] See also BH 15.74.4, where Dionysius could not outwit Fate. A good example of 'railing against Fate' is provided in *Zeus Catechized*, Lucian's satire on Fate.

[25] BH 11.89.3, where it is described as θείας τινὸς ἀνάγκης. See Busolt, 'Verhältnis' 298–9, and BH 5.71.3; but cf. 9.20.3, where it is said that μοῖρα is not charged to the account of the gods.

[26] This accords with the view of Posidonius that 'since all things happen by Fate, if there were a man whose soul could discern the links that joined each cause with every

the opposite of chance (BH 2.30.1). Fate is a teacher of humans (BH 1.8.9; 2.38.2; 3.18.7,19.2), but also teaches Nature (BH 3.15.7).[27]

Yet Diodorus also diminishes the power of Fate in two ways. More explicitly than Dionysius, he indicates that Fate does not hold complete sway over human history by recounting incidents in which human will is determinative of the resultant event.[28] Further, he equates Fate with Fortune,[29] the goddess whom he views as the predominant divine entity.[30] Diodorus does not seek to oppose two sharply contrasting entities (as does Dionysius, at RA 3.5.1–2, quoted above) so much as to smooth the sharp edges off the view of Fate which he opposes. Equating Fate with Fortune is a way of neutralizing the power of Fate.[31]

## 7.2 Fate and free-will in Josephus

Josephus makes an equation between Fortune and Fate similar to that made by Diodorus, when he reflects on the role of Fortune which some had perceived in the life of Herod, and asserts that, according to this view, 'human actions are dedicated by her [Fortune] beforehand to the necessity of taking place inevitably

other cause, then surely he would never be mistaken in any prediction he might make'; (Cicero, *De div.* 1.56.127; see also Theiler, *Poseidonios* F382a). Cf. BH 8.5.1, where an oracle is declared right by chance (ταὐτόματον), and see Cicero's rebuttal of Posidonius in *De fato* 3.5–7, where he asserts the ambiguity of omens which generally have 'some element of chance'.

[27] See also 15.48.4, where natural circumstances (φυσικάς are determined by necessary causes (κατηναγκασμένας). Compare two instances where Fate seems to be an agent of nature: Fate (πεπρωμένη) cut off the time allotted to Alexander by nature (φύσις) at BH 17.116.1, and necessity (χρεία) is imposed by nature (φύσις) at 3.19.2.

[28] Death is freely chosen by Prometheus (BH 1.19.1), Sosooesis (1.58.3), some Troglodytes (3.33.5), some Isaurians (18.22.4) and Marcius (37.29.4); ἑκούσς is often used of human actions (3.55.4; 4.31.5,44.1,54.3; 5.8.2,59.2,59.5,79.1; 8.8.2; 13.29.5; 14.8.6). Diodorus contrasts actions performed under constraint and freely chosen actions at 10.21.3 and 13.27.3.

[29] 'Nothing is stronger than ἀνάγκης καὶ τύχης' (BH 15.63.2); see also BH 14.20.3,76.1; 20.54.7. For the Stoic equation of Fortune with Fate, see *SVF* 2.966, 972; Seneca, *De benef.* 4.8.3; Busolt, 'Verhältnis' 301; Moore, 'Fate and Free Will' 376; Eitrem, 'Schicksalsmachte' 48–51; Walsh, *Livy* 55–9. On the relation between Fate and Fortune in astrology, see Gundel, *Beiträge* 74–81, and 'Heimarmene', PW VII.2.2632–4; Martin, 'τύχη' 456–7; Moore, 'Fate and Free Will' 385–7. Contrast the argument advanced by Cicero against Posidonius in *De fato* 3.6, to the effect that it is not necessary to have recourse to Fate when all things can be explained by means of nature or Fortune. Compare BH 16.5.6, where Fate and Fortune are distinguished.

[30] See chap. 3.1.3.

[31] Thus the polemic against Fate which we have noted in Dionysius' history is missing from Diodorus' work.

(ἀνάγκη), and we call her Fate (εἰμαρμένην) on the ground that there is nothing that is not brought about by her' (AJ 16.397). This enables him to repudiate the power of both Fate and Fortune, when they are compared with his own doctrine, 'according to which we attribute some part of the cause to ourselves and hold ourselves not unaccountable for the differences in our behaviour as has been philosophically discussed (πεφιλοσόφηται) before our time in the Law' (AJ 16.398). Josephus' own position is thus a mediating stance, affirming divine guidance whilst maintaining the freedom of humans to will events.

### 7.2.1 Philosophic views of Fate and free-will

This Jewish historian thus brings to the surface an issue which, as we have indicated, lay underneath the presentation of events in hellenistic histories which we have explored. The relation between Fate and human will had long been debated by the philosophers,[32] particularly the Stoics, who all asserted the existence of Fate whilst attempting to allow for some things being 'in our power'.[33] Chrysippus offered the most extensive discussion of this problem; he 'stood as unofficial umpire and wished to strike a compromise'[34] between the inevitability of divine Fate and the freedom of the human will, by seeking 'to escape Necessity and to retain Fate'.[35] He did this by distinguishing proximate causes (which are under divine control, and thus fixed) from principal causes (which are ἐφ' ἡμῖν, and

---

[32] On the origins of this question with Epicurus, see P. Huby, 'The First Discovery of the Free Will Problem', *Philosophy* 42 (1967) 353–62; Winston, *Wisdom of Solomon* 51 n. 67. For a broader examination of this issue and associated concepts, see Dihle, *Theory of Will* 20–67.

[33] ἐφ' ἡμῖν is the technical Stoic term for what lay within human power; it is first attributed to Zeno (*SVF* 1.175–7; see Amand, *Fatalisme* 7, and Gundel, *Beiträge* 2–3), but is most frequently associated with Chrysippus (*SVF* 2.979,981,984,988, 990,991,996,1001,1007); see Long, 'Freedom and Determinism' 180–1, 183–92, and 'Stoic Determinism' 260–5; Reesor, 'Necessity and Fate' 190–3; Stough, 'Stoic Determinism' 208–15; Gould, *Philosophy* 150–2. For the Latin equivalent (*in nostra potestate*), see *SVF* 2.115,943; 3.380.

[34] Cicero, *De fato* 17.39.

[35] Cicero, *De fato* 18.41, drawing a distinction between what will be (Fate) and what must be (necessity). Fate is contingent upon human actions and will not come to pass unless humans concur with it; necessity is absolute and will take place regardless of the decisions made by individuals. See the famous description of the dog, tied to a wagon, who must move not only because he chooses to run – what is fated – but also because the wagon, when it moves, compels him to run – what is necessary (*SVF* 2.975).

require our consent to be operative).[36] In order for human actions to occur, Chrysippus proposed that proximate and principal causes must join forces; and since human assent is required for principal causes to be effective, humans do have responsibility for their actions and at least a measure of human free-will is retained.[37] However, the success of this compromise solution has been debated without ceasing ever since Chrysippus proposed it.[38]

Whilst some awareness of these issues can be found in Jewish literature of the hellenistic era,[39] there is usually no clear resolution of the tension between determinism and free-will. In Philo's writings, the matter is addressed with greater awareness of the philosophical dimension.[40] Josephus provides the philosophical

[36] This distinction is examined by Cicero, *De fato* 18.41–19.45; Aulus Gellius *Noct. Att.* 7.2.6–13; Plutarch, *De Stoic. repugn.* 1056B; Alexander of Aphrodisias, *De fato* 13; and Plotinus, *Enneads* 3.1.7. See Moore, 'Fate and Free Will' 378–9; Long 'Freedom and Determinism' 180–3; Gould, *Philosophy* 149–51. On Stoic belief in a series of causes, see *SVF* 2.945–51.

[37] Chrysippus used the illustration of a cylinder which rolls because someone first pushed it – the proximate cause – but also 'because of its peculiar form and natural tendency to roll' – the principal cause (Aulus Gellius, *Noct. Att.* 7.2.11; Cicero, *De fato* 18.42–19.43); see Long, 'Freedom and Determinism' 186–8; Winston, *Wisdom of Solomon* 52–5; Dihle, *Theory of Will* 102–3.

[38] For ancient opposition, see n. 21. For the best modern exposition of how Chrysippus struggled to relate the two aspects, see the conclusion of A. A. Long ('Freedom and Determinism' 194), that 'a man can be free, can act as a man if and only if the external movements of his body follow from a decision which reconcile his own will and moral choice to what is necessarily the case'. Compare the assessment of Gould (*Philosophy* 152, following Aulus Gellius, *Noct. Att.* 7.2.15), that 'Chrysippus harbored two incoherent strands of thought, both of which he prized to the extent that he would give up neither, though he was unable to reconcile them'.

[39] See L. Finkelstein, 'Providence, Determinism and Free Will', *The Pharisees their Origin and their Philosophy* (Cambridge, Mass.: Harvard University Press, 1929) 195–260; D. Winston, 'Freedom and Determinism in Greek Philosophy and Jewish Hellenistic Wisdom', *Studia Philonica* 2 (1973) 40–50, and the expansion of this paper in his commentary, *Wisdom of Solomon* 46–58; Hengel, *Judaism and Hellenism* 1.119–21, 140–6; Tiede, *Prophecy* 27–8; Carson, *Divine Sovereignty* 41–74 (intertestamental literature), 84–109 (rabbinic literature). On the Dead Sea Scrolls, see F. Nötscher, 'Schicksalsglaube im Qumran und Umwelt', *Biblische Zeitschrift* (1959) 205–34, 4 (1960) 98–121; A. Marx, 'Y a-t-il une prédestination à Qumran?' *Revue de Qumran* 6 (1967) 163–81; Hengel, *Judaism and Hellenism* 1.218–24, 230–1, E. P. Sanders, *Paul and Palestinian Judaism: A Comparison of Patterns of Religion* (Philadelphia: Fortress Press, 1977) 257–70; Carson, *Divine Sovereignty* 75–83.

[40] Wolfson, *Philo* 1.424–62 (arguing for absolute free-will); Moore, *Judaism* 1.458–9; D. Winston, 'Freedom and Determinism in Philo of Alexandria', *Studia Philonica* 3 (1974–5) 47–70, reprinted with responses and discussion in Protocol of the Twentieth Colloquy of *Center for Hermeneutical Studies in Hellenistic and Modern Culture* (ed. W. Wuellner; Berkeley: The Center for Hermeneutical Studies

treatment to which he refers in AJ 16.398 on those occasions when he describes the Jewish sects. These descriptions are intended to enable Gentile readers to understand them in their own terms, for he presents them in a manner quite similar to certain Greek philosophical schools,[41] especially concerning their views of Fate.[42]

In the most succinct description, Josephus writes:

> As for the Pharisees,[43] they say that certain events are the work of Fate (εἱμαρμένης), but not all; as to other events, it depends on ourselves (ἐφ' ἑαυτοῖς) whether they shall take place or not. The sect of the Essenes,[44] however, declares that Fate (εἱμαρμένην) is mistress (κυρίαν) of all things, and that nothing befalls men unless it be in accordance with her decree. But the Sadducees[45] do away with Fate (εἱμαρμένην), holding that there is no such thing and that human actions are not achieved in accordance with her decree, but that all things lie within our power (ἐφ' ἡμῖν), so that we ourselves are responsible for our well-being.
>
> (AJ 13.172–3)

Thus, the position which Josephus himself adopts, as he has out-

---

1976) (arguing for relative free-will); Dihle, *Theory of Will* 90–8; Carson, 'Divine Sovereignty' *NovT* 23 (*passim*).

[41] The Esenes are equated with the Pythagoreans in AJ 15.371; the Pharisees with the Stoics in V 12. In rabbinic literature the Sadducees are equated with the Epicureans (see Sanh 10.1, Aboth 2.14; b. Sanh 99b–100a; b. Hag 5b; b. Bed 23a; T. J. Sanh 10.1, 27d); although Josephus does not draw this parallel explicitly, his depiction of the Epicureans at AJ 10.277–8 and CA 2.180 shares affinities with what he says of the Sadducees in the passages concerning Fate. See Blenkinsopp, Prophecy and Priesthood' 249; Rajak, *Josephus* 36–7, 99–101.

[42] BJ 2.162–4; AJ 13.172–3; 18.13,18. There has been extensive discussion of the philosophical significance of the passages in Josephus concerning Jewish views of Fate; see Bretschneider, *Capita theologiae* 31 4; Schlatter, *Wie Sprach*? 53–5; Montgomery, 'Religion' 287–90; G. F. Moore, 'Fate and Free Will' 371–89, and 'The Nature of Man', *Judaism in the First Centuries of the Christian Era, the Age of the Tannaim* (3 vols.; Cambridge, Mass.: Harvard University Press, 1927–30) 1.445–59, 3.139–40; L. Wachter, 'Die unterschiedliche Haltung der Pharisaen, Sadduzaen und Essener zur Heimarmene nach dem Bericht des Josephus', *ZRGG* 21 (1969) 97–114; L. H. Martin, 'Josephus' Use of εἱμαρμένη in the Jewish Antiquities XII, 171–3', *Numen* 28 (1981), 127–37.

[43] See also AJ 18.13; BJ 2.162–3.

[44] See also AJ 18.18; cf. BJ 2.159, where Josephus notes that the Essenes foretell the future with great accuracy.

[45] See also BJ 2.164.

lined it at AJ 16.398, is akin to the Pharisaic position,[46] which is to admit the existence of Fate but deny its inevitability.[47] However, the concept of Fate does not play a major role in his writings outside these three descriptive passages, for it is providence and the will of God which guides events, rather than a deterministic Fate.[48]

### 7.2.2 Divine necessity in Josephus

Thus we find in *Bellum Judaicum* that Fate is used infrequently,[49] almost invariably with the meaning of one's fated end, death.[50] Occasionally Josephus indicates that some believe in Fate as an inevitable force (BJ 5.355,572) or as a divine agent (BJ 6.108,250).[51]

---

[46] Despite Rajak's claim that Josephus 'did in truth identify himself with the upper strata of the priesthood' (*Josephus* 19; see the full discussion at 14–22), his descriptions of the Sadducees are particularly sarcastic, noting that 'they accomplish hardly anything' (AJ 18.17), they are unpopular (AJ 18.18), boorish and rude (BJ 2.166). His depictions of the Pharisees, by contrast, are positive, noting that they are 'affectionate to each other and cultivate harmonious relations with the community' (BJ 2.166), and the occupants of the cities have recognized the highest ideals and excellence practised by the Pharisees (AJ 13.15). For his affinities with the Pharisees see Cohen, *Josephus* 237–8; the survey of scholarship in Attridge, *Interpretation* 6–1 (but compare his own carefully guarded conclusions on 178–9); and, with particular reference to Fate and free-will, Carson, *Divine Sovereignty* 118–19.

[47] Thus Josephus, like Chrysippus, seems able 'to escape Necessity and to retain Fate' (Cicero, *De fato* 18.41). Cf. the discussion of the Stoic position above, n. 21.

[48] Martin ('εἱμαρμένη' 134–5) shows the clear distinction which Josephus draws between the deterministic εἱμαρμένη and the πρόνοια of God. For this distinction in Stoic philosophy, see Attridge, *Interpretation* 157 (esp. n. 3); cf. RA 3.5.1.

[49] εἱμαρμένη 14 times, χρεών 7 times, πεπρωμένη not at all. In addition, the terms δεῖ, ἀνάγκη and χρή, which usually refer to a generalized compulsion or necessity brought about by circumstances, do occasionally refer to Fate as a specific entity. For the various terms used by Josephus to indicate Fate, see Bretschneider, *Capita theologiae* 33 nn. 64–6; Carson, *Divine Sovereignty* 115–18.

[50] εἱμαρμένη refers to the death of the Romans Antigonus (BJ 1.79), Ananus (4.297) and Julianus (6.84), the death of Herod (1.628, 662), the threat of death upon Josephus (6.108), the destruction of Jerusalem (4.257), her Temple (6.250,257) and the whole nation of the Jews (6.428). χρεών refers to the death of Malichus (1.233), Herod (1.275), sick Jews who died while burying their relatives (5.514), and people in general (6.49,314).

[51] At BJ 2.162 Fate appears to be synonymous with God; see also AJ 19.347. This equation is widely accepted as determinative for Josephus' view of Fate; see Schlatter, *Theologie* 32–3, 215; Nötscher, 'Schicksal' 452–3; Theiler, 'Schicksalslehre' 46; Wachter, 'Haltung' 120; Finkelstein, *Pharisees* 195; Rajak, *Josephus* 99. Brün equates εἱμαρμένη with πρόνοια in various passages (*Flavius Josephus* 206); μεμορραμένη and βούλησις θεοῦ refer to the same thing at AJ 2.232 (*Flavius Josephus* 124) and τὸ χρεών guides human sins (BJ 4.573; AJ 9.199) just as God does (BJ 5.572; AJ 8.412–13; *Flavius Josephus* 206). If Thackeray's textual conjecture of ἄτροπος at AJ 4.113 is correct, then Fate is here equated with God's πρόνοια (AJ 4.114, 117). Against this consensus, see Martin, 'εἱμαρμένη' 134–5; Stahlin ('Schicksal' 335–42).

On one occasion – the successful campaign of Vespasian – he allows it to have a positive meaning, but only because he has identified it with both Fortune and providence.[52] Fate is almost completely absent from the biblical paraphrase of AJ 1–11, four times referring to the fated end of death.[53] The one significant occurrence comes after the death of Ahab, with an admonition 'to reflect on the power of Fate (χρεών), and see that not even with foreknowledge is it possible to escape it, for it secretly enters the souls of men and flatters them with faint hopes, and by means of these it leads them on to the point where it can overcome them' (AJ 8.419).

The deception worked by Fate, by which 'the false prophet [Zedekiah] seemed more convincing than the true one [Micaiah], in order to hasten Ahab's end' (AJ 8.409), appears to have been of such magnitude that it was even able to overcome 'the greatness of the Deity' (AJ 8.418).[54] Thus Fate is distinguished from the workings of God,[55] and although Josephus here seems to grant more power to Fate than to God, in fact the fate which befell Ahab was the fulfilment of the divinely inspired prophecy uttered by Micaiah,[56] since God provides, for our benefit, 'prophecy and the foreknowledge which it gives, for in this way God enables us to know what to guard against' (AJ 8.418).

In the latter part of *Antiquitates Judaicae*, Fate[57] is referred to either in connection with the philosophical views of the sects, or as

---

[52] 'Now that Fortune (τύχη) was everywhere furthering his wishes and that circumstances had for the most part conspired in his favour, Vespasian was led to think that divine providence (δαιμονίου προνοίας) had assisted him to grasp the entire empire and that some just destiny (δικαία τις εἱμαρμένη) had placed the sovereignty of the world within his hands' (BJ 4.622).

[53] χρεών for the deaths of David (7.383), Basanes (8.307) and Achab (8.412); πεπρωμένη, in a textual variant, for the death of Josiah (AJ 10.76). Attridge proposes that Josephus refrains from extensive reference to Fate in order to avoid deterministic overtones (*Interpretation* 101–2, 156–8).

[54] CF. RA 6.54.2 for the power of Fate over the gods.

[55] *Contra* Moore ('Fate and Free Will' 388–9), who identifies τὸ χρεών as 'neither Fortune (τύχη) ... nor Fate (εἱμαρμένη) ... but the will of God revealed by the prophets ... the "Must-be", the Inevitable, is the Deity'. But this would leave Josephus open to precisely the charge which he raises against the Greeks in CA 2.245, where he mocks that 'the Father himself [i.e. Zeus] ... is so completely at the mercy of Destiny (εἱμαρμένη) that he cannot either rescue his own offspring or restrain his tears at their death'.

[56] See chap. 6 nn. 46–7; and Stählin, 'Schicksal' 332, 336.

[57] εἱμαρμένη seven times (four times in relation to the philosophical views of the sects), πεπρωμένη once in a textual variant, χρεών not at all. Again, δεῖ, ἀνάγκη and χρή refer infrequently to Fate as a specific entity.

the fated end of death.[58] At AJ 16.397, as noted above, Josephus identifies Fate with Fortune and vigorously rejects the force of either element of popular belief. On occasion throughout the work, the activity of God is depicted as having a certain necessity about it, but on these occasions Josephus avoids the technical terms for Fate and uses instead terms such as compulsion[59] or necessity.[60]

Josephus is thus careful to avoid describing the divine guidance of history in explicitly deterministic terms, even though his view of the consistency of events appears somewhat similar to the rigorous conformity of events claimed by a deterministic viewpoint. The difference is actually to be found on those occasions when Josephus notes the freedom of humans to choose – a freedom which is not available in a deterministic system.[61]

## 7.3 Necessity and the plan of God in Luke–Acts

The problems involved in affirming divine providence yet retaining human free-will were not immediately addressed by the early Christians, for it was to be some time in the development of Christian thought before explicit steps were taken to clarify the philosophical issues inherent in the belief in providence and its relation to the

[58] εἱμαρμένη at AJ 12.279, the death of Mattathias, and εἱμαρμένη and πεπρωμένη at 19.347, the death of Agrippa. See also 15.287, 'the inevitable (ἀνάγκη) end of life'.
[59] ἀνάγκη, e.g. as the guide for Hagar (AJ 1.217), who is subsequently led by an angel of the Lord (1.219), or concerning Israel's desert travels (3.1). God compels the Nile to turn blood-red (3.86) and compels the Persian kings to have pity and compassion on the Israelites in exile (11.144). Daniel prophesies the destiny (ἀνάγκη) of Belshazzar (10.246). Frequently ἀνάγκη refers to a compulsion enforced by pagans against Jewish customs (2.345; 8.193; 12.253,268,384,385; 15.328; 16.27,130,154), or to the forces which compelled the Jews to fight wars (15.129; 17.240; 20.257,258). It is often contrasted with free-will (6.219; 8.69; 11.178; 12.280; 16.92; 18.17,186,265).
[60] δεῖ, with reference to the activity of God concerning the burning of Korah and his company (AJ 5.312); the misfortunes of Samson (5.312); David's kingship (6.335); choice of punishment (7.322) and his succession by Solomon (7.385); Rehoboam's advice to the people (8.215–16); Ahijah's answer to the wife of Jeroboam (8.268); God's advice to Elijah at Beersheba (8.351); Josiah's declaration of war (9.206); Jeremiah's prophecy of the capture of Jerusalem (10.89); the fate of Daniel (10.199, 293); and divine prophecy in general (10.142).
[61] See Carson, *Divine Sovereignty* 115, on the places where Josephus deliberately introduces the sovereignty/responsibility tension. Of the various words for will, προαίρεσις most frequently describes human decisions (BJ 2.207; 6.112; 16 times in AJ 1–11 and all but one of the 38 occurrences in AJ 12–20) and is often contrasted with decisions made under constraint (ἀνάγκης at BJ 6.230 ; AJ 6.219; ἀβουλήτους at AJ 4.293; ἀκουσίως at AJ 18.17; ἄκων at AJ 19.35). See also γνώμη at AJ 6.153; 17.129,240,243; 18.281; βούλησις at AJ 4.3,324; 6.61,237; 7.39,201; 19.137,166; and see the contrasts of βούλησις and ἀνάγκη at AJ 12.280; βούλευμα and ἀνάγκη at AJ 18.265.

notion of Fate. Nevertheless, Luke's history contains a strong expression of the necessity inherent in the events he reports, with certain indications which come very close to the hellenistic idea of Fate.

## 7.3.1 The necessity of the divine will

The two events which, as we have seen, are most clearly linked by Luke with the plan of God, are the passion of Jesus and the mission to the Gentiles. Both of these are emphatically defended as having been entirely necessary within the course of events as God had planned them. The theme of necessity thus reinforces Luke's apologetic purpose of asserting and expounding the Christian faith as he interprets the story of Jesus and the early church by means of the theme of divine providence.

### 7.3.1.1 Jesus and his Father's business

In each of the previous chapters, we have noted that elements in the prologue to Luke's Gospel establish themes to be developed more extensively in the body of the work. The necessity motif is alluded to in Simeon's oracle (Luke 2.33–4),[62] however, it is the first public utterance by Jesus which is more significant, when the twelve-year-old boy is in discussion with the temple teachers. In response to his parent's anxiety, Jesus declares, 'Did you not know that I must (δεῖ) be about my Father's business?' (2.49),[63] thereby revealing from the very beginning the inner necessity which drives his every action.[64] This motif is developed by Luke in several related ways which unfold by stages throughout his work.

(1)   Initially it entails Jesus' public proclamation of God's sovereignty: 'I must preach the good news (εὐαγγελίσασθαί

---

[62]   Tiede (*Prophecy* 27) notes that in his oracle, along with Luke 2.49, 'the matter of the character and content of this "necessity" is raised, but not yet defined'; the 'peculiar usage of the passive voice' indicates divine agency (*ibid.*, 29).

[63]   For this translation, see Fitzmyer, *Luke* 1.443–4; for linguistic parallels; see P. J. Temple, '"House" or "Business" in Lk. 2.49?', *CBQ* 1 (1939) 342–52. Marshall (*Luke* 129) rejects this translation; Brown (*Birth of the Messiah* 475–7) considers it possible but unlikely.

[64]   On the importance of δεῖ in Luke–Acts, see Grundmann, 'δεῖ', *TDNT* 2 (1964) 23–4; Conzelmann, *Theology* 153–4; Schulz, 'Vorsehung' 108; Haenchen, *Acts* 159 n. 8; Navone, 'Way of the Lord' 25–6; Marshall, *Historian* 106–11; Adams, 'Suffering' 37–40; Talbert, 'Promise and Fulfilment' 94; Richard, 'Divine Purpose' 192; Cosgrove, 'Divine ΔΕΙ' 173–4, 190; O'Toole, *Unity* 27–8.

με δεῖ) of the kingdom of God to the other cities also,
for I was sent for this purpose (ἐπὶ τοῦτο ἀπεστάλην,
(4.43). This summary of Jesus' preaching[65] is a thoroughly
Lukan redaction which places a double emphasis on
necessity.[66]

(2)   At the key turning point of his Gospel (9.51), Luke indicates that 'my Father's business' is marked not only by the
note of fulfilment[67] but also by an aura of determination
conveyed by the Septuagintal phrase, 'he set his face' (τὸ
πρόσωπον ἐστήρισεν).[68] A seemingly innocuous verb in
this verse (9.51) immediately assumes a significant role in
conveying the inevitability of the divine plan: Jesus sets
his face to go (πορεύεσθαι) to Jerusalem.[69] In the ensuing
ten chapters (9.51–19.44)[70] Luke repeatedly notes that
Jesus is journeying[71] to Jerusalem.[72]

[65] Luke 4.43 functions in the same way as Mark 1.15, introducing the public
preaching of Jesus. Luke here incorporates elements he previously omitted from his
version of Mark 1.15 (εὐαγγέλιον, ἡ βασιλεία τοῦ θεοῦ).

[66] Note the characteristic Lukan additions of δεῖ and ἀπεστάλην (Marshall, Luke
198; Fitzmyer, Luke 1.557; see chap. 3 n. 97 for the significance of the divine passive).
Conzelmann (Theology 154) notes that δεῖ is applied first to the passion, whence it
'spreads to other events in the course of redemptive history'; likewise, Adams,
'Suffering' 40 n. 63.

[67] G. Delling ('συμπληρόω', TDNT 6 (1968) 308–9) notes this 'is fulfilled according to God's plan'. On the characteristic link between necessity and scriptural
fulfilment throughout Luke–Acts, see Navone, 'Way of the Lord' 27; Marshall,
Historian 111 n. 1 and Luke 369, 690, 826, 905; W. J. Bennett, 'The Son of Man Must
...', NovT 17 (1975) 128; Johnson, Possessions 16.

[68] Cf. Jer 21.10; and nine times in Ezekiel, on which see K. K. Carley, Ezekiel
Among the Prophets: a Study of Ezekiel's Place in Prophetic Tradition (Naperville,
Ill.: Alec R. Allenson, 1974) 40–2. Carley (ibid., 42) concludes that to set one's face
'was a figurative way of saying that God's own power was active toward them,
whether for good or evil'. Marshall (Luke 405) views the phrase in Luke 9.51,53 as
'indicative of determination'.

[69] Within the space of seven verses, journeying is mentioned five times (Luke 9.51,
52,53,56,57). The same verb is used earlier of Jesus (4.30,42; 7.6,11) without any
suggestion of necessity. For its function as a technical term in the travel narrative, see
D. Gill, 'Observations on the Lukan Travel Narrative and Some Related Passages',
HTR 63 (1970) 201.

[70] For the end of the journey at 19.44, we follow F. V. Filson, 'The Journey
Motif in Luke–Acts', Apostolic History 70–2; Gill, 'Travel Narrative' 199; contra,
Conzelmann (Theology 63), who adduces the assessment of Karl Schmidt that the
journey ends at 19.27. Fitzmyer (Luke 2.1242) sees 19.28–48 as 'the climax of the
travel account itself'; cf. our comments below on 19.28–47a. Conzelmann
(Theology 75) later concedes that the Temple, not Jerusalem in general, is the
destination of Jesus' journey. For various attempts to analyse the structure and
purpose of the journey section in Luke's Gospel, see the literature cited by Johnson,
Possessions 104 n. 3.

Luke's extended account of the journey to Jerusalem then becomes a focus for the theme of the necessary plan of God. Through numerous redactional touches, Luke emphasizes the essentially inevitable nature of God's plan. This is especially so as the literary mid-point of the journey (13.31–5), when Jesus comments, 'I must go on my way, (πλὴν δεῖ με πορεύεσθαι) for it cannot be (οὐκ ἐνδέχεται) that a prophet should perish away from Jerusalem' (13.33). During his last supper with his disciples, Jesus again emphasizes that his journey was predetermined (22.22). Thus Jesus approaches Jerusalem, the city of his death, knowing that this is in accord with the plan of God. His entrance into Jerusalem (19.28–44) is the visitation (ἐπι-σκοπῆς, 19.44) of the divine messenger (19.38), who stands at last in the Temple (19.45–47a) where he can continue his Father's business.[73]

(3) What is required of this messenger by his divine Father, however, is not an easy task. In his first passion prediction (Luke 9.22 par Mark 8.31),[74] Jesus reveals the necessity of his suffering and death. During his journey to Jerusalem, Jesus senses the inevitability of his betrayal (μέλλει, 9.44)[75] and admits that he is totally governed (συνέχομαι, 12.50)[76] by the knowledge that he must suffer (δεῖ παθεῖν, 17.25; cf. 22.37). The necessity of the events of the passion is thrice recalled in Luke's resurrection accounts (24.7,26,44). The revelation of this necessity through the predictions of Jesus

[71] πορεύομαι occurs also at Luke 10.38; 13.22,31,32,33; 17.11; 19.28,36; for the sense of necessity it conveys, see Fitzmyer, *Luke* 1.169,539.

[72] Luke 9.51,53; 13.22,33; 17.11; 18.31; 19.28. Note also the use of ἐγγίζω, to heighten the tension as the journey reaches its end, at 18.35; 19.11,29,37,41. A sense of necessity pervades Luke's references to Jerusalem, for it is the city where Jesus' ἔξοδον is about to be fulfilled (ἤμελλεν πληροῦν, 9.31), where the prophet must perish (οὐκ ἐνδέχεται, 13.33), and where everything predicted of the Son of Man will be accomplished (τελεσθήσεται, 18.31).

[73] Aside from the location, in the Temple, there are similarities between Luke 19.45–8 and the earlier scene of 2.46–50. Jesus is a teacher (2.46; 19.47a) who evokes amazement (2.47; 19.48b) but also misunderstanding (2.48,50; 19.47b). He is clearly obedient to the divine authority (2.49; 19.46).

[74] W. J. Bennett ('Must ...', 113–29) examines attempts to distinguish Mark's use of δεῖ from an impersonal force such as Fate (see esp. 113–19, 128–9).

[75] For the sense of inevitability conveyed by μέλλω, see 9.31; 22.23; Schulz, 'Vorsehung' 107; Fasher, 'Beobachtungen' 239–40.

[76] For this translation, see the discussion of H. Koester, 'συνέχω', *TDNT* 7 (1971) 884–5.

(9.22,44; 17.25; 24.44), the angelic figures (24.7) and the ancient prophets (18.31; 24.26,44) reflects the way Fate is communicated through oracles in hellenistic histories.[77] Yet, as Tiede notes, 'when Luke uses impersonal verbs and passive constructions, it is not to counsel resignation to arbitrary fates and forces. Rather, it is to confront the reader with the determined purpose of God.'[78]

(4)   On the Mount of Olives, Jesus himself confronts the will of his Father (22.39–45), knowing that it will lead to his own death. Luke's redaction of this pericope emphasizes the necessity of the passion, presenting the incident as a temptation to oppose the divine will (22.40,46).[79] Although Jesus does not wish to die, Luke avoids reporting his distress,[80] presenting him rather in a dignified fashion[81] and emphasizing his obedience to the divine will (22.42).[82] This objectifying of the occasion seems to run counter to the picture of Jesus, sweating drops of blood (22.44).[83] However, his strengthening by the angel (22.43) is a characteristic Lukan

---

[77]   See above, n. 27, and chap. 7.2.2.

[78]   *Prophecy* 75.

[79]   The *inclusio* shows that Luke regards this whole incident as a temptation (πειρασμόν) with which Jesus had to struggle, but which he would ultimately overcome (cf. the similar *inclusio* which frames 4.1–13). On the pervasiveness of πειρασμός in Luke's passion account, see Conzelmann, *Theology* 80; Neyrey, *Passion* 59–62.

[80]   Luke omits the preceding conversation with his disciples (Mark 14.33–4) in which Jesus confessed to them his distress, sorrow and trouble. Instead of Jesus' being sorrowful (περίλυπος, Mark 14.34), it is the disciples who are grieved at what is certainly to eventuate, and Jesus rouses them from their 'sleeping for sorrow' (ἀπὸ τῆς λύπης, Luke 22.45). Neyrey ('The Absence of Jesus' Emotions – The Lucan Redaction of Lk 22,39–46', *Bib* 61 (1980) 154–7) regards this as having affinities with the Stoic manner of overcoming grief by courage.

[81]   Luke has Jesus kneel to pray (Luke 22.42) rather than throw himself on the ground (as in Mark 14.35); see Neyrey, 'Absence' 158.

[82]   The extended prayer of Mark 14.36–9 is reduced to the briefer account of Luke 22.42; instead of the introductory affirmation, 'all things are possible to thee' (Mark 14.36), which Luke has already used twice before (1.37; 18.27), he heightens the question of the divine will by having Jesus begin the prayer with a conditional request, 'If thou art willing, remove that cup from me' (22.42a), only to conclude swiftly, 'Nevertheless, not my will, but thine, be done' (22.42b). Neyrey (*Passion* 54) comments that 'Luke makes God's will the center of Jesus' prayer'.

[83]   For the evidence that 22.43–4 is not an original part of Luke's text, see K. Aland, 'Neue Neutestamentliche Papyri III', *NTS* 12 (1965–6) 199, 203; Fitzmyer, *Luke* 2.1443–4. Marshall (*Luke* 831–2) accepts them as original 'with very considerable hesitation'; so also Danker, *Jesus* 356. Neyrey (*Passion* 55–7) argues for their authenticity.

way of furthering the plan of God[84] and the phrase ἐν
ἀγωνίᾳ (22.44) suggests that Jesus accepts, and indeed pre-
pares for, the struggle which lies ahead of him. This depiction of Jesus shares affinities with the perspective of the
Stoics,[85] in which suffering is a crucial part of the divine
providential care, training one to cope with the vicissitudes
of life.[86]

(5) In an ironic twist found only in Luke's Gospel, as Pilate
sentences Jesus to be crucified he delivers him to the will
(τῷ θελήματι) of the Jewish leaders (23.25),[87] through
whose plan and deed (τῇ βουλῇ καὶ τῇ πράξει) the sovereignty of God is challenged (23.51). Although this seems
to undermine the earlier assertions that Jesus is obeying
God's will (θέλημα, 22.42) and that his passion was already
divinely determined (ὡρισμένον, 22.22), Luke reasserts this
foreordained nature of the crucifixion in the final chapter
of his Gospel (δεῖ, 24.7,26,46). Luke introduces another
distinctive way of emphasizing this aspect with the use of
προ- compounds in the early chapters of Acts.[88] The
Jerusalem believers acknowledge that the plot against
Jesus was predestined (προώρισεν, Acts 4.28)[89] and Peter

---

[84] See discussion of epiphanies in chap. 5.3.1.

[85] W. R. Paton ('Ἀγωνία [Agony]', *Classical Review* 27 (1913) 194) reads ἐν ἀγωνίᾳ in 22.44 as Stoic terminology ('anxiety' rather than 'agony'). For a comparison of various elements in Luke 22 with Stoic ideas, see Trompf, *Idea* 152–3 (esp. n. 176). On ἄγων in the Stoics, see Diogenes Laertius, *Lives* 7.112; *SVF* 3.394,407–9,416; C. M. Proudfoot, 'The Apostle Paul's Understanding of Suffering', Yale Ph.D. diss., 1956, 406–52; Malherbe, *Paul* 48. Neyrey (*Passion* 58–62) compares 22.44 with Philo's views on ἄγων without acknowledging the Stoic influences on him.

[86] Philosophic discussions of providence frequently dealt with the problem, 'Why do the good suffer while the evil flourish?'; see Philo, *De prov.* 2.14; 3.21–42; Cicero, *De nat. deor.* 3.32.79–34.85. The standard Stoic response to this question was that hardship trained the individual to enjoy life to the fullest; see Aulius Gellius, *Noct. Att.* 12.5.3; Seneca, *Ep.* 96.5; *De prov.* (*passim*, esp. 3.5–14). Note the similar perspective of Darius at AJ 10.258. For other ways in which the ancients responded to the question, see Wolfson, *Philo*, 2.280–3.

[87] Yet, in the light of Acts 2.23; 4.28, 'the question of whose will is actually being done has only been sharpened ironically' (Tiede, *Prophecy* 110).

[88] On the providential implications of the προ- compounds, see Schulz, 'Vorsehung' 105–6; Foakes Jackson and Lake, *Beginnings* 4.38.

[89] But 'this idea excludes notions of a closed, causally-connected history process' (Cosgrove, 'Divine ΔΕΙ' 184). L. C. Allen ('The Old Testament Background of (προ)ορίζειν in the New Testament', *NTS* 17 (1970) 104–8) argues that Acts 4.25–8 demonstrates that the New Testament use of (προ)ορίζειν is derived from Psalm 2; see esp. 105–6. In this way he accounts for each of the Lukan uses, except for Acts 11.29; 17.26. Nevertheless, ὁρίζω is used in classical Greek literature in association

declares that God had foreknown (προγνώσει) this predestined plan (τῇ ὡρισμένῃ βουλῇ, 2.23)[90] and had even foretold it (προκατήγγειλεν, 3.18) by all the prophets.

(6) The predetermined nature of Jesus' passion is further
emphasized by Luke's editorial notations concerning the
divine timetable of Jesus' passion. The devil leaves Jesus,
after tempting him, 'until an opportune time' (ἄχρι
καιροῦ, Luke 4.13), one of the times (καιρούς) determined
by God (Acts 1.7; 17.26).[91] Satan returns to enter Judas
(22.3), who leads the crowd as they arrest Jesus at their
'hour and the power of darkness' (ἡ ὥρα καὶ ἡ ἐξουσία τοῦ
σκότους, 22.53).[92] In these references, the necessity motif
has a strongly apologetic function, for it justifies the death
of Jesus as an entirely necessary act within the overall plan
of God.[93]

(7) This plan stretches beyond the death of Jesus, however,
incorporating the resurrection of Jesus as a further necessary element of the divine intention, as Paul indicates: 'the
Messiah must suffer and be raised from the dead' (Acts
17.3; see also 26.23).[94] Beyond his resurrection, Jesus must
enter his glory (Luke 24.26) in heaven (Acts 3.21) where he

with the decree of Fate; see Aeschylus, Choephori 927; Sophocles, Antigone 451–2
(and see 454–5, 465); Euripides, Frag. 218 (cited by LSJ, s.v. 'ὁρίζω').

[90] For the influence of Ps 2.7, see Allen, 'Old Testament Background' 106. God's
predestined purpose is affirmed by the Isaianic prophetic school (Isa 14.14–27;
34.16–17; 40.21–3 and throughout chapters 41–55); see Schubert, 'Areopagus Speech'
240. For the 'spezifisch heilsgeschichtlichen Sinn' of ὁρίζειν, see Wilckens, Missionsreden 124, esp. n. 3; similarly, Fitzmyer, Luke 2.1410.

[91] For the divine control of the καιρούς, see Luke 21.24; but as Danker (Jesus
335) notes, they are times of crisis also (cf. 8.13; 21.36).

[92] This suggests that this hour is not under divine control; but it is God who has set
the times ἐν τῇ ἰδίᾳ ἐξουσίᾳ (Acts 1.7) and humans are ignorant of 'the hour' (Luke
12.39,40,46; cf. Mark 13.32–3). Danker (Jesus 358) describes the hour as 'of the
heavenly Parent's permissive providence'. For an astute criticism of Conzelmann's
overreading of the divine timetable, see Minear, 'Birth Stories.' 123–5.

[93] In his speech before Agrippa, Paul declares his own pre-conversion belief, for
rather different reasons, in the necessity (δεῖ) of the opposition to Jesus which had
been demonstrated in his passion (Acts 26.9).

[94] Cadbury ('Lexical Notes on Luke–Acts. IV. On Direct Quotations with Some
Uses of ὅτι and δεῖ', JBL 48 (1929) 421–2) notes that although the construction of
26.23 is conditional, εἰ in effect stands for ὅτι. He is followed in this by Conzelmann,
Acts 211; Haenchen, Acts 684 n. 2, 687 n. 5. The translation of Bruce (Acts 493–4)
brings out this force: 'Must the Messiah suffer? Must he rise from the dead? Must he
bring the light of salvation?' Foakes Jackson and Lake (Beginnings 4.321) also note
the apologetic function of this verse: 'the suffering of the Messiah was a burning
question in the controversy of the Jews and Christians'.

is appointed (προκεχειρισμένον) as Christ (3.20) and divinely ordained (ὡρισμένος, 10.42; ὥρισεν, 17.31) as judge. This task of judgement will be accomplished, as predicted by scripture, at the return of 'the Christ appointed for you, Jesus' (3.20), whom 'heaven must (δεῖ) receive until the time for establishing all that God spoke by the mouth of his holy prophets from of old' (3.21). The most thorough statement of this post-resurrection dimension of the plan of God is announced by Paul at the end of his apologetic speech on divine providence, delivered to the Athenian philosophers. 'God has fixed (ἔστησεν) a day on which he will judge the world in righteousness by a man whom he has appointed (ὥρισεν), and of this he has given assurance (πίστιν παρασχών) to all men by raising him from the dead' (17.31).[95]

By these seven means, then, Luke insists on the inevitability of Jesus' preaching, travelling, betrayal, suffering, death, resurrection, return and judgement, as necessary elements in the plan of God. All of this, for Jesus, is the 'Father's business' which he must execute.

### 7.3.1.2 The apostles and obedience to God

In depicting the apostolic mission as being under the impulse of divine necessity, Luke continues to use the most characteristic terms which he has applied to Jesus: the impersonal verb δεῖ, as well as the προ- compounds and related verbs. The mission of the apostles begins with Judas' necessary death (ἔδει, 1.16), in fulfilment of the scripture (Pss 69.26; 109.8), and the consequent need to choose a replacement apostle who had been a witness to the whole of Jesus' earthly ministry (δεῖ, 1.21). Peter develops the necessity of the apostolic mission in his Caesarean speech, describing the apostles as 'chosen (προκεχειροτονημένοις) by God as witnesses' (10.41), divinely commanded (παρήγγειλεν) to preach to Israel (10.42) and

---

[95] Dibelius (*Studies* 27) mistakenly concludes 'the specifically Christian content of the speech is presented only in the last two verses'. Our analysis of the speeches has shown their common theological perspective (see chap. 3.3.3), including the cosmic scope of the divine plan (2.36,39; 7.48–50; 10.34,36,42–3; 13.39); we have also noted how Luke adapts his message to his listeners with special care in this speech (see also Flender, *Theologian* 66–72). In particular, the notion of resurrection need not have been totally alien to some of Paul's Stoic listeners; see Grant, *Miracle* 235–9; H. Chadwick, 'Origen, Celsus, and the Resurrection of the Body', *HTR* 41 (1948) 83–102; *contra*, Flender, *Theologian* 67, 71. On the apologetic function of 17.31, see Flender, *Theologian* 161.

authorized by the Holy Spirit to do likewise to the Gentiles (10.44–5).

Paul employs this terminology of necessity in recalling his call, describing himself as divinely appointed (προεχειρίσατο, 22.14; προχειρίσασθαι, 26.16)[96] to know the divine will and commanded (τέτακται, 22.10)[97] concerning what he is to do. Luke's initial account of Paul's call includes the necessity motif in the explicit command from the voice of Jesus to 'rise and enter the city, and you will be told what you are to do' (δεῖ ποιεῖν, 9.6); this is similar to the ways we have seen Fate revealed through portents in hellenistic histories. Paul is a chosen vessel (σκεῦος ἐκλογῆς, 9.15) whose subsequent actions are guided by the necessity of the same plan of God which had guided Jesus and the twelve apostles. This is emphasized immediately in the vision to Ananias, in which the Lord charges him to go to Paul, for 'I will show him how much he must suffer (ὅσα δεῖ αὐτὸν παθεῖν) for the sake of my name' (9.16). This presentation of Paul thus contains a propagandistic aim; by emphasizing the necessity of God's plan, Luke invites his readers to accept the inevitable course of their lives and believe the Christian message.[98]

Just as Jesus must suffer, so must Paul; and just as Jesus had to go to Jerusalem to meet that fate, so Paul had to go to Rome. Luke reports Paul's conviction about this in Ephesus, where Paul says 'after I have been there [Jerusalem], I must (δεῖ) also see Rome' (19.21).[99] As in hellenistic history, Fate is revealed in dreams, so on two occasions the Lord appears in epiphanies and affirms this necessity: 'you must (δεῖ) bear witness also at Rome' (23.11) and 'you must (δεῖ) stand before Caesar' (27.24).[100] The necessity of Paul's appeal to Caesar is implied in Agrippa's words to Festus (26.32)[101] and asserted by Paul when he arrives in Rome (ἠναγκά-

---

[96]  Used also for Jesus (3.20) and the apostles (10.41).

[97]  τεταγμένοι is used at 13.48 to indicate God's appointing of certain Gentiles 'to eternal life'.

[98]  For the proptreptic function of apology, see Malherbe, '"Preaching of Peter"' 205–6; for examples of self-presentation with a missionary purpose in apologetic literature of the second and third centuries, see J. Foster, *After the Apostles: Missionary Preaching of the First Three Centuries* (London: SCM, 1951) 86–91.

[99]  On the structural significance of 19.21, see Filson, 'Journey Motif' 72–3.

[100]  Cf. the reiteration of this necessity (δεῖ) at 25.10; 27.26. Conzelmann (*Theology* 154) notes the significance of the increasingly frequent use of δεῖ in the later chapters of Acts: here, 'the marks of Luke's composition can most clearly be seen'.

[101]  The conditional clause shows that the course is now irrevocable. The passive verb which follows (ἐκρίθη, 27.1) once again implies the divine decision.

σθην, 28.19). The necessity of Paul's journey to Rome thus resonates with the accounts of his call which he gives during this journey.

To these indications of necessity, consistent with the Gospel depiction of Jesus' ministry, Luke adds a third way of conveying the inevitability of the apostolic mission. The apostles' obedience to their commission to testify to what they have seen (Luke 24.49; Acts 1.8) is expressed in well-known hellenistic sayings in their public proclamations in Jerusalem.[102] Peter and John declare to the high priest that the choice they face is between listening to the council and being silent, or listening to God (4.19),[103] drawing the obvious conclusion that 'we cannot but speak (οὐ δυνάμεθα μὴ λαλεῖν) of what we have seen and heard' (4.20). Subsequently they repeat that they are under the impulse of necessity, echoing a saying well known among Greeks from Plato onwards: 'we must (δεῖ) obey God rather than men' (5.29).[104]

The implication of divine necessity is further conveyed by Gamaliel to his fellow council members as they contemplate punishing Peter and John. Luke puts into Gamaliel's mouth a clear statement of his own apologetic programme concerning the predominance of the plan of God,[105] that by rejecting their plan or undertaking, the council 'might even be found opposing God' (5.39). This saying expresses in a most concise fashion what Luke emphasizes in various ways, as we have seen; in this instance, the use by a Jewish

---

[102] Flender (*Theologian* 144–5) notes, rather generally, the hellenistic tenor of these sayings. On the awareness of classical Greek literature exhibited by New Testament writers, including Luke, see Renehan, 'Classical Greek Quotations' 17–45; A. J. Malherbe, *Social Aspects of Early Christianity* (2nd edn; Philadelphia: Fortress Press, 1973) 41–5.

[103] Haenchen (*Acts* 219 n. 11) regards this verse as an allusion to Plato, *Ap.* 29D, but later (p. 251) admits that the wording of 5.29 is closer.

[104] πειθαρχεῖν δεῖ θεῷ μᾶλλον ἢ ἀνθρώποις recalls the wording of Plato, *Ap.* 29D (πείσομαι δὲ μᾶλλον τῷ θεῷ ἢ ὑμῖν), leading Foakes Jackson and Lake (*Beginnings* 4.45) and Haenchen (*Acts* 25) to propose Plato as the direct model for this verse. However, the same idea is to be found in numerous works of antiquity (collected by Wettstein, *Nov. Test. Graec.* 478–9): see Sophocles, *Antig.* 450–5; Herodotus 5.63; Plutarch, *Sept. sap. conviv.* 152C; Epictetus, *Diss.* 1.30 (not 1.20 as Wettstein lists); Livy 39.367.17; Athenaeus, *Deipn.* 12.520A; for thematic, rather than linguistic, parallels, see Kurz, 'Proof from Prophecy' 137 n. 1. For the various nuances of the thought in the Stoics Epictetus and Marcus Antoninus, see R. Bultmann, 'πειθαρχέω', *TDNT* 6 (1968) 10 n. 1. Josephus has a similar idea at AJ 17.159; 18.268; indeed, the notion is not alien to the Hebrew scriptures (see Exod 1.17; Num 22.18; Sus 23; 1 Macc 2.22).

[105] Conzelmann (*Acts* 43) astutely comments, 'What Gamaliel proposes is the apologetic plan of Luke.'

leader of such a hellenistic commonplace[106] highlights the apologetic function which Luke intends to give to the theme of God's actions in the history of the early church. In more Jewish fashion, Peter later warns those who would oppose the spread of the Gospel among the Gentiles neither to oppose God (κωλῦσαι τὸν θεόν, 11.17)[107] nor to make trial of God (πειράζετε τὸν θεόν, 15.10).[108] Paul repeats this understanding of divine compulsion when he tells the Jews of Pisidian Antioch that even their own scriptures state concerning the apostles that God has set them (τέθεικα) to be a light for the Gentiles (13.47, quoting Isa 49.6) and therefore he must (δεῖ) speak to the Gentiles (13.46). Later, he tells the Ephesian Jews that his travels are entirely at God's behest; he can only promise to return to them 'if God wills' (τοῦ θεοῦ θέλοντος, 18.21). This striking phrase, 'a Hellenistic pious formula of strictly heathen origin'[109] without Jewish roots,[110] recurs in a more Christian form

---

[106] θεομαχέω is found in Euripides, *Iph. in Aul.* 1408–9; *Bacch.* 44–6, 325, 1255–6; the same idea, in variant terminology, appears at *Bacch.* 635–6; *Iph. in Aul.* 1396–7; *Iph. in Taur.* 1478–9; and two fragments (*Frags.* 491, 716, quoted by A. Vögeli, 'Lukas und Euripides', *ThZ* 9 (1953) 418–19 n. 14). For the question of Luke's literary dependence on Euripides, see chap. 2 nn. 71–2; Renehan, 'Quotations'. Again, this phrase reflects a common idea which appears in many works of antiquity (collected by Wettstein, *Nov. Test. Graec.* 489; see also Vögeli, 'Lukas und Euripides' 429–30 nn. 58–61); Xenophon, *Oecon.* 16.3; Pindar, *Pyth. Odes* 2.88; Cicero, *Tusc. disp.* 3.25; Plutarch, *De superstit.* 168C; *Apoph. Lac.* 225C; *Marcell.* 16.2 (307A); Josephus, *AJ* 14.310 (quoting a letter of M. Antonius); *CA* 1.246 (quoting Manetho); *CA* 1.263; Lucian, *Jupp. trag.* 45; Philostratus, *Vit. Apoll.* 4.44; see also 2 Macc 7.19 Especially important is its use by Epictetus (*Diss.* 3.24.21,24 (bis); 4.1.101) in the context of affirming Zeus' providential care of the universe (see 3.24.19, 24; 4.1.99–100). For its appearance in Diodorus Siculus, BH 14.69.2, see chap. 3 n. 30.

[107] Although this verb is common in the Septuagint, it is used only in relation to opposing humans (but cf. Eccl 8.8, 'no one has power to retain the Spirit'). Peter's use of the verb is uniquely Lukan; see also Acts 8.36; 10.47.

[108] The phrase is found in the Septuagint; see Exod 17.2,7; Num 14.22; Ps 77(78).41,56; 94(95).9; 105(106).14; Isa 7.12; Judg 8.12; Sir 18.23; ἐκπειράζω at Deut 6.16; Ps 77(78).18; cf. Exod 15.25.

[109] Thus, Foakes Jackson and Lake, *Beginnings* 4.231. The phrase is commonly called the *conditio Jacobaea* because of its use at Jas 4.15; the numerous parallels in Greek literature and papyri (as well as Latin equivalents) are noted by J. H. Ropes, *A Critical and Exegetical Commentary on the Epistle of St James* (ICC; New York: Scribners, 1916) 279 and M. Dibelius, *A Commentary on the Epistle of James* (Hermeneia; rev. of 11th German edition (1964) by H. Greeven; Philadelphia: Fortress Press, 1976) 233 n. 21 (first collected in Dibelius' German commentary of 1921); see also Wettstein, *Nov. Test. Graec.* 677 (on Jas 4.15) and 404 (on Heb 6.3).

[110] Foakes Jackson and Lake, *Beginnings* 4.213; Ropes, *James* 279–80. On the false attribution of the saying to first-century Jews and the misuse of later Jewish evidence (eleventh century), see Ropes, *James* 280; Dibelius, *James* 234 n. 21. Early Christian literature, however, provides evidence of its use by Christians of Jewish extraction; see Rom 1.10; 15.32; 1 Cor 4.19; Jas 4.15; with ἐπιτρέπω, 1 Cor 16.7; Heb 6.3; note also Mart. Pol. 7.1. See Dibelius, *James* 234 n. 22

in Caesarea, when Paul's companions and their hosts send him to Jerusalem with the blessing, 'the will of the Lord be done' (τοῦ κυρίου τὸ θέλημα γινέσθω, 21.14).[111] Luke has Paul then express his complete obedience to God's will (21.13) 'with a carefully chosen vocabulary' in classical Greek fashion.[112] The next time that Paul is in Caesarea, he vigorously asserts God's purposes for his life in his apology before Agrippa and Festus (25.23–26.32). The futility of his persecutions of the Way and the inevitability of his conversion are both encapsulated in the proverbial Greek saying that 'it hurts to kick against the goads' (26.14). Thus it is clear to Luke's hellenistic audience that events from the conversion of Paul to his journey to Rome are integral parts of God's inevitable plan.

### 7.3.2 The role of human will in the plan of God

This emphasis on divine necessity does not, however, eliminate human free-will,[113] for there are frequent moments when Luke notes what it means for humans to co-operate with the plan of God. William Beardslee observes that throughout Luke–Acts 'the firmness of the divine purpose is set in counterpoint to the peril and expendability of its instruments'.[114] He attributes this dynamic to Luke's extensive dependence on the Hebraic model of writing history; rather than a hellenistic struggle against Fate, Luke has taken hold of the Hebrew pattern of the struggle against 'a highly

---

[111] The use of θέλημα and γινέσθω recalls Jesus' words at Luke 22.42 (which in turn evokes the Lord's Prayer, if it was known to Luke's readers with this phrase included); the use of κύριος rather than θεός in this phrase can be seen at 1 Cor 4.19; 6.7; Jas 4.15. Foakes Jackson and Lake (*Beginnings* 4.269) incorrectly differentiate 1.14 from 18.21, calling the former a 'phrase of resignation'; *contra*, Conzelmann (*Acts* 178), who calls it 'a positive affirmation of the will of God'. Schubert ('Final Cycle' 14) equates θέλημα with βουλή.

[112] Haenchen, *Acts* 602. For parallels to the phrase ἑτοίμως ἔχω, see Wettstein, *Nov. Test. Graec.* 604; note esp. 2 Cor 12.14. Josephus uses this phrase to refer to a willingness to die at AJ 12.315; 13.6; cf. BJ 2.196,201; 5.419.

[113] Schulz ('Vorsehung' 110–11) correctly notes the Jewish belief in free-will alongside election of God, but incorrectly dismisses this from Lukan thought by depicting Luke as entirely hellenistic. Cosgrove ('Divine ΔΕΙ' 171) criticizes Schulz or his tendency to ignore the 'human dimension' of the divine will. Haenchen (*Acts* 62) claims that 'Luke virtually excludes all human decision'; see the criticisms of Junkett, 'Cornelius Episode' 473–4. The structural interplay of necessity and free-will in Luke 24.13–35 is explored by Radcliffe ('Necessity and Freedom' (*passim*), esp. 487–90).

[114] *Literary Criticism of the New Testament* (Philadelphia: Fortress Press, 1970) 1.

purposeful Yahweh'.[115] Indeed, it is true that the Hebrew scriptures are insistent on the freedom and right of human individuals to wrestle with God's will. Yet we have already noted the dangers of totally separating hellenistic from Hebraic; such an issue is common to both general cultural areas. Our own exploration of the hellenistic historians shows that they are, generally, not concerned to highlight the philosophical dimensions of the dynamic. It is only Josephus, of the writers we have examined, who is consistent and explicit about this interplay.

Luke, then, may well be placed in company with the hellenistic historians in his use of the necessity theme. Like them, he appears to be well aware of the broad issues involved in relating necessity to human free-will, but also quite content to avoid the technical terms and concepts of the philosophical discussion.[116] Although he is engaged in a similar apologetic process as Josephus, he falls away from any express treatment of the question. Rather, Luke is content to tell his story with no more than fleeting, but persistent, hints as to the broader philosophical issues which lie behind the narrative.

### 7.3.2.1 Philosophic views of Fate and free-will

As we have already noted, it is not until Justin Martyr that a clear awareness of the philosophical dimensions of faith is expressed in our extant Christian literature. Justin affirms God's foreknowledge (1 *Ap* 28) and justifies it by means of his characteristic proof from prophecy technique (1 *Ap* 32–53), emphasizing especially the necessity of Christ's passion (1 *Ap* 41, 49–50). However, he senses a possible objection, that 'whatever happens, happens by a fatal necessity, because it is foretold as known beforehand' (1 *Ap* 43.1). Using the terms of the philosophical discussions,[117] Justin rejects the claim that 'whatever happens, happens by a fatal necessity (καθ᾽ εἱμαρμένην) and asserts that there are 'things in our power (ἐφ᾽ ἡμῖν) for we are able to 'choose good by free choice' (προαίρεσι). Prophecy does not nullify such free-will, for the prophet

---

[115] *Literary Criticism* 45.
[116] Luke's avoidance, or ignorance, of the technical terms is illustrated by his use of a standard Epicurean term (αὐτομάτη) to describe the opening of the city gate s that Peter might escape his imprisonment (Acts 12.10). In context, however, this occurrence is anything but fortuitous – it is clearly a divine action, performed by the angel of God who is leading Peter.
[117] καθ᾽ εἱμαρμένην, προαίρεσιν and ἐφ᾽ ἡμῖν. The first two terms are combined with παρ᾽ ἡμῖν at 2 *Ap* 7.3–5; see also *Dial.* 141.

themselves emphasized personal responsibility and the opportunity to choose, in the same manner as Plato affirms choice.[118]

Justin returns to the same theme in 2 *Ap* 7, where he names the Stoics and specifies their doctrine that 'all things take place according to the necessity of Fate'. Just as their doctrine of the conflagration is to be rejected, so is their doctrine of Fate, for 'God in the beginning made the race of angels and men with free-will (αὐτεξού-σιον)'.[119]

Justin therefore provides an explicit discussion of Christian providence in conversation with philosophical beliefs. Likewise, Tatian asserts that human beings have free-will (*Or* 7) but that the doctrine of Fate was laid down by demons (*Or* 9), and concludes that 'we are superior to Fate … we do not follow the guidance of Fate' (*Or* 9), and explains sin as arising not from God, but from our own free-will (*Or* 11).[120] Because of the apologetic emphasis on providence, this objection (that free-will is denied) must be dealt with in explicitly philosophical fashion.

Luke is aware of the dilemma which his emphasis on divine providence produces; but he refrains from such an explicitly philosophical discussion of free-will and determinism.[121] Nevertheless, Luke does offer a resolution of the problem, for as well as the

[118] *Rep.* 10.617E, quoted at 1 *Ap* 44.

[119] This term recurs five times in Justin's Dialogue with Trypho: *Dial.* 88.5; 102.4 (three times); 141.1; and see 2 *Ap* 7.5 in *Dial.* 88.5 this comes in a discussion of prophecy which is fulfilled in the birth and baptism of Jesus; in *Dial.* 102.4 the word is used three times amidst strenuous affirmation of God's providential powers as creator, appointer of the καίρους and judge. In *Dial.* 141.1 such free-will is emphasized alongside God's foreknowledge and foretelling of punishment and blessing. See Osborn, *Justin Martyr* 152; Chadwick, 'Defence' 292; for other uses of this word in Hellenistic texts, see W. C. van Unnik, 'Josephus' Account of the Story of Israel's Sin with Alien Women in the Country of Midian (Num 25.1ff)', *Travels in the World of the Old Testament: Studies Presented to Professor M. A. Beck on the Occasion of his 65th Birthday* (ed. M. S. H. G. Heerma van Voss, P. H. J. Houwink ten Cate and N. A. van Uchelen; Assen: Van Gorcum, 1974) 256.

[120] See Amand, *Fatalisme* 208–11. Note also Theophilus, *Ad Autol.* 2.27 and Arnobius 7.10. Although Athenagoras also relates the Christian faith to philosophical belief, he does not address the specific issue of free-will. See chap. 3 nn. 91–2.

[121] For the philosophical discussion, see above, chap. 7.2.1. Tiede (*Prophecy* 84) comments on the cause of the judgement against Jerusalem (a topic we do not consider), 'the text repeatedly states it both ways'. This is the case wherever issues of free-will and causation arise in Luke's work. Radcliffe ('Necessity and Freedom' *passim*), deals with the relation between the two ideas on a highly abstract level, without adducing specific textual data dealing directly with this relationship. Cosgrove ('Divine ΔΕΙ' 185) explains the lack of systematic presentation of providence by Luke as due to his kerygmatic and contextual purposes; Haenchen (*Acts* 159 n.8) describes the juxtaposition of divine will and human free-will as 'not explicitly thought out'.

hellenistic language of cosmic determinism which he uses, we find a
balancing emphasis on human responsibility. Thus, immediately
after Paul emphasizes the inevitability of his call (Acts 26.14), he
repeats God's charge in terms which admit of human free-will.[122]
This juxtaposition is clearer than the tendency we have noted in the
hellenistic historians, to avoid addressing the fundamental concern
although not as directly philosophical as we have found in Josephus
or the apologists. Luke thus stakes a position remarkably close to
the Stoic viewpoint.

This interplay between divine and human actors throughout
Luke's two volumes can be seen especially in the possibility of
opposing the plan of God and through those individuals (especially
Jesus and Paul) who play significant roles in the plan of God, not
merely as human pawns of an arbitrary divine necessity, but as key
figures in implementing that plan. The inclusion of this aspect is
akin to the numerous instances in hellenistic histories in which
human will, rather than a fixed Fate, is determinative.[123]

### 7.3.2.2 Opposition to the plan of God

The possibility of opposing God by rejecting the divine plan,
expressed by Gamaliel (Acts 5.38–9), is raised by Luke earlier in the
Gospel, at the first appearance of the key phrase, 'the plan of God'
(Luke 7.30). The context within which we first meet this key phrase
is of great importance, for it alerts us to two vital aspects of the
theme. First, from the very start, the plan of God is understood in
terms of the opposition it encounters (here from the Pharisees and
lawyers); Luke's readers are thus prepared for the apologetic function which, as we have noted, it serves throughout the work.
Second, the freedom of the human will is asserted in the very same
phrase as the plan of God is introduced, and thus it is absolutely
clear that Luke is not utilizing a notion of an inexorable and
inevitable Fate.[124] Indeed, the 'purpose and deed' of those who
oppose the plan of God (23.51) is permitted to come to fruition,[125]

122 Paul is charged with inviting 'the people and the Gentiles' to turn to the light,
exercise faith and receive forgiveness, all of which assumes the ability of such people
to make such choices.
123 See above, nn. 20, 28, 48, 111–12.
124 Cf. the popular view of Fate noted above (pp. 157–8, 160–2).
125 Such opposition 'is never denied ... nor is [it] absorbed by a divine determinism' (Tiede, Prophecy 110). Tiede thus considers that Luke–Acts is clearly within
prophetic stream flowing through contemporary wisdom literature' (ibid.), but no

as the plotting by the scribes and Pharisees (Luke 5.21,30; 6.2,7,11; 7.30; 11.53–4; 13.14,17; 14.1; 15.2; 16.14), later joined by the priests and Sadducees (Luke 19.47–8; 20.1,19; 22.2,52,66; 23.10,13), leads to the death of Jesus.[126] Such opposition to the followers of Jesus continues throughout Acts, coming both from Jews[127] and from Gentiles[128] alike. The plan of God is not explained by the Stoic illustration of the moving wagon to which the dog is tied,[129] for there is a real freedom to choose for or against it.[130]

Although the Jerusalem leaders are held responsible for the death of Jesus,[131] the apostles continue to preach to them in the hope that they will change their minds about him and believe. The possibility that they acted in ignorance is raised both by Peter (Acts 3.17) and by Paul (17.30a),[132] both of whom link this with a clarion call to repentance (3.19; 17:30b). This is a common item in the apostolic proclamation (Acts 2.38; 3.26; 5.31; 8.22; 10.43; 11.18; 13.38; 14.15; 20.21; 26.18,20), which is familiar from the preaching of both John the Baptist (Luke 3.3,8; Acts 13.24; 19.4) and Jesus (Luke 5.32; 10.13; 11.32; 13.3,5; 15.7,10; 16.30; 17.3–4). Such repentance would

the similar polemic against Fate in hellenistic history which we have noted above (pp. 158–61, 163 5).

[126] Radcliffe ('Necessity and Freedom' 491) notes, 'the moment in which, for Luke, necessity and freedom ultimately coincide' is expressed at Luke 22.20–2; the death is both necessary and yet a free act.

[127] Although some Jews are helpful to Paul (Acts 9.8; 18.20; 19.33; 22.11), it is more frequent for a group within the Jews to oppose him, forcing him to move on to another city (13.50; 14.5–6,19; 17.5; 18.12; 19.9; 20.1,27–33; 23.12,21,33; 25.2,7; 26.21; see esp. 19.23–41 for Jewish opposition in Ephesus). There are positive notes concerning the Jews in Rome (28.17,22,23), but the final picture is of a divided Roman Jewry (28.21); see Jervell, *Luke* 44–9, 62–4; Johnson, *Possessions* 56–8.

[128] Some Gentiles hinder Paul, notably the centurion (Acts 27.11) and his soldiers (27.42), although the same centurion comes to Paul's defence against these latter soldiers, rescuing him from their plot (27.43). Usually the Gentiles are presented in a positive way, as helpful to Paul (21.32; 23.24,31; 27.3; 28.2). Both Festus and Felix are influenced by the Jews in a negative way (24.22,26,27; 25.2,9). See Jervell, *Luke* 157; Johnson, *Possessions* 57.

[129] See above, n. 35 (referring to *SVF* 2.975).

[130] Conzelmann (*Theology* 155–6) argues that 'the language of "predetermining" replaces that of "election"', but then denies that 'a doctrine of predestination' can be deduced from this. See Marshall's modification of Conzelmann's interpretation (*Historian* 111–13). Haenchen (*Acts* 180) approvingly quotes Holtzmann: 'thus human freedom and divine necessity here go hand in hand', but later (*Acts* 362) he tips the scales entirely in favour of Fate. Flender (*Theologian* 144–5) observes the correct balance between providence and freedom of choice.

[131] Acts 2.23; 3.14–15; 4.10; 5.30; 7.52; cf. 10.39b; and note esp. 4.25–8, quoting Ps 2.1–2.

[132] Cf. Luke 23.24. On ignorance in Acts, see Conzelmann, *Theology* 89–93; Wilckens, *Missionsreden* 133–4; Tiede, *Prophecy* 38–9, 84–5, 111; Radcliffe, 'Necessity and Freedom' 489–90.

not be possible were the human will not free to make such a decision. Luke never explicitly makes this connection between repentance and free-will, for he simply reports the apostolic call for repentance and depicts the usual response which followed, when 'those who believed turned to the Lord' (11.21),[133] assuming that such a freedom to respond is at all times possible. Nevertheless, it was understood that the assertion of free-will functioned as an invitation to adopt the way of life being presented, and so this affirmation provides an instance of apology functioning in a protreptic manner.[134]

### 7.3.2.3  Co-operation with the plan of God

To this call to repent and adopt Christian beliefs and practices, Luke adds a series of role models who actively engage in the divine plan. He persistently depicts Jesus as a human executor of the plan of God, having a more active role in implementing that plan than the emphasis on necessity and fulfilment would at first suggest.[135] Although obedient to his parents (Luke 2.51), he has a stronger tendency to obey God, and so he constantly aligns himself with the divine will. Instead of being driven into the wilderness by the Spirit (Mark 1.12), Luke's Jesus decides himself to go into the wilderness, and the Spirit accompanies him as his guide (Luke 4.1). Jesus' quotation of the 'physician, heal thyself' saying provokes the clash in his home town of Nazareth (4.23), his journey towards Jerusalem is the result of his conscious decision when 'he set his face to go to Jerusalem' (9.51), he remains in control throughout his struggle on

---

[133] For belief in response to preaching, see Acts 4.4; 8.12,35–7; 9.42; 10.43–4; 13.12,48; 14.1; 15.7; 16.15,31–4; 17.11–12,34; 18.8; 20.21; 26.16–18. For turning to God, see 9.35; 15.3,19; 20.21.

[134] For the freedom of the will as an integral part of a protreptic address, see Maximus of Tyre, *Or.* 16.4, 6 (translated in Malherbe, *Moral Exhortation* 76, 78); for the freedom of the philosopher, subsumed under providence yet functioning as example in protreptic fashion, see Epictetus, *Diss.* 3.22.38–49; 4.1.1–5.

[135] See Cosgrove, 'Divine ΔΕΙ' 179–81, for the 'creative initiative' of Jesus as executor of the divine necessity; similarity, Radcliffe ('Necessity and Freedom' 491) for his 'free appropriation of [his] destiny' and Tiede (*Prophecy* 61) concerning 'the volition of the agents'. The assertion of Haenchen (*Acts* 362) that Luke presents only 'the twitching of human puppets' and of O'Neill (*Theology* 178), that 'human decision was almost completely excluded at the crucial moments', are misguided. Flender (*Theologian* 76) notes, 'God has not created man to be the puppet of his will; God's will enhances the responsibility of the human will.'

the Mount of Olives, obediently seeking God's will (22.42),[136] he provokes his arrest by encouraging his betrayer to kiss him (22.49, cf. Mark 14.45), and at the end he hands over his spirit to his Father (23.46, alluding to Ps 30(31).6). These texts suggest that the Lukan Jesus has a consciousness that he must fulfil the plan of God. His own will is never opposed to that of God, but rather plays an active role, carrying out the plan of God.

Paul's own will is an important factor in the events recounted in Acts.[137] In Corinth, Paul resolves in the Spirit, 'after I have been there [Jerusalem], I must also see Rome' (Acts 19.21), thereby indicating the full extent of his mission. Upon receiving the advice of the believers in Tyre, who 'through the Spirit told Paul not to go to Jerusalem' (21.14), Paul asserts his complete readiness for what will ensue in Jerusalem (21.13) and submits himself to 'the will of the Lord' (21.14). The prophecy made by the Holy Spirit (21.11; cf. 20.23) is set to come true, now that Paul's will is aligned with God's will. So Paul goes to Jerusalem, 'bound in the Spirit' (20.22); through an act of his own will, he is completely subordinated to the divine πνεῦμα.[138]

Luke gives many further indications of the way in which Paul willingly co-operates with the divine will,[139] especially as he actively decides the direction to be taken on his journeys.[140] After the Jerusalem Council there is a sharp contention (παροξυσμός, 15.39) between Paul and Barnabas, concerning who should accompany them on their return to Syria (15.36–40); Paul's decision not to take John Mark is vindicated by the brethren (15.40).[141] In Lystra Paul's

---

[136] Neyrey, 'Absence' 158–9; disputed by Marshall (*Luke* 828), who nevertheless reads 22.39 as emphasizing 'the initiative of Jesus' (*ibid.*, 829).

[137] On Paul as a 'creative executor of the divine δεῖ', see Cosgrove, 'Divine ΔΕΙ' 81–3; Radcliffe, 'Necessity and Freedom' 491–2.

[138] ἐν τῷ πνεύματι (19.21) is interpreted as a reference to the Holy Spirit by Haenchen, *Acts* 568; O'Neill, *Theology* 67–8; more hesitatingly by Foakes Jackson and Lake, *Beginnings* 4.244; *contra*, Cosgrove, 'Divine ΔΕΙ' 178 n. 26.

[139] In the authentic letters of Paul, there are similar indications of the way in which Paul understood his missionary enterprises not only to be under the will of God (Rom 1.10; 15.32; 1 Cor 4.19; 16.7b; 2 Cor 1.17–22) but also to require his own active participation in the execution of that will (Rom 1.13; 15.23; 1 Cor 16.5–9; 2 Cor 1. 5–16; 2.1; 12.14; Gal 4.20; 1 Thess 2.18).

[140] Throughout Paul's journeys, his fellow believers also assist in guiding his movements; see Acts 9.25,27,30; 11.25–6,30; 17.10,14; 21.4,7,8,16; 23.16.

[141] The χάρις of God to which Paul is here commended functions to represent divine approval, as already in the cases of Mary (Luke 1.30), Jesus (2.40,52), all the Jerusalem believers (Acts 4.33; cf. 2.47), Stephen (6.8), the church in Antioch (11.23) and Paul when he was with Barnabas (14.3,26); see also Stephen's use of the term for

decision to have Timothy circumcised (16.3) so that he, too, migh
accompany Paul is vindicated by God (16.5). In Ephesus Pau
submits to the will of the Lord concerning his potential return tc
Ephesus after the request of the Ephesians to do so,[142] yet very
soon thereafter the travel arrangements are made by Paul with a
firm and decisive will (20.3,13) and it is his decision to bypass
Ephesus in order to be in Jerusalem (20.16). Once in Jerusalem
Paul is deliberate and insistent on his right to appeal to the
Emperor (25.9,11; 26.32; 28.19). When the decision to sail for Italy
is made (27.1), the advice of Paul on the journey is highly valued
(27.10,21,31–2,33–6).[143]

Thus, at every point in Paul's travels, humans have the freedom
to co-operate with the plan of God, or to dissociate themselves
from it. Without any explicit philosophic discussion of the matter
Luke has affirmed his stance on the matter: the plan of God
requires human acceptance and assistance for its implementation.
The language of necessity and foreordination must be read in a
context which still allows for human free-will and within which i
functions apologetically as an invitation to Christian belief.[144]

Yet even where such co-operation is not obtained, the divine wil
is not defeated. The two 'test cases' for this are, as always, the cru
cifixion of Jesus and the mission to the Gentiles. Although those
who killed Jesus opposed the plan of God (Luke 7.30), Luke is still
able to affirm that Jesus' death fits into the overall plan of God. H
apologetically depicts it as a fulfilment of God's predetermined
intentions. Although some Jews oppose Paul because they believ
he is forsaking the ancestral customs by associating with Gentile
(Acts 21.21), Luke adamantly maintains that such a mission i
integral to the divine plan; again, he apologetically depicts th
Gentile mission as a necessary fulfilment of prophecy. Divin

Joseph (7.10) and David (7.46) and 1 Sam 2.26 for its probable origin. See Haenche
Acts 366.
  [142] Cosgrove ('Divine ΔΕΙ' 187 n. 40) argues that this is 'an expression of willir
obedience to divine guidance ... not a resigned fatalism'.
  [143] Paul is thus 'an active protector of the divine δεῖ of his Roman destin
(Cosgrove, 'Divine ΔΕΙ' 179).
  [144] Put in this way, Luke's position is thus quite similar to the Stoic positic
outlined in chap. 7.2.1; see also Pohlenz, Die Stoa 1.106. Schubert ('Final Cycle' 1.
suggests that Paul's three-point summary of his conversations with Felix (24.2)
includes the Stoic ability of ἐγκράτεια which, according to Epictetus (Diss 1.1.1–
enables a person 'to choose between what is in a man's power and what cannot be
his power'.

providence rules supreme; the fitting response is to repent and believe.

## 7.4 Conclusions

The language of necessity is used often by Luke. Certain sayings and phrases, especially in the 'Jerusalem' section of Acts and most notably in Paul's final account of his call, are explicitly hellenistic sayings which were used to refer to the compelling force of divine necessity. Luke thus signifies the necessity of the plan of God in a way which was understandable to hellenistic readers. A comparison with similar themes in the hellenistic histories demonstrates a widespread awareness, shared by Luke, of the ways in which divine providence could be expressed in terms of Fate.

An apologetic purpose is evident in the various ways that the plan of God is described as necessary and foreordained. This is especially so in the two 'test case' incidents of the passion of Jesus and the mission to the Gentiles, which are apologetically asserted by this means. The theme of the necessary plan of God is a significant theological factor in Luke–Acts, providing a defence of Christian beliefs as well as functioning as apologetic assertion and exposition of those beliefs. However, Luke's conception of divine necessity is not entirely deterministic, but rather serves to reinforce the personal will of God in much the same way as we find in Josephus. A further apologetic purpose is served by this theme, for recognition of the inevitability of the divine will encourages repentance, that is the adoption of Christian beliefs and practices, in conformity with the divine plan.

An explicit philosophical discussion relating divine necessity to human free-will is avoided by Luke, in contrast to Josephus' use of Greek philosophical categories in describing the Jewish 'sects' of the first century. Yet Luke's appropriation of the language of necessity is stronger than we find in Dionysius and Diodorus, who give only generalized and imprecise indications of the philosophical issues. Luke demonstrates his awareness of these philosophical issues by addressing his hellenistic readers with familiar phrases designed to elucidate a popularist Stoic position without extensive argumentation.

# 8

## CONCLUSIONS

Our exploration of the theme of 'the plan of God' has demonstrated its central role in Luke–Acts. It is central because it is related to crucial events in the story which Luke narrates, namely the passion of Jesus and the mission to the Gentiles. It is central also in the sense that it provides a means of relating various strands in the story which have to do with the divine guidance of history. To claim that this is a central theme of Luke's two volumes is not to say that it is the one and only theme which structures the work,[1] but rather that it is one means by which Luke attempted to integrate his narrative and present his story in a cohesive manner.

This theme is prominent at strategic places throughout Luke's narrative; we have noted these texts from time to time in our explorations. With the benefit of hindsight, the significance for this theme of some key terms in the preface (Luke 1.1–4) can be appreciated (see chapter 2.3.1). However, the prologue (Luke 1.5–2.52) is quite clear and explicit in the way it sets forth divine providence as a principal motif for the whole work (see chapter 2.3.3.1). This prologue, whatever its origins, stands as an integral part of Luke's completed work. It highlights God's guidance of the events by various means which often recur later in the narrative. The epiphanies, prophecies, miraculous happenings, and straightforward statements about God's providential guidance of events all signal the way these features will recur throughout the ensuing two volumes.

In the first volume, the role played by the journey section (Luke 9.51–19.44) is significant; it is throughout this journey that a growing awareness of the precise nature of God's guidance of Jesus is made known. Especially significant are the redactional notes o

---

[1] See the disclaimer of Talbert ('Promise and Fulfilment' 101) with regard to the theme of prophecy and fulfilment; the claim is pertinent also for the theme of the plan of God.

necessity, and the predictions uttered by Jesus which unfold the fate which lies in store for him in Jerusalem (see chapter 7.3.1). Luke presents the passion of Jesus, from the very beginning, as part of God's plan. This understanding is consolidated in the very last chapter of the Gospel, when the strands of necessity and fulfilment of prophecy are drawn together in three recognition scenes (see chapter 6.3.1.1). The first volume ends with prophecies fulfilled; more promises awaiting fulfilment thus drive the narrative into the second volume.

In this volume, the missionary speeches attributed to Peter, and then Paul, play a major role. These speeches are also significant for the way in which they develop the theme of the plan of God (see chapter 3.3.3). Peter's speech on the day of Pentecost (Acts 2.14–36) stands at the start of a new era in the story, as the promise of power is fulfilled. Luke has Peter draw together portents, fulfilled prophecies and an understanding of God as the subject acting through the life of Jesus. These strands combine to emphasize the providential perspective which Luke brings to his accounts of the early days of the church (see chapter 3.3.3.1). The strand of portents is further developed in Acts 3 and 4, when the healing performed by Peter and John is emphatically declared to be a sign of God's guidance and care (see chapter 4.3.2).

The central concern of much of Acts is the mission to the Gentiles. The theme of the plan of God is used in a consistent manner to justify this mission. This is evident in the first account of Paul's conversion and call (Acts 9.1–19), but becomes emphatically clear in the extended narrative of the visions to Peter and Cornelius (Acts 10.1–11.18). In this pivotal section of Acts, Luke combines these epiphanies with a sermon about God's impartial providential care and comments about divine guidance, to establish that the mission to the Gentiles was always intended by God (see chapter 5.3.3).

The theme of God's guidance runs consistently throughout the narrative comments of Acts; 'the things that God has done' becomes an especially significant catchphrase (see chapter 3.3.2). In the final section of Acts – Paul's arrest, trials and journey to Rome (Acts 21.27–28.16) – Luke persists with this theme. Here he twice has Paul recapitulate his conversion and call, with the purpose of demonstrating apologetically that he has been carrying out God's intentions. Woven together in his apology before Agrippa and Festus (Acts 26.1–29), are epiphanies, fulfilled prophecies and a note of necessity. These are all signs of divine providence at work in the events which Luke has narrated and which he has Paul here recall (see chapter 2.3.3.2). The second volume ends, as it had begun, with a declaration of the fulfilment of prophecy, indicating that what takes place is under the providence of God (see chapter 6.3.3.2). Thus, the theme remains central throughout the two volumes.

Given the centrality of this theme, we return now to the three questions posed of 'the plan of God' at the beginning of our exploration of Luke–Acts, in order to offer answers to each in turn. After considering each of these questions, we shall also treat a fourth question which arises out of the answers we have discovered.

## 8.1 What logic holds the various strands together?

In chapter one we noted that various scholars had commented on some, or all, of the various strands which we identified as related to the plan of God. Close attention to the text of Luke–Acts has demonstrated the ways in which those various strands come into relation with one another. In the prologue to Luke–Acts, the theme of divine guidance is established most clearly; epiphanies of divine messengers and their oracular pronouncements indicate that God is to be at work in the events which follow, while a hint of the necessity of ensuing events is also given.

The passion of Jesus, narrated at length by Luke in the Gospel, is immediately and insistently interpreted in the early chapters of Acts as being a demonstration of the predetermined plan of God. The structure of Luke's Gospel is such that attention is especially directed towards the passion from the ninth chapter onwards, throughout the extended account of Jesus' journey to Jerusalem. During the narrative of this journey, explicit mention is made of the passion through prophecies spoken by Jesus. Less direct indications of the passion occur in the epiphanies in the Gospel. In Acts, explication of the necessity of the passion and its fulfilment of scriptural prophecies serve to underscore the notion that God has indeed been at work in Jesus' passion.

Likewise, the mission to the Gentiles is consistently presented as a part of the divine plan. It was foretold by Jesus, it conforms to scriptural prophecies, it is authenticated by epiphanies at critical points and is further undergirded by the signs and wonders performed by those engaged in the mission. The necessity of Paul's call to mission amongst the Gentiles and the necessity of his journeys strengthen the claim that God has been at work in the Gentile mission.

Thus, the various strands reinforce one another as explanations for the passion of Jesus and the Gentile mission. The interweaving of strands reinforces the function of the central theme of the plan of God as an interpretive key to the events which Luke narrates. Such interweaving of themes is particularly clear in specific passages which we have considered; the programmatic speeches delivered by Peter in Jerusalem and Paul in Pisidian Antioch especially show how the various strands cohere, although many of the speeches in Acts include a number of the strands. This phenomenon has already been noted in the prologue of Luke 1–2. There is, then, a general coherence of each of the strands, made stronger through frequent intertwining throughout Luke–Acts, for the specific purpose of interpreting the passion and the mission in particular.

The interweaving of these strands is also evident in our comparative analysis. The interrelation of providence, fate and the various means of divination (portents, dreams and oracles) is evident in the hellenistic historians, while Josephus demonstrates how this hellenistic perspective is congenial with the scriptural perspective of the Hebrew people. Luke's interweaving of the strands thus makes sense because they were already understood to be related to one another, as our survey of other hellenistic literature has demonstrated.

## 8.2 What understanding of providence informs Luke?

Our investigation of the broader hellenistic context within which Luke was writing offers some guidelines for interpreting the theme of 'the plan of God' in Luke–Acts. It is clear that Luke reflects many of the elements of the Stoic philosophy in the way he presents divine providence and comments on how one might become aware of (i.e., 'divine') such providential activity. It is also clear that Luke rarely makes an explicitly philosophical statement concerning this theme. In this regard, he is quite akin to Dionysius and Diodorus, who are also clearly aware of the philosophical context but choose not to make direct philosophical comments on events. Josephus largely follows this practice, although at particular times (and for particular reasons) he writes in an explicitly philosophical manner.

The understanding of providence which informs Luke's use of the theme of the plan of God might be called a basically Stoic understanding, moderated for popular consumption in the manner of the historians, and mediated to early Christians through hellenistic

Judaism such as we see in Josephus. Although this tends to depict Luke as somewhat removed from Stoic thought, it is not true that Luke was totally unaware of the Stoic position, for certain phrases and allusions indicate quite clearly his philosophical awareness. However, he presents not a theoretical philosophical argument, but rather an application of his philosophical position in so far as it helps him tell the story of Jesus and the early church with relevance for a hellenistic context.

### 8.3 What is the function of the plan of God in Luke–Acts?

Luke–Acts is to be regarded as a kind of cultural 'translation', an attempt to tell a story to people who are in a context somewhat different from the context in which the story originally took place. There is, however, no indication of any polemical context for Luke himself; there are no direct attacks on people who hold views alternative to Luke's own, such as we find Josephus confronting in AJ 10, for example.

This does not mean that polemic is entirely absent from Luke–Acts. Clearly, certain of the individuals in the story which Luke tells find themselves in polemical situations; for example, Jesus, both when exorcizing and when teaching in Jerusalem; Peter and John, when healing in Jerusalem; Stephen, when speaking in Jerusalem; and Paul, when preaching in numerous cities. Nevertheless, we must resist the temptation to make the opponents of these individuals into 'antitypes' for some alleged opponents in Luke's own time. It is sufficient to note only that Luke sees the relationship, in general terms, between faith and opposition (Acts 14.22).

We have already noted the complexity of themes in Luke–Acts; correlative with that is the complexity of purposes for this work. No one purpose can be regarded as the definitive, all-encompassing key to Luke's work, for the literature Luke writes is not a tract designed with only one purpose in mind. He is, rather, seeking to address a range of issues within the extended work which includes a variety of people, places and times. Nevertheless, whenever the purpose of Luke–Acts is considered, one or both of two clear aspects usually emerge as significant: (1) the Jewishness of Christianity throughout the whole of Luke–Acts, especially concerning the role of Hebrew scripture; (2) the hellenization of Christianity, especially (but not exclusively) in the appropriate sections of Acts. These two features each need to be heeded when attempting to account for Luke's purposes.

So it is that the model of Luke–Acts as a 'translation' from one context to another seems appropriate; Luke is attempting to explain Christianity in such a way that it might be more fully understood by hellenized Christians. His readers (typified by 'Theophilus') would have been personally aware both of the Jewish origins and heritage of Christianity and of the generally 'hellenized' context within which the Gospel spread and within which they now live. In such an enterprise, the apologetic task (as defined in its broadest sense) is particularly appropriate. Luke shows that apologetic is related to edification. He includes not merely polemic against others, nor solely a defence of Christianity, but in large measure he offers apologetic assertion and apologetic exposition of the Christian faith.

Thus, in a connection not unknown in the ancient world (witness Josephus and, most especially, Philo), aspects of a philosophical understanding of faith are pressed into the service of apologetic. The task of 'translation' is furthered by means of popular philosophical ideas, known to educated readers familiar with hellenistic histories, which are embedded into the story of Luke–Acts, serving to show how the gospel relates to the hellenistic world. Furthermore, the Jewish origins of Christianity also play a role in this task of 'translating' from one context to another. The prominence of the Hebrew scriptures and the insistently Jewish practices of Jesus, the early Jerusalem church and Paul each reinforce the notion (essential in the hellenistic context) that Christianity was 'no mere novelty', but was able to claim a long antiquity in Israel. This aspect of Luke–Acts should be recognized as a valid component of Luke's apologetic. It provided the possibility of a polemical attack on Judaism as not living up to the ideals imbedded in its scriptures; such ideals are fulfilled only by Christians. Wherever Luke mounts such an attack, it is grounded in specific accusations and does not attain the force of an overall motif. At points we have suggested that Luke's apologetic may have been in response to various criticisms of Christianity that might have been made, both by Jews and by pagans.

The genre of historiography is one which was particularly amenable to these interests which we find in Luke–Acts. Hellenistic historians were interested both in recording 'antiquities' and in offering something of 'usefulness' to their readers. For Luke to write in this genre was not only helpful but also probably inevitable; to convey an authentic sense of origins whilst at the same time pointing to moral and religious lessons from that history, was an integral part of the historian's task.

It is the theme of providence which, as we have seen, draws all of these interests and aims together. Providence was a central theme in hellenistic historiography, a theme which was also central to the Hebrew scriptures, albeit in different terminology. Providence was a central aspect of philosophical discussion and theory, and it had an apologetic function in the less technical writings of hellenism. Providence in the histories had a religious application; it emphasized certain rituals at the expense of others. All of these elements are found in Luke–Acts in association with the theme of 'the plan of God', which provides us with a key to unlock some of the complexities of Luke–Acts.

The function of 'the plan of God' in Luke–Acts can best be described in three related terms. (1) The theme confirms the faith of the readers of Luke–Acts. It provides a means of relating diverse elements into an overall story; it offers a cohesive interpretation of Christian origins, especially in its explanation of the passion of Jesus and the mission of the early church. (2) The theme thus encourages the readers to exercise their tasks as witnesses to the Christian faith, and especially equips them to present the Gospel to the hellenistic world in a way that will make it understandable, that is, already 'translated'. (3) The theme enables the readers to defend their beliefs in the face of objections which might arise within their own context. The story makes it clear that Jesus and the early church faced objections and offered plausible explanations in their own times; the readers of Luke–Acts are thus enabled to do the same should the need arise in their own times.

These three functions are each developments of the basic apologetic purpose which Luke has in mind as he writes Luke–Acts. It is appropriate, then, to add a fourth question to our initial list and to conclude with a final consideration of reasons for Luke's use of 'the plan of God' in such an apologetic fashion.

## 8.4  Why does Luke write apologetically?

Luke, we have argued, is engaged in the task of 'translating' the Gospel into its hellenistic context. An important tool that he uses in this process is an apologetic stance. We have noted various objections which might have been raised against Christianity. From a Jewish perspective, Christianity might have been attacked as a new religion unrelated to Judaism, and Jesus might have been dismissed as a leader who could not lay claim to messianic status because of his crucifixion. From a pagan perspective, Christian missionary efforts might have been equated with Jewish proselytism, or dismissed as preachings of mere novelties only, while Jesus might have been perceived as a failed leader. Luke offers a comprehensive strategy for dealing with these objections; each strand of 'the plan of God' which we have identified functions in an apologetic manner, rebutting these objections on various levels.

We have also noted that the umbrella term, apologetic, includes defence, polemic, assertion and exposition, and borders on missionary preaching. Each of these elements is to be found, to varying degrees, in the hellenistic histories we examined. Although it is not the case that Luke presents a fully fledged Christian apologetic in the style of second-century writers, nevertheless it is clear that Luke–Acts includes elements which would later become identified with Christian apologetic.

(1) Defence against attack became important in the more polarized setting of the second century. This feature is not prominent in Luke–Acts because there was no immediate problem of opposition to the Gospel for Luke and his readers. Nevertheless, the presence of other apologetic elements shows that Luke was aware that Jesus and the early Christians had faced opposition, and as an historian he faithfully reports those instances. In addition to such historiographical interest, however, Luke has a practical aim: knowledge of how to defend oneself against opposition is useful should such an occasion arise. Thus, Luke's 'translation' of the story contains the seeds of an apologetic stance.

(2) An assertion of the rightful place of Christianity has frequently been seen to be a basic purpose of Luke–Acts. That such events 'were not done in a corner' is integral to Luke's history; this does not mean, however, that Luke has a political agenda in mind. Rather, what is of note is that he often claims the rightful place of Christianity as a religion which has ancient origins and is no mere novelty. The constant presence of Jewish elements and, especially, citations of Jewish scripture, function as apologetic assertion of the antiquity of the Christian faith. Likewise, in Paul's Areopagus speech, this motive is present, although here (as in Stephen's speech) the antiquity of Christianity is proven by means of a venerable philosophical tradition.

(3) An apologetic polemic surfaces from time to time in Luke–Acts. The attack on idols in Acts 7 and 17 is the clearest expression of polemic; so also are the debates which take place after the

exorcisms of Jesus and the healings of the apostles. Each of these polemical examples functions as reinforcement for the central theme of divine providence. Indirect polemic occurs when Luke deals with the disciples' failure to interpret prophecy in a correct manner, and the assertion of human free-will. In each case, Luke hints at the stance which might be taken if such aspects were to be questioned.

(4) The exposition of central aspects of the faith is the major type of apologetic activity which is present in Luke–Acts. Two key events have recurred throughout our investigation, for it is these two events which are pivotal to the plan of God and which therefore need to be expounded in some detail. (a) The necessity and centrality of the passion of Jesus is asserted and expounded, in opposition to the deed of the Jewish leaders and the misunderstanding of the disciples, as being central to the plan of God. (b) The integral role of the mission to the Gentiles, as an important part of the plan of God, is asserted and expounded in opposition to Jewish objections and misgivings on the part of certain Christians. Each of these events is central to the plan of God; each of them is explained by recourse to divine providence.

(5) The apologetic aim which Luke has in regard to the passion and the mission flowers in the speeches in Acts, for in these sections we see that what was originally apologetic assertion has developed into an extended exposition which borders on missionary preaching. Although the context is polemical in the time when these events took place, in the time in which Luke is writing, the context is more one of apologetic exposition. He writes to assure his readers that these events were part of the plan of God and to provide them with the means of witnessing to the divine plan in such a way that it might be understood and appreciated in the hellenistic world. At times, the further apologetic purpose of protreptic comes into view, and whilst the primary audience for which Luke writes is the Christian community, his apologetic methods also serve to invite others to accept Christian beliefs and adopt Christian practices. Luke offers this missionary tool to his Christian readers with the intention that they might use the story which he tells to further the Christian cause and make converts to Christianity.

# A SELECT BIBLIOGRAPHY

## A Texts and translations

*Apostolic Fathers with Justin Martyr and Irenaeus.* Ante-Nicene Fathers 1; ed. A. Roberts and J. Donaldson, rev. A. C. Coxe. New York: Charles Scribner's Sons, 1913.

*Cicero.* Loeb Classical Library. *De divinatione,* trans. W. A. Falconer, 1923. *De natura deorum,* trans. H. Rackham, 1933. *De fato,* trans. H. Rackham, 1942. Cambridge, Mass.: Harvard University Press.

*Diodorus of Sicily.* Loeb Classical Library, 12 vols.; trans. C. H. Oldfather, C. L. Sherman, C. B. Welles, R. M. Geer and F. M. Walton. Cambridge, Mass.: Harvard University Press, 1933–68.

*Diogenes Laertius: Lives of Eminent Philosophers.* Loeb Classical Library, 2 vols.; trans. R. D. Hicks. Cambridge, Mass.: Harvard University Press, 1925.

*Dionysius of Halicarnassus: The Roman Antiquities.* Loeb Classical Library, 7 vols.; trans. E. Cary on the basis of the version of E. Spelman. Cambridge, Mass.: Harvard University Press, 1937–50.

*Dionysius of Halicarnassus: Critical Essays.* Loeb Classical Library, 2 vols.; trans. S. Usher. Cambridge, Mass.: Harvard University Press, 1974, 1985.

*Epictetus: The Discourses Reported by Arrian, The Manual, and Fragments.* Loeb Classical Library, 2 vols.; trans. W. A. Oldfather, Cambridge, Mass.: Harvard University Press, 1925, 1928.

*Fathers of the Second Century.* Ante-Nicene Fathers 2; ed. A. Roberts and J. Donaldson, rev. A. C. Coxe. Buffalo: Christian Literature Publishing Co., 1885 (includes Tatian, *Address to the Greeks,* and Athenagoras, *A Plea for the Christians*).

*Fathers of the Third Century.* Ante-Nicene Fathers 4; ed. A. Roberts and J. Donaldson, rev. A. C. Coxe. Buffalo: Christian Literature Publishing Co., 1885 (includes Origen, *Against Celsus*).

*Florilegium Patristicum: S. Iustini Apologiae Duae,* ed. G. Rauschen. Bonn: Sumptibus Petri Hanstein, 1911.

*Herodotus.* Loeb Classical Library, 4 vols.; trans. A. D. Godley. Cambridge, Mass.: Harvard University Press, 1920–5.

*Josephus.* Loeb Classical Library, 10 vols.; trans. H. St J. Thackeray, R. Marcus, A. Wikgren and L. H. Feldman. Cambridge, Mass.: Harvard University Press, 1926–65, 1981.

196     *A select bibliography*

*Lucian.* Loeb Classical Library. *How to Write History*, trans. K. Kilburn.
Cambridge, Mass.: Harvard University Press, 1959.
*Old Testament Pseudepigrapha*, ed. J. H. Charlesworth. 2 vols. Garden
City, N.Y.: Doubleday, 1983.
*Philo.* Loeb Classical Library, 10 vols.; trans. F. H. Colson and G. H.
Whittaker. Cambridge, Mass.: Harvard University Press, 1929–62.
*Plutarch: The Moralia.* Loeb Classical Library. *De Pythiae oraculis, De
defectu oraculorum*, trans. F. C. Babbitt, 1926. *De fato*, trans. P. H. De
Lacy and B. Einarson, 1959. Cambridge, Mass.: Harvard University
Press.
*Polybius: The Histories.* Loeb Classical Library, 6 vols.; trans. W. R. Paton.
Cambridge, Mass.: Harvard University Press, 1922–7.
*Poseidonios: Die Fragmente*, ed. W. Theiler. Texte und Kommentare
10/1–2. Berlin and New York: de Gruyter, 1982.
*Posidonius: I. The Fragments*, ed. L. Edelstein and I. G. Kidd. Cambridge
Classical Texts, Commentaries 13. Cambridge University Press, 1972.

References to ancient authors are taken from editions in the Loeb Classical
Library unless otherwise noted.

## B  Monographs

Adams, D. 'The Suffering of Paul and the Dynamics of Luke–Acts'. Yale
Ph.D. diss., 1979.
Amand, D. *Fatalisme et liberté dans l'antiquité grecque.* Amsterdam:
A. M. Hakkert, 1973.
Arnim, H. F. A. von. *Stoicorum Veterum Fragmenta collegit Ioannes ab
Arnim.* 4 vols. Lipsiae: Teubner, 1903–24.
Attridge, H. W. *The Interpretation of Biblical History in the 'Antiquitates
Judaicae' of Flavius Josephus.* HDR 7. Missoula, Mont.: Scholars
Press, 1976.
*First Century Cynicism in the Epistles of Heraclitus.* Harvard Theological
Studies 29. Missoula, Mont.: Scholars Press, 1976.
Aune, D. E. *Prophecy in Early Christianity and the Ancient Mediterranean
World.* Grand Rapids, Mich.: Erdmans, 1983.
*The New Testament in its Literary Environment.* Library of Early Chris-
tianity 8. Philadelphia: Westminster, 1987.
Avenarius, G. *Lukians Schrift zur Geschichtsschreibung.* Meisenheim/Glan:
Anton Hain, 1956.
Barnard, L. W. *Athenagoras.* Théologie Historique 18. Paris: Beauchesne,
1972.
Barrett, C. K. *The Holy Spirit and the Gospel Tradition.* London: SPCK,
1947.
*Luke the Historian in Recent Study.* London: Epworth, 1961.
Bassler, J. M. *Divine Impartiality: Paul and a Theological Axiom.* SBLDS
59. Chico, Calif.: Scholars Press, 1979.
Beardslee, W. A. *Literary Criticism of the New Testament.* Philadelphia:
Fortress Press, 1970.
Behr, C. A. *Aelius Aristides and the Sacred Tales.* Amsterdam: A. M.
Hakkert, 1968.

Betz, O. *Offenbarung und Schriftforschung in der Qumransekte.* Wissenschaftliche Untersuchungen zum Neuen Testament 6. Tübingen: J. C. B. Mohr, 1960.

Betz, O., Haacker, K. and Hengel, M. (eds.) *Josephus-Studien: Untersuchungen zu Josephus, dem antiken Judentum und dem Neuen Testament. Otto Michel zum 70. Geburtstag gewidmet.* Göttingen: Vandenhoeck und Ruprecht, 1974.

Bevan, E. *Sibyls and Seers: a Survey of some Ancient Theories of Inspiration.* London: George Allen and Unwin, 1928.

Bieler, L. *Theios Aner: Das Bild des 'Göttlichen Menschen' in Spätantike und Frühchristentum.* 2 vols.; Wien: Oskar Höfels, 1935–6, reprinted Darmstadt: Wissenschaftliche Buchgesellschaft, 1967.

Bomstead, R. G. 'Governing Ideas of the Jewish War of Josephus'. Yale Ph.D. diss., 1979.

Bovon, F. *Luc le théologien: vingt-cinq ans de recherches (1950–75).* Neuchâtel et Paris: Delachaux et Niestlé, 1978.

Brawley, R. L. *Luke–Acts and the Jews: Conflict, Apology and Conciliation.* SBLMS 33. Atlanta: Scholars Press, 1987.

Bretschneider, C. G. *Capita theologiae Judaeorum dogmaticae e Flavii Josephi scriptis collectae.* Lipsiae: Bahrdtium, 1812.

Brown, R. E. *The Birth of the Messiah.* Garden City, N.Y.: Doubleday, 1977.

Brüne, B. *Flavius Josephus und seine Schriften in ihrem Verhältnis zum Judentum, zur griechischen-römischen Welt und zum Christentum.* Wiesbaden: Sändig, 1969.

Burkert, W. *Greek Religion.* Cambridge, Mass.: Harvard University Press, 1985.

Bury, J. B. *The Ancient Greek Historians.* London: Macmillan, 1909.

Busse, U. *Die Wunder der Propheten Jesus: Die Rezeption, Komposition und Interpretation der Wundertradition im Evangelium des Lukas.* Stuttgart: Katholisches Bibelwerk, 1977.

Cadbury, H. J. *The Making of Luke–Acts.* New York: Macmillan, 1927.
*The Book of Acts in History.* New York: Harper, 1955.

Carley, K. W. *Ezekiel Among the Prophets: a Study of Ezekiel's Place in Prophetic Tradition.* Naperville, Ill.: Alec R. Allenson, 1974.

Carson, D. A. *Divine Sovereignty and Human Responsibility: Biblical Perspectives in Tension.* New Foundations Theological Library. Atlanta: John Knox, 1981.

Cassidy, R. J. and Scharper, P. J. (eds.) *Political Issues in Luke–Acts.* Maryknoll, N.Y.: Orbis, 1983.

Clarke, G. W. *The Octavius of Marcus Minucius Felix.* New York: Newman, 1974.

Cohen, S. J. D. *Josephus in Galilee and Rome: His Vita and Development as a Historian.* Columbia Studies in the Classical Tradition 8. Leiden: Brill, 1979.

Cohn, L. and Wendland, P. (eds.) *Philonis Alexandrini: Opera Qvae Svpersvnt,* vol. 7. Indices compiled by H. Leisegang. Berlin: Walter de Gruyter, 1926, 1930.

Conzelmann, H. *The Theology of St Luke.* London: Faber and Faber, 1960.

*Acts of the Apostles*. Hermeneia. Trans. of 2nd German edition (1972). Philadelphia: Fortress Press, 1987.

Danielou, J. *Gospel Message and Hellenistic Culture*. Philadelphia: Westminster, 1973.

Danker, F. W. *Luke*. Proclamation Commentaries. Philadelphia: Fortress Press, 1976.

*Jesus and the New Age*. Philadelphia: Fortress Press, 1988.

Dibelius, M. *Studies in the Acts of the Apostles*. ed. H. Greeven. London: SCM, 1956.

*A Commentary on the Epistle of James*. Hermeneia. Rev. of 11th German edition (1964) by H. Greeven. Philadelphia: Fortress Press, 1976.

Dihle, A. *The Theory of the Will in Classical Antiquity*. Berkeley and Los Angeles: University of California Press, 1982.

Dodd, C. H. *The Apostolic Preaching and Its Development*. London: Hodder and Stoughton, 1936.

Dodds, E. R. *The Greeks and the Irrational*. Sather Classical Lectures 25. Berkeley and Los Angeles: University of California Press, 1951.

*Pagan and Christian in an Age of Anxiety: Some Aspects of Religious Experience from Marcus Aurelius to Constantine*. Cambridge University Press, 1965.

Dupont, J. *Études sur les Actes des Apôtres*. Lectio Divina 45. Paris: Cerf, 1967.

*The Salvation of the Gentiles: Essays on the Acts of the Apostles*. New York: Paulist, 1979.

*Nouvelles études sur les Actes des Apôtres*. Paris: Cerf, 1984.

Easton, B. S. *The Purpose of Acts*. London: SPCK, 1936.

Eltester, W. (ed.) *Neutestamentliche Studien für Rudolf Bultmann*. Berlin: Alfred Töpelmann, 1954.

Esler, P. F. *Community and Gospel in Luke–Acts: the Social and Political Motivations of Lucan Theology*. Cambridge University Press, 1987.

Fascher, E. *Prophētēs: eine sprach- und religionsgeschichtliche Untersuchung*. Giessen: Alfred Töpelmann, 1927.

Finkelstein, L. *The Pharisees: their Origin and their Philosophy*. Cambridge, Mass.: Harvard University Press, 1929.

Fitzmyer, J. *The Gospel According to Luke*. 2 vols.; Anchor Bible 28, 28A. New York: Doubleday, 1981, 1985.

Flacelière, R. *Plutarque: sur la disparition des oracles*. Annales de l'Université de Lyon 3.14. Paris: Les Belles Lettres, 1947.

*Greek Oracles*. New York: Norton, 1961.

Flender, H. *St Luke: Theologian of Redemptive History*. London: SPCK, 1967.

Foakes Jackson, F. J. and Lake, K. (eds.) *The Beginnings of Christianity: Part I, The Acts of the Apostles*. 5 vols.; London: Macmillan, 1920–33, repr. Grand Rapids, Mich.: Baker, 1979.

Fornara, C. W. *The Nature of History in Ancient Greece*. Berkeley and Los Angeles: University of California Press, 1983.

Foster, J. *After the Apostles: Missionary Preaching of the First Three Centuries*. Philadelphia: Westminster, 1975.

Franklin, E. Christ the Lord: a Study in the Purpose and Theology of Luke–Acts. Philadelphia: Westminster, 1975.

Fridrichsen, A. *The Problem of Miracle in Primitive Christianity*. Minneapolis, Minn.: Augsburg, 1972.

Gärtner, B. *The Areopagus Speech and Natural Revelation*. Uppsala: Gleerup, 1955.

Garrett, S. R. *The Demise of the Devil: Magic and the Demonic in Luke's Writings*. Philadelphia: Fortress Press, 1989.

Gasque, W. W. and Martin, R. P. (eds.) *Apostolic History and the Gospel*. Exeter: Paternoster, 1970.

Geffcken, J. *Zwei Griechische Apologeten*. Leipzig and Berlin: B. G. Teubner, 1907.

Goodenough, E. R. *The Theology of Justin Martyr*. Jena: Walter Biedermann, 1923.

Goodspeed, E. J. *Index Apologeticus sive Clavis Iustini Martyris Operum aliorumque Apologeticrum Pristinorum*. Leipzig: J. C. Hinrich, 1912.

Gould, J. B. *The Philosophy of Chrysippus*. Albany: State University of New York, 1970.

Grant, R. M. *Miracle and Natural Law in Graeco-Roman and Early Christian Thought*. Amsterdam: North Holland, 1952.

*Gods and the One God*. Library of Early Christianity 1. Philadelphia: Westminster, 1986.

Guillaumont, F. *Philosophie et augure: recherches sur la théorie cicéronienne de la divination*. Collection Latomus 184. Bruxelles: Revue d'études Latines, 1984.

Gundel, W. *Beiträge zur Entwickelungsgeschichte der Begriffe Ananke und Heimarmene*. Giessen: Brühl University, 1914.

Haenchen, E. *The Acts of the Apostles: A Commentary*. Philadelphia: Westminster, 1971.

Hart, J. *Herodotus and Greek History*. London: Croom Helm, 1982.

Hengel, M. *Judaism and Hellenism: Studies in their Encounter in Palestine during the Early Hellenistic Period*. 2 vols. Philadelphia: Fortress Press, 1974.

*Acts and the History of Earliest Christianity*. Philadelphia: Fortress Press, 1980.

Hull, J. M. *Hellenistic Magic and the Synoptic Tradition*. Studies in Biblical Theology 2/28. Naperville, Ill.: Alec R. Allenson, 1974.

Hyldahl, N. *Philosophie und Christentum: Eine Interpretation der Einleitung zum Dialog Justins*. Acta Theologica Danica 9. Copenhagen: Prostant apud Munksgaard, 1966.

Jervell, J. *Luke and the People of God: A New Look at Luke–Acts*. Minneapolis, Minn.: Augsburg, 1972.

*The Unknown Paul: Essays on Luke–Acts and Early Christian History*. Minneapolis, Minn.: Augsburg, 1984.

Johnson, L. T. *The Literary Function of Possessions in Luke–Acts*. Missoula, Mont.: Scholars Press, 1977.

*The Writings of the New Testament: An Interpretation*. Philadelphia: Fortress Press, 1986.

Joly, R. *Christianisme et philosophie: études sur Justin et les apologistes grecs du deuxième siècle*. Brussels: University of Brussels, 1973.

Keck, L. E. and Martyn, J. L. (eds.) *Studies in Luke–Acts*. Philadelphia: Fortress Press, 1966.

Kee, H. C. *Miracle in the Early Christian World: A Study in Sociohistorical Method*. New Haven and London: Yale University Press, 1983.

Kessells, A. H. M. *Studies on the Dream in Greek Literature*. Utrecht: HES, 1978.

Killgallen, J. *The Stephen Speech: A Literary and Redactional Study of Acts 7,2–53*. Analecta Biblica 67. Rome: Biblical Institute Press, 1976.

Kremer, J. (ed.) *Les Actes des Apôtres: traditions, rédaction, théologie*. Bibliotheca Ephemeridum Theologicarum Lovaniensium. Gembloux: Duculot, 1979.

Krodel, G. *Acts*. Proclamation Commentaries. Philadelphia: Fortress Press, 1981.

Kurz, W. S. 'The Function of Christological Proof from Prophecy for Luke and Justin'. Yale Ph.D. diss., 1976.

Laffranque, M. *Poseidonios d'Apamée (essai de mise au point)*. Paris: Presses Universitaires de France, 1964.

Lieberman, S. *Greek in Jewish Palestine: Studies in the Life and Manner of Jewish Palestine in the II–IV Centuries CE*. New York: Jewish Theological Seminary of America, 1942.

*Hellenism in Jewish Palestine: Studies in the Literary Transmission, Beliefs and Manners of Palestine in the I Century BCE – I Century CE*. New York: Jewish Theological Seminary of America, 1950.

Lieshout, R. C. A. van. *Greeks on Dreams*. Utrecht: HES, 1980.

Lindner, H. *Die Geschichtsauffassung des Flavius Josephus im Bellum Judaicum*. Arbeiten zur Geschichte des antiken Judentums und des Christentums 12. Leiden: Brill, 1972.

Long, A. A. (ed.) *Problems in Stoicism*. London: Athlone, 1971.

Maddox, R. J. *The Purpose of Luke–Acts*. FRLANT 126. Göttingen: Vandenhoeck und Ruprecht, 1982.

Malherbe, A. J. *Social Aspects of Early Christianity*. 2nd edn. Philadelphia: Fortress Press, 1973.

*Moral Exhortation: A Greco-Roman Sourcebook*. Library of Early Christianity 4. Philadelphia: Westminster, 1986.

Malitz, J. *Die Historien des Poseidonios*. Zetema 79. München: C. H. Beck, 1983.

Marrou, H. I. *À Diognète*. Sources Chrétiennes 33. 2nd edn. Paris: Cerf, 1965.

Marshall, I. H. *Luke: Historian and Theologian*. Exeter: Paternoster, 1970.

*The Gospel of Luke*. Exeter: Paternoster, 1978.

*The Acts of the Apostles: An Introduction and Commentary*. Grand Rapids, Mich.: Eerdmans, 1980.

Meeks, W. A. *The Prophet–King: Moses Traditions and the Johannine Theology*. Novum Testamentum, Supplement 14. Leiden: Brill, 1967.

Mikalson, J. D. *Athenian Popular Religion*. Chapel Hill: University of North Carolina, 1983.

Moore, G. F. *Judaism in the First Centuries of the Christian Era, the Age of the Tannaim*. 3 vols. Cambridge, Mass.: Harvard University Press, 1927–30.

Moule, C. F. D. (ed.) *Miracles: Cambridge Studies in their Philosophy and History*. London: Mowbray, 1965.

Munck, J. *Paul and the Salvation of Mankind*. Richmond: John Knox, 1959.

Navone, J. *Themes of St Luke*. Rome: Gregorian University, 1976.

Neusner, J. (ed.) *Christianity, Judaism and Other Greco-Roman Cults: Studies for Morton Smith at Sixty*. Studies in Judaism in Late Antiquity 12, 4 parts. Leiden: Brill, 1975.

Neyrey, J. *The Passion According to Luke: A Redaction Study of Luke's Soteriology*. New York: Paulist, 1985.

Nicol, W. *The Sēmeia in the Fourth Gospel: Tradition and Redaction*. Novum Testamentum, Supplement 32. Leiden: Brill, 1972.

Niederwimmer, K. *Der Begriff der Freiheit im Neuen Testament*. Berlin: Alfred Töpelmann, 1966.

Nilsson, M. P. *Cults, Myths, Oracles and Politics in Ancient Greece*. Gleerup: Lund, 1951.

*Greek Folk Religion*. New York: Harper, 1961.

Nineham, D. E. (ed.) *Studies in the Gospels: Essays in Memory of R. H. Lightfoot*. Oxford: Blackwell, 1967.

Nock, A. D. *Essays on Religion and the Ancient World*. 2 vols.; ed. Z. Stewart. Cambridge, Mass.: Harvard University Press, 1972.

Norden, E. *Agnostos Theos*. Leipzig and Berlin: B. G. Teubner, 1913.

Norris, R. A. *God and World in Early Christian Theology*. New York: Seabury, 1965.

O'Neill, J. C. *The Theology of Acts in its Historical Setting*. 2nd edn. London: SPCK, 1970.

Osborn, F. F. *Justin Martyr*. Beiträge zur historischen Theologie 47. Tübingen: Mohr, 1973.

O'Toole, R. F. *The Unity of Luke's Theology: An Analysis of Luke–Acts*. Good News Studies 9; Wilmington, Delaware: Michael Glazier, 1984.

Palm, J. *Über Sprache und Stil des Diodoros von Sizilien*. Lund: Gleerup, 1955.

Parke, H. W., and Wormell, D. E. W. *The Delphic Oracle*. 2 vols. Oxford: Blackwell, 1961.

Pax, E. *Epiphaneia: ein religionsgeschichtlicher Beitrag zur biblischen Theologie*. Münchener Theologische Studien 10. München: Karl Zink, 1955.

Pease, A. S. *M. Tvlli Ciceronis De Natvra Deorvm*. 2 vols. Cambridge, Mass.: Harvard University Press, 1955, 1958.

*M. Tvlli Ciceronis De Divinatione*. University of Illinois Studies in Language and Literature 6 (1920) 159–500, 8 (1923) 153–474. Reprinted in 2 volumes; Darmstadt: Wissenschaftliche Buchgesellschaft, 1973.

Plümacher, E. *Lukas als hellenistischer Schriftsteller: Studien zur Apostelgeschichte*. Göttingen: Vandenhoeck und Ruprecht, 1972.

Pohlenz, M. *Die Stoa: Geschichte einer geistigen Bewegung*. 2 vols. Göttingen: Vandenhoeck und Ruprecht, 1949.

Proudfoot, C. M. 'The Apostle Paul's Understanding of Suffering'. Yale Ph.D. diss., 1956.

Puech, A. *Les Apologistes grecs du IIe siècle de nôtre ère*. Paris: Hachette, 1912.

Rajak, T. *Josephus: The Historian and His Society*. Philadelphia: Fortress Press, 1983.

Remus, H. *Pagan–Christian Conflict over Miracle in the Second Century.* Patristic Monograph Series 10. Cambridge, Mass.: Philadelphia Patristic Foundation, 1983.

Richard, E. E. *Acts 6:1–8:4: The Author's Method of Composition.* SBLDS 41; Missoula, Mont.: Scholars Press, 1978.

Richardson, A. *The Miracle–Stories of the Gospels.* New York: Harper Bros., 1942.

Rist, J. M. *Stoic Philosophy.* Cambridge University Press, 1969.

   (ed.) *The Stoics.* Berkeley and Los Angeles: University of California, 1978.

Rokeah, D. *Jews, Pagans and Christians in Conflict.* Studia Post-Biblica 33. Jerusalem and Leiden: Magnes and Brill, 1982.

Ropes, J. H. *A Critical and Exegetical Commentary on the Epistle of St James.* International Critical Commentary. New York: Scribners, 1916.

Sandbach, F. H. *The Stoics.* London: Chatto and Windus, 1975.

Sanders, E. P. *Paul and Palestinian Judaism: a Comparison of Patterns of Religion.* Philadelphia: Fortress Press, 1977.

Sanders, E. P. and Davies, M. *Studying the Synoptic Gospels.* London: SCM, 1989.

Schlatter, A. *Wie Sprach Josephus von Gott?* Beiträge zur Förderung christlicher Theologie 14. Gütersloh: C. Bertelsmann, 1910.

   *Die Theologie des Judentums nach dem Bericht des Josefus.* Beiträge zur Förderung christlicher Theologie 2/26. Gütersloh: C. Bertelsmann, 1932.

Schoedel, W. R. (ed.) *Athenagoras: Legatio and De Resurrectione.* Oxford: Clarendon, 1972.

Schultz, S. *Die Stunde der Botschaft.* Hamburg: Furche, 1967.

Seters, J. van. *In Search of History: Historiography in the Ancient World and the Origins of Biblical History.* New Haven, Conn.: Yale University Press, 1983.

Shutt, R. J. H. *Studies in Josephus.* London: SPCK, 1961.

Simon, M. *St Stephen and the Hellenists in the Primitive Church.* London: Longmans, Green and Co., 1958.

Spengel, L. (ed.) *Rhetores Graeci.* 3 vols. Leipzig: Teubner, 1853–6; repr. Frankfurt/Main: Minerva, 1966.

Stern, M. *Greek and Latin Authors on Jews and Judaism.* 3 vols. Jerusalem: Israel Academy of Sciences and Humanities, 1974–84.

Talbert, C. H. *Literary Patterns, Theological Themes and the Genre of Luke–Acts.* Missoula, Mont.: Scholars Press, 1974.

   (ed.) *Luke–Acts: New Perspectives from the Society of Biblical Literature Seminar.* New York: Crossroads, 1984.

Tannehill, R. C. *The Narrative Unity of Luke–Acts: A Literary Interpretation.* Vol. 1: *The Gospel According to Luke.* Philadelphia: Fortress Press, 1986.

Temporini, H. and Haase, W. (eds.) *Aufstieg und Niedergang der römischen Welt: Geschichte und Kultur im Spiegel der neuern Forschung.* Berlin and New York: Walter de Gruyter, 1972 onwards.

Thackeray, H. StJ. *Josephus the Man and the Historian.* New York: Jewish Institute of Religion Press, 1929.

*A Lexicon to Josephus.* Parts I–IV (incomplete). Paris: Librairie Orientaliste Paul Geuthner, 1930–55.

Tiede, D. L. *Prophecy and History in Luke–Acts.* Philadelphia: Fortress Press, 1980.

Trompf, G. W. *The Idea of Historical Recurrence in Western Thought: From Antiquity to the Reformation.* Berkeley and Los Angeles: University of California Press, 1979.

Unnik, W. C. van. *Flavius Josephus als historiches Schriftsteller.* Heidelberg: Lambert Schneider, 1978.

Usher, S. *The Historians of Greece and Rome.* New York: Taplinger, 1969.

Walaskay, P. W. *'And so we Came to Rome': the Political Perspective of St Luke.* Cambridge University Press, 1983.

Walbank, F. W. *Polybius: The Rise of the Roman Empire.* Harmondsworth: Penguin, 1979.

Walsh, P. G. *Livy: His Historical Aims and Methods.* Cambridge University Press, 1961.

Waters, K. H. *Herodotus the Historian.* London: Croom Helm, 1985.

Wilckens, U. *Die Missionsreden der Apostelgeschichte: Form- und Traditionsgeschichtliche Untersuchungen.* Wissenschaftliche Monographien zum Alten und Neuen Testament 5; Neukirchen: Neukirchener Verlag, 1961.

Wilken, R. L. *The Christians as the Romans Saw Them.* New Haven and London: Yale University Press, 1984.

Wilson, R. R. *Prophecy and Society in Ancient Israel.* Philadelphia: Fortress Press, 1980.

Wilson, S. G. *The Gentiles and the Gentile Mission in Luke–Acts.* Cambridge University Press, 1973.

Winden, J. C. M. van *An Early Christian Philosopher: Justin Martyr's Dialogue with Trypho Chapters One to Nine.* Philosophia Patrum 1. Leiden: Brill, 1971.

Winston, D. *Freedom and Determinism in Philo of Alexandria: Protocol of the Twentieth Colloquy of The Center for Hermeneutical Studies in Hellenistic and Modern Culture,* ed. W. Wuellner. Berkeley: The Center for Hermeneutical Studies, 1976.

*The Wisdom of Solomon.* Anchor Bible 43. New York: Doubleday, 1979.

Wissowa, G. (ed.) *Paulys Realencyclopädie der Classischen Altertumswissenschaft.* 24 vols., with supplement of 12 vols.; later vols. ed. W. Kroll, K. Mittelhaus and K. Ziegler. Stuttgart: J. B. Metzler, 1893–1963.

Wochenmark, J. *Die Schicksalsidee im Judentum.* Stuttgart: W. Kohlhammer, 1933.

Wolfson, H. A. *Philo: Foundations of Religious Philosophy in Judaism, Christianity and Islam.* 2 vols. Cambridge, Mass.: Harvard University Press, 1947.

Zehnle, R. F. *Peter's Pentecost Discourse: Tradition and Lukan Reinterpretation in Peter's Speeches of Acts 2 and 3.* SBLMS 15. Nashville: Abingdon, 1971.

## C Articles

Achtemeier, P. J. 'The Lucan Perspective on the Miracles of Jesus: A Preliminary Sketch', *JBL* 94 (1975) 547–62.

Aland, K. 'Neue Neutestamentliche Papyri III', *NTS* 12 (1965–6) 193–210.

Alexander, L. 'Luke's Preface in the Context of Greek Preface-writing', *NovT* 28 (1986) 48–74.

Allen, L. C. 'The Old Testament Background of (προ) ὁρίζειν in the New Testament', *NTS* 17 (1970) 104–8.

Andresen, C. 'Justin und der mittlere Platonismus', *ZNW* 44 (1953) 157–95.

Attridge, H. W. 'Josephus and His Works', *Jewish Writings of the Second Temple Period* (CRINT 2.2; Assen: Van Gorcum, 1984) 185–232.

Aune, D. E. 'Magic in Early Christianity', *ANRW* II.23.2, 1507–57.

'The Use of προφήτης in Josephus', *JBL* 101 (1982) 419–21.

Balch, D. L. 'Acts as Hellenistic Historiography', *SBLSPS* 24 (1985) 429–32.

'The Areopagus Speech: An Appeal to the Stoic Historian Posidonius against Later Stoics and the Epicureans', *Greeks, Romans and Christians: Essays in Honor of Abraham J. Malherbe* (ed. D. L. Balch, E. Ferguson and W. A. Meeks; Minneapolis: Fortress Press, 1990) 52–79.

Barnard, L. W. 'Justin Martyr in Recent Study', *SJT* 22 (1969) 152–64.

Barnett, P. W. 'The Jewish Sign Prophets – A.D. 40–70 – Their Intentions and Origin', *NTS* 27 (1981) 679–97.

Barrett, C. K. 'Paul's Speech on the Areopagus', *New Testament Christianity for Africa and the World* (ed. M. E. Glasswell and E. W. Fashole-Luke; London: SPCK, 1974) 69–77.

'Paul's Address to the Ephesian Elders', *God's Christ and His People: Studies in Honour of Nils Alstrup Dahl* (ed. J. Jervell and W. A. Meeks; Oslo: Universitetsforl, 1977) 107–21.

Bassler, J. M. 'Luke and Paul on Impartiality', *Bib* 66 (1985) 546–52.

Benko, S. 'Pagan Criticisms of Christianity During the First Two Centuries', *ANRW* II.23.2, 1054–118.

Bennett, W. J. 'The Son of Man Must ... ', *NovT* 17 (1975) 113–29.

Benoit, P. 'L'Enfance de Jean-Baptiste selon Luc', *NTS* 3 (1956–7) 169–94.

Berger, K. 'Hellenistisch-heidnische Prodigien und die Verzeichen in der jüdischen und christlichen Apokalyptik', *ANRW* II.23.2, 1428–69.

Best, E. 'The Use and Non-Use of Pneuma by Josephus', *NovT* 3 (1959) 218–25.

Bilde, P. 'The Jewish War According to Josephus', *JSJ* 10 (1979) 179–202.

Bizière, F. 'Comment travaillait Diodore de Sicile', *Revue des Études Grecques* 87 (1974) 369–74.

Blenkinsopp, J. 'Prophecy and Priesthood in Josephus', *JJS* 25 (1974) 239–62.

Boer, W. den. 'Some Remarks on the Beginnings of Christian Historiography', *Studia Patristica* 4 (1961) 348–62.

'Graeco-Roman Historiography in its Relation to Biblical and Modern Thinking', *History and Theory* 7 (1968) 60–75.

Braun, M. 'The Prophet Who Became a Historian', *The Listener* 56 (1956) 53–7.

Bruce, F. F. 'Paul's Apologetic and the Purpose of Acts', *BJRL* 69 (1987) 379–93.

Busolt, G. 'Diodors Verhältnis zum Stoicismus', *Jahrbücher für Classische Philologie* 139 (1889) 297–315.

Cadbury, H. J. 'Lexical Notes on Luke–Acts. IV. On Direct Quotations with Some Uses of ὅτι and δεῖ', *JBL* 48 (1929) 412–25.

Callan, T. 'The Preface of Luke–Acts and Historiography', *NTS* 31 (1985) 576–81.

Carson, D. A. 'Divine Sovereignty and Human Responsibility in Philo: Analysis and Method', *NTS* 23 (1981) 148–64.

Chadwick, H. 'Origen, Celsus, and the Resurrection of the Body', *HTR* 41 (1948) 83–102.

'Justin Martyr's Defence of Christianity', *BJRL* 47 (1965) 275–97.

Cohen, S. J. D. 'Josephus, Jeremiah and Polybius', *History and Theory* 21 (1982) 366–81.

Collins, J. N. 'Georgi's "Envoys" in 2 Cor 11:23', *JBL* 93 (1974) 88–96.

Cosgrove, C. H. 'The Divine ΔΕΙ in Luke–Acts', *NovT* 26 (1984) 168–90.

Daube, D. 'Typology in Josephus', *JJS* 31 (1980) 18–36.

Delling, G. 'Josephus und das Wunderbare', *NovT* 2 (1958) 291–309.

Dillon, R. J. 'Previewing Luke's Project from His Prologue (Luke 1:1–4)', *CBQ* 43 (1981) 205–27.

'The Prophecy of Christ and His Witnesses According to the Discourses of Acts', *NTS* 32 (1986) 544–56.

Dinkler, E. 'Earliest Christianity', *The Idea of History in the Ancient Near East* (ed. R. C. Dentan; New Haven: Yale University Press, 1955).

Downing, F. G. 'Ethical Pagan Theism and the Speeches in Acts', *NTS* 27 (1981) 544–63.

Drews, R. 'Diodorus and his Sources', *American Journal of Philology* 83 (1962) 383–92.

Dudley, M. B. 'The Speeches in Acts', *EvQ* 50 (1978) 147–55.

Dupont, J. 'La Structure oratoire du discours d'Étienne', *Bib* 66 (1985) 153–67.

Earl, D. 'Prologue-form in Ancient Historiography', *ANRW* I.2.842–56.

Eitrem, S. 'Schicksalsmachte', *Symbolae Osloenses* 13 (1934) 47–64.

Evans, C. F. 'The Kerygma', *Journal of Theological Studies* 7 (1956) 25–41.

'"Speeches" in Acts', *Mélanges bibliques en hommage au R. P. Beda Rigaux* (ed. A. Descamps and A. de Halleux; Gembloux: Duculot, 1970) 287–302.

Fascher, E. 'Theologische Beobachtungen zu δεῖ im A.T.', *ZNW* 45 (1954) 244–52.

Feldman, L. H. 'Hellenizations in Josephus' Portrayal of Man's Decline', *Religion in Antiquity: Studies in Memory of Erwin Ramsdell Goodenough* (ed. J. Neusner; Leiden: Brill, 1968) 336–5

'Josephus as an Apologist to the Greco-Roman World: His Portrait of Solomon', *Aspects of Religious Propaganda in Judaism and Early Christianity* (ed. E. Schüssler Fiorenza; Notre Dame, Ind.: University of Notre Dame, 1976) 69–98.

'Prophets and Prophecy in Josephus', *JTS* 41 (1990) 386–422.

Freudenthal, J. 'Are there Traces of Greek Philosophy in the Septuagint?', *JQR* 2 (1890) 205–22.

Gasque, W. W. 'The Speeches of Acts: Dibelius Reconsidered', *New Dimensions in New Testament Study* (ed. R. I. Longenecker and M. C. Tenney; Grand Rapids, Mich.: Zondervan, 1974) 232–50.

Gaventa, B. R. '"You will be My Witnesses": Aspects of the Mission in Acts', *Missiology* 10 (1982) 413–25.

George, A. 'L'Espirit Saint dans l'œuvre de Luc', *Revue Biblique* 85 (1978) 500–42.

Gill, D. 'Observations on the Lukan Travel Narrative and Some Related Passages', *HTR* 63 (1970) 199–221.

Glasson, T. F. 'The Speeches in Acts and Thucydides', *ExpTim* 76 (1964–5) 165.

Güttgemanns, E. 'In welchem Sinne ist Lukas "Historiker"?', *Linguistica Biblica* 54 (1983) 7–26.

Habel, N. 'The Prophetic Call Narrative', *ZAW* 77 (1965) 297–323.

Hackett, J. 'Echoes of the *Bacchae* in the Acts of the Apostles?', *Irish Theological Quarterly* 23 (1956) 218–27, 350–66.

Hamblin, R. L. 'Miracles in the Book of Acts', *South Western Journal of Theology* 17 (1974) 19–34.

Hamilton, J. R. 'Cleitarchus and Aristobulus', *Historia* 10 (1961) 448–58.

Hamm, D. 'Acts 3,1–10; The Healing of a Temple Beggar as Lucan Theology', *Bib* 67 (1986) 305–19.

Hanson, J. S. 'Dreams and Visions in the Graeco-Roman World and Early Christianity', *ANRW* II.23.2, 1395–427.

Hardon, J. A. 'The Miracle Narratives in the Acts of the Apostles', *CBQ* 16 (1954) 303–18.

Holte, R. 'Logos Spermatikos: Christianity and Ancient Philosophy according to St Justin's Apologies', *ST* 12 (1958) 109–68.

Horsley, G. H. R. 'Speeches and Dialogue in Acts', *NTS* 32 (1986) 609–14.

Hubbard, B. J. 'Commissioning Stories in Luke–Acts: A Study of their Antecedents, Form and Content', *Semeria* 8 (1977) 103–26.

Huby, P. 'The First Discovery of the Free Will Problem', *Philosophy* 42 (1967) 353–62.

Jacoby, F. 'Über die Entwicklung der griechischen Historiographie und den Plan einer neuen Sammlung der griechischen Historikerfragmente', *Klio* 9 (1909) 80–123.

Johnson, G. L. 'Josephus: Heir Apparent to the Prophetic Tradition', *SBLSPS* 22 (1983) 337–46.

Klein, G. 'Lukas I, 1–4 als theologischeProgram', *Zeit und Geschichte. Dankesgabe an Rudolf Bultmann zum 80 Geburtstag* (ed. E. Dinkler; Tübingen: Mohr, 1964) 193–216.

Kolenkow, A. B. 'Relationships between Miracle and Prophecy in the Greco-Roman World and Early Christianity', *ANRW* II.23.2 1470–506.

Kümmel, W. G. 'Luc en accusation dans la théologie contemporaine', *ETL* 46 (1970) 265–81.

Kurz, W. S. 'Luke–Acts and Historiography in the Greek Bible', *SBLSPS* 19 (1980) 283–300.

Lampe, G. W. H. 'The Lucan Portrait of Christ', *NTS* 2 (1955–6) 160–75.

Long, A. A. 'Stoic Determinism and Alexander of Aphrodisias *De Fato* (i–xiv)', *Archiv für Geschichte der Philosophie* 52 (1970) 247–68.

Lull, D. J. 'The Servant–Benefactor as a Model of Greatness (Luke 22:24–30)', *NovT* 28 (1986) 289–305.

Malherbe, A. J. 'Apologetic and Philosophy in the Second Century', *Restoration Quarterly* 7 (1963) 19–32.

   'The Apologetic Theology of the "Preaching of Peter"', *Restoration Quarterly* 13 (1970) 205–33.

   'Athenagoras on the Pagan Poets and Philosophers', *Kyriakon. Festschrift Johannes Quasten* (ed. P. Granfield and J. A. Jungmann; 2 vols.; Münster: Aschendorff, 1970) 1.214–25.

   'Pseudo Heraclitus Epistle 4: The Divinization of the Wise Man', *Jahrbuch für Antike und Christentum* 21 (1978) 42–64.

   '"Not in a Corner": Early Christian Apologetic in Acts 26:26', *The Second Century* 5 (1985/86) 193–210.

Martin, L. H. 'The Rule of τύχη and Hellenistic Religion', *SBLSPS* 15 (1976) 453–9.

   'Josephus' Use of εἱμαρμένη in the Jewish Antiquities XII, 171–3', *Numen* 28 (1981) 127–37.

Marx, A. 'Y a-t-il une prédestination à Qumran?', *Revue de Qumran* 6 (1967) 163–81.

McCasland, S. V. 'Portents in Josephus and in the Gospels', *JBL* 51 (1932) 323–35.

Miles, G. B. and Trompf, G. W. 'Luke and Antiphon: The Theology of Acts 27–28 in the Light of Pagan Beliefs about Divine Retribution', *HTR* 69 (1965) 259–67.

Mitton, C. L. 'The Will of God in the Synoptic Tradition of the Words of Jesus', *ExpTim* 72 (1960–1) 68–71.

Moehring, H. R. 'Rationalization of Miracles in the Writings of Flavius Josephus', *Studia Evangelica* 11 (1973) 376–83.

Momigliano, A., 'Greek Historiography', *History and Theory* 17 (1978) 1–28.

   'The Origins of Universal History', *The Poet and the Historian: Essays in Literary and Historical Biblical Criticism* (ed. R. E. Griedman; Harvard Semitic Studies 26; Chico, Calif.: Scholars Press, 1983) 133–54.

Montefiore, H. W. 'Josephus and the New Testament', *NovT* 4 (1960) 139–60, 306–18.

Montgomery, J. A. 'The Religion of Flavius Josephus', *JQR* 11 (1920–1) 277–305.

Moore, G. F. 'Fate and Free Will in the Jewish Philosophies according to Josephus', *HTR* 22 (1929) 371–89.

Nauck, W. 'Die Tradition und Komposition der Areopagrede', *ZThK* 63 (1956) 11–52.

Navone, J. 'The Way of the Lord', *Scripture* 20 (1968) 24–30.

Neyrey, J. 'The Absence of Jesus' Emotions – The Lucan Redaction of Lk 22,39–46', *Bib* 61 (1980) 153–71.

Nock, A. D. Review of M. Dibelius, *Aufsätze zur Apostelgeschichte*, *Gnomon* 25 (1953) 49–50.

Noetscher, F. 'Schicksal und Freiheit', *Bib* 40 (1959) 446–62.

'Schicksalsglaube im Qumran und Umwelt', *Biblische Zeitschrift* 3 (1959) 205–34, 4 (1960) 98–121.

Overbeck, F. 'Über das Verhältnis Justins des Märtyrers zur Apostelgeschichte', *ZWT* 15 (1872) 305–49.

Paton, W. R. 'Ἀγωνία (Agony)', *Classical Review* 27 (1913) 194.

Plessis, I. J. du. 'Once More: The Purpose of Luke's Prologue (Lk 1:1–4)', *NovT* 16 (1974) 259–71.

Plunkett, M. A. 'Ethnocentricity and Salvation History in the Cornelius Episode (Acts 10:1–11:18)', *SBLSPS* 24 (1985) 465–79.

Pohlenz, M. 'Paulus und die Stoa', *ZNW* 42 (1949) 69–104.

Praeder, S. M. 'Miracle Worker and Missionary: Paul in the Acts of the Apostles', *SBLSPS* 22 (1983) 107–29.

Radcliffe, T., 'The Emmaus Story: Necessity and Freedom', *New Blackfriars* 64 (1983) 483–93.

Rajak, T. 'Josephus and the "Archaeology" of the Jews', *JJS* 33 (1982) 465–77.

Ramaroson, L. 'Contre les "temples faits de mains d'homme"', *RPLHA* 43 (1969) 217–38.

Reiling J. 'The Use of ψευδοπροφήτης in the Septuagint, Philo and Josephus', *NovT* 13 (1971) 147–56.

Renehan, R. 'Classical Greek Quotations in the New Testament', *The Heritage of the Early Church: Essays in Honour of G. V. Florovsky* (Orientalia Christiana Analecta 195; ed. D. Neiman and M. Schatkin; Rome: Pont. Institut. Studiorum Orientalium, 1973) 17–45.

Richard, E. 'The Polemical Character of the Joseph Episode in Acts 7', *JBL* 98 (1979) 255–67.

'The Creative Use of Amos by the Author of Acts', *NovT* 24 (1982) 37–53.

'Luke – Writer, Theologian, Historian: Research and Orientation of the 1970's', *BTB* 13 (1983) 3–15.

'The Divine Purpose: The Jews and the Gentile Mission (Acts 15)', *Luke–Acts: New Perspectives from the Society of Biblical Literature Seminar* (ed. C. H. Talbert; New York: Crossroads 1984) 188–209.

Robbins, V. K. 'Prefaces in Greco-Roman Biography and Luke–Acts', *SBLSPS* 17 (1978) 2.193–207.

Sandmel, S. 'Some Comments on Providence in Philo', *The Divine Helmsman: Studies on God's Control of Human Events, Presented to Lo H. Siberman* (ed. J. L. Crenshaw and S. Sandmel; New York: KTAV 1980) 79–85.

Schmidt, D., 'The Historiography of Acts: Deuteronomistic or Hellenistic?', *SBLSPS* 24 (1985) 417–27.

Schreckenberg, H. 'Flavius Josephus und die lukanischen Schriften', *Wort in der Zeit, Neutestamentliche Studien, Festgabe für Karl Heinrich Rengstorf zum 75. Geburtstag* (ed. W. Haubeck and M. Bachmann; Leiden: Brill, 1980) 179–209.

Schubert, P. 'The Structure and Significance of Luke 24', *Neutestamentliche*

*Studien für Rudolf Bultmann* (ed. W. Eltester; Berlin: Alfred Töpelmann, 1954) 165–86.

'The Place of the Areopagus Speech in the Composition of Acts', *Transitions in Biblical Scholarship* (ed. J. C. Rylaarsdam; Essays in Divinity 6; Chicago: University of Chicago Press, 1968) 235–61.

'The Final Cycle of Speeches in the Book of Acts', *JBL* 87 (1968) 1–16.

Schulz, S. 'Gottes Vorsehung bei Lukas', *ZNW* 54 (1963) 104–16.

Schürer, E. 'Josephus', *The History of the Jewish People in the Age of Jesus Christ 175 B.C.–A.D. 135)* (trans., rev. and ed. by G. Vermes and F. Millar; Edinburgh: T. & T. Clark, 1973) 43–63.

Segalla, G. 'Gesù revelatore della volontà del Padre nella Tradizione Sinnotica', *Rivista biblica italiana* 14 (1966) 467–508.

Shutt, R. J. H. 'The Concept of God in the Works of Flavius Josephus', *JJS* 31 (1980) 171–87.

Sinclair, R. K. 'Diodorus Siculus and the Writing of History', *Proceedings of the American Classical Association* 6 (1963) 36–45.

Sneen, D. J. 'An Exegesis of Luke 1:1–4 with Special Regard to Luke's Purpose as a Historian', *ExpTim* 83 (1971) 40–3.

Sowers, S. 'On the Reinterpretation of Biblical History in Hellenistic Judaism', *Oikonomia, Heilsgeschichte als Thema der Theologie. Oscar Cullman zum 65. Geburtstag gewidmet* (ed. F. Christ; Hamburg-Bergstedt: Reich, 1967) 18–25.

Stolz, F. 'Zeichen und Wunder. Die prophetische Legitimation und ihre Geschichte', *ZThK* 69 (1972) 125–44.

Talbert, C. H. 'Promise and Fulfilment in Lukan Theology', *Luke–Acts: New Perspectives from the Society of Biblical Literature Seminar* (ed. C. H. Talbert, New York: Crossroads, 1984) 91–103.

Tannehill, R. C. 'Israel in Luke–Acts: A Tragic Story', *JBL* 104 (1985) 69–85.

Temple, P. J. '"House" or "Business" in Lk. 2.49?', *CBQ* 1 (1939) 342–52.

Theiler, W. 'Tacitus und die antike Schicksalslehre', *Phylobollia für Peter von der Mühl zum 60. Geburtstag am 1. August 1945* (Basel: Berno Schwabe, 1946) 35–90.

Thoma, C. 'Die Weltanschauung des Josephus Flavius', *Kairos* 11 (1969) 39–52.

Torrance, T. F. 'Phusikos kai Theologikos Logos, St Paul and Athenagoras at Athens', *SJT* 41 (1988) 11–26.

Townsend, J. T. 'The Speeches in Acts', *Anglican Theological Review* 42 (1960) 150–9.

Trocmé, E. 'The Beginnings of Christian Historiography and the History of Early Christianity', *AusBR* 31 (1983) 1–13.

Unnik, W. C. van. 'The "Book of Acts" the Confirmation of the Gospel', *NovT* 4 (1960) 26–59.

'Jesus the Christ', *NTS* 8 (1961–2) 101–16.

'First Century A.D. Literary Culture and Early Christian Literature', *Nederlands Theologisch Tijdschrift* 25 (1971) 28–48.

'An Attack on the Epicureans by Flavius Josephus', *Romanitas et Christianitas: Studia Iano Henrico Waszink* (ed. W. den Boer, P. G. van der

Nat, C. M. J. Sicking and J. C. M. van Winden; Amsterdam and London: North Holland, 1973) 341–55.

'Remarks on the Purpose of Luke's Historical Writing (Luke I 1–4)', *Sparsa Collecta: The Collected Essays of W. C. van Unnik* (3 vols.; Leiden: Brill, 1973) 1.6–15.

'Josephus' Account of the Story of Israel's Sin with Alien Women in the Country of Midian (Num 25:1ff)', *Travels in the World of the Old Testament: Studies Presented to Professor M. A. Beck on the Occasion of his 65th Birthday* (ed. M. S. H. G. Heerma van Voss, P. H. J. Houwink ten Cate and N. A. van Uchelen; Assen: Van Gorcum, 1974) 241–61.

Vögeli, A. 'Lukas und Euripides', *ThZ* 9 (1953) 415–38.

Wachter, L. 'Die unterschiedliche Haltung der Pharisaen, Sadduzaen und Essener zur Heimarmene nach dem Bericht des Josephus', *ZRGG* 21 (1969) 97–114.

Walbank, F. W. 'The Historians of Greek Sicily', *Kokalos* 14–15 (1968–9) 491–3.

Whittaker, M. '"Signs and Wonders": The Pagan Background', *Studia Evangelica* 5 (1968) 155–8.

Wilcox, M. '"Upon the Tree": Deut 21:22–23 in the New Testament', *JBL* 96 (1977) 85–99.

Wilken, R. L. 'Pagan Criticism of Christianity: Greek Religion and Christian Faith', *Early Christian Literature and the Classical Intellectual Tradition, in honorem R. M. Grant* (Théologie Historique 54; ed. W. R. Schödel and R. L. Wilken; Paris: Beauchesne, 1979) 117–34.

'The Christians as the Romans (and Greeks) Saw Them', *Jewish and Christian Self-Definition. vol. 1, The Shaping of Christianity in the Second and Third Centuries* (ed. E. P. Sanders; 3 vols.; Philadelphia: Fortress Press, 1980) 100–25.

Winden, J. C. M. van. 'Le Portrait de la philosophie grecque dans Justin, Dialogue I,4–5', *VC* 31 (1977) 181–90.

Windisch, H. 'Die Christus-epiphanie vor Damaskus (Act 9, 22 und 26) und ihre religions-geschichtlichen Parallelen', *ZNW* 31 (1932) 1–23.

Winston, D. 'Freedom and Determinism in Greek Philosophy and Jewish Hellenistic Wisdom', *Studia Philonica* 2 (1973) 40–50.

'Freedom and Determinism in Philo of Alexandria', *Studia Philonica* 3 (1974–5) 47–70.

Wright, D. F. 'Christian Faith in the Greek World: Justin Martyr's Testimony', *EvQ* 54 (1982) 71–87.

Zeitlin, S. 'A Survey of Jewish Historiography from the Biblical Books to the Sepher Ha-kabbalah, with Special Emphasis on Josephus', *JQR* 59 (1969) 171–214, 60 (1969) 37–68.

Zweck, D. 'The Exordium of the Areopagus Speech, Acts 17.22,23', *NTS* 35 (1989) 94–103.

# INDEX OF GREEK WORDS

# INDEX OF SUBJECTS AND AUTHORS

# INDEX OF BIBLICAL REFERENCES